Reader as Accomplice

SRLT NORTHWESTERN UNIVERSITY PRESS
Studies in Russian Literature and Theory

SERIES EDITORS
Caryl Emerson
Gary Saul Morson
William Mills Todd III
Andrew Wachtel
Justin Weir

Reader as Accomplice

Narrative Ethics in Dostoevsky and Nabokov

Alexander Spektor

NORTHWESTERN UNIVERSITY PRESS / EVANSTON, ILLINOIS

Northwestern University Press
www.nupress.northwestern.edu

Copyright © 2021 by Northwestern University Press. Published 2021.
All rights reserved.

Printed in the United States of America

10 9 8 7 6 5 4 3 2 1

Library of Congress Cataloging-in-Publication Data
Names: Spektor, Alexander, author.
Title: The reader as accomplice : narrative ethics in Dostoevsky and
   Nabokov / Alexander Spektor.
Other titles: Studies in Russian literature and theory.
Description: Evanston, Illinois : Northwestern University Press, 2021 | Series:
   Northwestern Unversity Press Studies in Russian literature and theory | Includes
   bibliographical references and index.
Identifiers: LCCN 2020022407 | ISBN 9780810142459 (paperback) | ISBN
   9780810142466 (cloth) | ISBN 9780810142473 (ebook)
Subjects: LCSH: Dostoyevsky, Fyodor, 1821–1881—Criticism and
   interpretation. | Nabokov, Vladimir Vladimirovich, 1899–1977—Criticism
   and interpretation. | Ethics in literature. | Literature and morals. | Narration
   (Rhetoric)—Moral and ethical aspects.
Classification: LCC PG3015.5.E74 S64 2021 | DDC 891.709353—dc23
LC record available at https://lccn.loc.gov/2020022407

In loving memory of Vitalii and Lyuda

The moral sense in mortals is the duty
We have to pay on mortal sense of beauty.
—Vladimir Nabokov, *Lolita*

Contents

Acknowledgments		xi
Introduction	Dostoevsky and Nabokov: The Case for Narrative Ethics	1
Chapter One	Between Sin and Redemption: Narrative as the Conduit for Responsibility in Dostoevsky's "The Meek One"	34
Chapter Two	From Violence to Silence: Vicissitudes of Reading (in) *The Idiot*	83
Chapter Three	The Metaphysics of Authorship: Narrative Ethics in Nabokov's *Despair*	102
Chapter Four	The Dangers of Aesthetic Bliss: The Double Bind of Language in *Bend Sinister*	144
Conclusion		174
Notes		183
Bibliography		223
Index		235

Acknowledgments

Its placement notwithstanding, this is the last and, without a doubt, most pleasurable part of the book to write. It also causes me considerable anxiety at the possibility of forgetting to thank any among those who helped with this work from its first to last stages. With that in mind, it might be easier to start from the back and get to the institutions first: I would like to thank the Franklin College of Arts and Sciences at the University of Georgia for its generous financial support toward the book's publication. The grant from the Willson Center for Humanities and Arts at UGA allowed me the necessary time to push the project into its final stages. Since the book uses parts of my dissertation, I would also like to thank the Harvard University Graduate School of Arts and Sciences, which in part funded its writing.

Now on to those without whom this work wouldn't exist. It was conceived ages ago when everyone was still alive in the tiny apartment of Vitalii Tabachkovsky and Lyudmila Anoshkina, my second parents and my guardian angels. This book is dedicated to you.

Since the Slavic field is considerably small, chances are the reader will immediately understand how fortunate I am to have been mentored by Stephanie Sandler, Caryl Emerson, and Irina Paperno. These three very special women have helped me in more ways than I can count, but especially when it counted most—in times of crisis. Their intellectual, moral, and emotional support is not only the spirit of this book but also makes up a large chunk of its body. Ever since my first class with her, Stephanie, with her highest sense of professional and intellectual integrity, has served as the ideal model of a scholar. I looked up to her as a graduate student, and I do now. Over more than a decade, I have been lucky to have been shaped by Caryl, while she has been somewhat less lucky to plow through pretty much all of my writing, patiently weeding out "Spektorisms," gently steering me away from banalities, teaching me to express myself clearly and concisely. It is from reading her work and from her reading mine that I continue to learn how to say complicated things simply. Doesn't mean that I've mastered the skill, though. Even a cursory glance through the "works cited" will easily tell

Acknowledgments

the level of my indebtedness to her thought. When the book suddenly fell apart, it was Irina who put it back together again. She spent tireless hours reading and rereading its numerous drafts. When I told Yuri Corrigan that Irina rejected draft number 7 of the introduction, he laughed and said that getting Irina as a reader was like winning the lottery. True that.

When this book was still in its teenage dissertation years, William Mills Todd III, Svetlana Boym, and Anna Lisa Crone shared with me their time and minds, a procedure that distilled into precious comments on drafts of my dissertation—comments without which its completion would have been impossible.

Since the book took its sweet time, I'm bound to neglect acknowledgment of numerous readers who provided me with important comments and advice on how to proceed. If you find yourself included in this category, please email me an angry letter. Among those who come to mind immediately are Yuri Corrigan, Jacob Emery, Irma Nuñez, Emily Finer, Chloë Kitzinger, and Julia Vaingurt. I would also like to thank my colleagues at the University of Illinois at Chicago, Vanderbilt University, and the University of Georgia—the vagaries of our profession!—for creating a productive and friendly atmosphere, which undoubtedly contributed to my ability to write. Also, special thanks to the editorial team at Northwestern University Press, whose high professionalism is the reason you're holding the physical book in your hands, and to the anonymous reviewers, whose comments helped realign everything into this work's present shape.

Since it takes a village, last—but, of course, first—I would also like to thank my family. There are lots of you (well, not as many now), so I won't list names. Mom, dad, that sort of thing. Your unremitting love and faith in me make everything else possible.

Reader as Accomplice

Introduction

Dostoevsky and Nabokov: The Case for Narrative Ethics

TOWARD THE MIDDLE of Nabokov's first English-language novel, *The Real Life of Sebastian Knight*, the narrator, V., tells an anecdote from the life of the elusive subject of his biography—his recently deceased half-brother. When a friend finds Sebastian prostrate on the floor after finishing a novel, the latter explains: "No, Leslie, . . . I'm not dead. I have finished building a world, and this is my Sabbath rest."[1] Since the novel is in large part about the impossibility of capturing someone's—anyone's—*real* life as a story, this episode, like almost all of the accounts in *Sebastian Knight*, comes to the narrator secondhand. It speaks, however, of the authorial mastery that V.'s own project continuously fails to achieve, the validity of which the novel constantly questions.

The tension of Nabokov's novel exists between these two extremes: the absolute—godlike—control that the author exerts over his creation and the impossibility of fully capturing a life through narrative means without losing something integral about it. As the novel moves along, it continues to vacillate between the temptation of representing one's life narratively as a totality of meaning and understanding that life is episodic, impenetrable, lacking order, and ultimately not one's own. V. operates under "the fundamental assumption that an author is able to discover anything he may want to know about his characters" (93), but at the same time, he continuously rejects all accounts of his half-brother's life because they belong to others and are thus corrupted and limited. The element of foreignness, Nabokov seems to argue here, will always inhabit the narrative account of the self, and his own extradiegetic traces scattered throughout V.'s story are perfect instantiations of this point.

Sebastian Knight ends up by affirming that inasmuch as it is a "real life" we are after, narrative will never capture it; reality will always contain an inassimilable remainder of otherness. When V. finally succeeds in inhabiting Sebastian's soul, he does so not by attempting to represent his half-brother's life *narratively* but by coming into close *physical* proximity to him. As V. sits

1

outside Sebastian's hospital room and listens to his breathing, he understands that one's pneuma cannot be confined to a single narrative account but has to be witnessed: "That gentle breathing was telling me more of Sebastian than I had ever known before" (201). Still, in accordance with the principles it has established, the novel risks annulling V.'s epiphany: as it turns out, V. was listening to the breathing of the wrong man.

Nabokov's insights about the alterity that is indelibly present in any narrative account ask us to attend to the relationships constructed between tellers and listeners. In this, Nabokov comes close to contemporary theoretical conceptualizations of the ethics of narrative. In his book *Narrative Ethics*, Adam Newton likewise proposes that an act of storytelling invariably creates a surplus that cannot be accounted for by the transfer of knowledge alone. As the site of address between two subjects, narrative always exceeds its referential function. The kind of attention that can respond to such recognition adequately, argues Newton, must be ethical. As the locus of the relationship between speaker and listener, narrating falls outside of the formal designs of text and, at the same time, makes ethical claims on the subjects participating in it.[2] As Newton puts it, "to be narrated by others taps into a play of ethical-discursive forces" (24). This, as Mikhail Bakhtin tells us, would be especially true of narrative fiction, where the distribution of narrative discourse happens within the built-in hierarchies that bind together authors and their characters.

I would like to offer my reading of *Sebastian Knight* as a portal into my justification for choosing to study narrative ethics through Dostoevsky and Nabokov, a pair that might strike some as odd. One of the main arguments of my book is that both authors seek to affect the moral imagination of their readers by creating a link between the morally laden situations dramatized within their prose on the level of content and the ethical charge of narrative fiction on the discursive level, that is, the relationships that literature forms among authors, characters, and readers. By doing so, Nabokov and Dostoevsky ask us to think about and respond to the ethical demands that narrative acts of representation and interpretation place on authors and readers.

The principle that the ethics of fiction is to be found by attending to the distribution of power at the site of narrative address has been most recently formulated and explored by Newton, whose work, in turn, draws in large part on Bakhtin's aesthetic philosophy. While Bakhtin was arguably the first to locate the ethical in a narrative act that brings together author and character, the evolution of his ideas on the interaction between aesthetics and ethics was considerably influenced by Dostoevsky's art. Thus, the first main goal of my book is to uncover the genealogy of narrative ethics that goes back to Dostoevsky's aesthetic solutions of effectively representing the ethical problems of interpersonal relationships.

The second goal is to bring to light the important, previously unexplored correspondences between Dostoevsky and Nabokov. Given Nabokov's notorious dismissal of Dostoevsky's art, as well as his ardent antimoralism, the choice of these two writers to be each other's "distant interlocutors," to use Osip Mandelstam's expression, can at first appear counterintuitive. Moreover, Dostoevsky's Christian ethics hardly finds its way into Nabokov's prose. Nevertheless, in this book I argue that Nabokov's examination of the ethical costs involved in narrating oneself and others and his awareness of the hierarchies of representation that exist in fiction allow us to see Nabokov as Dostoevsky's unexpected heir.

In their prose, both authors incite the reader's sense of ethics by exposing the risks but also the possibilities of narrative fiction. As such, ethical readings of Dostoevsky and Nabokov make their texts relevant in the context of contemporary critical debate on the ways in which literature has a formative influence on the ethics of its readers. Ultimately, I am aiming not so much to intervene in the theoretical field of literary ethics as to use its instruments to examine specific texts' unique place in ethical discourse and to discuss the terms of one's ethical engagement with these texts as a reader and critic.

AN ETHICAL TURN

The turn toward ethics in contemporary literary studies is not new. Theorists who tend to date such occurrences place it in the early 1990s, when American scholars, ending their half-century moratorium on any explicitly ethical criticism, renewed their interest in the ethical analysis of literary texts. Numerous volumes documented the reasons for literary theory's suspicion of ethics, as well as the newly recognized need to resume theoretical discourse on the subject.[3] Hence, in the resurgence of the ethical through the fissures of postmodernist discourse, scholars tend to see not so much a turn as a *return*. As the editors of *Mapping the Ethical Turn* explain in their preface: "ethical critics do not necessarily discover or make a territory but, instead, describe and give shape to what has always existed."[4]

Martha Nussbaum, a moral philosopher who argues that literature is "indispensable to a philosophical inquiry in the ethical sphere,"[5] locates the beginning of the rift between literary and ethical criticisms in early twentieth-century formalism and, later, in the New Criticism. If, as Tobin Siebers writes, "to criticize ethically brings the critic into a special field of action: the field of human conduct and belief concerning the human,"[6] then, according to Nussbaum, formalism imbued with Kantian aesthetics achieves exactly the opposite by losing touch with the human element.[7] Siebers, how-

Introduction

ever, suggests that the liberation of critical discourse from the presence of the human subject is itself ethical. He treats the theoretical turn toward language as an attempt to free the "human sciences" from the "human urge for colonization."[8] Nevertheless, like Nussbaum, Siebers advocates a return to the study of human subjectivity and deplores theory's exclusive focus on language, the character of which "makes extremely difficult the type of consciousness necessary to moral reflection."[9]

Some of the main preoccupations of contemporary ethical theory have been to properly redefine our understanding of the "human" and the ethical formation of the subject by taking into account the critique of Enlightenment notions of morality. It is here that scholars like Nussbaum find that imaginative literature can instruct us better than moral philosophy. As Nussbaum explains, unlike Kantian morality, fictional literature is all-inclusive, practical, stresses the continuous process over moments of choice, and, above all, is concrete, not abstract. This allows her to argue that literature belongs to "a family of related views" with the similarly all-inclusive Aristotelian inquiry.[10]

The sympathetic resemblance between fiction and Aristotelian ethics makes clear the kind of literature Nussbaum has in mind. It is mimetic and character-driven; and it should be concerned with a representation of concrete lives submerged in a "thick" context, where details triumph over generalities and abstractions. Though ethically instructive in a practical sense, it must also be able to encompass conflicting and incommensurate views of its characters and narrators. For Nussbaum, literature's formal characteristics become indispensable for an ethical inquiry because they correspond to human faculties that she, after Aristotle, considers most auspicious for the cultivation of a good life. Literature for Nussbaum is about choice-making; it is able to represent the particularities and intricacies of making a choice and to offer the reader a relationship with that particularity:

> [Literature] speaks *about us*, about our lives and choices and emotions, about our social existence and the totality of our connections. As Aristotle observed, it is deep, and conductive to our inquiry about how to live, because it does not simply (as history does) record that this or that event happened; it searches for patterns of possibility—of choice, and circumstance, and the interaction between choice and circumstance—that turn up in human lives with such a persistence that they must be regarded as *our* possibilities. And so our interest in literature becomes . . . cognitive: an interest in finding out (by seeing and feeling the otherwise perceiving) what possibilities (and tragic impossibilities) life offers to us, what hopes and fears for ourselves it underwrites or subverts.[11]

The reader's task, then, is to recognize the equivalence between the structure of literary patterning and the patterning that exists in her own life. The reader's ethical reflection focuses on the trajectory of choices that characters make within the thick texture of fictional circumstance and applies that analysis to her own choices in life. The pattern that literary characters carve with choice out of circumstance is the same one that, according to Nussbaum, distinguishes literature from history. Unlike moral philosophy, whose primary instrument is *reflection*, literature allows us to exercise *perception*, a faculty that does not exclude emotions and the ability to learn from and appreciate particularity (even at the cost of balance). Nussbaum's ideal reader uses perception over reflection, and here literature and philosophy come to form a symbiosis: literature is not just the most productive discursive field for an ethical inquiry governed by perception, it fosters it.

Nussbaum's perceptive reader, who uses fiction to understand the complexities of ethical dilemmas, is close to the figure of friendship between authors and readers that Wayne Booth declares to be foundational for ethical literary criticism.[12] For Booth, the company of texts (and their implied authors) with which we surround ourselves for the ethical improvement of our character also influences our subsequent choice of texts and the way we engage with them. But how do we choose in the first place, and what is the relationship between us and the company we keep? To instruct us, Booth proposes pluralism with discernment—a careful maneuvering between two strategies: one that excludes all which can be potentially harmful to us and another which is all-embracing, advocating immersion into everything that life offers:

> We must both open ourselves to "others" that look initially dangerous or worthless, and yet prepare ourselves to cast them off whenever, after keeping company with them, we conclude that they are potentially harmful. Which of these opposing practices will serve us best at a given moment will depend on who "we" are and what the "moment" is.[13]

The image that governs this relationship is one of friendship, and Booth notes that friendships are based on the production of pleasure and mutual gain, but the most important ones are those that "make life together worth having as an end in itself" (172, 174). This again puts us into an Aristotelian universe, to which Booth adds a pinch of Christian ethics: read me as you would like to be read by others (173).

The alternative view claims that literary experience makes possible a true encounter with the incommensurable and establishes a relationship that does not allow for the safety offered by either Nussbaum's perception or Booth's friendship but instead pushes the reader to abandon the protective distance between herself and the text. Hence, Charles Altieri takes Nussbaum to task for the way she simultaneously enlarges and delimits the role of the reader by including the importance of an emotional involvement with the text and at the same time containing it through the power of reason.[14] Altieri argues that if the best we can expect from the "reader as judicious spectator" is pathos, which is a result of the emotional energy of the text put through a crucible of reason, then we lose those "substantial values" of literary experience that are "very difficult to get elsewhere."[15] The singularity of the literary experience for Altieri is to be found in the appreciation of the affectual states that literature provides for us, "with no sanction beyond the intellectual, emotional, and intersubjective intensities a text affords."[16]

Instead, Altieri suggests, our ethical inquiry into literature should embrace the narrative's liminal states, moments when its rhetorical strategies can neither restrain nor constrain the pressures that inaugurate the narrative in the first place.[17] For this to happen, instead of the pathos of Nussbaum's reader, Altieri offers the ethos of a reader who is able to suspend "impersonal judiciousness" in order to allow an identification with how a particular text's "specific efforts at articulation provide a sense of discovery or sharpen what we thought we knew."[18] Shifting the ethical inquiry to a reflection on our "intense participation" with the text similarly shows the insufficiency of the ethics of friendship proposed by Booth.[19] As Altieri puts it, "our affective lives can be strongly touched by pleasures, fascination, and challenges that have their power because they refuse the domesticating ideal of friendship for other less stable and less comforting modes of presence."[20]

Yet, if we don't allow reason to govern the way imaginative literature affects us, what then can inform our ethics, which, after all, must be grounded in epistemology? Finding Booth's prescription of friendship with texts affectively confining, Altieri stops short of advocating an approach that is based solely on nonrestrictive phenomenology, and he is careful not to exclude the faculty of reason altogether. While the phenomenon of honoring "subtle differences in qualities of feeling" resists reason's authority, it still invites it.[21] Ultimately, Altieri proposes a convergence between an aesthetics of art based on phenomenology and on its ethics. While the first teaches us to appreciate the singularity of our affective states, the second "brings the aesthetic into the existential."[22]

Nussbaum's mistrust of language-based criticism, Booth's stress on the interpersonal relationship between readers and authors, and Altieri's preference for phenomenological and affective practices over epistemological ones all come together in the philosophical and aesthetic concerns of Mikhail Bakhtin. Bakhtin faulted the Russian formalists for treating aesthetic activity merely as a means of organizing and processing matter. In contrast, he proposed that aesthetic activity always contains human interest because any cultural product is an embodiment of its creator's valuational position toward the world.[23] As Bakhtin wrote in 1924, "What fails to be understood [in the formalist approach] is the emotional-volitional tension of form, the fact that it has the character of expressing some valuational relationship of the author and the contemplator to something apart from the material. For this *emotional-volitional relationship* that is expressed by form (by rhythm, harmony, symmetry, and other formal moments) is too intense, too *active* in character to be understood simply as a relationship to the material."[24]

Bakhtin's critique of the formalist exclusion of human subjectivity from the study of culture seems to suggest the inapplicability of formal analysis to ethical criticism—and yet it does not have to. Thus, Caroline Levine has recently called for a revision of the narrow definition of formalism as an instrument for analyzing culture as a reified form—a revision that would allow us to analyze valuational (ethical and political) positions. To bring under the auspices of formal analysis numerous ways of organizing *human* experience might help us to "understand sociopolitical life as itself composed of a plurality of different forms, from narrative to marriage and from bureaucracy to racism."[25] For Levine, recognizing that the forms and systems inherent to social relations and literary texts have the same ontological status (i.e., they are "equally real in their capacity to organize materials, and equally unreal in being artificial, contingent constraints")[26] can refocus formal analysis to include questions it does not usually ask: "what does each form afford, and what happens when forms meet?"[27]

Bakhtin fits well into Levine's appeal to study the transferability of forms and its effects. Elaborating on the concepts of his aesthetic philosophy, Bakhtin adopts a model for human relationships from his analysis of the structures and hierarchies that are inherent in literary texts. The dynamics of my relationship with others are the same as between author and hero, inasmuch as human beings both author one another and become heroes for one another's form-shaping (i.e., authorial) activity. The application of aesthetic structures to the analysis of the extratextual world invests aesthetic activity with ethical and political significance and calls for the kind of criticism that can adequately respond to it. Alternatively, Graham Pechey sees Bakhtin's turn to aesthetics as an argument with Kantian ethics, which denies the uniqueness of the interpersonal experience: "The aesthetic event always 'presupposes two non-coinciding consciousnesses' ["Author and Hero," 22]; anything in writing or reading that conflates or effaces these tends to syncretize the aesthetic, threatening to transform the event in the case of conflation into an ethical event and in that of effacement into an event of cognition."[28] The evolution of Bakhtin's evaluation of the relationship between author and hero—and, consequently, between two subjects—is intrinsically connected to Dostoevsky, and especially to the latter's considerations of how Christian ethics informs human relationships. Hence, in chapter 1, I argue that in his work on Dostoevsky, Bakhtin brings to light *as philosophy* what is implicitly present *in the prose*: the radical am-

Introduction

plification of the ethical charge of aesthetic and hermeneutic activity that unites all the participants in narrative prose—authors, characters, and readers. For now, a brief return to Newton's conceptualization of narrative ethics will help us appreciate the importance of Dostoevsky's investment of narrative discourse with moral value, as well as the relevance of the Dostoevsky-Bakhtin genealogy for contemporary ethical criticism.

Arguing for narrative *as* ethics, Newton proposes that narrative fiction is indispensable for ethical inquiry because of the unique way in which it structures relationships between authors, characters, and readers. For Newton, the conceptual core of narrative ethics consists of a triadic structure: "(1) a narrational ethics (. . . signifying the exigent conditions and consequences of the narrative act itself); (2) a representational ethics (the costs incurred in fictionalizing oneself or others by exchanging 'person' for 'character'); and (3) a hermeneutic ethics (the ethico-critical accountability which acts of reading hold their readers to)."[29] The first category, influenced by the ethical philosophy of Levinas, relates to "the dialogic system of exchanges at work among tellers, listeners, and witnesses, and the responsibilities and claims which follow from the acts of storytelling" (18). Drawing on Bakhtin for his second category, Newton correlates the aesthetic (representational) act of creating/becoming a hero with questions of responsibility that such acts necessarily entail: what "gains, losses and risks [are] taken up when selves represent or are represented by others"?[30] Newton's third category of interpretational, or hermeneutic, ethics concerns the reader's responsibility for "getting" someone else's story. This involves recognition of the costs of interpretation and the acceptance of one's responsibility for the act of reading.

Newton's is a powerful argument against versions of literary ethics grounded in structuralist analysis that tend to master the experience of reading by relegating meaning between the equidistant poles of an implied reader and writer.[31] Instead, Newton urges us to engage with texts by studying the hierarchical structures formed between writers, narrators, tellers, listeners, and readers through what Bakhtin would term "a surplus of vision": a consciousness that is shared between author and character but which also supersedes both. The ethics of such a narrative will be found in its relationship to alterity—with that other which this consciousness encounters at a given moment, be it author, character, or reader. It also calls for the subjectivities participating in a narrative act—fictional or otherwise—to accept responsibility for the unavoidable violence of such participation.

Newton's ethics "as pragmatics" also seems to be better equipped to deal with the ethical costs of hermeneutic procedures of reading than are posthumanist attempts to move past criticism that centers on the human subject. For example, Heather Love's instructions to read "close but not deep" might indeed avoid "engag[ing] the metaphysical and humanist concerns of hermeneutics," but they also miss an opportunity to explore the ethical costs inherent in any act of reading—even one that promises to faithfully "rely on description rather than interpretation."[32] Rather than escaping the risks of forming subjectivities through the act of reading, narrative ethics asks us to become *accountable* for the practice of representation and interpretation as it happens dialogically within the text and outside of it, orchestrating the relationships between the participants in the narrative scene of address. The presence of alterity and the dynamics of the subject's engagement with it are brought to the fore in the very structure of narrative fiction.

It is hardly an accident that Newton's framework of narrative ethics aligns so perfectly with how we read Dostoevsky today. Newton's first two categories correspond to the role that narrating oneself and others in Dostoevsky's fiction plays in the construction of his characters' identity. In the following chapters, I explore how Dostoevsky's representational and narrational ethics enter into a relationship with interpretational, or hermeneutic, ethics, which concerns the reader's responsibility for "getting" someone else's—in this case, Dostoevsky's—story.

Thus, in my exploration of Dostoevsky's narrative ethics in the first and second chapters of this book, I focus on two of its main aspects: the role that narrative acts of representation and interpretation play in the formation of subjectivity in his prose, and the responsibility these activities place upon author and readers. I seek to show that one of Dostoevsky's cardinal innovations is the understanding of narrative discourse as a moral category that circumscribes within its sphere author, character, and reader. As the title of my book suggests, the reader's accountability for the act of reading begins with the awareness that her interpretative activity belongs to the same discursive order as the representational activity of the author and the characters. In the book's third and fourth chapters, I argue that in his attention to the risks of narrative acts and his emphasis on the power dynamics created by the distribution of discourse between author, character, and reader, Nabokov emerges as Dostoevsky's direct successor and counterpart. I read Nabokov's explicit denunciation of Dostoevsky's poetics as a creative misreading, which reveals numerous implicit correspondences between the narrative ethics of these two seemingly opposed authors.

DOSTOEVSKY AND NABOKOV I:
A CASE FOR COMPARATIVE ETHICS

Most scholars who juxtapose the two writers see Nabokov's use of Dostoevsky—be it thematic or intertextual—as a case of parody.[33] This parodic appropriation, it has been argued, befits a wider paradigmatic shift from realism to modernism and from ethical, content-driven concerns toward aesthetic and formal ones.[34] At the same time, Nabokov's interdiction against reading his prose from a moral perspective has met with growing critical resistance.[35] In my own engagement with Nabokov, I build on such studies and argue that pairing Dostoevsky with Nabokov can further illuminate how narrative structures affect the moral formation of a reading subject. Furthermore, I extend the reach of the ethical inquiry into Nabokov's prose in order to propose that the reader's responsibility is not easily separable from that of the author.

Like Dostoevsky's fiction, Nabokov's prose is populated with protagonists whose crimes are directly connected to their aesthetic ambitions. Instead of Dostoevsky's moral ideal of Christ, however, Nabokov's narrators are pitted against the figure of the implied author. His absolute representational control over his characters and his insistence on interpretative control over his readers turn into a parodic fulfillment of the characters' own metaphysical and aesthetic aspirations. As such, Nabokov's prose stands as a modernist response to the radical conditions of narrative intersubjectivity set up by Dostoevsky's Christian ethics.

As I intend to show, Dostoevsky and Nabokov share similar ethical concerns about the function of narrative in the formation of subjectivity and the responsibilities it places upon those involved in the narrative process. To ask about the narrative ethics of these authors is to inquire about the role of narrating in the formation of a character, be it a literary character in their prose or the character of a reader. The two authors can be said to be each other's polar opposites in how they understand and utilize the authorial function in their prose. Dostoevsky, as Bakhtin tells us, forgoes discursive control over his characters, allowing them the possibility of "attaining the truth of [their] own consciousness."[36] Nabokov, by contrast, claims to maintain complete narrative authority over his characters, professing to treat them as "galley slaves."[37] Yet, as I argue in this study, the difference here is not determined by one's preference for ethics (Dostoevsky) or aesthetics (Nabokov). My analysis of their prose shows that both authors exhibit a keen awareness of the ethical responsibilities of authorship and, consequently, of readership. Both Dostoevsky and Nabokov insist that being a responsible author necessitates an acceptance of being authored by someone else, that the responsibility for authorship begins with an acknowledgment that one is also a character in someone else's story. Such is the ethical framework posited by the texts analyzed in this book: its space stretches between the narrative usurpation of authorship and silence. In this way, the prose of Dostoevsky and Nabokov can be seen as a narrative unfolding of Father Zosima's powerful assertion that "each of us is guilty before everyone, for everyone and everything."[38] Both writers present narrative fiction as an experience that requires an acceptance of such responsibility. In other words, narrative unfolds a space *of* and *for* ethics.

My inquiry into Dostoevsky's narrative ethics begins in chapter 1 with a reexamination of Bakhtin's theory and how it resonates with Dostoevsky's solutions to the problem of incorporating his Christian ethics effectively into the formal aspects of the prose. Setting Bakhtin's notion of polyphony against scholarship that emphasizes the importance of action in Dostoevsky's prose, I argue that the novel's dialogic sphere becomes an arena for the struggle among Dostoevsky's characters to dominate one another. The source of this struggle is the characters' lack of moral fortitude in the face of what Dostoevsky identifies as a spiritual and moral crisis in Russia in the latter half of the nineteenth century. In order to show the relevance of the author's and characters' ethical and religious worldviews—the ideological content—to the relationships between author, characters, and reader, I analyze Dostoevsky's short story "The Meek One" against the backdrop of Dostoevsky's discussion of suicide that enframes it in *A Writer's Diary*. Thus, in "The Meek One," the protagonist's inability to maintain his faith undermines the moral value of truth that emerges as the product of his monologue. Correlating discursive interactions in the story with the protagonist's social interactions, Dostoevsky underscores the moral dimension of the narrative act itself and asks the reader to consider the ethical costs of her own discursive participation with the text.

In chapter 2, I turn to *The Idiot* as an extreme case in Dostoevsky's oeuvre because of the radical emphasis it places on the ethics of narrative representation. The intense struggle for domination that takes place between most of the novel's characters once again occurs on the discursive level, through what Sarah Young has called "scripting."[39] Entering the novel as an ethically pure character, Prince Myshkin eventually learns that any discursive participation is ethically compromised and requires an acceptance of responsibility for the violence it inflicts on others. This significantly raises the stakes for the reader, whose participation in the text is by definition discursive. At the end, the reader is left with the impossible choice of either taking part in the discursive struggle of the novel, conscious of its effect, or withdrawing from the novel in nonparticipating silence. This choice, I argue, is an ethical one.

My investigation of Nabokov's narrative ethics begins in chapter 3 by focusing on the ethical responsibilities nested in the aesthetic relationship between author and characters. To do this, I turn to *Despair*, a novel in which Nabokov most thoroughly establishes the link between crime, writing, and one's metaphysical aspirations. The protagonist's desire for ontological certitude motivates both his crime and the practice of writing, enacting a metaphoric relationship between them. Hermann is pitted against the figure

Introduction

of the implied author, whose absolute representational control over the text and insistence on interpretative control over the reader mirror the desire for control of his protagonist. The position of authorship, thus compromised, similarly marks the reader's discursive activity with the text as ethically ambiguous.

In chapter 4, I proceed to tease out the complexities of Nabokov's conceptualization of art and the artist's role in the process of artistic creation. Pushing back against Dostoevsky, Nabokov envisions artistic practice as simultaneously mimetic and self-referential, dependent on the outside referent and existing as an autonomous aesthetic artifact. The correlative to this vision is a similar doubling in Nabokov's conceptualization of the writer as both a godlike creator of fictive worlds and a human agent whose perspective is by definition limited and imperfect. From this duality emerges the notion of language as an instrument of quasi-divine creation—if used by the authorial figure—and of control and subjugation when employed by the novels' protagonist-narrators. Such a moral distribution absolves the authorial figure from any responsibility and places the moral burden for the narrative violence on Nabokov's characters. The ethical reading, however, interprets the author's desire for control as being driven by the same source as the characters'. It insists that the author, in Bakhtinian terms, cannot have "an alibi in being" and must be answerable for his own participation in aesthetic activity.[40] To show how Nabokov's conceptualization of language generates the ethical ambiguities in the relationship between author and characters, I analyze the Shakespeare chapter from *Bend Sinister*, arguably Nabokov's most political novel. What my analysis brings to the fore is the role language plays in the distribution of power between the novel's different subjectivities. Nabokov makes the reader conscious of the ethical bind of language and the responsibility that such an awareness brings to the act of reading.

Exploring Dostoevsky and Nabokov, and the affinities between them, through the lens of narrative ethics allows us to reassess the importance of Dostoevsky for twentieth-century literature. Notwithstanding Nabokov's banishment of morality from his works and his claims to artistic autonomy, such an investigation points to the persistence of a literary tradition whose central preoccupation is the moral dimension of human life. An ever-skillful provocateur and manipulator of public opinion, Nabokov might indeed have donned the role of the "last patrician of world literature and supreme arbiter of artistic taste" who "transcended national roots, traditions, and influences."[41] At the same time, however, a careful exploration of Nabokov's later work shows a conscious and painstaking reconstitution of the Western modernist canon that places Russian literature at its center and Nabokov's own prose as its crowning achievement.[42] The kinship between Nabokov and Dostoevsky that I put forward in this book leaves little doubt that in this

Dostoevsky and Nabokov

transformation the moral dimension of Russian literature was paramount. What interests me most, however, is how each writer found a way to affect the moral imagination of the reader through specific formal innovations. I begin by drawing out the sources behind Dostoevsky's radical reshaping of the relationship between the ethics and aesthetics of the text.

THE ETHICS OF FORM

Dostoevsky's elaboration of new literary forms allowed him to produce fiction grounded in Christian ethics, while at the same time avoiding didacticism. In this sense, it is instructive to compare Dostoevsky with his most direct predecessor, Nikolai Gogol, whose project to do the same ended in failure.

Gogol's declaration of literature's moral efficacy comes from two nonfiction works, written as a result of his deep spiritual crisis in the mid-1840s: *Selected Passages from Correspondence with Friends*, published in 1847, and the "Author's Confession," published posthumously in 1855. Part homily, part confession, part literary study, *Selected Passages* grants literature a decisive role in the project of Russia's spiritual revival. In Gogol's vision, literature works as an instrument of the reader's spiritual regeneration; its task is to restore Russia and, ultimately, the world:

> Our poetry will be imbued with an angelic passion and, having struck every string there is in the Russian, it will move the most hardened soul with a holiness with which no power and no instrument in man can contend: it will evoke our Russia for us, our Russian Russia . . . and will display us in such a way that everyone, without exception, however different their ideas might be, of whatever education and opinions, will say with one voice: "This is our Russia; it is a warm refuge for us, and now we are really at home in it, under our native roof and not in a foreign land."[43]

At the same time, for Gogol, Russian poetry is a product of the new forms of statehood that appeared in Russia with Peter the Great: "Everyone in the young state was enthusiastic, uttering the same cry of astonishment that a savage utters at the sight of glittering treasures brought before him. This enthusiasm was reflected in our poetry, or, to put it better, *it created it*" (201, emphasis added). Moreover, literature is also answerable to the other indispensable agent of change that looms large over the pages of *Selected Passages*: the church.[44]

State service for Gogol becomes coterminous with religious service and takes priority over all other activity. Writing is just one of its many forms.

13

Introduction

In "An Author's Confession," Gogol similarly asserts that writing must be teleologically aligned with state service: the writer must "feel and be assured that in creating his work he is fulfilling precisely that duty for which he was called to life, for which he was given abilities and strengths and that by fulfilling it, he . . . serves his country as if in reality he were performing state service."[45] Importantly, Gogol explains his early hesitations about his ability to succeed with *Dead Souls* in a context that conflates state service and religious duty: "Whoever wishes to serve Russia honestly must have a lot of love for her . . . one must have a lot of love for the human being . . . and become a true Christian in the full meaning of this word. It is no wonder that without finding it in myself, I couldn't serve the way I wanted."[46] Only after having reformed himself can Gogol set out to create a work whose goal is to represent the whole of Russian man: "so that after reading my work, the Russian man would appear as if by himself, with all the variety of gifts and riches he received in comparison with other nations, and with all the multitude of his weaknesses that he has in himself also in comparison with other nations."[47] For Gogol, his own moral imperfections muddied the clarity of his intentions and hindered readers from understanding his novel properly. Not able to discern the whole from the part, readers who finished the first part of *Dead Souls* had assumed that he was "laughing not only at the weakness, but at the entire man."[48] His readers' experience of the first part of the novel refueled Gogol's doubts about his moral standing and sent him on yet another round of his quest for self-improvement, which finally brought him to Christ: "I was taken with everything that contained the knowledge of man and the soul of man, from the confession of a lay person to the confession of an anchorite and a desert-dweller, and on this road . . . I came to Christ, having realized that He contains the key to the soul of man, and not a single one of the wise men has ascended to that height of knowledge of the soul that he has."[49] Hence, in *Selected Passages*, the purpose of literature is cast in religious terms. In order to succeed, the writer's task is to improve his soul and the soul of his reader, preparing both for the high mission of spiritual resurrection, the example of which will become the second part of *Dead Souls*.

Gogol's instructions on how to be and how to read exemplified the growing pretensions of Russian writers in the second quarter of the nineteenth century to "become teachers, leaders, and lawgivers of Russian society."[50] At the same time, Gogol's implicit anxiety about his ability to control his readers' reactions was symptomatic of a new phase in the history of Russian literature, which saw the strengthening of the role of Russian literary critics as agents of competing authority. By the early 1840s, literary critics had become Russian fiction's most attentive and demanding readers and—to the extent of their willingness to interfere in the literary process—its coauthors.[51] One of the earliest and most dramatic episodes of the struggle between critic and author over the kind of literature Russia needed was the exchange of letters between Gogol and Vissarion Belinsky, triggered by Belinsky's scorching review of *Selected Passages* published in *The Contemporary* in 1847.[52]

If in *Selected Passages* Gogol proposes a utopian program that begins with personal transformation founded on Christian ethics and culminates in the triumphant unification of church and state, the heart of Belinsky's rejection of the book is what he finds to be Gogol's appallingly reactionary views on political and social issues, as well as his deplorable regression from a secular to a religious worldview:

> This is why you haven't noticed that Russia sees its salvation not in mysticism, not in asceticism, not in pietism, but in the successes of civilization, education, and humanism. She needs neither sermons (she has heard enough of them!), nor prayers (she has said enough of them!), but the awakening of the feeling of human dignity in her people, lost for so many centuries in dirt and manure. She needs rights and laws, in accordance not with the church and its teachings, but with common sense and justice, as well as their strict implementation, whenever possible.[53]

Belinsky's letter to Gogol marked a crucial turn in Dostoevsky's life: his copying of the letter and reading it to the members of the Petrashevsky circle became decisive in Dostoevsky's arrest, conviction, and punishment.[54] Moreover, both in terms of its ideology and its belief in the critic's right to influence the course of literary production, Belinsky's attack on Gogol signified a major line of development for the next generation of Russian literary critics. And it was against such professional heirs of Belinsky as Nikolai Dobroliubov and Nikolai Chernyshevsky that Dostoevsky would direct some of his most important philosophical and aesthetic polemics after his return to literary activity at the beginning of the 1860s. Dostoevsky's aesthetic innovations stand out prominently against the background of his constant struggle with these critics' endeavors to shape the course of literary production. Dostoevsky's critical writings also reflect his deep ambivalence toward Gogol's goal of seeing Russian literature as an instrument of religious and moral revival.

During Belinsky's short but intense career as Russia's leading literary critic, his personal and professional worldview underwent a series of dramatic changes—from the German romanticism and idealism of the late 1830s, to the utopian socialism of the early 1840s, to the socialist atheism of the late 1840s.[55] Among the members of the next generation of critics, however, the passionate theomachy that characterized Belinsky's last years morphed into a staunchly materialist worldview in which the romantic idealism of the previous generation gave way to rationalist utilitarianism.[56] Radical literary critics advocated a conscious transformation of society according to principles of social and economic equality. And since literature was the primary agent for implementing this program in real life, the main task of the new generation of utilitarian ideologues was to describe the parameters that would secure literature's utmost effectiveness.

By the time he had restarted his literary career at the end of the 1850s, Dostoevsky found the views of the radical critics objectionable both philosophically and aesthetically, and he attacked them in his journalistic writing and prose. In his important 1861 article "Mr. –bov and the Question of Art," Dostoevsky confronted the radical critics' mandate for a useful and utilitarian art by pointing out two key features of the human condition that expose any such program as untenable.

First, Dostoevsky argues that while humans exist in a state of conflict, what fills one's life with meaning and makes it worth living is not the conflict's successful resolution but one's striving to overcome it. This idea reappears once again in *The Idiot*, in Ippolit's confession as a cry against the finality of death and his fierce embrace of life:

> Oh, you may be sure that Columbus was happy not when he had discovered America, but when he was discovering it; you may be sure that the highest moment of his happiness was, perhaps, exactly three days before the discovery of the New World, when the mutinous crew in their despair almost turned the ship back to Europe, right around! . . . The point is in life, in life alone—in discovering it, constantly and eternally, and not at all in the discovery itself![57]

Such striving awakens in us a need for beauty. As Dostoevsky writes in "Mr. –bov": "The need for beauty develops most when a human being is in a state of discord with reality, in a state of disharmony and struggle, i.e., when he lives most fully, because a human being lives most when he searches and strives for something. It is then he develops the most natural desire for harmony and peace, and in beauty there is both: harmony and peace."[58] For Dostoevsky, the most vivid manifestation of beauty is art:

> The need for beauty and for art that embodies it is inseparable from humans, and without it humans perhaps would not want to live. A human being thirsts for it, finds it, and accepts beauty without any conditions only because it is beauty. Humans admire beauty with reverence, without asking whether it is useful and what can be bought with it. Perhaps the greatest mystery of art is that the image of beauty it creates immediately becomes an idol without any conditions.[59]

Thus, Dostoevsky concedes that art is useful, but he insists that its value far surpasses the narrow limits set by utilitarian aesthetics. The embodiment of beauty makes art as essential as "eating and drinking"; it also necessitates artistic freedom.[60]

The requirement of artistic freedom is warranted—and here Dostoevsky turns to the second feature overlooked by the radical critics—by the simple fact that human consciousness is an imperfect tool and cannot be used to measure what humanity really needs at any given moment. A couple of years later, Dostoevsky will give the same argument to the Underground Man, who convincingly uses it against the assumption of rational egoists that reason can realign our selfish interests with those that benefit society at large. Since we are unable to effectively determine our own needs, let alone the needs of humankind, we cannot know what kind of art is required to improve our lot: "That is why in determining ahead of time the goals of art and how it must be useful, we might make a terrible mistake and bring only harm instead of use, therefore acting against ourselves."[61]

In a notebook entry from April 16, 1864, Dostoevsky provides the raison d'être of his faith and names Christ as the most perfect ideal. With his wife's body lying in the next room, Dostoevsky writes down what he believes to be a logical proof for the existence of the afterlife:

> To love a person *as oneself* as Christ commanded is impossible . . . On earth the law of personality binds us. The *I* prevents us . . . Only Christ could, but Christ was an eternal ideal toward whom one strives and must continue to strive according to the laws of nature. After the appearance of Christ as an *ideal of man* in the flesh, it became clear as day that . . . the highest, the ultimate development of personality must be (at the end of development, at the very point of achieving the goal) in discovering and becoming aware with all the power of one's nature that the supreme application of personality, the fullness of the development of one's *I*—is to destroy this *I*, to give it completely to all and everyone indivisibly and unreservedly . . . This is Christ's paradise. . . . But if this is the ultimate goal of humanity . . . then in achieving it one ends his earthly existence. This means that on earth one is only a creature that is developing, that is unfinished and transitional. But achieving such a great goal . . . is completely senseless if after this everything expires and disappears, that is, if there is no more life after one achieves this goal. This means that there is a future, paradisiacal life.[62]

The argument Dostoevsky makes for Christian faith here is strikingly similar to his argument for the freedom of art in "Mr. -bov." What the article describes as aesthetic necessity, the diary entry expresses in ethical terms.

Introduction

In his belief that Christ is the foundation and the goal of any true personal transformation and that art—and literature in particular—must enact the ideal of Christ, Dostoevsky is not too far from the Gogol of *Selected Passages*. The proximity of Dostoevsky's and Gogol's views on a number of aesthetic and philosophic positions comes into relief by looking at the first draft of Gogol's response to Belinsky.[63] In numerous places in the draft, Gogol reproaches Belinsky for not knowing life and asserts that the latter's peremptory opinions are indefensible considering his "superficial journalistic education" (111). Having spent his life in St. Petersburg, Belinsky, in Gogol's opinion, had no right to pass judgment on the Russian church, Russian society, or the Russian people:

> I was also astounded by the brave arrogance with which you say that "I know our society and its spirit." How can you vouch for this ever-changing chameleon? What data do you possess that proves that you know society? . . . Have you ever shown in your works that you are a profound expert on the human soul? Living almost without contact with people and society, leading the peaceful life of a journalist . . . how can you have any concept of this enormous monster . . . (112)

This is the same rebuke that Dostoevsky addresses to Dobroliubov in his article fourteen years later: "The foundation of his convictions is just and evokes sympathy from the reader, but the ideas with which he expresses this foundation are often paradoxical and notable because of one important drawback: the smell of the lamp. Mr. –bov is a theoretician, sometimes a dreamer, and in many cases has a poor grasp of reality. Sometimes he treats reality too unceremoniously: he bends it any way he wishes, until he manages to make it concur with his idea."[64] Alienation from life with its accompanying symptom of "dreaminess" is one of the more serious conditions that afflict Dostoevsky's characters. Its moral dangers become obvious in *Notes from Underground* and most fully pronounced in *Crime and Punishment*.[65] Most importantly, like Dostoevsky in his argument with Dobroliubov, Gogol connects what he considers to be Belinsky's perverse understanding of human nature to a profoundly flawed conception of art. In the draft, Gogol reiterates the main point of *Selected Passages*, that the reformation of society must begin with the moral and spiritual rebirth of a single individual:

> Seeing that the society has chosen a wrong path . . . many think that reforms and changes . . . can improve the world. Others think that some special, mediocre literature . . . can influence society's development. It bears fruit, but such that more often than not the author recoils from it in fear . . . Society forms by itself, it forms from the individuals . . . Let a man remember that he is not

a material beast, but a sublime citizen of the sublime heavenly state, and until everyone starts to live the life of the heavenly state at least somewhat, the earthly state won't be rearranged either.[66]

Gogol's insistence on the importance of spiritual life and his warning that socially engaged literature will breed monsters bear an uncanny resemblance to Dostoevsky's aesthetic and ethical viewpoints—ones that remained unchanged from the early 1860s on. Still, regardless of whether Dostoevsky read Gogol's draft, he retained his negative opinion of *Selected Passages*, most vividly materialized in his merciless parody of Gogol's book in the 1859 novella *The Village of Stepanchikovo*.[67] One of the reasons for the consistency of Dostoevsky's attitude toward *Selected Passages* could have been his desire to overcome his predecessor's influence.[68] Yet another explanation is that Dostoevsky's treatment of Gogol's book was part of his search for a literary form that would not betray his Christian beliefs.

Gogol's failure to embody his ideals in the novelistic form might have strengthened Dostoevsky's opinion that in order to avoid didacticism and remain effective, the Christian morality he espoused must find its successful expression in a proper aesthetic form. The importance of this issue for Dostoevsky is present as late as November 1880, as Dostoevsky comes close to finishing his last novel. In a letter to Ivan Aksakov, he addresses the problem of finding the right *form* for communicating his views and puts it in the context of *Selected Passages*:

> Your thesis about the tone of spreading sacred things in society, that is without frenzy or abusive language, does not leave me. Obviously one could do without abusive language, but is it possible to not be oneself, to be insincere? . . . To shroud oneself in clouds of grandeur (that's Gogol's tone, for example, in *Specific Passages*)—is insincerity, and insincerity will be sensed by even the most inexperienced reader. It will betray you on the spot.[69]

Dostoevsky's discussion with Aksakov concerns the task of communicating his Christian beliefs in the journalistic setting of *A Writer's Diary*; still, Dostoevsky's preoccupation with the relationship between the medium and the message can be extrapolated into the wider question of his search for new literary forms that would present his views in the most effective and persuasive manner without corrupting them.

As is made clear by his polemic with Dobroliubov and by the expression of his credo in the notebook, Dostoevsky hoped that such forms would embody his convictions about human nature's incompleteness and the limitations of human consciousness. They would also account for Dostoevsky's prerequisite of freedom in a way that could correlate the aesthetic freedom

Introduction

necessary for art's "organic development" with the ethical freedom to follow the ideal of Christ. In one of his articles of the early 1860s, contemplating the legacy of Belinsky's last period, Dostoevsky stresses that a crucial literary achievement of that period was "literature's organic entrance into life."[70] Paraphrasing Dostoevsky, we can say that in his own prose he developed ways in which the ethics of fiction, the extent of literature's participation in life, could find its organic manifestation aesthetically. In his quest, Dostoevsky took on Gogol's appeal for religious literature and searched in his fiction for a proper aesthetic form that would make its moral lessons effective.

REALIGNING DIALOGISM

Dostoevsky's solution to the correlation between aesthetic and ethical freedom received its most famous analysis by Mikhail Bakhtin, who argued that Dostoevsky "opened" his prose by connecting the radical change in the relationship between author and character with his characters' ability to freely determine their own truth about the world. Such a dismantling of the hierarchy of representation between author and hero endows Dostoevsky's characters with discursive freedom. At the same time, however, as Dostoevsky makes clear in "Mr. -bov," incompleteness is never a final stage: life and art must be directed by our striving toward an ethical and aesthetic ideal. Any artistic form must then accommodate the dramatic tension between the character's freedom—the unfinalizability of one's personhood—and the ethical pull toward the completion of one's search for an ideal, which, if it were reachable, would also signify ethical and aesthetic closure.[71]

The implications of this tension for Dostoevsky's prose require a reconsideration from an ethical perspective of the relationship between the dialogic realm of the novel—what for Bakhtin establishes the unfinalizable freedom of the characters—and the progression of the plot that reflects the characters' movement toward or away from acting upon that freedom. With this in mind, I suggest pairing Bakhtin's formulations on Dostoevsky's narrative ethics with the notion that, in narrative prose, plot can reflect the state of the text's ethics at any given point of textual time. The idea of plot as an appropriate vehicle for ethics in narrative fiction was put into circulation by Geoffrey Harpham, a contemporary critic who works on ethics and literature. Contrasting morality with ethics, Harpham describes their relationship as a tense collaboration between overdetermined choices and underdetermined principles. Ethical discourse demands the acknowledgment of one's interior, interested motivations, or what Harpham calls "overdetermination," while morality can be seen as the "non-ethical" moment within ethics, a point in time when one must act as if a disinterested choice, or "underdetermination," were still possible. "Ethics," writes Harpham, "constitutes a general and categorical imperative to 'act on principle'; morality constitutes a further imperative nested within the ethical that commands us to act now and on the right principle, that is, the one we want to stand *as* principle."[72] Without morality, argues Harpham, "ethics would be condemned to dithering"; while without the sanctity of ethics, morality becomes "mere blindness and brutality" (30). In this relationship, each element works to exclude the other while simultaneously necessitating the other's existence.

Locating the difference between *ethics* and *morality* on a chronological axis, Harpham argues that plot can be viewed as a vehicle for the ethics of the text, since it accommodates both the categorical adherence of ethics to principle and morality's requirement to act on the right principle. An ethical inquiry construed as a temporal progression from ethics to morality always inhabits a narrative structure, whose plot, Harpham suggests, enacts the crossing of the distance from what *is* but *ought-not-to-be* to what *is* and *ought-to-be*.[73]

A similar relationship, I contend, exists between the discursive freedom of Dostoevsky's characters and the moral imperative that streamlines their trajectory through the text. The source of this relationship is Ivan's definition in the "Grand Inquisitor" of freedom as a gift that one receives from Christ in order to fulfill the imperative of destroying one's *I*. An illustration of this tension in *Notes from Underground* might be helpful here. One of the Underground Man's main arguments in part 1 depends on the opposition he establishes between the "normal man," a rational egoist, and "the man of heightened consciousness," that is, himself.[74] What allows normal men to act is their ability to make underdetermined choices, justified in their case by a blind reliance on natural law ("the stone wall"). For men of heightened consciousness, however, everything is overdetermined, since they cannot allow themselves to "take the most immediate and secondary causes for the primary ones, and thus become convinced more quickly and easily than others that they have found an indisputable basis for their doings" (17). The Underground Man finds himself stuck in a state of discursive inertia, which makes him unable to successfully complete his narrative. As we are told at the end, he "could not help himself and went on" (130). Yet, Dostoevsky purposefully follows the argument of the first part with the action-driven plot of the second part, in which the Underground Man's freedom *from* action is contrasted with Liza's freedom *to* act. What enables her to do so is the underdetermined justification of her actions based on the moral, not the natural, law.

Thus, one of my main goals in this book is to reconsider whether Bakhtin's notion of the polyphonic novel is compatible with Dostoevsky's transfer of his Christian ethics onto the formal features of his prose. To do so, I investigate the tension between the nonverbal elements of Dostoevsky's

Introduction

prose—images, characters' actions, or characters' bodies—and its dialogic realm or, in other words, between plot and discourse. To foreground the importance of dialogic interactions between Dostoevsky's characters, Bakhtin relegates plot to the secondary role of preparing the stage for the characters' dialogic exchanges. Yet, the discursive freedom of Dostoevsky's characters always comes with a responsibility to act, and this dynamic, in turn, energizes the progression of the plot. The reintegration of plot into an inquiry into Dostoevsky's narrative ethics invites a reassessment of the ethics of dialogism in Dostoevsky's prose and, consequently, has important ramifications for the author's and the reader's ethical engagement with the text.

Instead of treating the dialogic realm as a gift of freedom that Dostoevsky bestows on his characters, I propose that such unrestrained narrative freedom is a symptom of the moral and spiritual crisis that afflicts Dostoevsky's fictional worlds. In their striving toward Christ, Dostoevsky's characters suffer just as strongly from a loss of faith in Christ—the loss of an ideal. This loss, affecting the formation of hierarchies *within* Dostoevsky's prose, corresponds to the hierarchies formed *by* the prose, since the perceived absence of moral authority—Christ—is mirrored by the seemingly absent author.[75]

The beauty that, according to *The Idiot*'s Prince Myshkin, will save the world is rarely found in Dostoevsky's novels: with the exception of Zosima, Markel, and Alyosha from *The Brothers Karamazov* and Myshkin himself, hardly anyone attains a glimpse of the real thing. Nor does the epiphanic experience of these characters have the power to save the world from the catastrophic consequences of the loss of faith. Dostoevsky's prose is at best an arrow pointing toward the place where that beauty might be rediscovered after reading. The markers of Christianity in Dostoevsky's fiction are at once simple and easily noticeable: his characters and readers are offered the intercession of an iconic image. Such are the image of Raskolnikov and Sonya silently reading the "eternal book" together in *Crime and Punishment*; the icon depicting the Mother of God in the hands of the Meek One as she jumps to her death; the image of the nursing child and his smiling mother witnessed by Myshkin during his travels across Russia; and Christ kissing the Grand Inquisitor in *The Brothers Karamazov*. Indeed, Christian ethics, on the level of content, makes its entry into Dostoevsky's texts in a not particularly subtle way—no wonder it made Nabokov shudder with an aesthete's disgust.[76]

At the same time, the presence of Christ in Dostoevsky's fiction is marginal, in the sense that it sets the limits to the ethics of each text through images that promise salvation but also through ones that bespeak Christ's death: most notably, Holbein's portrait of the dead Christ in *The Idiot*. If the loss of Christ can be regarded as the *is* of Dostoevsky's fiction, salvation through Christ becomes its *ought-to-be*. The ethics spans the distance between these two extremes, and plot takes us from one to the other.

The hidden light of Dostoevsky's Christian ethics shines brightest in places that are mostly nondialogic. Dostoevsky's characters willingly engage in external and internal polemics with others, yet their dialogic interactions are for the most part coercive and antagonistic. The moral strength of female characters embodying the ideal in Dostoevsky's fiction, like Liza in *Notes from Underground* or Sonya in *Crime and Punishment*, comes from their ability to act, not speak. While Myshkin begins *The Idiot* with an exemplary eloquence, his ability to present his ethics verbally deteriorates as he becomes conscious of the ethical dangers of dialogic activity. Arguably, an example of verbal activity that does not finalize the other appears only in Dostoevsky's last novel.[77] The dynamics of dialogic coercion between characters prefigure acts of physical violence (either against oneself or others) or of self-sacrifice and compassion. Setting the dialogic interactions between these two extremes makes the moral status of what Bakhtin called the "big dialogue" of the novel highly problematic. Such a setup exposes the compromised ethics of the characters' ideology and shows their genuine search for a society in which salvation is not reached at the expense of others.

Moreover, the narratives—confessions, ideological speeches, arguments, and apologies—of Dostoevsky's characters frequently begin as a response to a crisis of faith, which can also, as in the case of the Underground Man or Mr. Goliadkin, have its origin in social humiliation. In Dostoevsky's fictional universe, the social sphere and religious metaphysics bleed heavily into each other: the characters' attempts to attain social justice parallel their desire to reconstruct a proper metaphysical hierarchy. In Dostoevsky's fiction, however, the desire for order is most often perverted into the desire for control, which materializes as a bid to control representation. Authorship thus becomes a placeholder for authority, and the struggle between the characters for control of authorship restages their metaphysical and social struggles for domination. Dostoevsky's radical repositioning of the author-character hierarchy intensifies the ethical value of the narrative representation through which characters attempt to author one another and instigates an intense rivalry among them about whose version of the truth will dominate.

The removal of the authorial "speech center" endows Dostoevsky's characters with the potential for resolving dialogic struggles through acts of self-sacrifice and compassion. The freedom of choosing to act responsibly—even if the act itself is not carried through—allows the prose to retain the possibility for reestablishing the moral order—the *ought-to-be* of the text. This prospect, however, remains a priori foreclosed to the reader, whose engagement with the text is by definition limited to discursive interaction, that is, participation in the exchange of ideas in the text or its hermeneutic analysis. The reader's awareness of her accountability for this participation constitutes the kernel of the ethical lesson of reading Dostoevsky and is meant to promote the correct course of action in the reader's own life. Ultimately, discursive activity in Dostoevsky's prose becomes a primary instrument in the construction of interpersonal relationships and calls for responsibility from all who participate in it—author, characters, and reader. As I argue in the next section, an analysis of the architectonics of Nabokov's fiction shows a result that is surprisingly similar.

DOSTOEVSKY AND NABOKOV II: A BAKHTINIAN APPROACH

The Vagaries of Pleasure

Much has been made of how Nabokov's dislike of Dostoevsky manifests itself in the differences between their aesthetics; still, the most obvious distinction between the two—the measure, quality, and function of authorial presence in the prose of each—has remained mostly unexplored. Bakhtin's proposition that in reading Dostoevsky we experience the conscious removal of the authorial field of vision has forever changed how we read Dostoevsky now, and while we might disagree with Bakhtin's conclusions, we can hardly dispute his method. As Nabokov writes at the end of *Speak, Memory*, once you see what the sailor has hidden, there is no going back; and arguing today about whether the imprint of Bakhtin's reading on Dostoevsky's prose has always been an intrinsic part of the work itself seems to be a moot point.

Reading Nabokov, however, we experience the opposite: authorial presence looms large over his texts, instilling an unshakeable hierarchy in which both characters and readers are definitively stationed below the author. If—according to Bakhtin—Dostoevsky's upending of the relationship between author and character has brought momentous changes to the whole novelistic genre, how do we account for the undeniable presence of authorial consciousness in most of Nabokov's prose? If Dostoevsky's reformulation of the author-character dynamic brings awareness of the ethics of relationships between author, character, and reader, what would be the ethical implications of the mastery of Nabokov-the-author over his characters, as well as his insistence on controlling the aesthetic effects of the text?

In what follows, I look for openings that allow for an ethical analysis of Nabokov's fiction. I begin by examining the strategies Nabokov employs to complicate ethical inquiry into his texts, as well as the different critical approaches to reading Nabokov that attempt to circumvent those strategies. Pointing out some of the drawbacks of current ethical approaches to

Nabokov, I push for a reading that treats the presence of Nabokov's authorial figure in his prose as comparable to its perceived absence in Dostoevsky's. While we can agree that Nabokov's characters are often guilty of rhetorical crimes, the inclusion of the authorial figure in the ethical analysis asks us to consider the author's own responsibility for rhetoric that bears an uncanny resemblance to that employed by his characters, as well as the reader's responsibility for enjoying its pleasures.

Nabokov not only presides over the interdictions and prescriptions of his lectures on literature, the prefaces to his novels, and his interviews, his authorial figure also makes itself known in the fiction itself, as he explores the practices of writing and reading—of representation and interpretation—by allegorizing them in his prose. Addressing Nabokov's "meta-concerns" was initiated by some of his earliest readers. Among the first, Vladislav Khodasevich suggested that Nabokov's characters are nothing but masks that allow Nabokov to explore "the life of an artist and the life of a device in the artist's consciousness."[78] Treating Nabokov's texts as complex allegories of reading, however, has obvious negative consequences for reading them ethically, if only because it diminishes the mimetic effect of Nabokov's prose. In Humbert's sexual desire for Dolores Haze, David Packman characteristically sees an inscription of the reader's desire to interpret the text of the novel—but turns a blind eye to the possible ethical side effects implied by this analogy.[79]

At the other end of the spectrum, there is the Nabokov whom Michael Wood calls "the theorist of pain" and whose affiliation with modernism lies not in undermining the mimetic bond between the text and the reader but in complicating it, forcing the reader to contemplate the tension between art, which supposedly "does not have a moral in tow," and life, which surely does.[80] According to this view, the self-conscious artificiality of his worlds does not lessen the author's concern for their inhabitants but asks the reader to acknowledge that "reality" (as Nabokov writes in the afterword to *Lolita*) means "nothing without quotes."[81] Our task as readers, then, is to understand and evaluate the ethical impact of the practice of art on life.

Nabokov's readers often find themselves in the space framed, on the one side, by the writer's promise to reward their interpretative industriousness with "aesthetic bliss" and, on the other, by the undeniable fact that some of his most pleasurable passages have been penned by narrators whose narrative endeavors begin with an announcement of the deep-rooted link between writing and crime.[82] I argue that the tension between the poles—of the aesthetic pleasure promised by the author and the crimes perpetrated by his characters—is ethical. Inasmuch as we try to orient ourselves in the space between, the answer to the question "How do we read Nabokov?" is not much different from the answer to "How do we read Nabokov ethically?"

Introduction

Critics agree that Nabokov's exclusion of morality from his fiction is but a starting point, a protective spell against the generalities and platitudes populating ideological abstractions, and an injunction to endow the prose with a complexity that would do the master justice. Hence, there are those like Richard Rorty, who argue that Nabokov's morally compromised narrators (Hermann of *Despair* and Humbert of *Lolita*, to name a couple) are not artists enough and that Nabokov's ethics is to be found in the reader's understanding of the limits to their artistic skill, no matter how subtle its instrumentarium. For others, Nabokov's moral lesson lies in warning his readers about the dangers of applying an aesthetic lens to life directly, without mediation. Here, Nabokov emerges as a satirist, exposing his character-narrators' inability to keep art and life separate.[83] The moral transgression of such protagonists is that rather than sublimating their desires into a pursuit of art, they choose to aestheticize life, turning people into characters and themselves into life's authors. As one recent study of *Lolita* argues, to avoid solipsism and cruelty, art requires tenderness and empathy, qualities that, while being adjacent to art, might not necessarily be its part and parcel.[84] Learning this lesson constitutes Humbert's moral journey in narrating—but not living—his relationship with Dolores Haze; it is for its completion that he receives from Nabokov a partial redemption (earning himself an annual walk "in the green lane of Paradise," as Nabokov writes in the preface to the English version of *Despair*).[85] The reader, in turn, must learn the hard but rewarding job of discernment between the novel's morals and its ethics, that is, between "the *categorical*" response, in which Humbert's crime against Lolita remains forever unpardonable, and "the *conditional*" one, which seeks to make sense of the rich complexity of his "person and circumstances": the difference between the two being proportional to the difference between Humbert-the-character, who rapes an adolescent girl, and Humbert-the-narrator, who tells about it.[86]

In general, in investigations of Nabokov's ethics, his character-narrators—whether because of their aesthetic callousness or compromised ethics—bear the brunt of moral responsibility, while Nabokov, providing his most attentive readers with clues on how to avoid aesthetic and ethical pitfalls, emerges as the model artist and a subtle moralist. This is certainly one of the solutions to a release of tension between the two poles of experiencing Nabokov's prose that I outlined above. It also comes with side effects, however.

First, it sets up Nabokov as his own most perfect reader, which, in turn, creates a strong pull to align the interpretation of the meta-diegetic level of Nabokov's prose—the linguistic winks and kinks that the characters are oblivious to but that the reader should not be—with Nabokov's extra-textual commentary on what constitutes proper and improper interpretative strategies. As Eric Naiman has argued persuasively, the games Nabokov plays with his readers are far less innocent than his prefaces and interviews would allow. In Naiman's reading, as in Packman's, the illicit sexual desires and practices of Nabokov's characters are indeed re-created as the reader's desire for the text. For Naiman, however—and this is where he differs from Packman—this recognition makes the reader—as well as the author—ethically complicit in the characters' transgressions.[87]

Second, there is the danger that scapegoating Nabokov's characters, by assigning to them all of the ethical culpability or aesthetic obtuseness, happens at the expense of the complex relationship between the texts' ethical and aesthetic dimensions. Such readings too readily accept what Maurice Couturier has called "the authorial law," through which the author "seeks to promote his ideal ego to the rank of the super ego in the eyes of the reader and absconds as completely as he can from his text."[88] As a result, the reader complies with the author's bid to displace his responsibility for textual violence (violence *of* the text and *in* the text) onto his characters. Nabokov himself described this relationship quite accurately:

> Some of my characters are, no doubt, pretty beastly, but I really don't care, they are outside my inner self like the mournful monsters of a cathedral façade—demons placed there merely to show that they have been booted out.[89]

As Couturier suggests, at the source of this act of exorcism is both authorial and institutional censorship, whose main function is to protect the authorial figure by preventing the reader's escape from "the black box of the text."[90] Instead, Couturier suggests that one should see the text as "a communicational interface where the author's and the reader's desires interact with each other" and that the reader's task is "to try and recreate the internal logic of the text . . . and therefore to reach for the authorial figure which looms behind the text and is different from the real author."[91]

Finally, readers who seek a release from the tension between the ethics and aesthetics of Nabokov's prose inevitably end up with either an uneasy conscience about the pleasure of reading or frustration from foregoing the pleasure for the promise of what Nabokov calls "aesthetic bliss." This, I believe, ultimately boils down to a choice between suppressing the pleasure from the style of the prose[92] or having to continuously reassess one's definition of "aesthetic bliss" until it fits in with Nabokov's.

Difficulty of reception being a staple in the modernist's bag of tricks, Nabokov admits that aesthetic bliss is the product of hard labor on either side of the textual divide, his or the reader's. This labor is symbolized by the famous image of the panting, sweating reader climbing the steep slope of interpretation to be rewarded with the author's embrace at the summit. There

Introduction

is also Nabokov's admission that the pleasure comes from bringing to life the complexity of the construct:

> Why did I write any of my books, after all? For the sake of the pleasure, for the sake of the difficulty. I have no social purpose, no moral message; I've no general ideas to exploit, I just like composing riddles with elegant solutions.[93]

It is tempting to align the distance between pleasure and bliss—and I think it is bliss that Nabokov is talking about in the quote above—with the space separating Roland Barthes's definitions of *plaisir* and *jouissance*. Not unlike Barthes, Nabokov would be highly critical of the passive gratification that makes one a consumer of texts. Yet, it is hard to imagine Nabokov willingly granting his readers the freedom to produce textual meaning that comes with *jouissance*. As Zadie Smith accurately observes, Nabokov "felt his work to be multiplex but not truly multivalent."[94] At the same time, it is not quite clear what kind of pleasure from Nabokov's texts we are actually to write off as too passive. Are we not supposed to enjoy Humbert's stylistic acrobatics? Or do we take to heart Nabokov's suggestion that his "elegant solution" in *Lolita* is the evocation of a human being in her absence, something akin to what Dostoevsky achieves in "The Meek One," intensified in Nabokov's case by the reader's inescapable pleasure from the narrating voice that so successfully solipsizes its victim? Couturier suggests that the bliss from reading Nabokov comes from navigating precisely these challenges: the reader seeks "to appropriate the literary object and use it as the lame depository of his intellectual, aesthetic, or erotic desire," while understanding that to succeed at this is to risk becoming not much different from the narrator.[95] Still, the argument that one's awareness of the deep connection between pleasure and cruelty is a necessary milestone on the road to aesthetic bliss is not an easy one to accept. By the time the reader reaches the final destination, it is unclear how much either pleasure or bliss is left to her. In the final analysis, what comes to mind is not Barthes's *plaisir du texte* but Montaigne's condemnation of rape:

> Of violences offered to the conscience, that against the chastity of woman is, in my opinion, most to be avoided, forasmuch as there is a certain pleasure naturally mixed with it, and for that reason the dissent therein cannot be sufficiently perfect and entire, so that the violence seems to be mixed with a little consent of the forced party.[96]

The experience of reading Nabokov from this perspective makes it obvious that the shorthand for Nabokov's art is not only "curiosity, tenderness, kindness, ecstasy" but also—perhaps more so than Nabokov would like to admit—endurance and resistance, muscles, exercising which the reader learns unpleasant but hopefully necessary truths about her own practices of signification. To do so, the reader must struggle to fulfill the authorial imperative to interpret the text and at the same time rise up against it, prolonging her pleasure of the text while at the same time condemning it, ultimately accepting that, independent of her definition of what aesthetic bliss is, her struggle against "authorial law" has been doomed a priori.

Such considerations should make us wary of the image of friendship between author and reader that Nabokov offers at the summit of the textual mountain. In Nabokov's case, Altieri's warnings about the restrictive nature of such friendships sound especially relevant. Yet, if we refuse Nabokov's invitation for friendship, what critical approach to his fiction would allow us to identify with his texts' affective energies and, at the same time, respond to the ethical dangers of such identification? In the next section, I put forth an argument for an ethical inquiry based on the Dostoevsky-Bakhtin framework I elaborated earlier. While the analysis of power relations formed by the distribution of discourse among author, characters, and reader does not shy away from emotional identification with the text, it also calls for responsibility from all of the participants for the connection between the violence *in* the text and *of* the text.

Possessed by Structure

Commenting on the acrostic written into the final paragraph of Nabokov's story "The Vane Sisters" (an acrostic of which the narrator is ignorant, but the reader must not be), Michael Wood writes that "the trick comes off, but . . . at the expense of the story."[97] For Wood, the acrostic threatens the fragile balance of the story, since it forces readers to vacillate between understanding the story "to mean merely what it grammatically and semantically says" and experiencing the text as if it were encrypted, "possessed not only by another person but by another system of signification" (79). The first choice feels too naive and artificially constructed: to read the story "as is" seems to me close to an impossible task for a *Nabokov* reader, and it somewhat lessens the import of Wood's otherwise eloquent argument. But it is the second choice that interests me here, and I would like to explore its implications more fully.

"Possession by another system of signification" is a curious hybrid of personal agency and structure—one that presumes subjectivity and otherness of a different kind and makes itself present not through a direct interpersonal experience but by lodging itself within, inhabiting, invading, making itself part of the narrative structure. My difficulty in choosing the correct

Introduction

verb to approximate the act of agency here is quite telling, since it points precisely to the paradox at hand: possession implies a force that is external in origin yet is understood here as a constituent part of the system. Wood makes a similar point on the otherness that is always already present within the narrative's folds by pointing to the relationship between the meanings of "hand"—Sybil's hand, in this case—and "script." Wood notes Sybil's presence in the story in places where "possession" points to itself and can produce symptoms not only of "referential mania" but also of "self-referential" mania, as, for example, when the narrator makes a note of Sybil's "usual combination of several demon hands." This makes Nabokov's interlacing of the acrostic into the story's final paragraph feel heavy-handed and fares poorly against the "enchanting and touching 'aura'" of otherness that envelops the story.[98]

And yet, the trick that "can be tried only once in a thousand years of fiction," as Nabokov writes in his notes to the short story,[99] might work after all, if we agree to entertain the notion that it is part of a different story, one that exists in a close relationship with the original but is separate from it, and whose protagonist, as far as I know, has mostly managed to stay outside of the fiction. This is none other than V.N. himself or, to be more precise, the figure of the *implied author*. In rejecting "The Vane Sisters" for the *New Yorker*, fiction editor Katherine White compared the story unfavorably to the earlier story "Signs and Symbols." Nabokov, disappointed, responded by pointing out that the two stories are not that dissimilar; their affinity lies in the additional layer of meaning superimposed onto the main one:

> Most of the stories I am contemplating (and some I have written in the past—you actually published one with such an "inside"—the one about the old Jewish couple and their sick boy) will be composed on these lines, according to this system wherein a second (main) story is woven into, or placed behind, the superficial semitransparent one.[100]

In his discussion of the two stories, Wood remarks that what appears as the desire for otherness in "The Vane Sisters" materializes in "Sign and Symbols" as fear. In the latter story, order becomes a menacing force that tramples over one's hope for coincidence; *syuzhet* seeks to destroy *fabula* and prove the paranoiac right. The distance between the two responses to this kind of narrative structuring marks the range of Nabokov's "main story." In other words, by weaving the "second story" into the first, Nabokov not only makes the reader peer into the *syuzhet* until he discovers in it the key to unlocking the riddle of the *fabula*[101] but also fosters in his readers the awareness of their desire for and fear of the author.

At first glance, the notion that the production of meaning on the level of characters is refracted in the reader's engagement with Nabokov's fiction might seem not too distant from Packman's argument that the characters' interpretative and sexual desires reflect and inform the reader's desire for the text. What such allegorical readings miss, however, is the intersubjective dimension of Nabokov's prose, in which the two tiers of the text are not so much parallel to each other as they are contiguous. Indeed, what our refocusing brings to the fore is that the relationships among the implied author, the multitudes of narrators and narratees, and the implied reader in Nabokov's fiction are, if not of kinship, then of responsibility. Andrew Gibson's proposal to view the distance between authors, narrators, and characters outside the logic of structuralist narrative schemas helps to solidify this point: "Suppose I try to think about narrative outside a 'language of appropriation, instrumentality and distanciation' which sets an author at a distance from a narrator, a narrator at a distance from a character, and then presents the first as appropriating the second, or using the second for certain ends."[102] As Gibson suggests, these distances divide not subjects with varying degrees of agency but *a* subject, and the lines between "me" and "not-me," between author, character, and narrator, become the very threads that make up the texture of narrative fiction.

To understand Nabokov's prose not as a self-contained artifact but as an intricate network of interpersonal relationships where the responsibility is shared among author, characters, and reader would allow us a better grasp of his fiction's double bind, as it offers both the promise of aesthetic *jouissance* and the risk of cruelty and enslavement. This must not necessarily mean reading Nabokov against the grain, however. The image—whether real or made up—of the ape that drew its own cage, which, as Nabokov attests, inspired *Lolita*, can be interpreted similarly: the charcoal drawing is a symbol of art's great potential and danger.[103] This, if we agree that narrative—to paraphrase Humbert—"is but the ancilla of art,"[104] would be especially true of narrative fiction.

The experience of narrative prose, especially as it concerns the degree of otherness that the author can allow and tolerate in relation to his hero and his reader, is, of course, Bakhtin's territory. It was Bakhtin who insisted that both aesthetics and ethics obey the same rules of life, inscribing questions of freedom and responsibility into the relationship between author and characters.[105] Or it was Dostoevsky, whose prose paid such unremitting attention to the intersection between authority and authorship. After all, it is Dostoevsky's characters who project the vacillations of the human spirit between its concurrent desires for freedom and submission, so accurately divined by the Grand Inquisitor, into the struggle for narrative control. In Dostoevsky, the staging of the death of an Author gives birth to authors not only in readers but also, and especially, in characters, whose narratives strive to re-create the collapsed order and, simultaneously, usurp the position of authorship.

Introduction

Either way, the fusion between aesthetics and ethics (to which Dostoevsky provides an ideological and Bakhtin a methodological foundation) is writ large all over Nabokov's oeuvre. In my analysis of Nabokov's narrative ethics that follows in chapters 3 and 4, his characters project the metaphysical loss of authority as the loss of original authorship, and in this they are no different from Dostoevsky's metaphysical and social rebels. In Dostoevsky, the reader encounters human characters who attempt to attain the quasi-divine status of an author, while the author himself appears to be absent; in Nabokov, the reader's ethics are engaged as the human author insists on his quasi-divine control over the world of the novel. The difference between the two authors might be best expressed in terms of the dominant: for Dostoevsky, metaphysical and social struggles clearly take the foreground, while their structuring of the narratological levels of the text remains implicit. In Nabokov, aesthetic concerns predominate over the ethical and metaphysical ones. In both, however, the discursive field of the prose is marked as ethical and calls for the reader's acceptance of responsibility for her participation in it. To validate this hypothesis, in my readings of Nabokov, I proceed with an approach that does not simply search for Dostoevskian motifs and themes in Nabokov's texts (evaluating them either as subject to Nabokov's parody or as proof of his implicit acceptance of Dostoevsky's ideas) but instead focuses on the analysis of the architectonics of Nabokov's fiction, taking into account the ethics of the relationship between author and hero, as well as between reader and text. This reading can accommodate a wide range of authorial statements, for example, Nabokov's expressions of control over his characters (and how these resonate with the similar desires of those same characters) or his apophatic belief in the revitalizing force of art. It would also reassess the role of intertextuality in his prose from the point of view of the text's possession by a subjectivity other than that of the author.[106] Finally, such a reading would not only provide a connection between art and crime but also investigate the metaphysical and ethical grounds for that connection. This remains a largely unexplored area in Nabokov criticism. Most importantly, it would allow for the tension between artistic endeavor and cruelty in his prose to remain dangerously taut.

Hence, using the framework of narrative ethics for Nabokov allows me to perform an interpretative trick that might be as risky as some of the narrative tricks Nabokov himself performed: I put Nabokov's authorial figure on . . . the list of his fiction's characters (whether or not it comes off, as Nabokov would say, is, of course, a separate question). Such a reading maintains that in his desire for representational and interpretative control, Nabokov's author must be held as responsible as his characters for their own rhetorical and aesthetic violence. In a sense, I propose to read Nabokov through the lens of Dostoevsky (at least in my reading of him). To acknowledge that discursive participation is ethically compromised is to accept Zosima's call for collective responsibility. Perhaps, however, the devil is not so black, and reading Nabokov ethically might be easier than it seems. After all, having learned to share "aesthetic bliss" with Nabokov, we might not be all that far from sharing ethical responsibility with him, too. The profit from this is clear, since ethical readings return to Nabokov's prose the tension and the urgency it deserves. Drawing parallels between his authorial persona and his protagonists, Nabokov similarly insists on the reader's ethical participation by making us aware that aesthetic pleasure can be procured only at the expense of others. The challenge then is to consider the figure of the author—both as a demiurge and as merely human—as a reflection of his ethically compromised narrators. What distorts the mirror is Nabokov's consciousness of this process; if anything, however, this should indicate an acceptance rather than a rejection of responsibility.

While in this book I do not claim that the framework of narrative ethics is the only possible one for comparing Dostoevsky and Nabokov, I argue that it provides us with a vision of what are implicit but nevertheless deep affinities between the two writers. It does so by correlating the relationships each author establishes between the ideology present in his work as content and its manifestation as form, particularly the way in which the prose organizes the discursive distribution of power between author and characters. Narrative ethics asks us to consider the moral weight these relationships add to our own engagement with the text through acts of interpretation. Hence, my goal is not so much to historicize Dostoevsky's and Nabokov's narrative ethics but to make its scope contemporary and timely by arguing for our complicity in and, consequently, responsibility for reading—quite possibly the only act with the power to unite us across space and time.

Chapter One

Between Sin and Redemption: Narrative as the Conduit for Responsibility in Dostoevsky's "The Meek One"

BAKHTIN AND DOSTOEVSKY: THE LIMITS OF DIALOGISM

The Promise of Polyphony

Toward the end of *Problems of Dostoevsky's Poetics*, Bakhtin speaks of the impact the polyphonic novel—whose creation he attributes to Dostoevsky—has on other literary forms. The genre of the polyphonic novel, concludes Bakhtin, does not replace the old ones but instead "makes [them] . . . more conscious; it forces them to better perceive their own possibilities and boundaries . . . , to overcome their *naiveté*" (271). In this encounter between the polyphonic novel and the monologic one, the former becomes that necessary other-for-me through which the Bakhtinian subject acquires the gift of identity. Without the self-awareness brought by the polyphonic novel, the older genres cannot sufficiently know themselves. Bakhtin talks about the consequence of this encounter in language that is both ethical and political: the polyphonic novel breaks apart the totality of monologic literary forms and takes away their absolute—because blind—power. Literature's task is to create the potential for freedom and responsibility.

At the same time, however, Bakhtin's inquiry into Dostoevsky's aesthetics famously begins with an argument against readings that use Dostoevsky's fiction merely as a vessel for ideology, ethical or otherwise. Hence, while Bakhtin declares Viacheslav Ivanov's thesis that "the affirmation of someone else's consciousness—as an autonomous subject and not as an object—is the ethico-religious postulate determining the content of [Dostoevsky's] novel" to be correct in general, it falls short precisely because it fails to address "how this principle of Dostoevsky's worldview becomes the principle behind Dostoevsky's *artistic* visualization of the world, the principle behind his artistic structuring of a verbal whole, the novel" (10–11, emphasis in the original). Instead, Bakhtin discusses Dostoevsky's works by focusing on their *aesthetics*, that is, the formal innovations of their prose. To be sure, the change of perspective Bakhtin undertakes in his study is no less groundbreaking than the one with which he credits his subject: he is the first to propose that the intersubjective dynamic between Dostoevsky's characters might be better understood not through the content of the characters' discourse but as it manifests itself in the formal features of the dialogic narrative exchanges between them.

To perceive the glow of ethics through the lens of aesthetic analysis is undoubtedly Bakhtin's great innovation and achievement. Critics might disagree whether Dostoevsky's novels are indeed polyphonic; still, Bakhtin's analysis of Dostoevsky's prose presents us with the possibility of a unique relationship with literature, the temptations of which are difficult to resist. Bakhtin's redefinition of the relationship between hero and author in Dostoevsky's prose allows characters to cross the fictional divide not only because of the mimetic illusion of realism but also because of the unprecedented freedom they obtain vis-à-vis the author.[1] We can surmise that this change similarly affects the experience of the reader, who is included in the discursive sphere of the novel not only by identifying herself with the characters but also by engaging them dialogically.[2] Nevertheless, I question Bakhtin's conclusions about the ethics of the relationship between author and hero—and consequently between reader and text—in Dostoevsky's works. I begin this chapter with a reassessment of Bakhtin's understanding of Dostoevsky's "dialogic imagination." Ultimately, I argue that the consequences of the shift in Dostoevsky's position toward his characters and, hence, the ethical value of the dialogic realm in his prose are far more ambivalent than they emerge in Bakhtin's conceptualizations. My goal is to reveal a relationship between Dostoevsky's ethics and aesthetics that does justice to his Christian beliefs. In his prose, Dostoevsky puts to the test the moral value of the dialogic realm, and through the actions—but rarely the dialogic exchanges—of his most innocent and morally sound characters, designates the possibility for an ethically responsible life. As a rule, the verbal interactions in Dostoevsky's prose are more often coercive than benevolent. In their dialogues with others, Dostoevsky's protagonists frequently engage in intense power struggles, and their ideological utterances are not so much an inquiry about the world as a demand that it be as they wish. While the characters' discourse, both internal and external, is directed toward others (and is, in that sense, dialogic), it is driven by a desire to assert a world that is monologic inasmuch as it refuses to tolerate the authorship of the other. Consequently, the reader's engagement with texts in which dialogic participation is ethically

Chapter One

compromised must also become a subject for ethical inquiry. Like ripples from a stone thrown into water, the reader's participation *with* such a narrative replicates the dynamics exposed *within* it.

After a reassessment of the moral import of Dostoevsky's change in the position of author toward hero, I proceed with a reading of Dostoevsky's 1876 short story "The Meek One," with which Bakhtin begins his discussion of Dostoevsky's aesthetic revolution. In my analysis of the story's narrative ethics, I pursue two objectives: first, I aim to determine the effect of Dostoevsky's religious views on the formal aspects of his prose. To do so, I analyze the story in the context of two suicide notes—one real, by Alexander Herzen's daughter, Liza Herzen, and the other fictitious—that frame "The Meek One" in *A Writer's Diary*. The analysis of the notes helps us to understand how, for Dostoevsky, one's worldview—one's religious beliefs and moral values—finds its way into the text not only as content but also as a factor that determines the dialogic directionality of the text itself. The character's system of values governs the manner of expression, its tone, but also their position toward the addressees of their utterance and the way it affects the formation of interpersonal relationships present in the narrative. My second objective is to analyze the dynamic between dialogic activity and plot in Dostoevsky's prose. Hence, I conclude with a reading of "The Meek One" that reveals how the narrative aggression of the story's protagonist-narrator, itself a product of his inability to maintain religious faith, impacts the advancement of the plot. Driven by the desire for authenticity and the urge to be the only author of his life, the pawnbroker is stuck in what appears to be an endless narrative loop. Incorporating plot into the analysis of the story allows us to reconsider Bakhtin's positive evaluation of dialogic freedom in Dostoevsky's prose and acknowledge the moral ambivalence of the dialogic realm. Such an acknowledgment, in turn, demands the recognition of the reader's responsibility for her own discursive participation with the text.

The Ethical Limits of Architectonics

In Bakhtin's philosophy, our interaction with one another is both a necessity and a philosophical problem. From within, I am both undetermined and unfinished. Only the other—from the outside—can bestow the gift of meaning and affirmation on me. In this lies the other's unique and irreplaceable (since no one else can take the other's place and time) responsibility to the world. Conversely, only I can bestow the same gift upon the other. As numerous scholars argue, this view is deeply Christian and presupposes man's initial state as postlapsarian, passive, or, in Bakhtin's terminology, "given."[3] To become actualized, or "posited," we require salvation through the kenotic activity of the other. Consequently, a refusal to accept my dependence on others and my insistence on autonomy are a sin of imposture:

> My justification is always in the future, and this justification, eternally standing in opposition to me, countermands my past and present as they are for me, with their pretension to prolonged already-presentness, to tranquility in givenness, to self-sufficiency, to true reality of being, with their pretension to be all of myself and my essential self, to define me exhaustively in being (the pretension of my givenness to declare itself to be myself in my entirety, to be my true self, the imposture of givenness).[4]

For Bakhtin, both sets of relationships—between author and hero and between two subjects—generate textual and social hierarchies: the dynamic of the author-hero model is reciprocal yet asymmetrical and unequal. The author's position provides him with a surplus of knowledge ("vision," as Bakhtin puts it) that is inaccessible to the hero and which demands the hero's submission. Authorship presupposes authority. The ideal other is God; hence, for Bakhtin, as Ruth Coates writes, "if we yield to the temptation to declare axiological independence from God, we cut ourselves off from the unity safeguarded for us in the future" (46). Coates argues that Bakhtin is aware of the power gap in I-other relations and that in his earlier essay "Author and Hero," he protects this structure from corruption by either party, the self or the other, providing it with the figure of Christ, the aesthetic and ethical model for human activity in the world. Christ's unique ethical position in the world ("for myself—absolute sacrifice, for the other—loving mercy")[5] makes him the ideal model for human behavior.[6]

The Johannine argument that Christ is the only model that can save humanity is most clearly formulated by Dostoevsky, in whose writing Christ is both the guarantor of and the foundation for ethical behavior, releasing human beings from the power struggle and mutual antagonism brought on by the incompatibility of their visions. Dostoevsky expresses this view in a notebook entry of 1880 on the difference between morality and honesty. Being true to one's convictions, insists Dostoevsky, is not morality but honesty.[7] To consider oneself moral, one must unceasingly question whether one's "convictions [are] true," and the only possible measure for this is Christ. Furthermore, Bakhtin's statement that Christ is distinguished by his absolute sacrifice of himself and by his mercy toward the other is resoundingly similar to Dostoevsky's belief that Christ represents the absolute apogee of human development, having sacrificed his own life out of love for humanity.[8]

Importantly, neither Dostoevsky nor Bakhtin sees Christ as someone who *forgives* humanity its sins. Christ's gift to the world is not forgiveness but *grace*, and the distinction between the two is crucial. Grace is understood as the precondition on the path toward forgiveness; it is the gift of freedom, of the choice to make a turn toward repentance. This is the role that the Church must play for its flock in Zosima's vision, providing it with what the State cannot: the freedom to begin the hard work of self-examination. Finally, Christ is Alyosha's only solution to Ivan's depiction of the abysmal corruption of power in the "Rebellion" chapter of *The Brothers Karamazov*. Ultimately, both Bakhtin and Dostoevsky share the notion that in Christ we have "the synthesis of *ethical solipsism* (man's infinite severity toward himself, i.e., an immaculately pure relationship to oneself) with *ethical-aesthetic kindness* toward the other."[9]

Whether Christian love is a sufficient solution for the problems arising from the valuational inequality built into Bakhtin's elaboration of intersubjectivity remains debatable. Numerous critics resist the temptation to resolve the aporia between what Erdinast-Vulcan calls the "centripetal" and "centrifugal" forces in Bakhtin's philosophy, the first marked by a "deep current of nostalgia for the narrative coherence of subjectivity, for some form of authorial grounding,"[10] and the second by "a bid for freedom" (41), which is necessary for the emergence of the hero as an ethical subject who is allowed "to live, to make choices and to act" (38).[11]

Bakhtin's anxiety about the dark side of the authorial "consciousness of a consciousness" makes itself present as early as *Problems of Dostoevsky's Art* (1929), which was the first version of his Dostoevsky book. Here, the charge of imposture shifts from the hero (who insists on autonomy and refuses to acknowledge the need for the other) to the author, whose surplus of vision now is not so much a gift of love as a tool for control through which the latter exercises his will to power. As Coates writes: "In [*Problems of Dostoevsky's Art*] Bakhtin is trying to accommodate the apparently new realization that ideological and personal closure is more often than not expressed not in withdrawal, but in aggressive self-assertion."[12] Once again, Bakhtin's changing attitude toward the position of the author can be easily traced against the background of his subject, Dostoevsky's prose.

Ivan's response to Alyosha's evocation of Christ's sacrifice and intercession as the means through which the abuse of power can be overcome is "The Legend of the Grand Inquisitor." There, all verbal activity belongs to the Grand Inquisitor; Christ responds with a nonverbal gesture, a kiss. Such a distribution of discourse (framed in its turn by Ivan's narration and Alyosha's silence) reflects Dostoevsky's general attitude to language, according to which, as Malcolm Jones aptly puts it, "human language is 'fallen discourse.'"[13] In Dostoevsky's prose, verbal expression is most often a tool of aggressive self-affirmation at the expense of others—and narrative violence prefigures physical violence. Dostoevsky's protagonists want to be authors, not heroes; sharing the position of authorship with others is not something they do willingly. Compared to Bakhtin's "Author and Hero," we can say that in Dostoevsky's fiction (and in Bakhtin's analysis of it in *Problems of Dostoevsky's Art*), the accent is radically different: people talk, while Christ remains silent.

That Bakhtin's proposed solution to the potential for violence hidden in the opposition of author and hero is unrealistic has been pointed out by a number of critics. Bakhtin protects the hero's freedom from the author's exercise of power by splitting discourse into monologic and dialogic or, as far as the novel is concerned, monologic and polyphonic.[14] To escape monologism (which represents bad authorship for Bakhtin), the polyphonic author takes himself out of the novel's parenthesis, no longer authoring the hero in the usual sense but instead limiting his activity to orchestrating the heroes' discourse.[15] Polyphony becomes the marker of authorial silence. Dostoevsky's ideal of silence on the level of his characters is transferred by Bakhtin to the level of the author.[16] Scholars have since questioned the nature of this proposition by pointing either to Dostoevsky's abundant image-heavy "monologism" or to the repressive nature of such a split. As one argument goes, splitting discourse into monologic and dialogic results in safely labeling the violence of representation "monologic," thereby releasing "dialogic" discourse from any responsibility.[17]

While Bakhtin's formulations about Dostoevsky's art might require readjustment, his method opens up the possibility of an investigation into how the dialogic interactions among Dostoevsky's characters impact the discursive activity of both author and reader, that is, the representational activity of the former and the hermeneutic activity of the latter. The goal of the polyphonic shift is nothing less than to preserve the characters' humanity, to allow them a hitherto unavailable autonomy vis-à-vis their creator. There emerges in Bakhtin's writing on Dostoevsky a clear *moral* opposition between a living voice offered by the polyphonic novel and the dead material of the monologic literary forms:

> The consciousnesses of other people cannot be perceived, analyzed, defined as objects or as things—one can only *relate to them dialogically*. To think about them means to *talk with them; otherwise they immediately turn to us their objectivized side*: they fall silent, close up, and congeal into finished, objectivized images. An enormous and intense dialogic activity is demanded of the author of a polyphonic novel: as soon as this activity slackens, the characters begin to congeal, they become mere *things*, and monologically formed chunks of life appear in the novel.[18]

Hence, on the one hand, Bakhtin chooses an *aesthetic* approach toward Dostoevsky's prose as a polemic with those who engage with the novels' ideological content rather than with their "artistic visualization." On the other hand, however, as the passage above implies, the philosophical opposition between objectified images/things and subjects, who have autonomous voices, is geared against formalist materialist aesthetics, which treats art—and literary texts in particular—as reified aesthetic objects. The success of Bakhtin's skillful navigation here between the Scylla of the content-based analysis of classical Dostoevsky scholarship and the Charybdis of formalism is safeguarded by his treatment of form as a manifestation of a *valuational* attitude of the artist toward the world that supersedes the understanding of form as matter. The distinguishing feature of the polyphonic novel is that it invites the reader to an admittedly unprecedented relationship with literature, in which the principles of intersubjectivity are set against the formalist treatment of literary texts as matter.[19] Nevertheless, considering the intensity with which Bakhtin insists on extracting any kind of moral evaluation from Dostoevsky's aesthetic activity, it is hard to say whether in the Dostoevsky book Bakhtin actually succeeds in escaping the snares of materialist aesthetics that he decries in formalist analysis. Driven by the desire to endow his characters with true freedom—a *valuational* intention, to be sure—the polyphonic author, abdicating his ability to evaluate definitively, finds himself coming perilously close to the same formalist materialism that Bakhtin was careful to avoid in the first place.[20]

Another side effect of the change in the polyphonic author's position vis-à-vis his characters is the imbalance between what Bakhtin calls Dostoevsky's novels' "great dialogue"[21] and their plots, as well as between the characters' "form-shaping" verbal activity and the visual and physical elements of the prose. The muting of the polyphonic author's voice and the focus on textual *poetics* at the expense of *content* is directly related to the prevailing emphasis on the word in Bakhtin's analyses of the novels, as a result of which plot, image, and body move into the background and become secondary to voice. For Bakhtin, Dostoevsky's plots are but a necessary backdrop against which the dialogic narrative exchanges of his characters can unfold:

> In Dostoevsky, the adventure plot is combined with the posing of profound and acute problems; and it is, in addition, placed wholly at the service of the idea. It places a person in extraordinary positions that expose and provoke him, it connects him and makes him collide with other people under unusual and unexpected conditions precisely for the purpose of *testing* the idea and the man of the idea, that is, for testing the "man in man." (105)

Not surprisingly, this demotion of plot extends to Bakhtin's neglect of the physical and the bodily. Even though Bakhtin states that Dostoevsky's characters are formed from both somatic and discursive constituents, in his reading the discursive component of the character comes to the fore, while the physical or somatic one loses in significance. The physical realm, for Bakhtin, becomes a stage on which a character's consciousness develops self-knowledge through a potentially endless dialogue with the consciousnesses of other characters. Hence, in Bakhtin's reading of "The Meek One," to take one example, the dead body of the pawnbroker's wife is understood as a trigger for her widower's dialogic search for the truth of their relationship.

A related issue concerns what Bakhtin calls "carnivalistic" overtones in Dostoevsky's plots—scenes of scandal and catastrophe, and traces of Menippean satire (transformed by Dostoevsky into a mystery play). For Bakhtin, these chronotopes place his protagonists "on the threshold of life and death, falsehood and truth, sanity and insanity," where they find themselves "for a moment outside the usual conditions of their lives, on the carnival square or in the nether world," as a result of which "there opens up another—more genuine—sense of themselves and of their relationships to one another" (145–47). Dostoevsky's characters, however, are not simply situated outside of the usual conditions of their lives; more often than not, they also enter into situations of extreme conflict with one another. For Bakhtin, this only intensifies the potential for their self-discovery vis-à-vis the world and one another. One commonsense criticism of this approach is that it removes the sting from Dostoevsky's conflict-ridden worlds by rendering them harmless, suggesting that indeed—as in a carnival setting—death is nothing more than a spectacle. Bakhtin's description of the function of the plot seems to suggest that although the characters participating in this spectacle do so in all seriousness, they are also aware of its theatricality and use this knowledge to stage their endless dialogues.

To revise Bakhtin's conceptualization of Dostoevsky's aesthetics, I concentrate on two interrelated points. First, I argue that the dialogues of Dostoevsky's protagonists are ambivalent, in the sense that they manifest their carriers' split intentions. On the one hand, the verbal activity exposes the characters' will to power; they seek to subjugate others, upon whom they wish to impose their image of the world. On the other hand, this activity reflects their spiritual strivings, their attempts at reconstructing the world left without a moral center. Second, I hold that the relationship between the characters' verbal exchanges and the plot is more dynamic than Bakhtin allows. As Bakhtin argues, Dostoevsky purposefully makes his characters engage in narrative exchanges without being overpowered by the ideological weight of the authorial consciousness. This transfer of authorship, however—and here is where I diverge from Bakhtin—enables Dostoevsky to test his characters' moral fortitude by placing on them the burden of responsibility for their discursive activity. Moreover, the ethics of Dostoevsky's prose is revealed not only through the decrease of the authorial presence but also in the changes that his characters' discourse generates on the level of the plot. In this sense, the physical violence of the novels is not merely a background for the center-stage dialogues but a manifestation of ideological, verbal aggression. In short, the characters' narrative conflicts prefigure the physical ones. At the same time, physical, nonverbal actions of willful self-sacrifice and compassion can lead one out of the endless narrative struggle and show a way toward potential redemption. Finally, by intensifying the tension between nonverbal actions and discursive exchanges, Dostoevsky presents his readers with the conditions upon which their own responsibility for the act of reading must rest. A proper understanding of these conditions testifies against polyphonic tolerance and instead asks the reader to close off the dialogue with the text and make an ethical choice to act in the reader's "real" life. We could say that the relationship between the reader and the text parallels the discursive dynamics of Dostoevsky's characters.

The Double-Voiced Word

In the editor's preface to *Problems of Dostoevsky's Poetics*, Caryl Emerson notes that "translation . . . was for [Bakhtin] the essence of all human communication . . . To understand another person at any given moment is to . . . translate."[22] In Bakhtin's Dostoevsky book, this principle finds its conceptualization in the notion of the double-voiced word that becomes both the emblem and the expression of the inherent dialogism of human consciousness. "Every internal experience ends up on the boundary," writes Bakhtin in his 1961 notes "Toward a Reworking of the Dostoevsky Book"; it "encounters another, and in this tension-filled encounter lies its entire essence."[23] In Bakhtin's notion of dialogism, states Michael Holquist, "consciousness is otherness";[24] it is intersubjective in its very structure, and the double-voiced word is the visible trace of that intersubjectivity, a spark with which consciousness enters history.

For Bakhtin, the use of the double-voiced word by Dostoevsky is necessary to successfully realize the kind of discourse that enables his characters to fully represent themselves without the authorial intervention. The double-voiced word of the characters remains outside of the author's discourse; nevertheless, it addresses it in a hidden polemic (196).[25] The less we sense the objectification of the double-voiced word, the more we can experience the merging between the voices of the character and the author. The disappearance of distance between the two endows the character's consciousness with autonomy vis-à-vis the consciousness of the author and gives birth to true selfhood. "In such discourse," writes Bakhtin, "the author's thought no longer oppressively dominates the other's thought, discourse loses its composure and confidence, becomes agitated, internally undecided and two-faced" (198). The presence of the double-voiced word in Dostoevsky's novels secures the aesthetic and the ethical success of this principle: unlike other novels, where the inherent discordance of the double-voiced word is eventually trampled on by the single monologic "speech center" of the author, in Dostoevsky the inner indeterminacy of the double-voiced word becomes a marker of freedom.

The difference between hidden and overt polemics (or between internal and external manifestation of the double-voiced word), however, is important enough to analyze in more detail. Dostoevsky showcases the contrast between the two in the conversation between Prince Myshkin and Keller in *The Idiot*. Keller comes to mooch money off the Prince and in the ensuing dialogue proceeds to confess his intentions to Myshkin. Although externalized, Keller's dialogue with Myshkin does not exactly qualify as an example of overt polemics: it is simultaneously a sincere confession and a tool to coax Myshkin into still giving him money (although a smaller sum than he intended to ask for previously):

> I stayed because I wanted, so to speak, by imparting to you my full, heartfelt confession, to contribute thereby to my own development; with that thought I fell asleep past three, bathed in tears. Now, if you'll believe the noblest of persons: at the very moment that I was falling asleep, sincerely filled with internal and, so to speak, external tears . . . an infernal thought came to me: "And finally, after the confession, why don't I borrow some money from him?"

Myshkin responds:

> "It's probably also not true, and the one simply coincided with the other. The two thoughts coincided, it happens very often. With me, constantly . . . It's as if you had told me about myself just now. I've even happened to think sometimes," the prince went on very seriously, being genuinely and deeply interested, "that all people are like that, so that I even began to approve of myself, because it's very hard to resist these *double* thoughts; I've experienced it. God knows how they come and get conceived . . . What then is to be done? Best of all is to leave it to your own conscience, don't you think?"[26]

Directed and formed by his relationship with Myshkin, Keller's decision to confess is thoroughly dialogic. Yet, the dialogic tonality itself is not enough to help Keller choose a moral course of action; it only brings him to the crossroads where the choice between his "own development" and hoodwinking the prince must be made. Although Myshkin suggests that help can come only from Keller's own conscience, Keller's externalization of his internal dialogue in front of Myshkin helps him lessen the degree of his selfish intentions. Alas, only lessens, since Keller's confession leaves the decision to the Prince, and after this second confession Keller manages to put Myshkin's kind thoughtfulness to good use and still ends up borrowing money from him. Still, we sense that there is a significant difference in the character's actions depending on whether this dialogue is taking place—inside the character or in the reality inhabited by real, physical others. While Keller's initial impulse to confess establishes the need for the I-for-the other and, in this sense, allows him to be "authored" by Myshkin, it is overridden by the I-for-myself's need for supremacy—in this case, manifested comically by Keller's selfish greed. As Myshkin states, to choose between the double thoughts is not easy, and only by disclosing this internal dynamic to Myshkin, by submitting himself to Myshkin's "penetrated word," does Keller finally get a chance to act in accordance with his conscience.[27] Keller's candor also prefigures the caring form that Myshkin's words take. Significantly, the self-discovery of "the man in man," which for Bakhtin is the ultimate goal of polyphony, happens not within Keller's consciousness but between Keller and Myshkin, or rather from Keller to Myshkin and back: Keller describes himself to Myshkin, and the Prince, in turn, recognizes himself in Keller. It would hardly lessen the initial altruistic quality of Myshkin's character to say that what allows him to see himself in Keller is the form of Keller's narrative. Both the confession and the response become "penetrated words" for their addressees. Keller "authors" Myshkin by revealing himself, and Myshkin does the same.

Hence, while accepting Bakhtin's claim that one's internal utterances are always dialogic, we should also agree that one can be internally dialogic yet remain monologic in one's attitude toward others. Bakhtin's primary opposition in *Problems of Dostoevsky's Poetics* is not between a dialogue and monologue but between a polyphonic consciousness that tolerates different worldviews and a monologic one that strives to occupy a position of a single authorship vis-à-vis the world. Dialogism in itself is not a guarantee of an exchange that would be beneficial to both participants; it only represents the tension inherent in any verbal communication, a point of encounter between two different worldviews. Since the scene from *The Idiot* is a comic one, the result of Keller's double confession is insistently insignificant: instead of 150 rubles, he gets only 25. Yet, this comic situation is paradigmatic in Dostoevsky's prose and in more dramatic circumstances represents the characters' choice between life and death, sanity and insanity, integrity and baseness.

To better understand the character of the difference between the internal and the external dialogue as ethical, I suggest comparing Dostoevsky's and Bakhtin's evaluations of the relationship between one's belief system and its expression in a dialogue with another person. Dostoevsky's characters, posits Bakhtin, consist of two principal attributes. The first is their absolute unselfishness, inasmuch as their acts correspond to their ideology:

Between Sin and Redemption

> All of Dostoevsky's major characters, as people of an idea, are absolutely unselfish, insofar as the idea has really taken control of the deepest core of their personality. This unselfishness is neither a trait of their objectivized character nor an external definition of their acts—unselfishness expresses their real life in the realm of the idea . . . ; idea-ness and unselfishness are, as it were, synonyms. In this sense even Raskolnikov, who killed and robbed the old pawnbroker, is absolutely unselfish, as is the prostitute Sonya, as is Ivan the accomplice in his father's murder; absolutely unselfish also is the *idea* of the Adolescent to become a Rothschild. We repeat again: what is important is not the ordinary qualifications of a person's character or actions, but rather the index of a person's devotion to an idea in the deepest recesses of his personality. (87, emphasis in the original)

The second is the inherent dialogism of their consciousness:

> The idea begins to live, that is, to take shape, to develop, to find and renew its verbal expression, to give birth to new ideas, only when it enters into genuine dialogic relationships with other ideas, with the ideas of *others*. Human thought becomes genuine thought, that is, an idea, only under conditions of living contact with another and alien thought, a thought embodied in someone else's voice, that is, in someone else's consciousness expressed in discourse. At that point of contact between voice-consciousness the idea is born and lives. (87–88)

On the one hand, then, there is a full correspondence between the character's external life and his or her ideology—what Bakhtin calls the "real life in the realm of the idea"—and, on the other hand, the ideology lives and takes form only by entering into an "essential dialogic relationship" with the ideology of others. For Bakhtin, the two components are complementary to each other; he does not mention, however, the potential tension that can arise between them.

Bakhtin explains this complementarity in his discussion of the "architectonics" of human existence. Humans seek an aesthetic finalization by one another. Since our own vision of ourselves—the I-for-myself—cannot be finalized by definition, we require an outside consciousness—an I-for-the other, which can only come from without, so that it can author us. The ensuing relationship between the two consciousnesses is necessary for the construction of the Bakhtinian subject. While we are given an opportunity to correlate our perpetually unfinished I-for-myself with a finished, aesthetic vision of I-for-the other, in return we provide the other with the Other-for-me, which she requires in order to situate herself in the world. In Bakhtin's early writing, I-for-the other and the Other-for-me are gifts—of love—that

Chapter One

we exchange with each other for our mutual benefit. In the Dostoevsky book, the anxiety about the potential conflict that can arise out of such a relationship—when one of the dialogic participants insists that his or her version of the world is the only correct one—is present, inasmuch as Bakhtin protects the characters of the polyphonic novel from the finalizing word of the author. Yet, the side effect of safeguarding the characters from the authorial monologizing consciousness is an unwarranted enthusiasm about the intradiegetic discursive dynamic. Dostoevsky's characters, however, hardly fit into Bakhtin's optimistic mold. As Emerson observes, "For the great ideologues of the novel, the act of speaking out passionately (even if their topic is radical doubt) is largely a way of securing the floor and silencing others."[28] The most common scenario in Dostoevsky's prose is when the Other-for-me becomes not so much a gift of love but an act of aesthetic silencing, coercion, and, at times, even violence.

Dostoevsky is clear that a mutually rewarding dialogue appears only if there is a possibility of doubt, a crack—no matter how small—between one's ideology and its verbal expression. Only when I am able to question the ultimate authenticity of I-for-myself for the benefit of I-for-the other, when I allow the other to author me even potentially, can I afford to hear the other. In one of his notebook entries, Dostoevsky is blunt that the character's unselfishness—the complete correspondence between the character's actions and his or her ideology—is a recipe for an immoral society:

> It is not enough to define morality as fidelity to one's own convictions. One must continually pose oneself the question: are my convictions true? Only one verification of them exists—Christ. But this is no longer philosophy, it is faith, and faith is a red color . . .
>
> I cannot recognize one who burns heretics as a moral man, because I do not accept your thesis that morality is an agreement with internal convictions. That is merely *honesty* (the Russian language is rich), but not morality. I have a moral model and an ideal, Christ. I ask: would he have burned heretics?—no. That means the burning of heretics is an immoral act . . .
>
> Christ was mistaken—it's been proved! A scorching feeling tells me: better that I remain with a mistake, with Christ, than with you . . .
>
> You say that to be moral one need only act according to conviction. But where do you get your convictions? I simply do not believe you and say that on the contrary it is immoral to act according to one's convictions. And you, of course, cannot find a way to prove me wrong.[29]

Discussing this passage in *Problems of Dostoevsky's Poetics*, Bakhtin insists that what is important here is not Dostoevsky's Christian creed but his dialogic directionality toward Christ: Dostoevsky does not try to unite with

Christ but *poses a question* to him. In the notebook entry, there are two dialogues, however, not one. One is an imagined dialogue with Christ, and the other is a real one with the historian Konstantin Kavelin, Dostoevsky's intended interlocutor. And the first is fundamentally different from the second. For Dostoevsky, the "intersubjective relationship" with Christ is predicated on faith: Christ is not only absent but is also immeasurably higher in hierarchy than his human interlocutors. The relationship is defined by Dostoevsky's complete submission before Christ, his absolute agreement to be "authored" by a superior being: Christ is a "moral model and an ideal." Once this ideal is absent, the dialogue risks turning into potentially endless bickering between two rivaling I-for-myself's—in this case, between Dostoevsky and Kavelin. Without an agreed-upon arbitrator (Christ), who is an *unquestionable authority* for both, the argument has no possible resolution. The knowledge of each about the world and himself can appear as truth, yet this is the truth *for oneself*—not both—and it conceals one's desire for domination. One may object that each of the interlocutors' Christs might be vastly different from each other; it is important, however, that for the dialogue to work, the first step is its participants' faith that there is an authority which exists outside each person's horizon and which has the ability to take them out of their respective solipsism.

Thus, for Dostoevsky, the only way out of the dialogic deadlock is to restructure the dialogue into a conversation formed by the presence of the agreed-upon third, albeit silent, authority. Both participants have to acknowledge the authority of Christ in order to overcome their conflict. Importantly, Bakhtin focuses on Dostoevsky's questioning of Christ, that is, his verbal interaction with the authority. What remains unaddressed in Bakhtin's argument is the behavioral—performative—aspect of Dostoevsky's attitude toward Christ: for Dostoevsky, Christianity is not a set of dogmatic prescriptions that his interlocutor (in this case, Kavelin) has to accept on faith. Instead, Dostoevsky imagines what Christ would *do*, not say; Christ is first of all "a moral model and an ideal" of behavior. It is not Christ's teachings that for Dostoevsky have the potential to take us beyond the borders of our consciousness but Christ's actions, narrated in the Gospels. Likewise, in his fiction Dostoevsky tries to forge the idea of faith and ethical life in his readers by creating narratives in which a correct course of action has to be chosen in order to leave the battleground of the dialogic power struggle.

Dialogue vs. Plot

Dostoevsky's protagonists, writes Bakhtin, are all given the task to "'think and seek higher things'; in each of them there is a 'great and unresolved thought';

all of them must, before all else, 'get a thought straight.'"[30] Throughout *Problems of Dostoevsky's Poetics*, the unresolvable thought serves as evidence for the characters' freedom from the ideology of the author. In Dostoevsky's fiction, worldviews—and among them Dostoevsky's Christian ideas—are defined as "an ultimate position in the world in relation to higher values . . . embodied in voices" (296) and "enter the great dialogue of the novel on *completely equal terms* with other idea-images" (92, emphasis in the original). Yet, the experience of reading Dostoevsky consists not only of the vertiginous unwinding of the dialogic spiral but equally of the persistent progression of the plot, a relentless torrent of events and ethical choices prefigured by dialogic deliberation. Without action, the dialogic exchanges would lose their dramatic intensity; instead, it is more productive to use Harpham's definition of the plot as a criterion that measures ethical shifts within the text, registering the transfer of value from *is*—the way things are, to *ought*—the way they should be.

Hence, to give one example, the analysis of this dynamic between dialogue and action in *Crime and Punishment* would pay attention to how action in the novel alters the nature of Raskolnikov's dialogues with others and how, in turn, the dialogues prefigure and prepare acts by Raskolnikov and other characters. The physical and visual world of the novel—the murder of Alyona and Lizaveta, Raskolnikov's psychosomatic sickness, his dreams throughout the novel, his sensations of looking into Sonya's eyes, the landscape of St. Petersburg that Raskolnikov observes from the Nikolaevsky Bridge, the unknown woman's attempted suicide, the death of Marmeladov, Luzhin's attempt to set up Sonya, Raskolnikov and Sonya's joint act of reading the Bible, and so on—greatly affects the intensity and tenor of the dialogues. And vice versa—the dialogic activity of the novel directly influences the course of the action. This complex interrelationship between action and dialogue asks the reader to consider the moral weight of Raskolnikov's choices, especially in the first part of the novel. Do Raskolnikov's encounters with others lead him to the murder, or is their selection subordinate to his "new word," the idea of extraordinariness that drags Raskolnikov through the first part "as if a piece of his clothing had been caught in the cogs of a machine"?[31] How does the murder determine the succession and order of the verbal exchanges that follow in its wake? Finally, how does each successive dialogue prepare Raskolnikov for "[flinging] himself down at [Sonya's] feet" in the novel's epilogue (549)? Dostoevsky emphasizes the contrast between this *silent* act of submission and the verbal activity of the rest of the novel, by adding that neither Raskolnikov nor Sonya could speak after it. Raskolnikov's embrace of Sonya, which he does without being conscious of his actions—"as if something lifted him"—finally resolves the ideological tension, at least within Raskolnikov's consciousness, and serves as the novel's closure (549).

Yet, how do we properly respond to the moral ambiguity, suggested by the description of his lack of agency here, that points back to the similar passivity Raskolnikov exhibits on his way to murder?

Raskolnikov's ability to "act himself out" of the discursive solipsism at the end of *Crime and Punishment* is a rather unusual trait among Dostoevsky's characters. In Dostoevsky's universe, much more frequent are cases where the characters remain in their dialogic imprisonment. Refusing to acknowledge a hierarchically higher authorship of the world and authority other than their own, they attempt to force the other into accepting their form-shaping ideology as the only authentic one. The source behind these quests for domination is the subject's desire for authenticity, yet, in Dostoevsky's prose, this desire is condemned to remain forever unfulfilled, trapping the subject in a state of ressentiment from which there is rarely an escape.[32]

Dostoevsky does provide his characters with an exit from the dialogic struggle for power, but to see it we must shift our focus to physical, nonverbal actions of the plot and understand how they embody his Christian ideals. Paradoxically, in Dostoevsky the ability to let go of coercive dialogism can only be achieved by acknowledging the inherently dialogic nature of the word, that is, that it always equally belongs to the other. While acceptance of the other as an equal participant in the dialogue is a necessary precondition for achieving a state of wholeness, it by no means guarantees that the dialogizing subject will be able to abandon the state of conflict permanently or even at all. If characters like Raskolnikov are able to leave the realm of coercive dialogic activity, those like the Underground Man remain stuck in the dialogic hell even after the intercession of Liza, the ideal other.

What seals the fate of the Underground Man is his inability to allow a different consciousness to make a crack in his solipsistic worldview. For the duration of his narrative, he continues to interpret only *from his particular angle of vision*. By entering the dialogic vicious circle of the Underground Man, the reader must accept responsibility for the Underground Man's discourse, especially since its only other participant, Liza, is doomed to remain silent. In this matter, the reader does not exactly have a choice.

Writing in his notebook of 1863–64, Dostoevsky ascribes the inability to love another as oneself to the presence of the ego, which separates humans from one another. The appearance of Christ, writes Dostoevsky, "as *an ideal of a man in flesh*" makes apparent the ultimate goal of the ego's development: its voluntary self-sacrifice and self-destruction, which one attains by giving it "to each and everyone humbly and undividedly."[33] Dostoevsky concludes that reaching this ideal "is contrary to one's nature" (175). To do so, one has to "sacrifice *through love* one's *I* to other people or a person" (175, emphasis in the original). Importantly, Dostoevsky's idealized characters, like Liza, Sonya, Myshkin, and Alyosha, hardly sacrifice their ego in the

Chapter One

sense that Dostoevsky implies in his notebook. They have barely any ego to begin with. Instead, they exist as incarnated ideals, whose acts mark the ethical distance that other characters must cross in order to achieve a resolution of their struggles with themselves and others.[34]

In *Notes from Underground*, the fulfillment of the Christian ideal renders any other continuation (narrative or otherwise) obsolete. As Dostoevsky affirms in his notebook, "If this is the final goal of humanity (attaining it, humanity would not need to develop anymore, i.e., to continue to achieve, struggle, try again to recover . . . one's ideal, and to strive toward it eternally—thus, it would not need to live)—this means that reaching it, one would finish one's earthly existence" (172). As Emerson astutely observes, "at crisis times, Dostoevsky's protagonists must choose. They can elect the logic of reason (which usually works horizontally, that is, in the form of discussions with a familiar voice, although these discussions can be dialogues with the devil as readily as interpolations by a prince ever eager to see everyone's best side), or they can choose the much more risky leap of faith."[35] The Underground Man and Liza perfectly align with the two axes of Dostoevsky's prose: the horizontal one of dialogic interactions and the vertical one of action.

While Bakhtin prioritizes the dialogic realm of the novel over the physical one, in Dostoevsky's works we encounter a much more dynamic relationship between the two. Oftentimes, physical actions reenact the verbal intersubjective dynamic: the latter precedes and prefigures the former. Turning Bakhtin's notion of the relationship between plot and dialogue on its head, we can surmise that the "big dialogue" of Dostoevsky's prose becomes a platform from which the characters must choose to act. In Dostoevsky's chiaroscuro universe, such acts are usually the polar opposites of each other—one reveals its performer's aggressive ressentiment, and the other is an act of love and compassion. Put simply, the liberated self acts out of love, while the imprisoned self is doomed to continue speaking. In Dostoevsky's fiction, the distance that separates them can be crossed only by a leap of faith—an act that forecloses the narrative. This dynamic, I believe, does not exclude Dostoevsky's own text by treating the prose to be of a different order; after all, Dostoevsky still *writes* about the glimpsed images of the potential state of salvation. The movement of Dostoevsky's prose repeats the evolution of the ego he described in the notebook entry that contains the expression of his Christian faith: the ethically compromised narrative diachronically crosses the distance that separates it from the point of its destination at which it ought to give itself up voluntarily. The all-embracing responsibility that Zosima preaches in Dostoevsky's last novel is enacted here on the formal level: Dostoevsky assigns responsibility to both parties involved in the production of the narrative: the listener and the teller, the author and the reader. At the same time, by providing us with an example of how such characters as Liza respond to the dialogic entrapment of their interlocutors, Dostoevsky offers his readers a possible course of moral action. The leap of faith that the reader has to perform is from the narrative to action, from text to life, in which she herself is invested with the task of becoming a hero. The ethical polarization of the narrative interpersonal dynamic and the physical, nonverbal actions of voluntary sacrifice of the ego constitutes the space within which the reader must find her own ethically appropriate response to the text. It also, as Dostoevsky concludes in the notebook entry, necessitates faith, the only support through which the movement from *is* to *ought* becomes possible. As far as Dostoevsky is concerned, the final step is always a leap into action.

ETHICS OF AN AESTHETIC VISION

The Truth of One's Own Consciousness

Bakhtin's discussion of Dostoevsky's aesthetic revolution begins with an almost complete citation of the preface from Dostoevsky's "The Meek One," a short story written in 1876 and included in the November issue of *A Writers' Diary*. With the exception of the preface, "The Meek One," from its first word to the last, is the direct speech of a husband, whose wife's corpse is lying in the front room of their apartment. Unlike the confessions of the Underground Man, jotted down as notes and coming to the reader via an anonymous editor, "The Meek One" allows no chronological distancing and comes to us in all of its immediacy: the events which gave birth to the story have just taken place. The wife committed suicide only a few hours prior to the husband's first word; we hear his soliloquy as he paces in his rooms, trying to arrange and control his emotions by retelling the story of his marriage and the tragedy that has just occurred.

The story's subtitle calls it "fantastic." In the preface, Dostoevsky explains that the "fantastic" element is formal: the husband's voice appears to the reader as if it were overheard by an invisible stenographer and merely touched up by the writer some time later. Because of how unusual this device is, Dostoevsky deems it necessary to forewarn his readers:

> Now, a few words about the story itself. I called it "fantastic," even though I consider it to be realistic to the highest degree. But it truly does contain something fantastic, which is the form of the story itself, and it is this which I find necessary to explain beforehand.[36]

Chapter One

The story is fantastic because of its increased verisimilitude, and the preface shows Dostoevsky's awareness that the effect of reporting the events "as is" will at the very least surprise his readers. For Bakhtin, the explanations of the preface "are of extraordinary importance for understanding Dostoevsky's creative method."[37] Dostoevsky "retains for himself . . . not a single essential definition, not a single trait, not the smallest feature of the hero: he enters it all into the field of vision of the hero himself, he casts it all into the crucible of the hero's own self-consciousness" (48).

For Bakhtin, the profit of such an exercise is clear:

> The "truth" at which the hero must and indeed ultimately does arrive through clarifying the events to himself, can essentially be for Dostoevsky only *the truth of the hero's own consciousness*. It cannot be neutral toward his self-consciousness. In the mouth of another person, a word or a definition identical in content would take on another meaning and tone, and would no longer be the truth. Only in the form of a confessional self-utterance, Dostoevsky maintained, could the final word about a person be given, a word truly adequate to him. (55)

Hence, the relationship between the formal and the content levels of the story is that of function. The formal device enables Dostoevsky to represent his hero's painful search for truth as a confession without, as Bakhtin puts it, "destroying the fabric of the story" (56). The benefit is the concrete possibility for the hero to attain truth, knowledge arrived at through the process of a confessional self-expression. Bakhtin calls this truth "the truth of one's own self-consciousness." The story gives its readers an opportunity to witness the private, documentary confession, an illusion achieved through the innovative formal framing of a fictional account.

It is formal solutions like these that for Bakhtin make Dostoevsky a "realist in the highest sense," allowing him to depict his characters' true coming into being. Endowed with a new kind of vision, the polyphonic author is able to peer into the pure internality of his characters and deliver this uncontaminated internal discourse to his readers.

In my analysis of "The Meek One," I will argue against the grain of the Bakhtinian reading. I claim that the removal of authorial mediation is a complex rhetorical device through which Dostoevsky questions not only the validity of truth thus obtained but also its ethical value. Moreover, it also pushes the reader to become aware of her own responsibility for the discursive participation with the text. Narrative self-representation indeed brings the pawnbroker to self-understanding. Yet, just like his actions before his wife's suicide, it brings nothing but cruelty and injustice to those who come within his sphere. The same desire for power and control that orchestrated his marriage hides underneath the confession. By allowing his protagonist to come to the truth of his own self-consciousness, Dostoevsky shows that one's worldview directly affects the limits of self-knowledge one can acquire.

"At Least as Far as He Is Concerned": The Ethics of Truth

Dostoevsky's justification for the immediacy of "The Meek One" is its double claim to truth: one to be found in the story's form, the other in its content. On the level of content, the author explains the immense impact his wife's death has had on the narrator:

> Imagine a husband whose wife only a few hours earlier has killed herself by jumping out a window; her body now lies on the table before him. He is in a state of bewilderment and still has not managed to collect his thoughts. He paces through the apartment, trying to make sense of what has happened, to "focus his thoughts."[38]

As the story begins, the reality of what has happened is too fresh for the narrator; he still has not been able to "collect his thoughts." The narrative of the pawnbroker is going to be a process of understanding; the distance that it will traverse is from his complete inability to comprehend his wife's suicide to the place in which he can finally "focus his thoughts." Thus, one generator of the husband's speech is his search for meaning, and the narrative moves him toward an articulation of meaning—from chaos to order. Furthermore, as the author of the preface makes it implicitly clear, the husband understands that if this meaning is to be found, it must be sought within the moral sphere. Even before we hear the story of the unhappy marriage, the preface tells us that the pawnbroker knows that to understand the suicide means to allocate responsibility for it. Hence, the second impulse behind the husband's story is his desire to avoid responsibility. In the preface, Dostoevsky conveys this indirectly by addressing the mode and the dynamic of the pawnbroker's narration:

> Despite the apparent coherence of his speech, he contradicts himself several times, both logically and emotionally. At times he justifies himself and blames her, then he launches into explanations of things which have little to do with the case: we see here the crudity of his thoughts and spirit, and we see deep feeling as well. (677)

The live broadcast of the narrative is required because only through the *process* of narration will the pawnbroker be able "to make . . . clear to himself"

Chapter One

what has really happened (677). The husband has to navigate his narrative ship between intelligibility and moral sensitivity. Painful but necessary, this process finally pays off: as the author explains, "a series of memories he has evoked irresistibly leads [the narrator] to *truth*; and truth irresistibly elevates his mind and his spirit" (677–78, emphasis in the original).

It can be said that Dostoevsky makes the first argument for the particular form of the story on the level of its content. One arrives at the truth of events through persistent attempts to responsibly interpret one's participation in them. The form of the narrative is necessary for the elucidation of meaning. This necessity is perhaps assumed by the reader—otherwise, there is no story to read—yet it should not be: the "irresistible" attainment of truth signifies interpretative work without which the pawnbroker would have remained in the dark. And this work, whether it contains logical, psychological, or chronological sequencing, has to be presented in that particular narrative form which appears in front of the readers. Dostoevsky asserts the same in the preface:

> But so it always happens in real life. If a stenographer had been able to eavesdrop and write down everything he said, it would be somewhat rougher and less finished than I have it here; still, it seems to me that the psychological structure would perhaps be just the same. (678)

The second argument for the story's "fantastic" form also proclaims truth to be the end that justifies the means, but on a purely formal level. The integrity of the story paradoxically hangs on its literary improbability. It is as if the truthfulness of the story comes from the pressure created by the tension between the impossibility of overhearing one's private laments over the dead body of a loved one and the author's insistence on doing just that. In the preface, Dostoevsky calls to witness Victor Hugo as his literary predecessor for his similar confusion of the epistemological borders between reality and fiction. In *The Last Day of a Condemned Man*, Hugo, Dostoevsky attests, traverses an even more improbable territory, supposing that during the course of the condemned man's last day—hours, and even minutes before his death—he is able to keep a record of his final thoughts. But by allowing this fantasy, concludes Dostoevsky, Hugo created "the most real and most truthful work out of all his writings" (678).

This argument for the chosen form corresponds to the previous one for the chosen content: to convey one's true state of being, the writer needs to unpack the narrative hidden within it. The veracity of truth, the preface implies, is achieved by transcending verisimilitude: the device of overhearing a narrative that cannot be witnessed allows Dostoevsky to portray the true, not literary, reality and the reader to experience it through reading.

Justified by a literary precedent, the chosen method brings to the fore those extreme states of being that resist or defy narration. "Realism in its highest sense," as Dostoevsky called his art, gives voice to those who literally cannot be heard and claims to depict the hidden reality of our lives—the reality that cannot otherwise be observed and witnessed. "The Meek One" is the story of the pawnbroker's journey to truth; the narrative that follows the preface is the Jack hidden in the box of an affirmative "I understand."

Yet, what is the nature of the pawnbroker's truth? Presented with "the most real and most truthful" work, how do we, the readers, understand this truth and relate to it? What is asked of us by the claims of the preface? One way to read the pawnbroker's narrative would be in terms of its salutary effects—as a working-through after which the widower begins to accept the loss of his wife. The "therapeutic" intent behind the search for truth resembles that of Dostoevsky's earlier protagonist—the Underground Man—who spins his tale in order to get rid of its haunting presence. The preface to "The Meek One" promises more than that, however: it connects the possibility of recovery from a trauma to serious ethical considerations. The suicide calls for responsibility, and the husband starts out by placing it on his wife and absolving himself. The fact that by doing so he cannot stop and continues "for a couple of hours" suggests that the original attribution of blame is a displacement, which he, in the course of narration, manages to overcome. At the end, the attainment of truth "elevate[s] [the pawnbroker's] mind and spirit." Since the pawnbroker begins his story by resisting responsibility, the reader can reasonably expect that the narrative will eventually produce not only the promised emotional and intellectual reaction but also a moral accounting. Must the reader, then, learn from the story the process of repentance that she can now practice in her own life? In other words, if the suicide puts forth an imperative for the pawnbroker to interpret it, what are the guidelines for interpreting the text itself? Since the preface implies that the narrator's truth must be found within the realm of intersubjective experience, can we ask how the narrator's truth stands in relationship to us, the readers? In other words, does the author expect the reader to agree with the truth of his protagonist?

An answer to these questions will hopefully lead us to a better understanding of Dostoevsky's narrative ethics: What are the ethical limits of his characters' narrative acts? What determines these limits? And finally, what are the guidelines for the interpretative procedures through which we can come up with an ethically proper response?

Dostoevsky mentions the possible limitations of the pawnbroker's potential understanding of the events almost in passing: "The truth is revealed quite clearly and distinctly to the unhappy man—*at least as far as he is concerned*" (678, emphasis added). This modification, however, threatens to

Chapter One

void the rest of the statement. At first, its addition seems superfluous. The husband is already alone, and by the end of the story, he either understands things clearly and distinctly or he does not. Are the readers possibly asked to share the pawnbroker's truth? And if yes, does this sentence imply that while the narrator understands things clearly at the end of the story, the reader might not? Yet, the formal condition on which the author presents the story to us promises that the progression of the husband's thought *is* his speech, that there is no difference between internal and external monologues. The quoted sentence is the first indication by the author (as well as the last one, since "The Meek One" has no postscript) that the elevation of the pawnbroker's mind and heart can possibly occur *only within his own* consciousness. If this is true, what are we, as readers, to make of it? Does this mean that the husband's confession, even made in a state of uncontrollable emotional stimulation, might still be false?

Whether conscious or subconscious, this lie would be different from the one Dostoevsky points to previously. The pawnbroker might have lied before, by "justifying himself and blaming [his wife]," but we are told that he eventually overcomes this lie. Yet, in directing our attention to the fact that truth might, or might not, be shared, the author casts a shadow on the integrity of the whole truth-producing procedure: the possessive qualifier in the quotation above tests the "truthfulness" of the pawnbroker's narrative endeavor. The pawnbroker's narrative is a discourse of the self and is said to produce the previously unavailable self-awareness. In the preface, we are asked to understand the process that leads to self-knowledge as a gradual articulation of the relationship between the social and the private realms. The formal aspects of the story make sure that the process is truthful. As the author of the preface tells us, however, the truth also has to endure the test of intersubjectivity.

The distance between the two kinds of truths implied in the preface calls to mind the distinction Dostoevsky makes between "morality" and "honesty" that we discussed earlier: "I do not accept your thesis that morality is an agreement with internal convictions. That is merely *honesty* (the Russian language is rich), but not morality."[39] In the preface, the qualifier "at least for himself" plays the same role: it draws our attention to the difference between the pawnbroker's honesty—secured by the narrative process—and morality, which, in order to be attained, must be shared by all the participants.

To sum up: in explaining the formal aspects of the story, Dostoevsky also gives his readers pointers on what might be their task of interpretation. The subtlety with which Dostoevsky chooses to expose his rhetorical strategies suggests that while proclaiming an almost complete abdication of authorial power on the denotative level, the preface, in fact, shows an increase of the author's control on the connotative level. In offering his readers the unmediated account of the pawnbroker, Dostoevsky asks them to suspend their disbelief for a fictional account that presents itself as larger than fiction. This, however, requires readers to give up the protective distance that separates them from the text and take on the role of the pawnbroker's "invisible listeners." To understand the preface is to become entrapped by it; as the story begins, we find ourselves locked up in the claustrophobic space of the apartment, in whose living room there lies the body of the narrator's wife. Though meant to explain, the preface simultaneously cloaks the author and pushes the narrator and the reader into an intersubjective struggle for meaning. To find the truth of the story, the reader must agree to share the responsibility for it with the narrator.

Dostoevsky's "Narrative Imperative": Is There an Implied Author After All?

To better understand what kind of moral responsiveness Dostoevsky expects from his readers, we must take a look at how his ideology and religious beliefs actualize in the formal features of his prose. In her study of the relationship between the author, the narrator, and the reader, Robin Feuer Miller finds behind what she calls Dostoevsky's "narrative imperative" a strong pedagogical initiative and a belief that "the narrative . . . had an aesthetic obligation to be the best possible mode for the expression of the author's intent."[40] Working within the structuralist approach, Miller applies Wayne Booth's "implied author–implied reader" schema. Simplified, it consists of three stages: (1) Dostoevsky (the poet) conceives of the idea; (2) Dostoevsky (the artist/entertainer) gives the idea a narrative form that will "attract and hold the reader's attention"; and (3) through careful reading, the implied reader eventually "starts to uncover the poet's idea" (26). The process here is one of deduction: through the careful analysis of the details of the text, the implied reader comes to understand the unifying idea behind it. In Miller's reading, while not explicitly expressed *in* the text, Dostoevsky's ideology frames the narrative. Building the bridge between Bakhtin's reading of Dostoevsky as an artist and a more traditional interpretation of Dostoevsky as a religious and ideological thinker, Miller quips that Dostoevsky was not so much "a writer of *ideas* as a *writer* of ideas" (48). The reader's job is to resist the temptation of the narrative and keep her interpretative distance from the narrating characters' ideology in order to reach the ideological impulse of the implied author.

I would argue, however, that such an approach cannot account for the full impact that Dostoevsky's radical aesthetics have on the moral dimension of his prose, if only because the approach transfers the burden of narrative violence from the author and reader onto the characters. As we saw from our analysis of the preface, such scapegoating risks repeating similar strategies that the narrator undertakes in order to escape the blame for his wife's suicide. Defining discourse as a moral category, the preface insists that the responsibility for the destructiveness of discourse must be shared by all participants. This circle of responsibility must inevitably include the author, whose justifications for giving up control of the text achieve the opposite effect and, in fact, betray an intensification of control over the reader's range of responses to the pawnbroker's story. Dostoevsky's authorial strategies purposefully echo the discursive practices of the narrator, whose dialogic activity continues to imprison his wife even as he promises her freedom. This is not to say, of course, that the measure of responsibility between different participants of the narrative act is equal. Still, I would argue that the properties of discursive activity in Dostoevsky's prose demand responsibility from all those who partake in it. To better understand the moral claim such narratives put on participating subjects, it would pay to remember Alyosha's explanations to Dmitry of why he also shares responsibility for Dmitry's acts and thoughts. As Alyosha explains, they both stand on the same moral ladder, even if he is "on the lowest [step], and [Dmitry is] above, somewhere on the thirteenth."[41]

The connection between the moral limitations of the pawnbroker's dialogic activity and his worldview becomes apparent as we look at the texts that frame "The Meek One" in the *Writer's Diary*. In the issue that immediately precedes "The Meek One," Dostoevsky includes two suicide notes: one real, written by Alexander Herzen's daughter, and the other fictitious, by a male narrator Dostoevsky calls N.N. In the December issue that follows the short story, Dostoevsky engages with some of his readers' responses to these texts and then gives his own, "correct" reading of them. The analysis of Dostoevsky's interpretative technique applied to events, his characters' discourse about events, and, finally, his readers' failure to grasp the ideas behind them helps us make the connection between Dostoevsky's Christian beliefs and the moral dimension of his characters' narratives. Dostoevsky's religious views define the moral framework of his characters' narrational experience; they also affect the dialogic directionality of the narratives. Simply put, having lost a belief in the immortality of the soul, Dostoevsky's characters through their dialogic activity become engaged in the vicious circle of violence against the self and others. A vision of the world without faith in transcendental authority locks characters such as the pawnbroker within a plane of interaction in which they lead narrative battles with others for the ultimate authority of their worldview. As I discussed above, Dostoevsky contrasts such narrative rivalry with physical acts of compassion and sacrifice, which establishes a vertical, nondialogic (in the Bakhtinian sense of the word) mode of interaction. Only in this mode are Dostoevsky's characters able to leave the dialogic rivalry and overcome their existential anxiety by reestablishing communication with an ideal other (Christ). In the contraposition of these two modes of interaction—the horizontal mode of dialogic interactivity and the vertical, nonverbal striving for the Christian ideal—we can witness the presence of what Yuri Kariakin calls the "double-voiced word's third 'voice' assigned permanently to Dostoevsky as author, and, as it were, stage director."[42] This voice in all of its finalizing force becomes explicit in Dostoevsky's journalism, where he concedes to the disliked role of a "psychologist" and explains the philosophical and moral reasons behind his characters' narratives.

TWO SUICIDES

The Meek Death of Mar'ia Borisova

Dostoevsky expands on the nonfictional sources for "The Meek One" at the end of the first chapter of the *Diary*'s October issue. In the third section of the chapter, titled "Two Suicides," Dostoevsky tells of two female suicides, whose reasons for dying he finds to be polar opposites of each other and exemplary of the contemporary zeitgeist. One, Liza Herzen, committed suicide in December 1875 by poisoning herself with chloroform; the other, Mar'ia Borisova, a seamstress who had moved to St. Petersburg from Moscow, killed herself in October 1876 by jumping out of a window. In the process of killing themselves, both women left traces, which allow Dostoevsky to offer an explanation for the suicides' motives. In these nonfictive accounts, by focusing on the particular details of the two deaths, Dostoevsky prepares his reader for the moral ambiguities of the fiction that follows.

In the case of Liza Herzen, the trace is her farewell note, which she wrote in French, and Dostoevsky translates it for his Russian-speaking readers:

> I am setting off on a long journey. If the suicide should not succeed, then let everyone gather to celebrate my resurrection from the dead with glasses of Clicquot. *If I do succeed*, I ask only that you not bury me until you have determined that I am completely dead, because it is most unpleasant to awaken in a coffin underground. *That would not be chic at all!*[43]

In the case of Mar'ia Borisova, the trace is an icon of the Mother of God, her parents' blessing, which the seamstress held in her hands as she jumped. Borisova's "jump with an icon" torments Dostoevsky with its apparent incongruity (suicide was declared a sin by Orthodox law, yet the woman was obvi-

Chapter One

ously a believer) and finds its way into "The Meek One," whose unnamed heroine commits suicide in the same fashion. For Dostoevsky, Liza Herzen's note and Mar'ia Borisova's icon tell of the enormous difference between the two women: "But how different these two creatures are—just as if they had come from two different planets!" (653). Liza Herzen died because of her soul's indignation at the "'stupidity' of man's presence on Earth, at the senseless unintentionality of his appearance here, at the tyranny of brute causality with which they cannot reconcile themselves" (652).

Dostoevsky interprets the icon in the hands of Mar'ia Borisova as a sign of utter despair, a sign powerful enough to make Dostoevsky reconsider his prior attitude toward suicide. The icon pushes Dostoevsky to construe the untold life of the seamstress as a life of submission, not rebellion. Using the icon as a clue, Dostoevsky deduces the painful path that led the young woman to her fateful jump, which at last put an end to a life of suffering. The icon is proof of the suicide's faith: the woman knew that choosing to die is sinful, yet life was unbearable, and the icon tells of the dying woman's hope of divine forgiveness for the sinful act of suicide. "Here," writes Dostoevsky, "apparently, there was no grumbling or reproach: it was simply a matter of being unable to live any longer—'God did not wish it'—and so she died having said her prayers" (653). It is this *meek* suicide—oxymoronic within the context of Dostoevsky's discourse on suicide—that becomes the subject of "The Meek One," which was published in the next month's issue.[44]

Significantly, in "The Meek One," the icon does not play a role in the husband's understanding of his wife's suicide. It makes its first appearance at the beginning of the husband's story, when the young woman tries to pawn it to the pawnbroker, her husband-to-be. The recognition of the icon's significance for the young woman indicates to the pawnbroker the extent of her financial misery and ignites his desire to pursue her. After the marriage, he puts the icon into the pawnshop's icon case and seems to forget about it. It reemerges only at the very end of the narrative, as the pawnbroker remembers the servant's report about the details of her mistress's death. As we read the description of the wife's final moments, the striking similarity between Mar'ia Borisova and the Meek One becomes apparent. Alas, in the pawnbroker's fictional St. Petersburg, however, Dostoevsky's *Diary* is not published, and the pawnbroker fails to see the icon as a detail that, once analyzed, could help him "focus his thoughts" (677). In fact, religiosity is completely absent from the pawnbroker's monologue, and the religious markers that Dostoevsky emphasizes for readers of the *Diary* pass unrecognized by the narrator. One of the more obvious examples of the husband's religious ignorance is his inability to cite his biblical quotations: "'Love one another.' Who said that? Whose commandment is that?" (717). For Dostoevsky, such moral amnesia was, undoubtedly, one of the main symptoms of the contemporary religious crisis.[45] It is also present in the "materialistic testaments" that precede the novella and stand in contrast to the religious suicide of Mar'ia Borisova.

Unlike Mar'ia Borisova's "humble" death, Liza Herzen's suicide is committed out of indignation at what Dostoevsky calls "the 'linearity' of things" (652). Dostoevsky ends his comparison of the two deaths with a rhetorical question to his readers: "which ... of these two souls bore more torment on this earth—if such an idle question is proper and permissible?" (653).

The first chapter of the October issue concludes with a fictional suicide note (titled "The Sentence") in which its author, N.N., explains the reasons for the suicide he is about to commit. Dostoevsky links this suicide to Liza Herzen: "By the way, here are the thoughts of one person—a materialist, of course—who committed suicide *out of boredom*" (653, emphasis in the original). The intent here is obvious, as the reader is meant to connect the note with the description of Liza Herzen's death that precedes it: "And so she simply died from 'chilly gloom and tedium,' in animal, so to say, and unaccountable suffering" (653). "The Sentence" is offered as an explanation of what Dostoevsky intuits are the reasons behind Liza Herzen's death. Both notes—Liza Herzen's and N.N.'s—are examples of a materialist discourse, and the fictitious one is called upon to explicate the real one.

Liza Herzen

Dostoevsky reads Liza Herzen's note as intentionally rude and provoking. Correlating what he knows about the Herzen family with Liza Herzen's suicide, he proposes that the causes of such aggressive despair are emblematic of the whole generation: a child of an atheist brought up in a socialist household, Liza Herzen grew to adulthood without faith in the resurrection of the soul.[46] The suicide note allows Dostoevsky to infer that the young woman's internal suffering came from her lack of belief.[47] He insists on this as he responds in the December issue to an anonymous correspondent who argues that Liza Herzen's insolent desire for champagne is a sign of the absence of suffering. As Dostoevsky explains, the tone of the suicide note points more than anything else to Liza's presuicide anguish. In her desire to offend, Dostoevsky sees evidence of Liza's great suffering.[48]

Dostoevsky's interpretation of Liza Herzen's suicide note is indeed both more generous and more accurate—and certainly more interesting—than that of his correspondent. However, in explaining the note, Dostoevsky does more than give us a lesson in reading. He also exposes and critiques the worldview that Liza Herzen's discourse actively constructs. Dostoevsky's compassion toward Liza does not alleviate his judgment of her materialistic philosophy, which he explicitly blames for the suicide. Moreover, he suggests

Chapter One

that her ideological upbringing—and since she is but a representative of the whole generation, that of thousands of others like her—made her demise inevitable.[49]

Dostoevsky recognizes a crucial difference between the generation of Alexander Herzen, whose "socialist and atheist convictions were a matter of ardent belief and replaced the Christian faith of its early years," and Liza's generation, which "was altogether deprived of spirituality."[50] Dostoevsky's logic at first appears counterintuitive: within one's life, he argues, a change in belief—even if it is one as radical as from religiosity to atheism—does not necessarily destroy the individual's faith altogether. Second-generation atheists, however, imbibing their values from early childhood, are set on a course of life governed by a lack of faith that is eventually bound to bring them to a self-destructive end. Switching from faith in God to faith in social change, Alexander Herzen was able to retain faith's life-sustaining potency. His daughter, however, grew up with lack of religious belief, which she took for granted. The absence of what Dostoevsky calls "conscious doubt" overwhelms Liza's soul and drives her to perdition. In both the preparatory materials and the *Diary* itself, Dostoevsky insists on the pernicious effect such certitude has on the children of the "first-generation" atheists:

> The most hideous thing of all is that she died, of course, without any apparent doubt. Most probably, there was no conscious doubt in her soul, no "questions." It is most likely of all that she believed everything she had been taught since childhood, without question.[51]

> In the linearity of all that she imagined, she, of course, was absolutely assured. But she couldn't endure it unconsciously, as something that was beyond doubt, that she discovered in her father's home. And what for the father was life and a source of [life] thought and consciousness, for the daughter turned into death.[52]

While Alexander Herzen might not have believed in the resurrection of the soul, within his consciousness there was still room for vivifying doubt. For Liza Herzen, this doubt could have become a life-sustaining valve; without it, Dostoevsky concludes, she suffocated:

> It was as if she could not get enough air and she began to suffocate. Her soul instinctively could not tolerate linearity and instinctively demanded something more complex.[53]

Dostoevsky unequivocally attributes Liza Herzen's interpretative failure to her inability to think dialogically. Unlike Bakhtin's insistence on the inherent dialogic nature of consciousness, for Dostoevsky, while being necessary for life, it is hardly a given: its presence, as in the case of Alexander Herzen, can save a person's life, while its absence may drive one to suicide. Or, to put it another way, unable to tolerate a dialogue with a system of beliefs different from her own within her own consciousness, Liza Herzen "dialogically" acts out against the world by killing herself. In his account of the Herzens' family tragedy, Dostoevsky depicts a process of progressive disintegration, with each generation suffering more than the preceding one. For Alexander Herzen, the dialogic movement between religious belief and atheism has already been internalized: it exists only within his consciousness. Externally, however, atheism reigns uncontested in the Herzen household. Without dialogic engagement, Liza Herzen stands no chance. Armed only with dangerous self-assurance, her "linear" consciousness cannot offer her despairing soul the hope that is necessary for its salvation.

Dostoevsky presents us with an in-between case in Alexander Herzen, yet, in these pages of the *Diary*, he does not give an example of what a truly faithful discourse would look like and how (if such a thing were at all possible) a discourse that lacks doubt in the immortality of the soul could avoid the risk of "linearity." After all, Mar'ia Borisova—whom Dostoevsky considers a true believer—chose to die remaining silent. Perhaps it makes sense to see Dostoevsky's representation of atheism as a discourse that constructs undialogic "linearity"; unlike faith, faithlessness produces an interpretative framework that is bound by the irrefutable and merciless logic which suffocated Liza Herzen.

In these pages of *A Writer's Diary*, Dostoevsky presents literature as a therapeutic practice and, as such, one not epistemologically different from other, nonliterary modes of observation and interpretation. Dostoevsky does not so much lower the bar for art as he raises it for life: to comprehend life in a truthful and life-sustaining way, one does not necessarily need to become a writer, but one must strive for artistry in life. The discussion of the qualities that distinguish a true artist occurs in the beginning of "Two Suicides" and can help us understand Dostoevsky's success at interpreting Liza Herzen's story, as well as her own failure at interpreting life.

Dostoevsky begins by agreeing with a statement by an unnamed opponent[54] that "real" life will always be infinitely richer and more complicated than any possible representation of it through art:

> I had known this ever since 1846, when I began writing, and perhaps even earlier, and this fact has struck me more than once and has caused me no small bewilderment: what is the use of art when we can see it so lacking in power? In truth, if you investigate some fact of real life—even one that at first glance is not so vivid—you'll find in it, if you have the capacity and the

vision, a depth that you won't find even in Shakespeare. But here, you see, is the whole point: *whose vision and whose capacity*? Not only to create and to write a work of literature, but merely even to pick out the fact requires something of the artist. (651)

To be aware of life's complexity, Dostoevsky asserts, one must have artistic sensitivity, and what differentiates one artist from another is a combination of two strengths: of vision and endurance. The first makes one capable of perceiving and registering the true significance of the event; the second helps the artist withstand the all-too-human tendency to appease one's mind with superficial explanations. Working together to strengthen "the artist's eye," these two strengths affect the range of possible reactions to a single event:

> For some observers, all the facts of life pass by in the most touchingly simple manner and are so plain that it's not worthwhile to think about them or even to look at them. Those same facts of life will sometimes perplex another observer to the extent that he (and this happens not infrequently) is at last incapable of simplifying and making a general conclusion about them, of drawing them out into a straight line and so setting his mind at rest. He resorts to simplification of another sort and *very simply* plants a bullet in his head so as to quench at one stroke his tormented mind and all its questions. These are only the two extremes, but between them lies the entire range of the human intellect. (651)

Significantly, Dostoevsky doesn't discriminate between the artist's representational process and that of everyone else. We are all engaged in the same task, trying to comprehend life and come to terms with its complexities. This task consists of two parts: noticing and interpreting. "Human intelligence" is produced through an act of interpretation. To come to terms with life's difficulties, one can either refuse to acknowledge them or give them an interpretation commensurate with one's fortitude. As Dostoevsky proclaims ironically, his interpretation of Liza Herzen's suicide, where "everything . . . is a riddle" (651–52), can also be seen as an attempt "'to pause and rest [his] mind'" (652) with a simple solution. In Dostoevsky's world, however, the dictate to "simplify, simplify" vacillates between the poles of blind indifference to human suffering and extreme interpretative frustration. At one pole, a person turns her back on life and lives in a state of blind contentment; at the other pole, she faces the difficult questions that life sooner or later poses and potentially becomes obsessed with them to a point of unbearable torment. The combination of mental and emotional suffering with one's inability to understand the reasons behind a distressing event leads one to stop the interpretative process by any means possible. Ergo: suicide. For

Dostoevsky, the desire to synthesize, "to draw [the events] out into a straight line" and produce meaning shares space with one's inability to explain these events adequately. This creates an internal conflict that can potentially lead to self-destructive violence. Liza Herzen's suicide note was formed—or, to follow Dostoevsky, misinformed—by her undoubting atheism; it constricted her interpretative range to a "linear" understanding of life without "higher meaning." It is also, however, a "riddle" on its own terms that now both Dostoevsky and the readers of the *Diary* have the task of deciphering.

Dostoevsky's purpose is pedagogical. To be perplexed by life is to be human, and in his description of Liza Herzen's death, Dostoevsky instructs by giving an example of a vision that is doomed to fail because of the limits of its interpretative framework. To engage in the process of understanding life, he stresses, is to be aware that interpreting necessitates an articulation of distance between two subjects. One can read Dostoevsky's story of Liza Herzen's death as a warning about the consequences of a failure to do exactly that. Liza Herzen's linearity comes from her powerlessness to allow any doubt—or, to use Dostoevsky' metaphor, "any air"—into her convictions. The indignation and anger that we read in Liza Herzen's suicide note tell of her unconscious rebellion against the self which cannot afford self-reflection, which cannot achieve a position of alterity in relation to its own convictions. The absence of internal space in which, had she properly understood the word's "double-voiced" nature, Liza Herzen could have had a dialogue with herself translates into sarcasm and an intentional vulgarity in her final interaction with others.

While Dostoevsky does not provide his readers with an answer to what would have allowed Liza Herzen a life-sustaining dialogue with herself, he makes the connection between the causes of her suicide and her family's loss of faith in Christ, the ideal other, who alone could have provided her soul with life sustenance. Having never acknowledged the loss of Christ, Liza cannot begin to mourn it in order to restore her internal balance. The haughtiness of her suicide note is a symptom of her inability to cope with the lack of higher meaning that the absence of Christ casts over her life. The most desperate and heartrending detail in Liza Herzen's final note is the note itself, its physical presence. Life is not worth living, yet silence is impossible. An ideological suicide par excellence, Liza still needs to communicate with others, and while she might consider her note "chic," Dostoevsky is able to perceive through its vulgar polish the cry for help of its author's suffering soul.

In contrast, Mar'ia Borisova—whose death Dostoevsky compares with Liza Herzen's—commits suicide silently. This difference is highly significant, since it connects Borisova's seemingly "undialogic" behavior with her Christian faith. She doesn't have to address anyone because, as the icon in her hands proves, Borisova has an internal interlocutor already—the Mother of God.

Chapter One

"The Sentence"

To make an even stronger connection between the collapse of nourishing intersubjectivity and one's lack of faith, Dostoevsky follows up his discussion of the two suicides with another suicide note, this time a fictional one. The final note of N.N. has the structure of a direct exposition, which explains the author's reasons for suicide with logical consistency. If the source of Liza Herzen's death is her lack of self-awareness, N.N. commits suicide knowingly because it appears to be the only solution to the problems tormenting his consciousness. Dostoevsky outlines the author's interpretative range in the note's truncated beginning: "In fact, what right did this Nature have to bring me into the world as a result of some eternal law of hers?" (653). N.N. lives in a materialist universe, where the only eternality is the perpetual constancy of physical laws and the only certainty one can have is life's finality. Such a realization makes life futile: happiness is worthless if it is not eternal. The combination of two factors—the possession of consciousness and the knowledge that striving for happiness is pointless—brings N.N. to turn against nature, which he faults for giving him life without higher meaning. Unwilling to obey nature's inhuman laws, N.N. rebels against it; not being able to destroy it, however, he destroys himself:

> I condemn this Nature, which has so brazenly and unceremoniously inflicted this suffering, to annihilation along with me . . . Since I am unable to destroy Nature, I am destroying only myself, solely out of the weariness of enduring a tyranny in which there is no guilty party. (656)

Except for a short introduction, Dostoevsky leaves the note without commentary. In the next issue, however, he picks up the topic again, lamenting the fact that his readers could not understand the moral of N.N.'s note, which he now has to explain. Dostoevsky ascribes his readers' failure to comprehend his true intentions to the power of the formula he found for the "logical suicide" of N.N. Blinded by the coherent irrefutability of his suicide's argument, his more simpleminded readers "miss the *inner sense* of the article, its intent and its moral," and are instead seduced by its logic (729). Dostoevsky cites a letter whose author, Mr. N.P., claims that N.N.'s fictional explanation of his suicide is but an "anachronism" in "an age whose banner bears the motto: 'To live by all means! . . .'" and is not worth a discussion (731). Taking up the discussion of the note again, Dostoevsky aims to help his audience avoid the "linearity" and the unsophisticated naïveté of Mr. N.P.

The moral of N.N.'s suicide explicitly restates Dostoevsky's convictions about Liza Herzen. N.N.'s suicide is brought on by his lack of doubt, expressed by the implacable logic of his argument. N.N.'s inability to believe in the afterlife robs him of the possibility of salvation: even if a universal harmony were to be achieved, he would not be able to participate in it. Dostoevsky states this explicitly: "The trouble was entirely in his loss of faith in immortality" (735). Such a worldview makes despair imminent, since the idea of the soul's immortality, the only idea that can reconcile one to life, cannot be perceived by the materialist vision.

Here, however, I would like to focus not so much on Dostoevsky's religious beliefs as on how they affect his relationship with his readers. Continuing his polemic with Mr. N.P., in whose opinion, as Dostoevsky puts it, N.N.'s suicide is an irrelevant exception to humans' desire to "stay alive by all means!" (731), Dostoevsky draws an important correlation between atheism and one's inability to love life and humanity. Dostoevsky's thoughts here are very close to what Ivan Karamazov declares in *The Brothers Karamazov*: "love for humanity is even entirely unthinkable, incomprehensible, and *utterly impossible without faith in the immortality of the human soul to go along with it*" (736, emphasis added).

As I wrote above, the most striking fact in both suicide notes—the real one of Liza Herzen and the fictional one of N.N.—is the presence of the notes themselves. Inherent in any suicide note is the tension between its content and form: an explanation of the decision to sever one's ties with the world coexists with a desperate—and final—attempt to establish contact with others. Once its intention is fulfilled, the suicide note plays the role of a magic circle meant to protect its author from outside intrusion: its message searches for an addressee, yet at the same time it refuses to hear a response. The implicit goal of the suicide note is to frustrate: the relationship it builds between its author and reader is by definition unbalanced; the price for such an advantage, however, is absolute: one's life. Unlike Mr. N.P., who writes that Liza Herzen's desire to drink champagne testifies to the superficiality of her emotional life, Dostoevsky explains its aggressive nature as proportional to its author's suffering. In the December issue of the *Diary*, Dostoevsky argues for the existence of the same dynamic between N.N. and the potential readers of his note. Directing our attention to the "inner sense" of N.N.'s note, Dostoevsky suggests that the young man's arrogance coexists with and is evidence of his great internal torment. As such, N.N.'s note can be seen as a condensed version of Ippolit's confession in *The Idiot*, just as N.N. shares with Ippolit a desire for salvation hidden beneath a surface of resentment. As with Ippolit, there is a striking similarity between Dostoevsky's representation of the subject, N.N., and the text of the note. The relationship between the surface meaning of the note and its "inner sense" corresponds to the relationship between N.N.'s consciousness, which develops the logical argument for suicide, and his soul, which suffers intently and silently without the possibility of an internal dialogue with Christ.[55]

Chapter One

N.N.'s note is an account of a failed philosophical inquiry; it appeals to all whom it may concern. Yet, its apparent all-inclusiveness is deceptive: N.N.'s materialist universe is governed by an evolutionary hierarchy, which also determines his choice of audience and his relationship to it. The possession of a highly developed consciousness separates N.N. from the rest of the human community; for him, society is divided into those like "cows," who "willingly consent to live, but on the condition that they live like animals," and those like N.N., who suffer from consciousness and the knowledge it brings about humanity's terrible fate.[56] This is the same interpretative range that Dostoevsky outlines in his polemic with Saltykov-Shchedrin: between bovine suppression and intolerance. N.N.'s aggressive inquest personifies nature and treats it as a contested authority with whom he competes for unrivaled superiority: "what *right* this Nature had to create me in this world as a result of its eternal laws" (653). While it is true that one of N.N.'s professed reasons for suicide is a refusal to accept the meaninglessness that his atheistic worldview suggests, it is also true that what draws his strongest discontent is his inability to be in full control of his existence. The courtroom atmosphere in which the distribution of roles is strict and where the response of the interrogated is mandatory governs the tone of the note. Dostoevsky's title for the chapter ("The Sentence") is hardly accidental: N.N. does not ask, he demands. What hides underneath N.N.'s logic and carries the emotional charge of his note is his soul's unreciprocated request for dialogue that coexists with his desire to reach a position of authority from which dialogue is no longer required. N.N.'s indignation with "a tyranny in which there is no guilty party" is deceptive here, inasmuch as it is driven by the desire to take over the highest rung in the hierarchy. The note is explicit that its author does not consider dialogue to be an option with those whom he accuses of being blindly content with their lot. N.N. addresses us, the readers, but the roles he makes available for his potential interlocutors are not many. The tone of the note, which re-creates the atmosphere of a courtroom with its predetermined power dynamics, pushes his readers into a relationship governed by courtroom hierarchies. If N.N. is a plaintiff, as he seems to think, then we must become judges. The paucity of choice here is aggravated by the inherent antagonism between different roles. Within the structure of the court offered to us by N.N., we can find security in the law; yet, we have just witnessed N.N.'s refusal to obey the laws of nature. As N.N. admits at the end, his suicide is a displacement of violence that was originally meant to be committed against nature. Refusing to submit to any laws and unable to tolerate any version of sociality in which a nurturing intersubjectivity can exist, N.N. kills himself. As such, the logic of his note is monological. There is no place in his narrative for an alternative opinion, a worldview that might differ from his own. Moreover, there is a direct connection between N.N.'s physical violence against the self and the narrative violence of the note. What hides behind N.N.'s monologic idea, what camouflages itself as logic, is a demiurgic desire to monopolize interpretative space. The strength of the note's logic can, in fact, be seen as a symptom of N.N.'s monologism. This becomes especially apparent once we compare the algorithmic exposition of his argument with Dostoevsky's unsubstantiated claims for the necessity of the belief in the soul's immortality.

What confounds Dostoevsky's readers such as N.P. is the blurring of boundaries separating the fictional and documentary accounts, which exist side by side on the pages of the *Writer's Diary*. To formulate a response to N.N.'s note, as if it were a real note of a real suicide, is to put oneself under the spell of its logic. The only way to safely and correctly respond to the note is to present it with an idea that exists outside its author's horizon. Dostoevsky cannot and does not prove the soul's immortality and the essential role that belief in an afterlife plays in sustaining life. Instead, he positions this argument alongside N.N.'s—his argument can only come from without and has to be accepted on faith. Since faith is not a given but a task, the least we can hope for is to allow for the existence of both worldviews, the atheist and the religious. This sustained Alexander Herzen; its absence, on the other hand, proved disastrous for his daughter. Importantly, Dostoevsky does not *respond to* N.N., or, to put it differently, he relates to N.N. as a monologic author (in Bakhtin's terminology) relates to a character, whose flaws he explains using the authorial surplus of vision. By showcasing N.P.'s angry response to N.N.'s note and by contrasting it with his own understanding of its author's philosophy, Dostoevsky shows the readers of the *Diary* the necessary steps needed in order to become implied readers. Significantly, the distance that readers need to traverse to interpret the note correctly corresponds to the distance between the materialistic worldview of N.N. and the religious one proposed by Dostoevsky. Since N.P. fails to become such a reader, he is punished on the pages of the *Diary* by becoming yet another one of its characters. According to Dostoevsky, only religious faith can withstand the materialist logic of N.N. and others like him. Yet, in order to bring this point across, Dostoevsky, misunderstood by Mr. N.P., has no other recourse than to continue explaining. Dostoevsky's need to continue the conversation with his readers points to a certain anxiety about leaving his fictional accounts as they are, without additional clarifications. At the same time, it also suggests his unease about the effectiveness of communicating with his readers directly. As Dostoevsky attests to Ivan Aksakov in a letter written in 1880, the monologic voice of the journalistic writing of the *Diary* can be problematic in successfully conveying his Christian ethics.[57] The absence of such a voice in fiction, however, threatens to muddle the clarity of the message. To see how Dostoevsky solves the problem of effec-

Chapter One

tively actualizing his Christian vision in his prose, we must turn once again to "The Meek One."

The Body and the Voice

What first arrests one's attention in reading "The Meek One" is the overbearing presence of the narrator's voice. By the time we tune into the story, the narrator has found a way to manage his initial incoherence by deciding to address his thoughts to an invisible audience. As in N.N.'s suicide note, here Dostoevsky once again puts us into the courtroom with the subtlest of means. The promise of the eventual order appears more or less concurrently with the first apostrophe:

> It's been six hours now, and I still can't focus my thoughts. The fact is that I just keep on walking, back and forth, back and forth . . . This is how it happened. I'll just tell it in order. (*Order!*) Gentlemen, I'm certainly not a literary man, and you'll see that for yourselves; but never mind: I'll tell you what happened as I understand it myself. That's what I find so horrible: I understand it all! (678, emphasis added)

The story begins once the narrator chooses his audience, and as long as we are reading it, we have to play the part. Yet, even as we begin finding out about the pawnbroker's married life, our focus is strangely doubled: we follow the story, but the immediacy of the narrator's voice also forces us to pay attention to the manner in which it is being told. The intermittent flow of the pawnbroker's speech, its jagged tempo, the narrator's constant references to his present physical situation, as well as the heightened dialogic tonality of his narrative in relation to his audience—all this asks us to concentrate on the form of the narrative as we are following its content.[58] As Dostoevsky warns us in the preface, the story's frequent interruptions, as well as the fragmented style of its telling, require us to concentrate on the story's form and on the way it corresponds to the narrator's state of being. The pawnbroker's failure to get his thoughts together is contagious and forces itself on the reader. Presented with the narrator's inability to create order out of a chaotic stream of consciousness, the reader is forced to struggle with the same task.[59]

Aside from the pawnbroker's psychological difficulties in telling the story, however, there exists the strong presence of a physical dimension that affects both the manner in which the story is narrated and its outcome. The reader is drawn to the physical space inhabited by the narrator as much as to the story of the narrator's life with his wife. From the very beginning of "The Meek One," as the pawnbroker synchronizes his own pacing across the room with the pace of his story ("I just keep on walking, back and forth, back and forth . . . This is how it happened"),[60] the nature of the physical interruptions that sequence the narrator's speech creates the effect of a direct correspondence between the physical state of the narrator and the manner in which his narrative is told. Hence, the second section of the first chapter ends with: "I'd better go to bed. My head aches" (687). The third section begins: "I couldn't get to sleep. Anyhow, how could I sleep with this throbbing in my head" (687)? As the physical environment of the story—the pawnbroker's apartment—becomes the sole locus for the story of the narrator's relationship with his wife, it begins to bear a direct influence on the style of the narrative. While the content of the story takes place in the narrator's head (as a series of remembrances), its form is trapped by his immediate physical surroundings.

The importance of physicality is similarly underscored by the narrative's abrupt conclusion. "The Meek One" ends as the pawnbroker's narrative "catches up" with his present and once again reenters the apartment it "left" in the beginning. The circle is complete and the tale ends just as it began, as though there is nothing else left to say. Here is its beginning:

. . . So as long as she's still here everything's all right: every minute I go up to have a look at her; but they'll take her away tomorrow, and how will I ever stay here by myself? (678)

And here is the end:

. . . No, in all seriousness, when they take her away tomorrow, what will become of me? (717)

The "physical object" that simultaneously gives the initial impulse to the pawnbroker's narrative and condemns its author to its endless repetition is, of course, his wife's body. In the story, it creates a force field strong enough to direct the narrator's physical movements around the apartment, as well as the spasmodic movement of his story. The extent to which the Meek One's body affects the narrator is made evident by the story's first sentence, and its influence does not diminish until the story ends. As long as the body is lying on top of the card tables in the living room, the pawnbroker is chained to it in both his physical whereabouts and his story. The transformation of the Meek One into a lifeless body causes an eruption of energy that consumes the narrator and forces his narrative out of him. The connection between the body and the text in "The Meek One" brings to mind Peter Brooks's dictum that "we are forever striving to make the body into the text,"[61] with the caveat that here the pawnbroker's story is constantly (and unsuccessfully) striving to make his text back into his wife's body, or, to put it differently, to have his seemingly chaotic and circular narrative fill the void caused by his wife's death.

Hence, the pawnbroker's narrative is not a response to his wife's words. The Meek One's dialogue with her husband—if it could be called a "dialogue" at all—has ended much earlier in their marriage, as the pawnbroker's aggressive responses to her attempts at communication have eventually bullied her into an almost complete silence. Even in his postmortem narrative, we never know exactly what the Meek One has "argued against" in the initial stages of their marriage—this omission testifies that whatever the pawnbroker's narrative is, it is *not* a response to the Meek One's "open-ended word." Nor is his word *about* his wife: yes, there is his promise of not letting the servant Lukeria leave his household so he can question her about his wife's last winter, but the present narrative is certainly more of an apologia than an attempt at biography.[62]

The Meek One's body's silently directs and comments on the pawnbroker's speech. This power to signify silently can be compared to the pawnbroker's alleged silence during their short life together, which became one of his tools for the subjugation of his wife:

> I'm an expert at speaking while barely saying a word; I've been speaking without saying a word all my life, and have endured whole inner tragedies without saying a word . . . I just kept silent, and especially with her I kept silent, right until yesterday.[63]

Hence, the story resists the Bakhtinian model for dialogue, according to which the participants of the dialogic exchange always have an ability to continue it. Such is the function of the famous "word with a loophole" with which one can always escape the finalization brought about by the external I-for-the other. Death for Bakhtin becomes the dialogue's only final word, transforming dying into one's dialogic gift to the other—an ultimate and final submission to the other's word. In transferring to the other the power of an uncontested response, death opens up space for the complete aestheticization of a person's life.[64] From the moment of death, the word can be *about* the person; it can no longer be *to* the person. At the same time, while death takes away the possibility to continue the dialogue, it does not have the power to erase what has been said before. My life ends, but my word, my ideas remain. As Bakhtin argued, the persistence of one's discourse, which does not diminish even after one's death, is a feature peculiar to Dostoevsky's polyphonic novels. The characters' ideas are to be addressed by others and do not disappear after their death. In his notes on the revisions to the Dostoevsky book, Bakhtin states: "Personality does not die. Death is a departure . . . The person has departed, having spoken his word, but the word itself remains in the open-ended dialogue."[65]

To endow the Meek One with the ability to "get back" at the narrator after her death would mean to interpret the relationship between the husband and wife as a dialogic battle, in which the husband wins the first couple of rounds but ultimately loses.[66] If the death of one of the participants is treated as the next response in the ongoing communication, then the dialogue between the husband and wife indeed has the possibility to continue ad infinitum. This reading of "The Meek One" follows the Bakhtinian "open-ended" model, albeit without the optimism. Lacking the promise of freedom, this is not so much dialogic imagination as dialogic coercion and becomes a locus for a potentially unending conflict. Once we line up the dialogic violence with the class difference between the pawnbroker and his wife, "The Meek One" can take its place within what Aaron Fogel identified as "a set of great nineteenth-century *anti*-conversational, yet extremely dialogical, [texts] which fix on a more coercive and authoritarian dialogue regime to return it incessantly upon the reader."[67] As Fogel notes, these narratives drive home the notion that "dialogue between the classes, as opposed to 'conversation,' which takes place within a class, will involve more 'drama,' more actions like coercive inquiry, detection, selling, negotiating, blackmailing, and so on" (175). This reading implies that in her death, the Meek One avenges herself upon the narrator. The pawnbroker's initial "strict" silence forces aggressive verbal outbreaks from his wife; her final silence now condemns him to an incessant verbiage. Indeed, there is a strong resemblance between the anxiety felt in the manner of the pawnbroker's narrative and the angry outbursts of the heroine that we hear about in the beginning.

In a contrasting reading, Harriet Murav concentrates on nonverbal markers of agency that point at the presence of the Meek One's subjectivity within a story in which she is almost completely deprived of a voice. Murav questions the ability of the Meek One's corpse to signify, let alone comment on her husband's narrative. In her death, argues Murav, the pawnbroker's wife is "'finalized' in all senses of the word."[68] In his hunger for self-creation, the pawnbroker has appropriated not only the Meek One's life but also her death.[69] In Murav's reading, it is not the body but the act of suicide that marks both the foreclosure of dialogue—since it underlines the limits of knowledge of another's consciousness—and, paradoxically, its reopening as a possibility of polyvalence. Yet, as Murav insists, "to be the condition of discourse or the limit of discourse is not . . . to be a participant in discourse" (49). The presence of an icon in the suicide's hands, however, is a different matter, and signifies an understanding of the self "not as a speaking subject, but as a creation in the image and likeness of God, who bears the image of the divine" (50). By putting an icon into the Meek One's hands, or rather by noticing it in the hands of Mar'ia Borisova, Dostoevsky contrasts the limits of an utterance with a nonverbal gesture, which has the power to escape and transcend the dialogic entrapment.

Indeed, there seems to be a world of difference between the pawnbroker's silence with which he used to train his wife and the silence of her corpse. To present the Meek One's death as a subsequent reply in the dialogue with the pawnbroker is to devalue the fact that it is irreversible. On the other hand, a simple opposition of the verbal, dialogic "form-shaping" activity of the pawnbroker to the nonverbal, image-based self-representation of his wife does not address the question of the reader's participation with what is, after all, a narrative. I have argued earlier that in his fiction Dostoevsky contrasts the coercive nature of dialogic exchanges between characters with leaps of faith, most often represented by nonverbal markers, such as the Meek One's icon, or acts of compassion, such as Liza's jump across the room toward the Underground Man. Yet, here I would like to push our understanding of Dostoevsky's narrative ethics beyond the static allocation of right and wrong, and the narrative strategies through which these designations become distributed among his characters. To leave the text by posthumously canonizing the Meek One and by pronouncing a verdict on the pawnbroker seems to me premature for a couple of interconnected reasons. In his discussion of the death of Mar'ia Borisova—the real-life Meek One—Dostoevsky makes a disconcerting note: "One cannot help but to continue thinking about some things, no matter how *simple* they seem. As though you are to blame for them. This meek soul which destroyed itself tortures the thought."[70] What can Dostoevsky expect from us other than compassion and understanding? Why should our thoughts about Mar'ia Borisova continue being tortured? And why should *we*, Dostoevsky's implied readers, feel guilty for an unknown woman's death?

As I have argued in my analysis of the preface, the reader's participation with the text of "The Meek One" has been set up by the story's formal features. For Dostoevsky, the production of knowledge through the interpretation of "facts" is not an endeavor from which one can come out unscathed. The sharpness of the interpreter's eyes should always be correlated with one's endurance. To accept that the truth promised by the author to the pawnbroker can be accessed and potentially shared by the reader is to accept the responsibility for its search and the narrative it creates.

While the wife's body might not have the power of signification, to argue that the narrator's discourse has completely absorbed the Meek One's death is to write off as insignificant the tremendous sense of anxiety spread over the whole of the pawnbroker's narration. Instead, I would like to suggest that the Meek One refuses to be "dead," in the Bakhtinian sense of the word, by remaining "the body"—something that resists narrative appropriation. Its most disruptive quality is its perfect physicality, against which the pawnbroker displays his absolute helplessness. The Meek One's death might very well be a necessary condition for the pawnbroker's confession, yet, as the ending shows, it also constantly threatens to nullify all of the narrator's strenuous effort. By killing herself, the Meek One eliminates herself as a participant in her husband's not-quite-dialogue, thus forcing him to permanently cross the threshold beyond which he has no other option but to transform his life with his wife into a story, the flow of which he fails to control. In this sense, it might be useful to compare this endless narrative to the comparatively quick narrative relief that Dostoevsky found after the death of his own wife. While Dostoevsky begins his thoughts on his wife's passing in an almost identical fashion to the pawnbroker ("Masha is lying on the table"),[71] his conscience is not burdened with guilt, since he locates the future meeting place for himself and his wife—in Christ. Faith allows the narrative to cease.

The pawnbroker's unsuccessful attempts to mark at least a portion of the narrative as finished are scattered, like scar tissue, over both the story itself—where he, time and again, struggles to anchor his partial understanding of what has happened—and the manner of telling it, as his internal anxiety compels him to talk without any respite. Such are his efforts to allocate at least some blame to his wife: "And so, I'll tell the truth; I'm not afraid to face the truth head on: it was *her* fault, *her* fault!"[72]

These thoughts correspond to his inability to stop: "I spent five minutes on my knees in prayer. I wanted to pray for an hour, but I kept thinking and thinking, and all my thoughts were painful. My head aches—so how can I pray? It would only be a sin!" (701).

The pawnbroker's narrative doesn't collapse; instead, like a screw with a stripped thread, it is doomed to perpetually revolve on its own axis. The story is finite, but its telling might continue interminably. Significantly, it is no longer directed at the Meek One; her death deprives him of his only witness and listener. And it is a listener that the pawnbroker needs more than anything else. The pawnbroker's tragedy is that he is no longer able to address his wife and is forced to send his narrative toward an invisible and imagined interlocutor. For him, this is hardly a sufficient substitution. Yet, even in the imagined dialogue with his audience, his authorial strategies have an uncanny resemblance to his "form-shaping" activity during the course of his marriage.

Like N.N. from the *Diary*, the pawnbroker suffers from an unacknowledged loss of an ideal—the world in which he lives does not have a supreme author who could give direction to its progress and meaning to its existence. Acceptance of this kind of uncontested external authority would provide him with an I-for-the other, which he then could successfully internalize without having to rise against it. Deprived of such a possibility, the pawnbroker reads

Chapter One

all other versions of I-for-the other as tyranny. This is how he interprets the incident that, as he insists, initiates his ordeals, after which he was forced to leave his regiment:

> You see [*Vidite*], there had been one terrible external event in my life which up to this point—that is, until the catastrophe with my wife—had oppressed me every day and every hour: this was my loss of reputation and my leaving the regiment. To put it briefly, there had been a tyrannical injustice committed against me. It is true that my fellow officers did not like me because I was not an easy person to get along with . . . Oh, even in school people never liked me . . . That same incident in the regiment, while a consequence of the general dislike for me, still was largely a matter of chance. I mention this because there is nothing more offensive and painful than to be ruined by a matter of chance, by something that might or might not have happened, by an unlucky conglomeration of circumstances that might have simply passed over like a cloud. For an intelligent creature this is humiliating. (702)

Everything in this passage betrays the narrator. The pawnbroker's absence of faith, his insistence that he is the ultimate author of his life, brings him to a catastrophe once he encounters a sociality which has the power to enforce its own version of what and who he should be at that moment. Pointing out the sources of his hero's hubris, Dostoevsky is very direct: the one whose only armor is intellect has no other choice but to see external intrusions as accidental and humiliating and to react to them with proud indignation. But the most telling detail about the pawnbroker's situation is the apostrophic "You see," which reveals the painful need this primordial author has for an audience.

Dostoevsky's mastery, however, is not so much in pinpointing the root of the problem but in the subtlety with which he shows its dynamics. The story the pawnbroker desperately tries to tell the invisible "gentlemen" is a representation of his life with his wife. Yet, that life itself is already a fictional creation, a theater, which the pawnbroker tries to perform "for real," with his wife as both its heroine and the only audience. The events that occurred from the moment of his meeting the Meek One to the moment of her death are authored by the pawnbroker, in the sense that they are prefigured by and are an embodiment of his preexisting worldview. Consider, for example, the purely formal attributes of the generic act of choosing the Meek One, during which the pawnbroker "distributes" the roles. There is an almost fairy-tale quality to the "three particularities" that make him decide her fate:

> It was then that I *particularly* noticed her for the first time . . . And that was my second thought about her at the time; that I remember . . . This was my third *particular* thought about her. (679–80, emphasis added)

The narrator's fantasies of seclusion in a Crimean idyll together with "a friend" also speak to the urgent need he has for bracketing his life within a fictional frame, whose signification only he can control. His wife's misfortune is that within the private theater of his life, she has to share the roles of both the character and the audience:

> *She* knew, and that meant everything to me, because she herself meant everything to me—all my hope for the future of my dreams! She was the only human being whom I was developing for myself, and I had no need of any other. (704)

Of course, such a friend, as the pawnbroker tells us, had to be "trained" and "conquered." The "accident" with the revolver helps the husband to achieve both. It helps him to create a complete structural imposition between the macrocosm of his whole life and the microcosm of his life with his wife, the crucial difference being that here he gets a chance to finally be in control of the external fortuitousness. (Noticeably, now he praises the accidental nature of the events: "For example, how could I, without the chance assistance of the terrible catastrophe with the revolver, have convinced her that I was not a coward and that my regiment had unjustly accused me of cowardice? But the catastrophe came along at the right moment" [704].) Moreover, by winning the duel with his wife, the pawnbroker manages to simultaneously conquer his wife and make her a witness of his triumph. The screens with which he limits her physical space only repeat her ideological encirclement. His fantasy world finally achieves the desired physicality.

It is more important and more terrifying, however, that the pawnbroker's awareness that he has broken his wife's will does not interfere with his sincere belief in her independent and unbiased (*sic!*) judgment of his character. In the pawnbroker's solipsistic world, he is able to combine both functions: that of an author and of a naive reader, which he then projects onto his wife. As much as the pawnbroker relishes the knowledge that his wife finally understands him correctly, he is the first one to take pleasure in his own fictionalization. The pawnbroker does not witness his life vicariously through his wife's eyes but, on the contrary, sincerely believes in his own creation and then, un-self-aware, assumes that his interpretation of events must be shared by both of them.

This is why the Meek One does not stand a chance. Not because her husband consciously usurps the authorship of their world and demands that she accept its fiction as the only one possible. While in the beginning of their marriage the Meek One attempts to stand her ground against her husband (her resistance to his tyranny culminates in the duel scene), toward the end the Meek One accepts (hence the name) her moral and physical defeat, as long as he "lets her go on like that" (709). But the pawnbroker's ultimate desire is not just to be the author but to be *the polyphonic author*, that is, to author and not to author at the same time, or, to put it differently, to completely submerge into the process of creation without leaving outside any authorial surplus of vision, which would allow him to have the consciousness that his form-shaping activity breeds fictions, not truths. The pawnbroker's project is nothing less than the total destruction of the inertia of life; he has to be an active participant in life's creation. What he cannot allow himself to see is that he, like all of us, is a monologic creator: an author of truth limited by his own angle of vision, who needs to share this truth with other monologic authors. Solitude is the pawnbroker's scariest nightmare, yet, without the possibility of an internal dialogue, to share the power of authorship with somebody else is, for him, tyranny.

To read "The Meek One" is a deflating experience. Over the course of the whole story, there is no distance between the pawnbroker and his voice—his incessant demand for authenticity turns him into a two-dimensional figure, all of which is "on the line." As such, he joins ranks with Dostoevsky's other split characters—like Mr. Goliadkin or, during his delirium, Ivan Karamazov. While one part of his self creates the world, the other part blindly experiences it in all of its authentic fascination. The doubling of the pawnbroker into author and reader becomes evident in his sincere incapacity to understand what has happened to him and his wife. While we should undoubtedly suspect the pawnbroker's sincerity, his understanding and ignorance of what has happened are emotionally on the same level. Hence, we can either reject the whole story as a lie or accept it as truth (at least "as far as he is concerned"). The pawnbroker's initial self-identification with Mephistopheles is ironic, not only because he, unlike his German counterpart, is a petty demon but also because functionally the comparison is true: each part of his self does not know what the other one is doing; it constantly wills one thing but surprisingly gets another.

The pawnbroker's predicament is not that his life lacks authenticity and is a theater but that he, while performing it, cannot afford to accept that he designed its course in the first place. Hence, none of the Meek One's strategies of evasion work, since the pawnbroker always manages to incorporate them into his life, the script of which he is both creating and living. Significantly, the narrator experiences all of the visible peripeteias of the plot—places in which his wife attempts to stake out her relative independence—as accidental, yet at the same time they are incredibly suitable for the narrative he is in the process of producing. Thus, for example, the Meek One attempts to assume some degree of agency in their household by appraising the pawned articles at a higher value. The pawnbroker needs to teach her a lesson in frugality. "Suddenly" the captain's widow "turns up" and provides him with that opportunity (693). The above-mentioned episode with a revolver also falls into his lap as if by accident, and of course he cannot afford to see that he himself puts the revolver on the table, tempting her to begin the duel that occurs the next morning.[73] As I have been suggesting here, rather than being an example of the pawnbroker's incredible hypocrisy, this inability to acknowledge his authorial function has metaphysical sources.

That the pawnbroker's goal is not to triumph over his wife but to participate in the creation of life through dialogic interactions with her becomes clear by his reaction to his wife's singing. Unlike her husband, the Meek One can be by herself even in the tiny space he allots her for self-expression; she does not depend on being dialogically interconnected with her husband. This becomes the cause of his melodramatic outburst, and the pawnbroker momentarily rewrites their relationship in a way that could accommodate his wife's autonomy, as long as it secures her continuous participation in their dialogic interaction. By investing her with overbearing power over him, he takes away her sovereignty. The complete reversal of their roles, once the "shroud" of pride falls from the husband's eyes, and the intensity of his cathartic moment when he realizes his offenses against her—on the surface level, both testify to his realization of the truth. Yet, at the same time, what can be more exciting and more meaningful than a sudden reversal of fortune in the continuous drama of one's life? The pawnbroker's epiphany inaugurates yet another round for the soap opera and kills his wife.

The Meek One's suicide takes her out of the unbearable dialogic hyperreality that the pawnbroker has constructed out of their lives. The story of his marriage is told. His need for dialogic interactivity, however, connects the story of the marriage with his address to invisible listeners. It also threatens to engulf the servant: "Oh, now I'll never let Lukeria go; she knows everything. She was here all winter; she'll be able to tell me" (713).

The reader, then, is presented with the uneasy task of having to respond to the pawnbroker's story, knowing that such a response, formally speaking, will continue the dialogue—which is precisely what the pawnbroker so obsessively desires—regardless of the Meek One's death. Thus, readings of "The Meek One" that demonize the narrator by revealing and focusing on his strategies of subjugation actually submit to his incessant need to continue his narrative, no matter what role is assigned to him in the new retelling. During his narrative, the pawnbroker exhibits a truly ingenious ability to internalize all possible I's-for-the other and still emerge a victorious author at the end. Since the pawnbroker is not aware of his usurpation of the authorial function, he never needs to take responsibility for it: events happen to him from the outside. The pain that he endures in the course of his life is a small price to pay for the ultimate security such an intersubjec-

Chapter One

tive dynamic provides; moreover, this pain only intensifies his belief in the authenticity of the process. The incident with the regiment, as torturous as its consequences were, only taught the pawnbroker to "endure whole inner tragedies without saying a word."[74] It is all the better if these tragedies can be endured with someone else to witness and participate in them—as it happened in his life with the Meek One and as is happening with the reader after her death. It really doesn't matter if in the ensuing story the pawnbroker is a villain or a hero—he "gets his" either way, as long as he ensures our dialogic participation. To respond to him with angry understanding or compassion (which is unlikely, but possible) or to his wife with empathy and compassion (undoubtedly) is to step inside the vicious circle of his narrative, at both ends of which we encounter his pathetic theatrical props: the white *gros de Naples* of the Meek One's coffin but also her little shoes standing by her cot, on which—oh, poor reader!—she spent the final days of her tragic existence. We can compare the range of our responses with that of the Meek One herself, who, as Robert Louis Jackson writes, "hurls herself out of [the] 'setting,' out of the mundane, temporal, profane frame of her life."[75] The frame out of which the Meek One "hurls" herself is, of course, also the fictional frame of the pawnbroker's story, and by jumping out, she finally takes her living body out of his authorial control. It is the icon that secures the Meek One's passage, but it also provides us with a model (unattainable, I would argue, for the reader) for a verbal response. The Meek One does not speak to the pawnbroker, but we do hear her speak before death. The fact that the speech is reported, in this story of exemplary unreliable narration, gives it more credence, not less:

> "What is it, ma'am?"
> "It's nothing, Lukeria, you may go . . . Wait, Lukeria."
> She came up to Lukeria and kissed her.
> "Yes, Lukeria."
> "The master should have come to ask your forgiveness a long time ago, ma'am. Thanks be to God you've made it up."
> "That's fine, Lukeria," she said. "You may go now."
> And she smiled, but oddly somehow.[76]

Having decided on the suicide, and mentally already "out of the frame," the Meek One simply does not react to her husband's actions. Her dialogue with him is over. The reader's dialogue, however, is just beginning.

As I have argued above, the reader does not have access to the choice of leaving the narrative framework. Unlike such Dostoevskian narratives as *Crime and Punishment*, in which the third-person perspective allows the reader to engage with the character of Raskolnikov from the safe distance of compassion, the first-person narrative in "The Meek One" forces the reader to experience the true power of narrative violence. The first-person voice used in "The Meek One" allows Dostoevsky to strengthen the reader's emotional identification with the consciousness of the narrating protagonist. Whether revolted or compassionate, whether as a judge or a victim, in both cases we become complicit in perpetuating the narrative cycle.

In his reading of Joseph Conrad's *Heart of Darkness*, Aaron Fogel demonstrates how the reader's response to the text is prepared by the disproportionate hierarchy of dialogic exchanges within it. Like the natives who are overwhelmed by the ship's whistle, the Russian is overwhelmed by Kurtz's powerful speech. In the same way, writes Fogel, "Marlow's silent audience (representing ourselves) falls—at least potentially—into this field."[77] Whether or not we accept the reader's silence as part of the ongoing dialogic coercion, Fogel argues that "Conrad asks the reader to think about dialogue as formal and proportional rather than simply expressive: by seeing and hearing the parallel ratios so as to find startling affinities among apparently discrete dialogue scenes" (177). Similarly, in my reading of "The Meek One," I argue that Dostoevsky addresses the reader's responsibility by creating a structural correspondence between the narrative dialogic exchanges within his prose and the dialogic relationships between narrators and readers. In Dostoevsky's fiction, the relationships built between characters through dialogic interaction define and prepare, but also transfer into, the reader's relationship with the text. To understand and allocate responsibility for the physical violence of the prose is, then, to become implicated in the dialogic violence of the text that prefigures it. Dostoevsky locates the origins of dialogic violence in our inability to have a dialogic relationship with ourselves. Crucially, for Dostoevsky, the collapse of internal intrasubjectivity is brought about by the individual's inability to have faith. In Dostoevsky's world, to have faith is to begin the hard work of forgiving oneself. Since forgiveness represents a redemptive internalizing of one's relationship with Christ, faith renders the endless external dialogic engagement with others obsolete. Such a state of forgiveness, however, is an ideal rarely attainable for Dostoevsky's characters. When it is, as I have argued above, its markers are primarily nonverbal. It is with this simple equation that the monk Tikhon tries in vain to convince Stavrogin not to publish his confession:

> "If you believe that you can forgive yourself and can attain to this forgiveness in this world, then you believe everything!" Tikhon exclaimed rapturously. "How is it that you say you do not believe in God?" . . .
>
> "I have glad tidings for you about that," Tikhon spoke with tender feeling. "Christ too, will forgive, if only you attain to forgiving yourself . . . Oh, no, no, do not believe that I have spoken a blasphemy: even if you do not attain to

Chapter One

reconciliation with yourself and forgiveness of yourself, even then He will forgive you for your intention and for your great suffering."[78]

Sin, however, encloses all who have knowledge of it and asks for responsibility from everyone. And so, after reading Stavrogin's manuscript, Tikhon asks Stavrogin for forgiveness. As he tells Stavrogin,

> "In sinning, each man sins against all, and each man is at least partly guilty for another's sin. There's no isolated sin. And I'm a great sinner, perhaps more than you are." (708)

For Dostoevsky, it is narrative prose that becomes the conduit uniting people in sin and responsibility.

Chapter Two

From Violence to Silence: Vicissitudes of Reading (in) *The Idiot*

BETWEEN CONSCIOUSNESS AND IDIOCY

Among Dostoevsky's later novels, *The Idiot* has notoriously divided its critics, especially in their evaluation of the novel's main protagonist, Prince Myshkin. The difficulty lies, first of all, in the reader's lack of access into Myshkin's mind; it is compounded by the narrator's ever-increasing unreliability, as well as his apparent inability to keep the narrative structure together. The lack of narrative coherence transfers into an interpretative anxiety in the reader, who is forced into making an ethical assessment of *The Idiot*'s similarly incoherent protagonist, even as the novel makes it progressively more difficult to do so. The reader's predicament mirrors similar efforts on the part of the novel's characters, who, through the course of *The Idiot*, continuously offer conflicting accounts of Myshkin's actions and motivations.

One such attempt is made toward the end of the novel, soon after the disastrous encounter between Aglaya and Nastasya Filippovna, amid the narrative confusion in which the world of the novel is embroiled. Speaking with the Prince, Evgeny Pavlovich Radomsky identifies in Myshkin a "democratic" and "magnanimous" impulse to protect a publicly dishonored woman from scorn. But he protests against the overwrought, self-congratulatory intentionality of Myshkin's altruism:

> You yourself will agree . . . that your relations with Nastasya Filippovna from the very beginning had something conventionally democratic about them . . . It's clear that, drunk with rapture, you fell upon the opportunity of publicly proclaiming the magnanimous thought that you . . . did not find dishonorable a woman who had been disgraced through no fault of her own, but through the fault of a loathsome high-society debaucher. Oh, Lord, it's so understandable! But that's not the point, my dear Prince, the point is whether there was truth here, whether your feeling was genuine, was it natural, or was it only a

Chapter Two

cerebral rapture? . . . Let her be innocent now . . . but can all her adventures justify such unbearable demonic pride as hers, such insolent, such greedy egoism?[1]

Radomsky faults Myshkin for his exaggerated and pathetic sense of responsibility. For him, Myshkin's insistence that a fallen woman is a victim and not beneath the saving love of an honorable man is didactic and discounts the reality of Nastasya Filippovna's proud and self-destructive nature.

In many important ways, the dialogue between Radomsky and Myshkin parallels Porfiry's final conversation with Raskolnikov in *Crime and Punishment*. During their final meeting, the magistrate tells Raskolnikov that he knows both the murderer's identity and his motivations. Predictably, Porfiry's explanations coincide with those discovered by Raskolnikov himself during the course of the novel. Much more dialogic than Radomsky's condescending evaluations, Porfiry's words are accurate, yet still lacking. What is missing from Porfiry's account is, of course, what Bakhtin calls the unfinalizability of Raskolnikov's character—his absolute unselfishness in the service of the idea.[2] "I-for-the other"—my discursive identity framed by those outside me—is by definition insufficient in comparison with "I-for-myself," the limitless and unframed identity that I provide for myself. More importantly, Porfiry's understanding is a secular—"psychological," as the narrator of *The Idiot* would put it—attempt to explain what is ultimately a religious impulse. Paradoxically, what exposes the limits of Porfiry's vision is its completeness and accuracy. As Raskolnikov envisions in his fourth dream at the end of the novel, the field of understanding of an individual's consciousness is necessarily limited: consciousness lies precisely when it believes it is telling the truth. As the narrator of *Crime and Punishment* underscores in the epilogue, what releases Raskolnikov from the prison of his consciousness comes from outside it. The epiphany happens without and against understanding.

Similarly, while Radomsky's insights into the psychological underpinnings of the relationship between Myshkin and Nastasya Filippovna are accurate, they are also misleading, not because they are incorrect but because they are missing some larger truth of the novel that is beyond understanding and thus cannot be adequately expressed in words. Here the novel once again frustrates the reader by promising to lead her to truth through narrative development, while at the same time insisting that the nature of this truth is inexpressible. Although, in comparing Nastasya Filippovna with Mary Magdalene, Radomsky correctly identifies the original model behind Myshkin's actions, he fails to respond in a way that would do justice to Myshkin's desire to return humanity to a prelapsarian state. Or rather, what becomes apparent here are the limitations of human justice in comparison to Christian ethics. In his response to Radomsky, Myshkin manages, in Avital

Ronell's words, to be "at once uncomprehending and magically perceptive."[3] While not making much sense, Myshkin, at the same time, claims knowledge that Radomsky cannot access:

> You see, Evgeny Pavlych, I can see that you don't seem to know everything . . . You see: neither of them talked about the right thing, not about the right thing at all, that's why it turned out like this . . . There's no way I can explain it to you . . . I now understand everything I didn't understand before . . . Oh, if Aglaya knew, knew everything . . . that's the first thing! Why can we never know *everything* about another person when it's necessary, when the person is to blame![4]

Myshkin's exchange with the "sensible" Radomsky is an extended version of the conversation he has with "a certain S.," an atheist and a "true scholar," of whom he tells Rogozhin during their meeting at Rogozhin's house: "Only one thing struck me: it was as if all the while he was talking about something else . . . I said this to him right then, but it must be I didn't speak clearly, or didn't know how to express it, because he didn't understand anything" (219, translation amended).

In both of these conversations, there is a striking juxtaposition between the ability to make sense of events (expressed by Radomsky and S.) and a Christian vision of the world in which the violence Dostoevsky's characters inflict upon one another is not part and parcel of that vision. These conversations become examples of the most radical opposition within the world of the novel—that between the act of expression and Christian morality: while Radomsky and S. fail to grasp Myshkin's vision, he, ostensibly carrying the vision within himself, fails to express it. If the product of consciousness is knowledge, then Myshkin is ridiculous. His idiocy, of course, is of a divine kind, and it is through Myshkin that Dostoevsky, as Ronell argues, "recognizes, in order to affirm, the ridiculous in Christ."[5] If, following Bakhtin, we see the novel as a great dialogue between participating consciousnesses, each of which struggles to impose narrative order upon the world, then idiocy—as consciousness's antimatter—frames *The Idiot*. A destabilizing force, a refusal and/or inability to secure meaning, this idiocy is intrinsically tied to the growing disintegration of Myshkin's consciousness as a self-aware and form-shaping entity. Myshkin enters the world of *The Idiot* with his consciousness intact, but during the course of the novel it undergoes a process of unraveling, and by the time he talks to Radomsky, his consciousness is already in a state of twilight. At *The Idiot*'s end, the act of exegesis—as a manifestation of consciousness—is incompatible with the kenotic Christian morality embodied by Myshkin. In this sense, Myshkin's trajectory through the novel involves the process of the gradual destruction of his conscious-

Chapter Two

ness, the slow and painful return to the original state of idiocy that is inextricably tied to the divine.

BETWEEN WORD AND IMAGE

The exchange between Radomsky and Myshkin stands at the intersection of two interconnected theoretical inquiries into Dostoevsky's moral philosophy and poetics. In this chapter, I continue to address the relationship between the narrative dynamics of Dostoevsky's texts and their ideological—moral and philosophical—content. First, I use *The Idiot* to examine how Dostoevsky's moral philosophy expresses itself through the narrative intersubjective exchanges between his characters. Second, I show how in this novel Dostoevsky's Christian ethics is actualized not only as a set of abstracted ideas but also in *The Idiot*'s formal features and through the reader's diachronic engagement with the text. As *The Idiot*'s energies form around problems of human freedom and responsibility, how do these energies hold the reader responsible for the process of interpreting the text? Dostoevsky's prose—and *The Idiot* in an extreme way—affects its reader's moral consciousness, not only by dramatizing a philosophical argument but also by forcing on the reader the awareness of the moral ambivalence of the acts of representation and interpretation. This, in large part, is what determines my choice of *The Idiot* as the text in which readers are faced with potentially unresolvable questions concerning the ethical formation of their subjectivity.

In Bakhtin's notes on reworking his Dostoevsky book, he writes that the polyphonic author's activity is "the activity of God in His relation to man, a relation allowing man to reveal himself utterly (in his immanent development), to judge himself, to refute himself."[6] At the same time, the absence from the novels of a single speech-center creates a power void, forcing the characters into a state of existential anxiety. Situated between "the Crucifixion and the Resurrection," that is, after the collapse of the external source of authority and before its ultimate reconstitution, Dostoevsky's protagonists suffer from a split consciousness.[7] Although they are engaged—as Emerson writes—in "a *search* for . . . higher authority," they also desire to replace God themselves.[8] In their search for an authority they would be willing to submit to voluntarily, Dostoevsky's protagonists also struggle to seize total control over their selfhood. Ultimately, the dialogic activity of Dostoevsky's ideologues can be identified as both a projection and an expression of the split within their consciousnesses.

How, then, do we solve the conflict between the apparent moral ambiguity of the polyphonic novel and its Christian ethics realized artistically? Jackson does this by contrasting the concepts of word and image. While

Christ's word exists on equal terms with other voices in the novel, it also provides, "in the figurative sense, above all," an exit for the desperately struggling consciousnesses.[9] Jackson points out that just as Bakhtin focuses not on the content of Dostoevsky's novels but on the artistic visualization of his ideas, for Dostoevsky an image of Christ takes precedence over Christian ideology. In his novels, this vision finds its place in iconic images of transcendence and is counterposed to the verbal activity of the protagonists. Jackson distinguishes between the silent visual—the vertical—dimension of Dostoevsky's works and their horizontal dimension of dialogic struggles between the characters.[10] The first is present in the novels not as a word but as an image and is only available to the characters as a momentous state of epiphany, miraculous and illogical. Nevertheless, these images serve as beacons, directing the characters' permanent striving.[11]

We can posit, then, that silence, contrasted to the morally compromised dialogue, acquires decidedly positive connotations in Dostoevsky's art and becomes a marker of the divine, which would lose its divine characteristics if expressed through any other means. This reading aligns Dostoevsky's use of silence with the role it receives in the apophatic theological tradition within Russian religious philosophy, according to which "God . . . eludes any definitions provided by consciousness."[12] Hence, Christ's silence set against the verbal onslaught of the Grand Inquisitor in *The Brothers Karamazov* becomes the purest manifestation of this principle through which, as Mikhail Epstein states, "the divine being declares itself in the image of silence" (193).

The motif of the silent, iconic image in *The Idiot*, serving as the marker of the unreachable ethical ideal, connects Myshkin with Christ and, at the end of the novel, belatedly becomes a template for ideal ethical action. The first in the series of images is Myshkin's vision of the heavenly city in Switzerland, during which, as he tells the Epanchins, the Prince experiences transcendence. He narrates the second image—of the mother taking care of and smiling at her newborn—to Rogozhin. The two images merge in Nastasya Filippovna's imagined painting of the silent Christ directing his gaze at the horizon with his hand on the shoulder of the child, who watches him. In the world of the novel, the distant echo of these images can also be perceived in Myshkin's "motherly" caresses of Nastasya Filippovna after her meeting with Aglaya, which in turn points to his silent caressing of Rogozhin after the murder.

At the same time, however, if silence is where the dialogic nature of discourse finds its final resolution, it can become—and, in Dostoevsky's work, indeed often is—not only an expression of the spiritual fullness of being but also its direct opposite, the utter absence of spirituality.[13] The cessation of verbal interaction turns into a harbinger of physical violence, as it does, for example, in Rogozhin's ominous admonition to Ippolit to be silent and not to read his "Confession": "That's not how the thing should be handled, man, that's not."[14] The most powerful counterexample of silence as a positive manifestation of the divine in *The Idiot* is the image of the loss of an ideal, Hans Holbein's *The Body of the Dead Christ in the Tomb*, the painting that becomes the novel's main symbol of spiritual stagnation and despair, producing a devastating effect on the faith of those who view it. Taken together, these polarized images indicate, on the one hand, the hope of bringing about the liberation the struggling characters seek through dialogue and, on the other hand, their spiritual defeat, the giving up of the struggle altogether. Hence, the images of hope and redemption, as well as of loss and perdition, frame the dialogue of the novel, which correspondingly finds the resolution of its story in the characters' acts either of sacrifice and compassion or of physical violence against the self or others. Together, word and image draw out the novel's moral coordinates, the distance between *is* and *ought*, the space of ethics that the characters have to traverse.[15]

It is tempting to see acts of compassion and violence as a realized potentiality that is latent within the characters, an external manifestation of their split internality. As Malcolm Jones puts it, Dostoevsky's "characters live (whether they are conscious of it or not) on the cusp of the fullness of faith and the abyss of nothingness."[16] Or, as Dmitry Karamazov famously tells Alyosha, "Here the devil is struggling with God, and the battlefield is the human heart."[17] Hence, Dostoevsky's belief in the split nature of the human personality is reflected in the concept of the dialogic word, which always carries the imprint of the conflict between "I-for-myself" and "I-for-the other." It is clear that Dostoevsky—from *The Idiot* to *The Brothers Karamazov*—is increasingly preoccupied with the possibility of introducing into the novel the word capable of releasing the tension between the two parts of the consciousness at war with itself, rather than exacerbating it. Such are his attempts at the morally uncontaminated discourses of Prince Myshkin, Zosima, and, toward the end of *The Brothers Karamazov*, Alyosha Karamazov, which are aimed, in Jones's words, at forging a unity between "authoritative discourse and inwardly persuasive discourse."[18] The importance for Dostoevsky of the search for a word that does not promulgate the split within the consciousness of the other but heals it can be seen by the central position this quest takes in all of his fiction, but especially in *The Brothers Karamazov*. While Zosima's life story and teachings stand their ground against the verbal aggression of the Grand Inquisitor, the philosophical drama of the novel consists in figuring out whether Zosima's word retains its power once it trickles down from above into the world and is taken on by Alyosha and other characters.[19]

Yet, more often than not, the end result of dialogic activity in Dostoevsky's texts is not a liberated consciousness but physical violence, committed by a solipsistic consciousness against a subjugated one. If it comes at all, the release from the dialogic struggle is not of the verbal order. Like Liza's embrace of the Underground Man or Sonya's and Raskolnikov's exchange of bows, the acts and images that are able to bridge the split parts of the struggling consciousness are, for the most part, silent. Thus, while the divided self actualizes in the dialogic utterance, any hope for making the self whole again is not of the verbal order and can come only from outside the dialogic interactions between characters.

This moral accentuation created by Dostoevsky's orchestration of discourse poses at least two questions that bring us straight into the center of the problems concerning *The Idiot*. The first question addresses the possibility of a noncoercive narrative structure within the framework of the novel, the existence of a voice—and, thus, of a self—that does not attempt to coerce or finalize others. *The Idiot* is Dostoevsky's first major experiment with creating an unambiguously positive male character; yet, the problem of the ethical status of Myshkin's voice (which is clearly the most ethical voice in the novel, even if we judge by the divided camps of the novel's critics) is far from being resolved. The paradox of Myshkin's participation in the novel's dialogue is not that he veers away from the Christian, self-abnegating morality that constitutes the core of his worldview but that for the duration of Myshkin's existence in Russia, his voice, which is already a manifestation of his growing attachment to the world, causes as much destruction as the Prince hopes to prevent. In this sense, we can perhaps understand Dostoevsky's opinion of the novel as a failed one; it is also what makes this text such a radical novelistic experiment: *The Idiot* establishes any participation in the novel's dialogue as a priori morally inadequate.

The second question follows from the first and relates to the reader's participation in the novel's dialogue, the moral status of which is compromised. Dostoevsky's "aesthetic revolution," as a result of which the characters are able to speak without authorial subjugation, affects the freedoms of not only the characters but also the reader. As the reader's role in the process of reading changes, so does her accountability for participating in the text's dialogic activity. Once the borders of the text become porous, the reader must accept that the moral accounting for the dialogue in the novel is not different from the moral accounting for her dialogue with the novel as the process of interpretation begins.

BETWEEN TEXT AND READER

Hence, *The Idiot* complicates the process of interpretation in a way unlike any of Dostoevsky's other novels, not so much by the polyphony of its voices, but by its insistence that any kind of finished interpretation is morally inadequate. This happens on one level, as Miller and Jones demonstrate in their studies of the novel, through the supreme unreliability of the narrator, who, by switching between a plethora of voices, each of which has a different take on the novel's events, makes impossible any stable framework from which to interpret the novel.[20]

Robin Miller's reading of *The Idiot* uncovers the narrator's betrayal of Myshkin in the later part of the novel. This realization causes the physical reader to split into the narrator's reader and the implied reader. While the narrator's reader is duped by the narrator's tricks and moral imperfections, the implied reader learns to see through them. Here, the physical reader's hermeneutic journey backward is completed, and the understanding of Dostoevsky's cherished idea of compassion becomes her reward for the labor of reading. Recognizing the simultaneous existence of good and evil within ourselves, we can in turn be merciful to others.

The dangers of reading *The Idiot*, however, are at least commensurate with its rewards, and the net profit of the implied reader that such structuralist readings strive to afford is not something that one can count on easily. Out of all of Dostoevsky's novels, *The Idiot* problematizes contractual relationships like no other. Monetary transactions and predetermined rights and values accompany virtually all human relationships in the novel, and the price one has to pay for extracting the objectified meaning—even if this meaning corresponds most closely to the one implied by Dostoevsky in our own construction of "the implied author"—can be rather high. As Lebedev warns Nastasya Filippovna, when living under the black horse and the rider with balances in his hand, one cannot hope to preserve one's freedom of spirit and a clean heart. Or, as Newton puts it somewhat less ominously: "The responsibility [for reading] is twofold. In part it means learning the paradoxical lesson that 'getting' someone else's story is also a way of losing the person as 'real,' as 'what he is'; it is a way of appropriating or allegorizing that endangers both intimacy and ethical duty. At the same time, however, one's responsibility consists of responding to just this paradox."[21]

If Miller salvages the meaning of *The Idiot* through the figure of the implied reader, Malcolm Jones goes further to suggest that such recuperative readings might be simply untenable, since the text forcing readers to confront "the problem about their own identity" offers no resolutions.[22] The reader's inability to achieve a resolution is paralleled by the novel's characters' failure to reach a conclusion about Myshkin's identity. Jones claims that the reader's choices are not the same as those available to the novel's characters, who continuously deliberate whether Myshkin is an idiot or a saint. Yet, what connects the reader's acts of interpretation with those of the characters, as I see it, is Dostoevsky's insistence that discourse in the novel is a moral category.

With regard to *The Idiot*, the ethics of discourse has been most thoroughly analyzed by Sarah Young, who argues that the characters' desire to establish and control their identity through dialogic activity—or what Young aptly calls "scripting"—is *The Idiot*'s most fundamental feature.[23] The protagonists in the novel are not only concerned with scripting their own roles but are also intent on forcing the others to accept them. As Young persuasively argues, this emphasis on the intersubjective narrative dynamic and the way it influences and coerces the characters' actions "endows narrative activity with an ethical dimension, because it pertains not simply to characters' textual existence as isolated entities . . . but precisely to their being *with* the other, and the effect of this on the narrative" (18, emphasis in the original). In short, in *The Idiot*, the most common source for the struggle between "I-for-myself" and "I-for-the other" is the desire for domination and the inability to tolerate authority. Discursive violence prefigures physical violence: hence, Rogozhin cannot help but kill Nastasya Filippovna because both she and—especially—Myshkin believe that he will. Indeed, contrary to Bakhtin's conception of plot as a platform necessary for and secondary to the dialogic exchange of ideas between characters, in Dostoevsky's texts, more often than not, we witness the opposite: narrative violence precedes and leads to physical violence.[24] In *The Idiot*, as we trace out the consequences of Myshkin's participation in the big dialogue of the novel to its tragic end, this point is driven home with a dispiriting intensity.

BETWEEN SIGN AND MEANING: FALLEN LANGUAGE

Discourse in *The Idiot* invariably re-creates and promulgates the characters' internal struggles, projecting these struggles into the social sphere. This feature is inherent in Dostoevsky's conception of language as a manifestation and a restaging of the characters' (and our) metaphysical situation. The most consistent elaboration on the role of discourse in the novel occurs during the discussion of "double thoughts" between Myshkin and Keller.[25] Here, the inherent distance between the signifier and signified—the quality particular to our understanding of secular language—is aligned with the split between a selfish motivation and a selfless one. Keller's confession will always be both selfless and selfish, since this, as J. M. Coetzee demonstrates, "is the characteristic movement of self-consciousness," which, in the very desire to purify its motives, hides a kernel of impurity.[26] With any confessional utterance, Coetzee argues, "we are at the beginning of a potentially infinite regression of self-recognition and self-abasement in which the self-satisfied candor of each level of confession of impure motive becomes a new source of shame and each twinge of shame a new source of self-congratulation" (222). Dostoevsky's belief that to narrate oneself imperils one's moral integrity is similar to Paul de Man's description of the linguistic curse in which "the simplest of wishes cannot express itself without hiding behind a screen of language that constitutes a world of intricate intersubjective relationships, all of them potentially inauthentic."[27] While for de Man, language always perverts the original purity of the wish, for Dostoevsky, through language comes the realization that the purity of the wish is an impossibility. Language always both exposes and obscures motivations; in *The Idiot*, this attitude toward language becomes evident through the anxiety that most characters exhibit about their desire to control meaning and their utter inability to do so. Language reveals both the desire to submit to an ideal and a fantasy of usurping the ideal's place within the hierarchy.

Significantly, the foray into the nature of double thoughts between Myshkin and Keller begins with Myshkin's apparent inability to grasp the double bind of language. Keller interprets Myshkin's readiness to take his confession at face value as an indication of the Prince's "Swiss" naïveté, which is contrasted here to Keller's Russian "realism."[28]

Myshkin's voice plays a unique role for others, and it is not accidental that characters in the novel choose Myshkin as their confessor. While truth and discourse are set against each other and, as Coetzee states in his analysis of Ippolit's confession, "the only truth is silence,"[29] what sets *The Idiot* apart from Dostoevsky's other novels is that it stresses the moral ambiguity of discourse while simultaneously introducing a character whose voice attempts to bridge the gap between signifier and signified, inasmuch as it is able to convey the purity and sincerity of Myshkin's intentions. Yet, the paradox of the novel is that while ethically pure, Myshkin's voice upon entering the novel is inevitably subjected to the rules and conditions of the novel's discursive sphere. The distance between signifier and signified secures the doubling of interpretations directed at Myshkin. As long as the Prince's voice is part of the novel's discourse, it is bound to be interpreted, and while the most common doubling of Myshkin into a saint and an idiot is obviously inadequate, it is emblematic of how discourse functions in the novel. As Ronell writes, "the ridiculous enables the manifestation of the Prince's goodness, and ridicule is what must be risked in the elaboration of extreme good: the good cannot be restricted to the merely innate, but must be public, exposed."[30]

This is not the first time that goodness appears in Dostoevsky's novels; the difference here is that this time, and for the first time, it appears as a voice. Myshkin begins his journey in the novel, not unlike Raskolnikov, with "a new word," but while in *Crime and Punishment*, a word is a symbol of a hubristic misappropriation of power and is used to enforce one's ego at the expense of others, in *The Idiot*, Myshkin attempts to use discourse to save others while sacrificing himself. Unlike Sonya, whose explanations of her worldview are limited to stock quotes from the Bible and whose salutary effect on Raskolnikov is achieved mostly through silent gestures, Myshkin starts by trying to affect others through dialogic interactions with them. In analyzing Myshkin's stories told to the Epanchins at the beginning of the novel, Sarah Young identifies Myshkin's strategies of "reading . . . , narrating and scripting" as "a model for the coexistence and interaction of all the protagonists."[31] The philosophical foundations of what Young calls Myshkin's "saintly scripting" (93) are to be found in Dostoevsky's belief in the endless self-renunciation of the self for the sake of others. Young cites the famous passage from Dostoevsky's notebooks written in 1864 just after the death of his first wife, in which he writes that "the highest use a man can make of his personality, of the full development of his *I*, is, as it were, to annihilate that *I*, to give it totally and to everyone, undividedly and selflessly."[32]

Hence, in the first part of the novel, we have an example of what Jones calls "Christian poetics,"[33] the purpose of which is not to participate in the characters' struggle for control but to introduce the paradigm in which such struggles become obsolete. Ultimately, both Jones and Young see the sources of Myshkin's failure to sustain his practice of "saintly scripting" in his experience of the epileptic fit, during which his attainment of a vision of universal harmony is surrounded by feelings of doubt and despair. It is indeed possible (although debatable) that the core of Myshkin's personality, like that of all the other characters, contains the seed of division as well. Nastasya Filippovna's destruction, however, occurs not only because Myshkin, after his return to St. Petersburg, is seized by doubt about his ability to save her but also because she cannot withstand the demands placed on her by his Christian vision. Myshkin's parables told to the Epanchins, on the one hand, express the hope that harmony among people can be restored; on the other hand, they tell of a world in which people live in harmony with themselves. As such, the Swiss are free from the internal divisions that plague the Russians of *The Idiot*. From Myshkin's first appearance in the novel, Dostoevsky constantly stresses that Myshkin's understanding of the vagaries of discourse is indeed "Swiss." This is especially visible in the graphological exercises with which Myshkin impresses General Epanchin. Myshkin's ability to infer the characters of the authors of the various scripts he copies plays on the notion that the Prince believes that a sign expresses a certain concrete meaning, not a co-presence of conflicting ones. His reading of Nastasya Filippovna's photograph similarly exhibits a belief that one can "be saved," as long as one is kind.[34] This is, perhaps, why Dostoevsky presents us not with a portrait—which is already an interpretation—but with a photograph, which, at least symbolically, insists on presenting the image "as is." Myshkin is wrong, of course, not because Nastasya Filippovna is not kind—she is, at least toward Myshkin—but because she is both kind and proud, and his insistence that

Chapter Two

"she's not like that" creates an irresolvable tension in her that persists as long as she is alive.

BETWEEN SELF AND OTHER

In *The Idiot*, acts of interpretation by the characters who attempt to secure meaning by imposing narratives of control on one another result in violence. This understanding is brought home in the novel through a thorough depiction of the destruction that Myshkin brings on those he attempts to save. It also leads us to a major potential problem for Dostoevsky's moral philosophy: can there exist a discourse free from violence, can humans as discursive subjects create a sociality that does not destroy itself in its struggle for power? More specifically, does Myshkin's failure to save himself and others (no matter how ethically pure his voice) indicate Dostoevsky's implicit admission of Christianity's inability to protect contemporary humanity from its own destructive impulses? This reading has been proposed by Val Vinokur, for whom Myshkin's Christian ethics, symbolized by his obsession with faces, leads to destruction because the Prince conflates the plurality of individual faces in the world of the novel with a transcendent, iconic, and thus, in Vinokur's words, "non-ethical" face of the ideal other; that is, the face of Christ. Vinokur juxtaposes Myshkin's—and Dostoevsky's—Christian vision of the iconic face as the incarnation of the divine with Levinasian ethics. For Emmanuel Levinas, we carry an infinite obligation toward the radically unique face of the other, while at the same time having to respond to the existence of the multitude of faces. It is precisely this impossible-to-fulfill dual obligation that gives birth to justice, which although inevitably violent and, as Vinokur puts it, "unethical in the pure sense,"[35] is necessary if ethics is to become a praxis.

Unlike Jones and Young, Vinokur argues that the source of Myshkin's failure lies not in the Prince's inability to sustain the purity of the voice but in the Christian vision from which the voice originates.[36] While I agree that Myshkin's participation in the novel is indeed destructive, it is hard not to see Vinokur's argument as an implicit projection of Levinas's Judaism-informed criticism of Christianity. Such a reading is problematic, however, since it is difficult, if not impossible, to understand how Levinas's "'vision' without image" would find its place within a novel, an art form, in which the self is constituted through language and image and which Levinas criticizes on a similar theoretical ground as Christianity.[37] The argument that Myshkin fails to recognize Aglaya's or Nastasya Filippovna's concrete, unique faces is hardly tenable, since the possibility of having a face in the Levinasian sense does not exist for Aglaya, Nastasya Filippovna, or indeed for any character in any novel. Alas, such is the difference between a character, who is irredeemably mediated and distorted by discursive representation, and a person.

When set against Levinas, Myshkin inevitably comes up short. In contemplating Myshkin's alternatives, however, Vinokur comes out not on the side of Levinas's radical alterity but on none other than Evgeny Pavlovich Radomsky: "[Myshkin] ruins both [Aglaya and Nastasya Filippovna] through his almost comically democratic compassion. Marriage, like justice, is a socially binding decision to give one person somewhat more compassion than another."[38] In analyzing Myshkin's moral shortcomings, Vinokur succumbs to the same weakness as Radomsky, who can neither comprehend nor endure the tension that exists between Myshkin's "Christian" vision and the versions of human justice presented in the novel.

Vinokur's forceful imposition of choice on Myshkin fails to acknowledge the high dramatic tension in *The Idiot* created by the presence of Dostoevsky's Christian ideal as an embodied voice—an experiment destined to fail, not only because pure forms of Christianity are destructive to life as we know it but also because it creates an irresolvable (at least within this novel) conflict between Christian ideals and any form of human sociality.[39] Dostoevsky hardly needed to write a novel to show that Christian ideals—as he espoused them—are antithetical to life here and now. One only needs to remember the famous letter to Fonvisina in which Dostoevsky soberly announces himself "a child of this century," not impervious to the epoch's doubts and religious skepticism.[40] What Vinokur calls "brutal intellectual and artistic honesty in his depiction [of Myshkin's] ultimate failure,"[41] Dostoevsky delivers directly in his notebooks, the same entry in which he announces that one's sacrifice of the ego is a necessary step in achieving the sought-for brotherhood in Christ. It is precisely marriage—which both Radomsky and Vinokur proclaim to be at the pinnacle of values—that Dostoevsky perceives to be both the highest achievement of our civilization and an absolute moral failure—as a social institution that separates a married couple from the rest of humanity—if judged from the point of view of Christ.[42]

Indeed, as long as Dostoevsky's Christian beliefs are conceptualized in theoretical form—as in his 1864 notebooks—they are clearly incompatible with human life. Dostoevsky is unambiguously clear on this matter: "Christ himself preached his teachings only as an ideal; he prophesized himself that there will be struggle and development until the end of the world" (173). What makes reading *The Idiot* such a unique experience, however, is that in Myshkin's verbal participation with others, these ideals incredibly become part of life for the duration of the novel. If for Dostoevsky language—as that which delineates and creates boundaries—is indispensable to the social construction of the self, then Myshkin's existence as a character becomes an ontological anomaly, at least within the framework set by Dostoevsky's Christian vision, which separates self and language from manifestations of ultimate goodness.[43] Myshkin's participation in the novel is an impossibility precisely because, while ethically pure, it begins with a voice, which in Dostoevsky's moral universe is an emblem and a product of the fall. A selfless voice, Myshkin is an oxymoronic creation; as Walter Benjamin puts it, "[Myshkin's] individuality is secondary to his life, just as a flower's is to its perfume, or a star's to its light."[44] For Benjamin, Myshkin is present to create a contrast between what Benjamin calls "psychology" and "immortal life." In Benjamin's reading of the novel, Myshkin's life points to the pure innocence of childhood, an unreachable ideal that remains set apart from life and toward which other characters direct their metaphysical strivings. Similarly, what inspires Myshkin to believe Keller's intentions is, in Myshkin's words, Keller's "childlike trustfulness and extraordinary honesty."[45] In the novel, Switzerland and childhood are the unreachable regions where a human being can still be whole, while Russia and adulthood are the markers of the fallen state, where the reader resides together with the novel's characters. Not surprisingly, Myshkin prefers to be with children, and those who, like Lizaveta Prokofyevna, are "childlike" follow Myshkin readily, or at least, more willingly than others. It is also children's souls that Myshkin saves from perdition in Switzerland, the only place where his presence is able to save anyone. Still, for the duration of the novel, Myshkin engages others in dialogue and thus unavoidably affects their existence. This engagement, on the one hand, makes this Christ-like character susceptible to extreme ridicule, while on the other hand, the dramatic tension arising from Myshkin's dialogic participation in the novel and the danger this causes for others' "individuality" uncovers the destructive force inherent in Christ's very meekness and childishness.

The novel's dramatic tension arises out of vacillations between selfless silence and ever-selfish dialogue, or as Benjamin puts it, "the relationship of human life to the living."[46] The catastrophic effects of Myshkin's narrative interactions with other characters push us to contemplate a curious paradox: while Dostoevsky's Christian beliefs might express the truth about higher forms of human life, any attempt to follow them in the novel proves disastrous. As Aglaya tells Myshkin in one of her brighter moments, truth without tenderness is cruel.[47] *The Idiot* is even more radical, however; Myshkin is forced to learn the hard lesson that truth with tenderness may be no less harmful.

In this way, one can see the novel as an inversion of a bildungsroman, in which a truly responsible hero gradually discovers that a correct understanding of the corrupt world is not enough and can in fact destroy any hope of that world's salvation. As the novel progresses toward its final chapter,

Myshkin grows increasingly suspicious of his verbal powers. Having started his nightmarish journey by teaching parables, Myshkin eventually learns—for what else can he do?—that the only proper outcome of pronouncing truth is to assume responsibility for what that truth implies. The Prince's answer to Aglaya's reproach is to abandon attempts to articulate the disembodied truth of discourse altogether and become tenderness incarnate. Rogozhin's crime becomes Myshkin's own in part because he foretells it, and as he silently caresses Rogozhin's face next to the corpse of Nastasya Filippovna, Myshkin himself becomes a living parable waiting to be interpreted by the reader.

It is in *The Idiot*'s radical insistence on the moral inadequacy of any form of dialogue that the novel presents its biggest challenge to the reader. How should the reader form an identity of and through a novel that posits any construction of identity—inasmuch as it is mediated by language—as ethically suspect? In this self-destructive renunciation of the dialogic, discursive self, *The Idiot*'s narrative ethics stands much closer to Levinas than Vinokur suggests. By exposing the moral bankruptcy of the dialogue, which envelops the other to ultimately reinforce the primacy of the self, *The Idiot* insists on an impossible reading that points beyond its own identity. The affinity between Dostoevsky and Levinas lies in their works' radical critique of the formation of narrative identity and the ethical demand that such a critique puts on the work itself, as well as on the range of the reader's responses to it. Indeed, as Jill Robbins argues, Levinas's requirement that his work "must not remain identical to itself but must go out to the other in a movement without return"[48] possibly creates a condition that neither the work nor its reader can effectively satisfy. Thus, as Robbins suggests, Levinas's texts are at risk of producing what she calls "a double bind": "Levinas says that the work ought to be nonself-identical. But if his work is nonself-identical in the way that his work says that the work ought to be nonself-identical, then it is self-identical. In fact, if Levinas's work does not do what it says about the work, if his work is thus nonself-identical, then it does what it says about the work, and it is self-identical" (12). As Robbins proceeds to show, this insistence of the work on the primacy of the other and its unremitting direction toward alterity puts the reader under an obligation that she a priori cannot fulfill. The same can be said about *The Idiot*, a novel whose identity emerges as highly unstable, not only because of its narrative incoherence and unreliability but also because its philosophical argument is centered on the idea that any discursive identity—even if it is selfless like Myshkin's—is wrought with violence. The impossible ethical conditions that this "constitutive" aporia within Levinas's work puts on the reader succinctly encompass the impossible choices that stand before the reader of *The Idiot*. For this novel to make itself comprehensible is ultimately to lower the reader

Chapter Two

to Radomsky's level. The Prince's appeal made to Radomsky to "understand everything" seems to imply a chance for the conflict's resolution. Yet, it could be argued that the sole reason for the conflict between Aglaya and Nastasya Filippovna is to present Myshkin—and the reader—with a situation that in principle cannot be resolved without violence caused to either of the parties. Since the novel intrinsically connects meaning with violence, the moment this understanding of the insolubility of the knot between the Prince and the two women is secured, we end up once again—as Vinokur does—in the Radomsky camp. Thus, we can say that if the verbal activity in the novel stands for the novel's *is*, its *ought* points to that which lies beyond signification and is symbolized by Myshkin's idiotic babbling at the end.

For Myshkin, this knowledge is acquired—although whether we can speak of "acquiring knowledge" in Myshkin's case remains a question—as he moves through the novel; the scene that especially stands out is his unavoidable participation in the first coerced death in the novel, that of General Ivolgin, a death all the more singular because of the completely discursive quality of the murder weapon. The damage that Myshkin's response inflicts on the poor general after his final story of misrepresentation is certainly not a determining blow, but it is all the more noteworthy as Myshkin finds himself in a position similar to that of the novel's reader: his reply to the general's made-up autobiography—regardless of what the reply is—helps to bring about the latter's demise. To abstain from replying, however, is not an option. Such dialogic entrapment becomes with growing intensity the main paradigm of the novel. It is perhaps in the first part of the novel that Myshkin's voice is most unambiguously salutary, and his meek presence, making the ripe conflicts explode, leads to a temporary resolution. Still, it is also in the first part where the intrigue and rivalry that beset the rest of the book begin to germinate. Even here, Myshkin's voice manages to seduce both of the female protagonists. In this sense, while the story of Marie is irresistible, its asexual dynamics prove to be unsustainable in the world of the novel. In short, starting and ending with Rogozhin, but with most of Myshkin's interlocutors as well, including Burdovsky, Ippolit, Nastasya Filippovna, and Aglaya, the Prince finds himself in a situation where to understand means to coerce, yet not to understand is to not participate. This, I argue, is the position of *The Idiot*'s reader as well.

Throughout the course of the novel, as even the most accurate readings of others prove disastrous and the act of "understanding others" is put on trial, the reader is subjected to the same experience. To narrate the most vivid scene of Myshkin's fall after his return to St. Petersburg, Dostoevsky, using what Miller identifies as the gothic mode, suspends the revelation of the Prince's condemnation of Rogozhin until the latter's sudden appearance on the other side of the street. Myshkin's compulsive desire to visit Nastasya

Filippovna at the start of the second part of the novel coincides with the reader's desire to get into the Prince's head and become privy to his "sudden idea."[49] As Myshkin fights with his undisclosed temptation, the reader falls prey to one of his own. To understand Myshkin's pre-epileptic scream "Parfen! I don't believe" (234) as a confession of sin against Rogozhin, and to say that Myshkin monologizes others, is ethically responsible only if we agree that by so doing we commit the same sin, since the pair of fiery eyes that follow Myshkin through his fever-induced path belong equally to Rogozhin and the reader.[50] But how to make sense of a world in which consciousness and goodness are mutually exclusive remains unclear, and will remain so until Dostoevsky's last novel. At the end of *The Idiot*, the reader is left with a rather uneasy choice between "understanding" the novel Radomsky-style and not participating in it, at which point, perhaps, a true realization of what it means to be an idiot in its original, Greek sense of an "outside person" occurs for the very first time.

BETWEEN WORD AND SILENCE

Like an arrow piercing *The Idiot*'s loose center, the novel's denouement brings us back to its very beginning. The silent vigil that Myshkin and Rogozhin keep on either side of Nastasya Filippovna's corpse stands as the novel's most powerful symbol, not only of Myshkin's failure to prevent the murder but also more generally of the failure of words—that is, of nonphysical interference—to be effective against the violent urges inherent in our nature. Myshkin's sudden realization "that . . . for a long time now, he had not been talking about what he needed to talk about"[51] testifies to the same problem: on the one hand, the choice of words here reverberates with the conversation he has previously held with an atheist, S., while on the other hand, it is unclear at this point whether there is or has been anything to say that would be what he needed to discuss at all, whether words can even get to *that*. Myshkin's verbal range in the novel has been surprisingly broad—extending from his quasi-religious and allegoric parables in the beginning to his almost complete vocal incoherence at the end. What else could the Prince say now that he has not said before and that somehow this time would miraculously affect the miserable status quo of the novel's protagonists?

As numerous critics have pointed out, this silent tableau-like scene corresponds to an earlier meeting between Myshkin and Rogozhin when the two looked at and spoke about Holbein's *The Body of the Dead Christ in the Tomb*.[52] As the novel's anti-icon, the painting transcends the register of secular communication: its meaning, as with any religious art, even art as apparently blasphemous as Holbein's painting, tends to overwhelm the sign.[53] For those who attempt to interpret it in the novel, the painting is a symbol of matter's utter dominance over spirit (Ippolit) and is powerful enough to make one "lose his faith"[54] (Myshkin/Rogozhin). For Ippolit, in particular, this painting represents the triumph of nature and progress over spirituality: "Nature appears to the viewer of this painting in the shape of some enormous, implacable, and dumb beast, or to put it more correctly, . . . in the shape of some huge machine of the most modern construction, which has senselessly seized, crushed, and swallowed up, blankly and unfeelingly, a great and priceless being—such a being as by himself was worth the whole of nature and all its laws, the whole earth, which was perhaps created solely for the appearance of this being alone!" (408). The novel's final scene supports Ippolit's interpretation: his conceptualization of the painting is dramatized by the actions of the novel's characters. The result of the battle within Rogozhin's heart is as obvious as it is tragic: assuming that Rogozhin, like everyone else, is a split personality, it is clear that matter has utterly destroyed whatever sparks of spirit he has held on to through his interactions with either Myshkin or Nastasya Filippovna.

If the power of the last scene is achieved through the final merging of Dostoevsky's Manichean opposites, it also comes from highlighting what has been at stake in the novel: as the novel's dialogue fails, it ends with representatives of two types of silence that frame it. Rogozhin, who has been barely able to tolerate alterity and whose dialogic participation has been both awkward and unwilling throughout the novel, finally succumbs to the action that has been tempting him all along. Myshkin, who, as I argued above, has by this point moved beyond any words, his own or others', silently accepts responsibility for the murder. His caresses of Rogozhin echo, perhaps unconsciously, the iconic motif of the novel: the mother rejoicing over her baby smiling for the first time whom Myshkin met on his journey through Russia, Nastasya Filippovna's unpainted vision of Christ holding his hand over the child's head, and Myshkin's own "maternal" soothing of Nastasya Filippovna after her verbal duel with Aglaya. Not surprisingly, in all of these, the physical gesture stands in opposition to words.

The contraposition of silent action and the word is played out in the dynamic between all three interpreters of Holbein's painting—Myshkin, Rogozhin, and Ippolit. Significantly, it is Ippolit who is associated in the novel with the most powerful verbal outrage, and it is through his confession that Dostoevsky most strongly undermines the possibility of an authentic discourse.[55] Both Myshkin and Rogozhin retain their symbolic function of ethically charged silence as each attempts to stop Ippolit from speaking. Rogozhin goads Ippolit to simply commit suicide, while Myshkin, recognizing the dangers of discourse, is afraid that Ippolit's verbal exposure will provoke his suicide.

Hence, on the one hand, discourse—secular discourse—in *The Idiot* causes and prefigures violence. On the other hand, it finds its original source in violence, the most powerful symbol of which is the dead body of Christ. As with most verbal utterances in *The Idiot*, the tragedy of Ippolit's confession is that it carries two functions at once, each of which undermines the integrity of the other: it is both a desperate appeal to what is best in us against violence, and, at the same time, an attempt to authenticate the primacy of the self vis-à-vis and against others. Rogozhin and Myshkin symbolically frame discourse in the novel as its two alternatives: murder and compassion. Holbein's painting, like a perfect membrane, contains both types of silences, that of a murderous nature and that of Christ, whose dead, silent body offers the promise of resurrection. Likewise, Nariman Skakov, writing on the rhetorical significance of silence in *The Idiot*, argues that the painting represents an ambivalent symbolic opening through which discourse enters the novel. As such, it is both ethically insufficient and ethically indispensable. As Skakov shrewdly puts it, "the discursive muddle is directed against the petrification of the spiritual debate, which has to remain open since the dead body of Christ manifests a threshold between complete decomposition and ultimate resurrection."[56] Hence, the big dialogue of the novel is both necessary and inescapable; to play a part in it is to be implicated in the violence it produces. While the painting becomes that which needs to be interpreted by the novel's protagonists, by the end of *The Idiot* the reader is forced to begin her interpretation of the novel. This ultimately secures our participation in the common lot, yet is tragic enough to make us lose faith.

Chapter Three

The Metaphysics of Authorship: Narrative Ethics in Nabokov's *Despair*

THE CHARACTER OF AN AUTHOR

Ever since Richard Rorty's proposition that aesthetics and ethics are interconnected in Nabokov's prose and that the bad moral judgment of Nabokov's immoral protagonists comes out as their *aesthetic* callousness, the most common solution to the correspondence between the activity of Nabokov the author and his cruel narrators was either to gather evidence of the characters' lapses as authors or to point out that, unlike themselves, those they treat as characters are, in fact, live human beings (at least within the diegetic world of the text).[1] This approach, however, risks overlooking the superb aesthetic agility of Nabokov's narrators. More importantly, it essentializes Nabokov's prose by drawing an ontological distinction between life and fiction that—even if we forget that his texts fail to support it—inescapably works to reduce the ethical tension of the prose. Instead, I propose to launch my inquiry into Nabokov's narrative ethics by looking at the ethical costs of aesthetic activity that extend to the authorial figure, the characters, and ultimately—as acts of interpretation are measured against acts of representation—the reader. I begin this chapter by examining how Nabokov's authorial intrusions into the world of his prose affect the relationship between author and characters. I continue by turning to *Despair* as a text in which Nabokov most clearly draws out the metaphysical temptation behind aesthetic activity. The connection the novel establishes between aesthetics and metaphysics invites us to also consider the ethical implications of the metaphysical aspirations of Nabokov's authorial figure.[2]

The moral quandaries of Nabokov's characters are inseparable from their creator's aesthetic concerns and can be seen as a commentary on the *ethical* role that aesthetics—and verbal rhetoric, more specifically—have in the construction of subjects both within the diegetic world of the novel and across the diegetic border. The observation that Nabokov's universe is filled with artist-protagonists is a truism; what is less frequently explored, however, is the relationship between their aesthetic endeavors vis-à-vis others and their artistic practice in general, which certainly includes the artistry of their own creator.

My discussion of Dostoevsky's narrative ethics, which circumscribes author, characters, and reader within a single field of ethical tension, rests on the Bakhtinian theory of characterization. In it, the ethics of a literary work revolves around the question of freedom that determines the relationship between author and character.[3] For Nabokov, however, or at least for the authorial persona found in the texts surrounding his fiction, authorial control over characters seems to be a nonissue. "My characters," as Nabokov famously quips, are "galley slaves."[4] Authorial intention seemingly reigns supreme in Nabokov's prose. Hence, when discussing the probability of his characters charting their own course in an interview, Nabokov dismisses the problem of the characters' freedom as irrelevant: "Writers who have had [this experience] must be very minor or insane. No, the design of my novel is fixed in my imagination and every character follows the course I imagine for him" (69).

The effect of Nabokov's dismissal of his characters' autonomy is intensified by the subtle yet undeniable presence of his own authorial persona on the extradiegetic level. Consider, for example, the list of Lolita's classmates, which Humbert provides for us with such enviable thoroughness. Humbert's inclusion of the list in full turns it into an *objet trouvé*, which now, framed by the text of the novel, acquires aesthetic significance of its own and allows a series of readings—simultaneously ironic and sincere—across different modal levels. On the forefront, we have Humbert reading the list as a poem, which he proceeds to do in an act that is both earnest and self-ironizing ("A poem, a poem, forsooth!"),[5] but behind Humbert we sense the presence of a different subjectivity. In a similar twofold gesture of irony and earnestness, this authorial presence pokes fun at the overzealous readers who, like the students in a Stanley Fish class, are ready to inject meaning into any text, but it also hints at the importance of the reader's active participation in the production of meaning. It is also the authorial figure who—by allowing us to witness the creation of a poem out of the list by sheer force of Humbert's desire for Lolita—points to the relationship between reading of/in *Lolita* and erotic desire, prefiguring the "cryptogrammic paper chase" (252) of the second part of the novel.[6] The authorial figure also proposes that, not unlike Humbert with the class list, reading the text of the novel (including the list) is to be done by paying attention to the novel's form as much as its content. In learning interpretative strategies from Humbert, who, for example, reads the rhyme into the two names surrounding "Dolores Haze" ("pretty Rosaline; dark Mary Rose"), the reader is to look not simply for *thematic*

Chapter Three

correspondences and echoes between different parts of the novel but also for traces of consciousness left on a different nondiegetic order. If in order to find Quilty, Humbert has to conduct a cryptogrammic paper chase, here we have a strong indication that the reader would not be amiss to begin a similar chase of her own, this time looking for traces on the meta-narrative level. One such trace, as Alfred Appel writes in his annotations to the novel, Nabokov leaves in the middle of the list itself; this trace is the character of Aubrey McFate.[7]

Here, in Aubrey McFate, we have a case of the author's *possessive* presence that appears solely on the meta-narrative level and creates an impression of form parasitically living at the expense of content. I will open up and explore this concept of possession, and especially the way Nabokov interconnects different modalities of his fiction, later on in this chapter; for now, I would like to point to another—albeit related—obstacle that makes it a challenge to ground Nabokov's prose in a Bakhtinian character study. Leaving the boundaries of realist prose often takes care of the issue of the character's freedom simply by eliminating literary characters' humanness. After all, Nabokov's insistence on absolute control over his characters is rooted not only in his privilege of authorial omnipotence but also in his belief that his characters are not human. For him, they are building blocks, one of the many tricks in the novelist's bag, or, as he describes them in the afterword to *Lolita*, "discarded limbs and unfinished torsos."[8]

Yet, here too, as with almost every aspect of Nabokov's art, we have to put on bifocals and exercise double vision, since, as I discussed previously, Nabokov is equally prone to affirm his characters' humanity. The ambiguity of such an authorial position is built into Nabokov's understanding of the double function of art—which strives to both present and *re*-present reality—and corresponds to the tension between the modernist and the realist poetics of his texts.[9] Reading between different narrative modes has been, of course, part and parcel of our reception of much of modernist literature; it is also, for the most part, a well-traveled road in Nabokov criticism. Yet, with few notable exceptions, a common critical solution to the conspicuous presence of the meta-narrative level in Nabokov's fiction is either to treat it as a final solution to the intradiegetic insolvability (using it as a guide that helps to resolve the tension of the text) or to leave it out from the critical discussion altogether.[10] Yet, in Nabokov's fiction, the authorial presence unavoidably becomes part of our study of characters by insisting on the close relationship between the intra- and extradiegetic levels of the text. Without including both levels into the implied world of the novel, our analysis of the complexities of characterization risks remaining incomplete. To do it justice would require an understanding of the relationship between different levels of diegesis and the role that the figure of the author on the extradiegetic level plays in structuring the power dynamics on the intradiegetic one. This ultimately returns us to a Bakhtinian framework. In Nabokov's case, an analysis that includes the figure of the author in the discussion of the ethics of power relations in the text also asks us to attend to the parallels between the monologizing characters and the monologizing author.

In order to see what the inclusion of "author" into the list of "characters" might give us in our reading of Nabokov's fiction and to shed light on the relationship between different diegetic levels, I suggest looking at a Nabokov text in which possession once again indicates authorial intrusion. In what follows, I propose a reading of *Despair* that focuses on the metaphysical underpinnings of the artistic aspirations of Hermann, the novel's protagonist-narrator. My goal here is to see how Hermann's conflation of authorship and authority reflects on the hierarchical relationship between author and character in the novel.

THE DESIRE FOR PRESENCE

As multiple critics have shown, there are numerous instances where Nabokov's presence, of which Hermann has no inkling, makes itself visible throughout the text of *Despair*; it is in this sense that we can speak of Nabokov's possession of the protagonist as the latter is composing his narrative.[11] I would like to begin with one such instance when Hermann seems to sense the presence of another consciousness directing his actions and pen. While Hermann is not aware of the possession of his hand by the author, one discerns his considerable anxiety about being able to remain not so much in control of the text he is composing as being the *only* one who is able to control it. This distinction is an important one, since the source of Hermann's existential turmoil—and in this he comes closest to Dostoevsky's protagonists—is both social and metaphysical. What he desires most of all is control:

> There is yet another reason why I cannot, nor wish to, believe in God: the fairy tale about him is not really mine, it belongs to strangers, to all men . . . If I am not master of my life, not sultan of my own being, then no man's logic and no man's ecstatic fits may force me to find less silly my impossibly silly position: that of God's slave; no, not his slave even, but just a match which is aimlessly struck and then blown out by some inquisitive child, the terror of his toys. There are, however, no grounds for anxiety: God does not exist, as neither does our hereafter, that second bogey being as easily disposed of as the first. Indeed, imagine yourself just dead—and suddenly wide awake in Paradise where, wreathed in smiles, your dear dead welcome you.
>
> Now tell me, please, what guarantee do you possess that those beloved

Chapter Three

ghosts are genuine; that it is really your dear dead mother and not some petty demon mystifying you, masked as your mother and impersonating her with consummate art and naturalness? There is the rub, there is the horror; the more so as the acting will go on and on, endlessly; never, never, never, never, never will your soul in that other world be quite sure that the sweet gentle spirits crowding about it are not fiends in disguise, and forever, and forever, and forever shall your soul remain in doubt, expecting every moment some awful change, some diabolical sneer to disfigure the dear face bending over you.[12]

In this passage, Hermann becomes almost conscious of his own maker. More importantly, the novel aligns his metaphysical turmoil with the author-character hierarchy as well as with his self-identity as an author. In the first paragraph, Hermann connects his refusal to believe in God with the desire to have full control over the origin story; in the second, he switches to identifying a force that can take over the shapes of those he used to know in order to impersonate them "with consummate art and naturalness." The boundary separating the physical from the metaphysical here parallels the one between the intra- and extradiegetic levels of the text. What terrifies Hermann is that this supernatural performance will never admit to the presence of the fourth wall, acknowledging the mystification; it will always, he fears, insist on its authenticity, thereby undermining his own. Significantly, Hermann identifies the author here not with the divine, omnipotent force of God but with the figure of the "petty demon."

The passage suggests a close link between the metaphysical and aesthetic issues raised in the novel. Indeed, in the novel's beginning, Hermann in both his guises of a narrator and a character appears to be a person for whom life has no higher meaning. This is emphasized for the first-time reader by the fact that in not yet understanding Hermann's situation at the point of writing, we easily collapse the distance between his two roles in the novel. Hermann's is a reality that has been flattened to the two dimensions of the chocolate wrapping from which he draws the details of his (pseudo-)biography. It consist not only of literary sources (Hermann hints at the metonymic proximity of imprisonment to literature as he mentions that his literary education took place during wartime internment) but also of second-rate literature: stock phrases and advertising clichés find their way into the text both as images (Hermann's initial biography of the mother) and familiar turns of phrase ("Chocolate, as everybody knows . . ." [5]). Hermann's bookish imagination, of course, points to his closest relative, the Underground Man, whose bookishness is also intrinsically tied to his existential condition of alienation and lack of spontaneity. Nabokov hints that the latter is a literary source for the former by having Lydia, like Lisa with the Underground Man, comment that Hermann's account of his suicidal brother can "only happen . . . in books" (142).[13]

Hermann's writing in the beginning indeed resembles a draft, not only because his life in the novel is circumscribed by the winds of extradiegetic origin[14] but also because it is composed of stock phrases that he—in his incessant attentiveness to form—is quick to point out and cross out. This, of course, is the state of Hermann-the-narrator, who is bored "to death" by having to tell his own story (the Russian text of the novel gives a much more ominous *"убийственно скучно"*), but the description of the state of Hermann as he walks toward his first encounter with Felix is just as literary and flat.[15] Lilac from the chocolate wrapping appears as a detail of the Prague landscape; it is followed by directions on how to interpret it: "The public garden, where invalids were hand-pedaling about, was a storm of heaving lilac bushes. I looked at shop signs; picked out some word concealing a Slav root familiar to me, though overgrown with an unfamiliar meaning" (6). Here nature itself becomes a demon-mystifier: the landscape deceives Hermann ("Its splendor proved to be a deception"); the wind fills objects with "sham life" (6).

For Hermann, the inability to penetrate the drab reality he inhabits is a symptom of a crisis that has aesthetic *and* metaphysical sources. The external world he describes assumes features of second-rate decorations without substance. Noticeably, his internal world is not much different. He compares himself "to some translucent vessel doomed to receive contents as yet unknown" (8). Moreover, his internal and external worlds overlap with each other and become indistinguishable: the smoke of the chimneys he notices from the hill blends with "whiffs of thoughts" that play "on the outside of [his] mind," while inside himself he feels the echo of "some force driving him along" in his "vast inward wilderness" (8).

A lot has been said on the topic of Hermann-the-failed-artist, who assumes that the world can become the product of his artistic endeavors.[16] I would like to stress, however, that the source of his creative aspirations is to be found in the alignment of the metaphysical and aesthetic levels of the text.[17] Herein lies the origin of his perception of the similarity he notices between himself and Felix, which Hermann describes as an experience of transcendence:

> Incredible! I doubted the reality of what I saw, doubted my own sanity, felt sick and faint—honestly I was forced to sit down, my knees were shaking so. [. . .] I was too dazed by the mystery implied. While I looked, everything within me seemed to lose hold and come hurtling down from a height of ten stories. I was gazing at a marvel. Its perfection, its lack of cause and object, filled me with a strange awe.[18]

For Hermann, the discovery of the likeness between himself and Felix becomes an event of a higher order, and evidence that such an order exists. Its lack of causality allows Hermann to experience the identity between himself and Felix as a miracle, proof of the existence of cosmic order in a world of chaos. Significantly, Hermann's rapturous reaction to the person he believes to be his perfect double is strikingly similar to the awe Nabokov expresses at nature's "nonutilitarian delights" as he contemplates the mysteries of animal mimicry. For Nabokov, the "mimetic subtlety, exuberance, and luxury" that he discovers in mimicry and that supersede "a predator's power of appreciation"[19] become an argument against Darwin's evolutionary theory, which is governed by what Nabokov considers to be the law of cause and effect.[20] Both Hermann and Nabokov appear here in the role of nature's perfect readers, recognizing and appreciating the magical subtleties of its nonutilitarian aesthetics.

Hence, Hermann's treatment of reality as a text acquires a relative value in the context of the novel. On the one hand, it releases him from the cause-and-effect prison of the mundane routine of necessity and allows him the aesthetic appreciation of life that fills his world with meaning and order. This essentially romantic sensibility, in which recognition of the world's beauty is understood as a source of transcendence necessary for creative production, Hermann shares with his creator.[21] On the other hand, being "flattened" into a text (the most appropriate symbol of which is the recurrent image of the chocolate box) threatens to empty life of authenticity. Once authored, reality loses its anchoring and becomes in danger of incessant rewriting. This possibility of becoming a character in someone else's story is intolerable for Hermann and determines most of his actions in the novel. Hermann attempts to control his existential anxiety first by becoming reality's perfect reader and then its only author. Nabokov's merging of metaphysics and aesthetics is much more conscious than Dostoevsky's; still, the latter undoubtedly emerges here as a precursor of the former. Both present us with characters whose attempts to solve the crisis of authority take place in the realm of *authorship*.[22] This alignment of aesthetics and metaphysics and its side effect of the collapse of distance between life and text is the main axis of *Despair* and becomes the governing principle in its plot progression.[23]

Hermann's unwillingness (and inability) to distinguish material reality from the textual one is apparent in his relationships with most others, but especially his wife. In Hermann's description, Lydia appears first of all as a bad reader of both daily events and history, with an inadequate interpretative apparatus:

> She believed in dreams: to dream you had lost a tooth portended the death of someone you knew; and if there came blood with the tooth, then it would be the death of a relative. A field of daisies foretold meeting again one's first lover. Pearls stood for tears. It was very bad to see oneself all in white sitting at the head of the table. Mud meant money; a cat—treason; the sea—trouble

for the soul. She was fond of recounting her dreams, circumstantially and at length...

She hates Lloyd George; had it not been for him, the Russian Empire would not have fallen; . . . Germans get their due for that sealed train in which Bolshevism was tinned, and Lenin imported to Russia. Speaking of the French: "Do you know, Ardalion [a cousin of hers who had fought with the White Army] says they behaved like downright cads in Odessa during the evacuation."[24]

Symptomatically, Lydia's ineptitude when it comes to interpreting the text of life is indistinguishable from her shortcomings as a reader of literature. Her reading habits show the same vulgarity and lack of depth:

> She is a great gobbler of books, but reads only trash, memorizing nothing and leaving out the longer descriptions. She goes for her books to a Russian library; there she seats herself down and is a long time choosing; fumbles at books on the table; takes one, turns its pages, peers into it sideways, like an investigative hen; puts it away, takes up another, opens it—all of which is performed on the table's surface and with the help of one hand only; she notices that she has opened the book upside down, whereupon it is given a turn of ninety degrees—not more, for she discards it to make a dash at the volume which the librarian is about to offer to another lady; the whole process lasts more than an hour, and I do not know what prompts her final selection. Perhaps the title.
>
> Once I brought back from a railway journey some rotten detective novel with a crimson spider amid a black web on its cover. She dipped into it and found it terribly thrilling—felt that she simply could not help taking a peep at the end, but as that would spoil everything, she shut her eyes tight and tore the book in two down its back and hid the second, concluding, portion; then, later, she forgot the place and was a long, long time searching the house for the criminal she herself had concealed, repeating the while in a small voice: "It was so exciting, so terribly exciting; I know I shall die if I don't find out—"
>
> She has found out now. Those pages that explained everything were securely hidden; still, they were found—all of them except one, perhaps. Indeed, a lot of things have happened; now duly explained. Also that came to pass which she feared most. Of all omens it was the weirdest. A shattered mirror. Yes, it did happen, although not quite in the ordinary way. The poor dead woman. (23–24)

As Sergei Davydov shrewdly notes, in Lydia's detective novel "one can easily recognize the book *Despair*."[25] It is similarly striking that Hermann's description makes Lydia not only the novel's reader but also its unintentional author, who is now actively but unconsciously participating in hiding the criminal on the extradiegetic (vis-à-vis the text of the novel) level by ripping the book apart. For Lydia, however—and this might be the key to the disdain Hermann feels for his wife—such authorship remains unintentional, while he quite consciously proceeds from being merely reality's reader to becoming its author. In the final analysis, for him she is nothing but a (minor) character in his own text, in which her actions foreshadow her future. Calling Lydia a "poor dead woman," Hermann once again collapses the figurative and the literal meaning of the expression Lydia had just used. Here are the first intimations of *Despair*'s fundamental irony and its lesson: the subject's attempts to control textual meaning are futile. While Lydia manages only too successfully (if accidentally) to hide the criminal, Hermann names his victim too prematurely. The "shattered mirror" with its simultaneous figurative and physical existence, echoes the torn-apart book and points precisely to the metaphoric and metonymical role that textual reality plays in *Despair*.

For Hermann, Lydia is an accidental author and a naive reader who lacks the necessary memory to keep track of his lies about himself. Hermann classifies her as a chaotic arranger, spreading "disorder" in the "cosmos of [his] beautifully arranged things."[26] Expectedly, in his own ordering of reality, Hermann exhibits a penchant for a noticeably more literary coloring: "when June and moon rhymed . . ." (26). For Hermann, Lydia's activity creates circular rather than spiral patterning, as in his anecdote of her "search for the telephone number which she had jotted down on one of the pages of a library book, borrowed by the very person whom she wished to ring up" (27).

For Hermann, Lydia similarly treats reality through an aesthetic lens (he notes her preference for "everything 'to be echoed'" [25]); she is just much worse at it than he is. Hence, Lydia's "world is locked" and she lacks the talent for creative rearrangement of the world that Hermann ascribes to himself (26). Hermann sees Lydia as his own inferior double. Quite intentionally, Nabokov follows Hermann's analysis of Lydia's shortcomings as an author and a reader with the scene in which Hermann describes his sexual intercourse with Lydia as a "certain aberration."

Hermann's practice of dissociation during the sexual act exposes the full extent of his paradoxical relationship with reality: in order to fulfill his desire for presence, he must be in total control of reality; yet, in order to be in control, he has to perpetually distance himself from direct experience, treating life as if it were an aesthetic object. Hence, to achieve "ecstasy" from the sexual act, he has to observe his own sexual actions from a distance. Earlier in the novel, the fulfillment of this desire takes the shape of the perceived identity between himself and Felix in which he conflates the imagined and the real. In the description of his sexual dissociation, the desired identity is similarly revealed as Hermann attempts to double himself: "the sensation of being in two places at once gave me an extraordinary kick" (27). The boundaries between reality and imagination become increasingly blurry in his description, as the unclear chronological sequencing makes it difficult to say which of the two realms remains "real": reality or fantasy. At first, his "magical point of vantage" from which he observes himself and Lydia is imagined; yet, at some point, the observer and the observed switch places:

> For example, I would be in bed with Lydia, winding up the brief series of preparatory caresses she was supposed to be entitled to, when all at once I would become aware that imp Split had taken over . . . The sensation of being in two places at once gave me an extraordinary kick; but this was nothing compared to later developments. In my impatience to split I would bundle Lydia to bed as soon as we had finished supper. The dissociation had now reached its perfect phase. I sat in an armchair half a dozen paces away from the bed upon which Lydia had been properly placed and distributed. (27)

This passage becomes another example of the novel's *mise-en-abyme* structure, in which individual scenes prefigure the larger concerns of the novel: the relationship between two Hermanns participating in the act of dissociation is structurally identical to the relationship between Hermann-the-character and Hermann-the-narrator, as well as between the narrative of Hermann's life and his lived experience. His sexual practices have the same intent as his writing: to secure his metaphysical presence by being the only one in control of his life. His sexual practice allegorizes the practice of writing and stages the novel's most important philosophical paradox: Hermann's writing originates with the desire for control and stability, which he hopes to achieve by imposing identity between the real and the imagined; at the same time, writing is the very practice that removes him from presence, making it virtually impossible to have any measure of real participation.[27] Hermann himself is conscious of this: "I have grown much too used to an outside view of myself, to being both painter and model, so no wonder my style is denied the blessed grace of spontaneity."[28]

Of course, Hermann's world is as "locked" as, in his opinion, Lydia's. The narcissistic or, rather, solipsistic nature of his sexual practice comes out as his focus on his own "muscular back" prevents him from seeing anything more than the fragments of his wife (27). The complex relationship between the autoeroticism of this experience, in which the other disappears almost completely, and its aesthetic dimension points to yet another way in which *Despair* anticipates *Lolita*. Just like Humbert who "solipsizes" Lolita on the couch by forcing her into the imprisonment of his aesthetic fantasy, Hermann reaches ecstasy by turning the sexual act into a staged performance.

Chapter Three

(In a similar manner, he prefers to frame Felix: "I longed for him to find work: it would have been sweeter to know that he were snug and warm—or at least safe in prison" [31].) Hermann's subsequent attempts to achieve control over reality by dislodging himself completely from the sexual act coincide with the increasing aestheticization of his perception. The experience reaches its apex as Hermann turns the act into a staged performance, imagining himself observing it from an ever-increasing distance through a "tremendous telescope, or optical instruments of yet unknown power that would grow larger in proportion to [his] increasing rapture" (28). At the peak of his fantasy, we see the extent of the connection the novel makes between aesthetics and metaphysics, as well as the ultimate hopelessness of Hermann's endeavors:

> I longed to discover some means to remove myself at least a hundred yards from the *lighted stage* where I *performed*; I longed to contemplate that bedroom *scene* from some remote *upper gallery* in a blue mist under the swimming allegories of the starry vault; to watch a small but distinct and very active couple through opera glasses, field glasses, a tremendous telescope, or optical instruments of yet unknown power that would grow larger in proportion to my increasing rapture. (28, emphasis added)

It is not difficult to understand what role Hermann-the-observer has prepared for himself here. As the opera house turns into a representation of the cosmos, we recognize that the "magical vantage point" is none other than the point of view of God, the ultimate author. Yet, it is also here that we get the first indication of the ineffectiveness of Hermann's actions:

> Actually, I never got farther back than the console in the parlor, and even so found my view of the bed cut off by the doorjamb unless I opened the wardrobe in the bedroom to have the bed reflected in the oblique speculum or *Spiegel*. (28)

Hermann's admission of his inability to make his vision autonomous from external reality is an indication of his awareness that life cannot be treated as an encased, aesthetic object, which one can fully detach from its physical environment. Moreover, inasmuch as Hermann's dissociation practice can be said to allegorize the process of writing, it becomes clear that within the world of *Despair*, such a juxtaposition of physical and textual realities once again proves that writing produces ontological absence rather than presence. The mirror that Hermann cannot directly name, as if it were a taboo object, acts here as a telling indication of the limits of mimetic practice. Through its ability to represent reality, the mirror allows Hermann to continue the fan-

The Metaphysics of Authorship

tasy from an extended distance (his attempts to turn the mirror into a word, a mere text, by calling it *Spiegel* are of the same order); the mirror simultaneously insists, however, on its own physicality, resisting being appropriated into the metaphoric world of Hermann's optical instruments.

Noticeably, what breaks the spell of Hermann's fantasy is the intrusion of Lydia's voice:

> From the distant bed, where I thought I was, came Lydia's yawn and voice stupidly saying that if I were not yet coming to bed, I might bring her the red book she had left in the parlor. It lay, in fact, on the console near my chair, and rather than bring it I threw it bedward with a windmill flapping of pages. This strange and awful jolt broke the spell. (28)

The effect of Lydia's voice on Hermann can be better understood if we compare it to Humbert's final realization that the biggest source of his anguish was "the absence of [Lolita's] voice from the concord" of other children's voices at play.[29] The presence of others prevents Hermann from successfully solipsizing life . . . for the time being, of course. The physicality of the book that Hermann hurls across the room attests to the same. The physical world surrounding Hermann belongs to the same semantic paradigm as other people: both resist Hermann's attempts to erase their materiality by transforming them into a text—*his* text.

Hence, in *Despair*, the physical dimension of life is used to underscore the futility of the subject's desire to secure metaphysical certainty. This interpretation is supported by the novel's take on the idea of *ekphrasis* as a verbal exercise in which one attempts to conjure presence at the site of absence. The desire to secure meaning through writing and Hermann's despair at his inability to do so is the source of the tension between the visual and the verbal dimensions of the novel that also extends to the rivalry between Ardalion and Hermann, the painter and the writer. According to the latter, "an author's fondest dream" is to create an illusion of presence, "to turn the reader into a spectator."[30] Predictably, while prizing this ability in himself, Hermann also conveys his underlying anxiety about the success of his project:

> How I long to convince you! And I will, I will convince you! I will force you all, you rogues, to believe . . . though I am afraid that words alone, owing to their special nature, are unable to convey visually a likeness of that kind: the two faces should be pictured side by side, by means of real colors, not words, then and only then would the spectator see my point. (16)

Significantly, it is the book, not the canvas of nature, that contains within its cover the nuances detailing the discrepancies between Felix and Hermann;

Chapter Three

physical features which, according to Hermann, only prove their remarkable likeness:

> You must not suppose, however, that I am ashamed of possible slips and type errors in the book of nature. Look nearer: I possess large yellowish teeth; his are whiter and set more closely together, but is that really important? On my forehead a vein stands out like a capital M imperfectly drawn, but when I sleep my brow is as smooth as that of my double. And those ears . . . the convolutions of his are but very slightly altered in comparison with mine: here more compressed, there smoothed out. We have eyes of the same shape, narrowly slit with sparse lashes, but his iris is paler than mine. (17)

Hermann's fantasy is for words to have the power of a visual image, which ensures and requires the spectator's presence (noticeably he calls himself a painter, not a writer). In order to do so, he insists that his writing has the immediacy of real life, while simultaneously representing reality as a text. Hence, after suggesting that Lydia's love for him manifested itself in her adoring examination of his face, Hermann proceeds with a detailed self-portrait:

> Our eyes alone were not quite identical, but what likeness did exist between them was a mere luxury; for his were closed as he lay on the ground before me, and though I have never really seen, only felt, my eyelids when shut, I know that they differed in nothing from his eye-eaves—a good word, that! Ornate, but good, and a welcome guest to my prose. No, I am not getting in the least excited; my self-control is perfect. If every now and again my face pops out, as from behind a hedge, perhaps to the prim reader's annoyance, it is really for the latter's good: let him get used to my countenance; and in the meantime I shall be chuckling quietly over his not knowing whether it was my face or that of Felix. Here I am! and now—gone again; or maybe it was not I! (29–30)

The sequence of sentences here makes it purposely hard to distinguish the referent of "my face," since it can refer either to the portrait of Hermann-the-character or, equally, to the sudden burst of self-conscious commentary on his own style, in other words, to the unexpected appearance of Hermann-the-narrator from behind the hedge of his narrative. In the context of the novel, the former belongs to the order of the allegedly lived experience of the protagonist, while the latter belongs to the textual reality of the narrator. Most telling here is Hermann's enviable certainty that for the reader the text possesses a visual dimension—that the reader's experience of this narrative is predicated on presence, or rather, on both presence and absence—since his writing, on the one hand, secures the reader's inability to check the reliability of the likeness between him and Felix and, on the other hand, like a painting, it possesses a visual dimension that proves their likeness beyond any doubt. Of course, Hermann's overstated self-assurance only betrays his epistemological fears. The passage ends with a clause in which he acknowledges them: "however fanciful and absurd it might seem . . ." (30). In Russian, the aesthetic nature of his utopian project is stressed even more strongly: "как бы *искусственно и нелепо это ни казалось*" (349). Expectedly, Hermann imagines that his *writing* makes him a better *painter* then Ardalion: "Ah, enough, enough about my fool Ardalion! The ultimate dab is laid on his portrait. With a last flourish of the brush I have signed it across the corner" (207).

Hermann's self-referential asides frequently employ metaphors in which the distance between the text and reality is collapsed, and the physical reality is treated as if it were a semantic unit ready to be processed into a trope: "I have now boarded that bus (mentioned at the beginning), and, what is more, I have a comfortable window seat. And thus, too, I used to drive to my office, before I acquired the car" (32). Here the bus *of* the story is the same as the bus *in* the story; similarly, we are invited to interpret his purchase of the car as symbolic of his progress in the story. That he christens his car "Icarus" is telling not only of his status as a failed author but also of his desire for and proximity to the sun—the image of the absolute metaphysical presence.

The understanding that Hermann's project is driven by his efforts to eliminate the distance between the ideal and the real also helps explain his frequent declarations of affinity with Communist ideology. For Hermann, the interchangeability and uniformity of Soviet citizens becomes a large-scale materialization of the same identity that he discovers between himself and Felix and through which he seeks to establish his own existential security. One can discern the metaphysical sources of Hermann's embrace of Marxism, an ideology which, as he states, is "getting the nearest to Absolute Truth" (124), by tracing it to Dostoevsky's belief that behind socialism hides a religious impulse, a desire of man to build the kingdom of Heaven here and now, usurping the place of God. In Hermann's rejection of God, one can feel the same ambivalent utopian longing that Dostoevsky inscribes into the character of his theomachist protagonists. In *The Brothers Karamazov*, this notion becomes crystallized as the narrator explains that Alyosha's decision to join the monastery is born out of a position that is similarly uncompromising, yet is also completely opposite that of his atheist contemporaries:

> As soon as he reflected seriously and was struck by the conviction that immortality and God exist, he naturally said at once to himself: "I want to live for immortality, and I reject any halfway compromise." In just the same way, if

he had decided that immortality and God do not exist, he would immediately have joined the atheists and socialists (for socialism is not only the labor question or the question of the so-called fourth estate, but first of all the question of atheism, the question of the modern embodiment of atheism, the question of the Tower of Babel built precisely without God, not to go from earth to heaven but to bring heaven down to earth).[31]

Here, in discussing Alyosha's faith, the narrator detects at the source of an atheist rejection of God a similar—even if polar opposite—transcendental impulse, as if the desire for equality and sameness cannot be distinguished from the desire to replace God.

The same yearning underlies Hermann's use of literary texts in which he shows a clear preference for texts with a "utopian" theme. Such are his numerous references to Pushkin's "'Tis time, my dear, 'tis time."[32] In this poem, the lyric subject longs for a "remote abode of work and pure delight," while at the same time realizing that the desired realm of aesthetic contemplation will remain forever unattainable. Pushkin conveys this idea by ending the first part of the poem, corresponding to the lyric subject's present situation, with the verb "die"—a powerful indication that if it can be achieved at all, the stasis of "peace and freedom" ("покой и воля" in the original) can only be achieved in death. For Hermann, however, the poem, which in a parodied state reappears throughout the novel ("I'm sick of everything and yearn for a remote land, where I'll devote myself to contemplation and poultry breeding, so let us use this rare chance"[33] or "Long have I, weary slave, been planning my escape to the far land of art and the translucent grape" [62]), turns into a kind of hymn to his project of solipsizing reality.[34] Similarly telling is Hermann's reference to Pushkin's "The Shot" (absent from the English translation). Indeed, there is a strong characterological affinity between Hermann and Sylvio: both attempt to force life into literary patterns. Just like Hermann, Sylvio makes his life meaningful by living it in accordance with literary templates, as if it were a romantic text. The genealogy between the two is hardly accidental: Sylvio (along with Hermann's namesake from "The Queen of Spades") is one of Pushkin's "metaphysical" protagonists: his real enemy is not just the lucky Count, but fate itself.

We witness a similar blurring between reality and text, as well as its metaphysical underlining, behind the reasons Hermann gives for keeping the story of his encounter with Felix from Lydia:

Why did I not tell her of my incredible adventure? I, who would fake wonders for her by the million, seemed not to dare, with those polluted lips of mine, tell her of a wonder that was real. Or maybe something else withheld me. An author does not show people his first draft; a child in the womb is not referred to as Tiny Tom or Belle; a savage refrains from naming objects of mysterious import and uncertain temper; Lydia herself disliked my reading a book she had not yet finished.[35]

His discovery of an almost complete identity between himself and Felix is the first draft, but what is the final one, the version he intends for publication? In the passage above, is Hermann referring to the act of assuming Felix's identity after his murder or to the narrative of the novel itself, the book we are reading? Life here undoubtedly imitates art, but art also ceases to be a mere representation of reality and becomes an act of conscious transformation of life. Hermann's belief that art is a transcendental force that affects life directly and has the potential to revitalize it secures his special standing vis-à-vis others: "If the deed is planned and performed correctly, then the force of creative art is such, that were the criminal to give himself up on the very next morning, none would believe him, the invention of art containing far more intrinsical truth than life's reality" (122). Thus, *Despair* follows the modernist ideal of art as a process of pure creation to its logical end.

Another side of Hermann's treatment of reality emerges as we analyze his relationship to time. The treatment of reality as a text eradicates the chronology between events by investing them with an order and meaning they might otherwise lack. Hence, instead of random events, we are presented with foreshadowing and plot progression that not only appear on the level of the narrative but are also experienced by the protagonist in narrated reality:

> That yellow post . . . I have the feeling today that I recognized it, when seeing it for the first time: familiar to me as a thing of the future. Perhaps I am mistaken; perhaps the glance I gave it was quite an indifferent one, my sole concern being not to scrape the mudguard against it while turning; but all the same, today as I recall it, I cannot separate that first acquaintanceship from its mature development. (35)

What we have, then, is another instance of a "locked world" in which the past is only a repetition of the future; or, to put it differently, the past's only raison d'être is to fulfill the future. Thus, life itself acquires narrative features of which Hermann is not simply a participating character but also an author.[36] At its roots, the process contains the temptation to escape the randomness of events that so plagues the pawnbroker in Dostoevsky's "The Meek One," a character who similarly perceives the randomness of existence as a metaphysical scandal. Here, the yellow post becomes meaningful only once it reappears in the future, once life reacquires its lost order and *fabula* becomes *syuzhet*:

Chapter Three

> Well, I can swear that I felt as if I had known it already. Yes, that's it, now I am getting it clear—I certainly did have that queer sensation; it has not been added as an aftertouch. And that yellow post . . . How meaningly it looked at me, when I glanced back—as if it were saying: "I am here, I am at your service."[37]

The effect here is also strengthened by the chronological flattening, since projected onto the past, images of the future overlap with Hermann-the-protagonist's presence:

> . . . and that bare birch tree on the forest's edge (now, why did I write "bare"? It was not winter yet, winter was still remote), and the day so balmy and almost cloudless, and the little stammering crickets zealously trying to say something beginning with z . . . Yes, it all *meant* something—no mistake. (36)

The quest for order and meaning with which Hermann seeks to revitalize his existence is the secret of his self-mystification: as he perceives himself to be the author of his life, it becomes "*meaningly*" and the world around him ordered. The overlap between the future and past, the feeling that "the future shimmers through the past," occurs not only on the page but in life itself, and the future snows onto the summer landscape of the past: "The pines soughed gently, snow lay about, with bald patches of soil showing black" (37). Even as Hermann understands the absurdity of his description, he refuses to correct it, absolving himself of responsibility, displacing the agency onto his "impatient memory" (37). He justifies his refusal to correct the dictate of memory because it is "wicked to erase" (37); the Russian original gives an even stronger indication that his activity here has metaphysical sources: "[Снег] бы следовало вычеркнуть. Нет,—*грешно*."[38] The visual image of the snow-covered ground "with bald patches of soil showing black" seals the representation of reality as a page.

Inasmuch as the past prefigures the future, the unraveling of the story at the end into a diary is another indication of Hermann's failure: as a potentially endless genre, the diary becomes evidence of Hermann's inability to continue to produce order either in his life or on a page (significantly, the diary appears at the chronological point of convergence between the narrated life and the real one). In "The Meek One," Dostoevsky shows the futility of the pawnbroker's attempts to achieve order by creating a circular—hence, endless—narrative that finishes where it has begun. Nabokov's solution is to turn Hermann's ordered plot into a disordered record of events, to downgrade *syuzhet* back into *fabula*.

While Hermann's ontological instability translates at the end of the novel into narrative instability, the same process takes place as he frequently slips into the meta-narrative mode, as, for example, during his numerous unsuccessful attempts to reignite his narrative in chapter 3. The freedom that the position of authorship affords him is terrifying *and* illusory; as I mentioned above, the total control he perpetually attempts to acquire over his life paradoxically becomes the very thing that alienates him from it. The image of the author who, like "a kind of spirit, [is] hovering over the page," becomes the symbol of Hermann's metaphysical uprootedness.[39] The correlative of his metaphysical situation is, of course, his complete physical lack of freedom. Just as Hermann is unable to completely separate himself from the physical world during his sexual practice, in his writing he is powerless to escape the constraints of his environment: "One moment I was copying that letter and now it has vanished somewhere. I can continue; it had slipped under the table" (61). This, of course, is the true source of his despair: Hermann hovers over his narrative like an angel *and* is chained to a specific time and place of his writing. Presence proves to be elusive and unattainable and, as Hermann realizes at the end, cannot be achieved through writing: "Indeed, it is not really possible to set down my incoherent speech, that tumble and jumble of words, the forlornness of subordinated clauses, which have lost their masters and strayed away, and all the superfluous gibber that gives words a support or a creep hole" (89–90). In short, Hermann desires presence yet is unable to accept that writing is predicated on absence. His treatment of reality is indeed *ekphratic*, and he laments his inability to convey presence in writing: "No, our conversation was not such as is set down here; that is, the words maybe were exactly as stated (again that little gasp), but I have not managed or not dared to render the special noises accompanying it; there occurred queer fadings or clottings of sound; and then again that muttering, that susurration, and, suddenly, a wooden voice clearly pronouncing: 'Come, Felix, another drink'" (88–89).

Another point of convergence between Hermann's metaphysical malaise and his writing is what I would call his "semantic aphasia," that is, his "anagrammatic" aptitude. Renate Lachmann points to the "baroque" source of Hermann's wordplay, a tradition placing a particular focus on the similarities and differences between the signs. What strikes me in Hermann's wordplay, however, is its complete and ostentatious *meaninglessness* and *randomness* (at least on the diegetic level):

> I liked, as I like still, to make words look self-conscious and foolish, to bind them by the mock marriage of a pun, to turn them inside out, to come upon them unawares. What is this jest in majesty? This ass in passion? How do God and Devil combine to form a live dog? (46)

Hermann's practice of forcing words into a "mock marriage" is an obvious expression of the same strategy he applies to himself and Felix. His questions

Chapter Three

about the affinities he discovers—rhetorical as they might be—bespeak the same desperate attempt to eradicate randomness, to find and secure meaning between the signifier and the signified.

The semantic quicksand against which Hermann struggles is another guise of the metaphysical emptiness against which he directs his plan of killing Felix. At the same time, however, it is also an outcome of his actions, chilling evidence of the futility of his effort, which results not in freedom but in complete alienation. It appears as a narcissistic vicious circle of a consciousness with a stripped thread; its outcome is a thorough transformation of the other into a reflection of Hermann's consciousness:

> He listened, that was certain. I listened to his listening. He listened to my listening to his listening. Something snapped. I noticed that I was not thinking at all of what I thought I was thinking; attempted to catch my consciousness tripping, but got mazed myself. (96)

In the novel, the most disturbing vision of Hermann's empty, meaningless productivity is his nightmare. An interminable dream within a dream within a dream, it is another image of Hermann's entrapment and becomes a symbol of his initial state of metaphysical meaninglessness in which reality appears as spiritless matter, a condition that Hermann cannot escape no matter how much he tries. A re-creation of Hermann's inner state, the dream of a monstrous dog references and parodies Ippolit Terent'ev's dream in which his dog Norma battles a reptilian creature. Yet, unlike Norma, who sacrifices herself in order to save her master, the dog here appears as a worm-like monster:

> I dreamed a loathsome dream, a triple ephialtes. First there was a small dog; but not simply a small dog; a small mock dog, very small, with the minute black eyes of a beetle's larva; it was white through and through, and coldish. Flesh? No, not flesh, but rather grease or jelly, or else perhaps, the fat of a white worm, with, moreover, a kind of carved corrugated surface reminding one of a Russian paschal lamb of butter—disgusting mimicry. A cold-blooded being, which Nature had twisted into the likeness of a small dog with a tail and legs, all as it should be. It kept getting into my way, I could not avoid it; and when it touched me, I felt something like an electric shock. I woke up. On the sheet of the bed next to mine there lay curled up, like a swooned white larva, that very same dreadful little pseudo dog . . . I groaned with disgust and opened my eyes. All around shadows floated; the bed next to mine was empty except for the broad burdock leaves which, owing to the damp, grow out of bedsteads. One could see, on those leaves, telltale stains of a slimy nature; I peered closer; there, glued to a fat stem it sat, small, tallowish-white, with its little black button eyes . . . but then, at last, I woke up for good. (96–97)

Just like Ippolit, Hermann is a man fruitlessly trying to find a foothold in a world deprived of higher meaning. Both Ippolit and Hermann see the monster plaguing their dreams as Nature, a force which for Ippolit becomes an agent of destruction that is bound to crush the human spirit. Yet, Hermann's dream is more of a dark parody of Ippolit's dream rather than its direct echo: its most striking quality is its utter lack of drama and progress. Instead of the intense spiritual struggle we find in Ippolit's dream, here we have the empty, soulless mimicry of formless matter, an image prepared by Hermann's dehumanization of Felix earlier. Hermann's "triple ephialtes" also parallels the labyrinthine nightmares of Svidrigailov before his suicide, and for both characters a dream becomes a clear indication of their state of spiritual stagnation.[40] Finally, the absence of movement in Hermann's nightmare is strengthened by what might be another reference to *The Idiot* and its "apocalyptic" theme in which "time is no more": Hermann's unmoving watch ("My wristwatch had stopped" [97]).

Hence, on the one hand, Hermann's dream can be interpreted as a symptom of his perception of the world without higher meaning and, on the other, as evidence that his attempts to inject life with meaning by treating it as a text of which he is the only author will end in failure. Hermann calls the dream "a vile will-o'-the-wisp," a ghostly apparition that, according to legends, tempts travelers away from the chosen path. The metaphysical (and religious) sources of Hermann's enterprise become more apparent if we compare his use of this metaphor to Emily Dickinson's treatment of a similar image in her poem "Those—dying then":

> Those—dying then,
> Knew where they went—
> They went to God's Right Hand—
> That Hand is amputated now
> And God cannot be found—
>
> The abdication of Belief
> Makes the Behavior small—
> Better an ignis fatuus
> Than no illume at all—.[41]

In Dickinson's poem, the will-o'-the-wisp, or ignis fatuus, is the marker of mankind's precarious position as the pillars of faith crumble; it is an ambivalent symbol of the divine, a remnant that points to the absence of the whole yet also offers a glimmer of hope, however ephemeral. In *Despair*, the nightmare vision of the endless dream shows the fundamental futility of Hermann's metaphysical aspirations to reinstate himself into the now-vacant position of transcendental authority. The religious connotations of the dream become apparent not only as it comes up in his rejection of eternity ("I refuse to undergo the tortures of everlasting life, I do not want those cold white little dogs")[42] but also in the context of Hermann's predilection for word games, especially his earlier anagrammatic suggestion that "God and Devil combine to make a live dog." Whether or not this is another parodic reference to Dostoevsky (this time to Dmitry's dynamic vision of man's spiritual struggle, which he imagines as a fight between God and the Devil on the battlefield of man's heart), the statement shines a light on the limit of Hermann's endeavors, as well as on their religious subtext. As Hermann leaves the hotel, he compares his experience of the dream to masturbation, another image that directly points to the autoeroticism of his actions but also connects the dream as a symbol of his literary activity to an idea of empty creation, the product of which is a formless, homunculus-like creature, devoid of spirituality.[43]

Hermann's self-mystification becomes a solution for his state of ontological uprootedness; by discovering his perfect double in Felix, he finally hopes to attain the stability he seeks.[44] The stakes of Hermann's project become evident in the following passage:

> "Please, God!" I said with force, and failed to understand, myself, why I said so; for did not the sense of my whole life consist now in my possessing a live reflection? So why then did I mention the name of a nonexistent God, why did there flash through my mind the foolish hope that my reflection had been distorted?[45]

Through Hermann's slip of the tongue we see the metaphysical underside of his actions, the despair of a man without faith, as well as a shadow of awareness of the violent toll such a project incurs. The awareness that his activity in the novel is Sisyphean reappears as Hermann comments on his ability to put down his account of events: "Well, I hardly know if I shall stand the strain of writing it at all" (158). Yearning to claim the function of the transcendental signified for himself alone, Hermann violates the rules of Nabokov's universe in which the manifestations of God are to be authored by a petty demon, a creator conscious that the product of his creation will be a deception no matter how divine it appears.

THE CLOSURE OF DEATH

Within the parameters of Hermann's project, Felix's death becomes, of course, obligatory. Hermann's metaphysical desire to secure and validate the similarity between himself and Felix brings about the latter's death, since in

The Metaphysics of Authorship

Hermann's fantasy, only in death can the resemblance between the two of them remain perfect. Life, on the contrary, threatens to erase the similarity Hermann perceives: "If he were to attain old age, I reflected, his grins and grimaces would end by eroding completely our resemblance which is now so perfect when his face freezes" (75). While Hermann is looking for a perfect form, life is formless, chaotic, unshaped. In order to secure his control over the text of reality, time needs to stop, and not just on Hermann's watch. To become an author, Hermann needs to sacrifice his character, Felix. By killing Felix, Hermann hopes to fulfill his desire to become an authentic creator, to get rid of—in Dostoevsky's words—the inertia of life. To do so, Hermann plays out the myth of Pygmalion backward: his project begins with Felix's awakening and is fulfilled with his death. Notably, Hermann sculpts Felix as he prepares him for death: "My dear fellow, you do look funny, it's a regular makeup! . . . In the cold wood there stood in front of me a naked man" (164). Likewise, after the murder, as he is contemplating the sight of Felix's corpse, Hermann rejects the thought of its decomposition, since it possesses "a marble quality" (186). And, after Hermann shoots him: "he terminated a movement still related to life, and that was a full turn almost" (171). The novel goes a long way to demonstrate that Hermann's desire for form necessitates death, since he believes that only in the other's death will he achieve the permanent control of the transcendental signified.

In *Despair*, death is shown to be a predictable consequence of Hermann's mission to seize control over the process of signification. Its correlative is a vision of perfect form, a narrative "locked world" which appears throughout the novel in numerous images that suggest completeness and enclosure. Such are the scenes in which Nabokov exposes the autoeroticism, narcissism, and solipsism of Hermann's actions. Such is also Hermann's proclivity for a form in which narrative order reigns supreme and which aims to eradicate randomness and loose ends. In accordance with this logic, Hermann bemoans Conan Doyle's missed opportunity to make his Sherlock Holmes cycle come full circle by ending it with the discovery of a true killer—Dr. Watson. Moreover, Hermann views his own form-shaping activity through which he packs the *fabula* of his life into a *syuzhet* of his project as further proof that he is following a higher, preordained plan:

> As I sat on that bench and clasped those letters in my burning embrace, I was suddenly aware that my scheme had received a final outline and that everything, or nearly everything, was already settled; a mere couple of details were still missing which would be no trouble to fix. What, indeed, does trouble mean in such matters? It all went on by itself, it all flowed and fused together, smoothly taking *inevitable* forms, since that very moment when I had first seen Felix. (121, emphasis added)

It is, of course, to be expected that while Hermann desires absolute control, he shifts all responsibility for his actions onto the "conscience of fate" (70).

In observing the relationship between writing and crime in *Despair*—as in the above example in which Watson's candidacy for a murderer is perfect *because* he is a writer—Claire Rosenfield suggests that both are driven by the "impulse for immortality."[46] At the same time, we can discern the metaphysical component of Hermann's endeavors in the extent to which writing is connected to his desire for order and power. In the novel, Hermann initiates and participates in three interrelated practices, all of which fail to bring him the measure of stability he desires: dissociation, the project of killing Felix, and an attempt to secure his experiences in writing. These exist in a metonymic—inasmuch as the failure of one gives birth to another—and a metaphoric—since each can ultimately be said to be a variation of the other two—relationship with one another. Writing down his experiences is a logical end to the progression of the novel's plot, in which failure of each practice to produce the desired result can be seen as a necessary impulse initiating the next practice. Writing also constitutes an integral part of *Despair*'s *mise-en-abyme* structure, which makes it quite difficult to say which of the practices is the primary one. Each is meant to be an instrument of Hermann's triumph over the world of chaos, which he hopes to achieve by establishing an inviolable order:

> But what are they—Doyle, Dostoevsky, Leblanc, Wallace—what are all the great novelists who wrote of nimble criminals, what are all the great criminals who never read the nimble novelists—what are they in comparison with me? Blundering fools! As in the case of inventive geniuses, I was certainly helped by chance (my meeting Felix), but that piece of luck fitted exactly into the place I had made for it; I pounced upon it and used it, which another in my position would not have done.[47]

Here, in one grand gesture, Hermann erases the boundary between literature and life, announces his superiority over both characters and authors, and testifies that the nature of his genius is to be the master of his own destiny. Hermann's desire for perfect form is apparent as he insists that his plan has a flawless mirror-like structure: "My accomplishment resembles a game of patience, arranged beforehand; first I put down the open cards in such a manner as to make its success a dead certainty; then I gathered them up in the opposite order and gave the prepared pack to others with the perfect assurance it would come out" (122).

Fitting reality into the vise of form brings similar creative frustrations that plague Hermann once his narrative inescapably begins to overflow the formal boundaries he has assigned it. It is hardly accidental that the news-

The Metaphysics of Authorship

papers compare (to his chagrin) his Procrustes-like project to a similar crime in which the murderer had to saw off part of his victim's feet, "as the corpse turned out to exceed in length his, the car owner's, measure" (193). Felix similarly turns out to be too big for Hermann's clothes.

As we discussed above, the novel demonstrates the futility of Hermann's actions: instead of helping him to regain a lost authenticity, they deprive his reality of "life" by flattening it into a text, a two-dimensional surface devoid of originality and meaning. Hence, Felix's murder, on one level, is the outcome of Hermann's aesthetic activity in the novel and, on another, its perfect metaphor. In a way, we can say that by treating it as a text, Hermann "kills" reality, just as he kills Felix.

In *Despair*, the signs that Hermann's treatment of reality as a text deprives it of life appear in the cluster of images of flatness and death that are closely related to the theme of doubling. The first evocation of reality being "flattened" comes in the very beginning of the novel as Hermann weaves his personal history out of the wrapper of the chocolate box. It resurfaces once again in the image of the deck of cards in the passage I quoted above, in which Hermann plans to "put down . . . in such a manner as to make its success a *dead certainty*" (122, emphasis added). As a metaphor for the two-dimensional reality, cards appear once again as Ardalion and Lydia play *durachki*. The name of the card game, which references the Russian idiom "*ostavat'sia v durakakh*" ("to be fooled"), ironically points to the principle at hand: while Hermann desires to take control of his life and anticipates "duping" others, he is not only being duped by his wife and her lover but ends up duping himself. The stock imagery of the cards resonates with the two-dimensional, "modern" representation of Hermann's portrait, and as Ardalion and Lydia speak of Hermann in the third person, the latter begins to feel reduced to the status of a character, a shadow:

> In the dining room the lamp illumined my hideous portrait . . . I returned indoors.
> "Whither is our pretty one going?" asked Ardalion without addressing either of us.
> "To Dresden," replied Lydia. They were now playing *durachki*, dupes.
> "My kindest regards to the Sistine," said Ardalion.
> "No, I can't cover that, I'm afraid. Let's see. This way."
> "He'd do better if he went to bed, he's *dead-tired*," said Lydia. "Look here, you've no right to feel the pack, it's dishonest."
> "I didn't mean to," said Ardalion. "Don't be cross, pussy. And is he going for long?"
> "This one too, Ardy dear, this one too, please, you haven't covered it, either."

> So they went on for a good while, talking now of their cards and now about me, as though I were not in the room or as though I were a shadow, a ghost, a dumb creature; and that joking habit of theirs, which before used to leave me indifferent, now seemed to me loaded with meaning, as if indeed it were merely my reflection that was present, my real body being far away. (65)

The unease Hermann feels here has the same source as the metaphysical anxiety he experiences in his discussion of God as the demon-mystifier. Here, of course, he is "mystified" by his unfaithful wife and her lover, who continuously present themselves to Hermann as *not who they are*. This is also one of the many instances where the metaphysical problematic of the novel reveals its social dimension. As Hermann overhears Lydia and Ardalion, he experiences—and cannot tolerate—what it is to be a character in someone else's story. This, of course, is precisely what he does to Felix, who is continuously described as less than human. Consider, for example, the following passage, the beginning of which marks Felix's body as animalistic, while the end suggests that he is not human at all, just a puppet:

> When he turned I could not help wincing at the sight of his big knobbed navel—but then mine is no beauty either. I doubt he had ever in his life washed his animal parts: they looked fairly plausible as these things go but did not invite close inspection. His toenails were much less abominable than I had expected. He was lean and white, much whiter than his face, thus making it seem that it was my face, still retaining its summer tan, that was affixed to his pale trunk. You could even discern the line round his neck where the head adhered. (93)

For Hermann, images of death are closely associated with the theme of doubling and narcissism. The resemblance that he feels exists between him and Felix is the resemblance of their *dead* bodies: "That man, especially when he slept, when his features were motionless, showed me my own face, my mask, the flawlessly pure image of my corpse" (15) and, later on, as he leaves for the meeting with Felix: "It should be said, to my justification, that the question of the suitcase was really the only point which I decided to alter: all the rest went just as I had designed it long, long ago—maybe many months ago, maybe that very second when I saw a tramp asleep on the grass who exactly resembled my corpse" (151). Similarly, as Hermann's request to meet Felix flutters away in a letter, he imagines himself as a dead leaf that encounters its own reflection by falling into water:

> After posting the letter, I felt what probably a purple red-veined thick maple leaf feels, during its slow flutter from branch to brook . . . When a slow leaf

fell, there would flutter up to meet it, out of the water's shadowy depths, its unavoidable double. Their meeting was soundless. The leaf came twirling down, and twirling up there would rise toward it, eagerly, its exact, beautiful, lethal reflection.[48]

This connection between doubling and death is echoed once again as Hermann notices a "decanter of dead water,"[49] although whether he himself realizes the weighty irony of his description within the context of the novel's thematics remains unclear.

The three interrelated themes of the novel—Hermann's metaphysical anxiety, his refusal or inability to recognize the boundary between textual and physical reality, and his desire for form, which he hopes to fulfill by killing Felix—converge, as if in a prism, in the scene of Felix's murder. In Hermann's account of the murder, the connection between these themes becomes most apparent and reaches its highest intensity.

The prelude to the murder is Hermann's arrival at Ardalion's lake, which he describes as if the murder were a performance and the landscape a decoration: "To my right, beyond the field, the wood was painted in a flat grey on the backdrop of the pale sky" (163). In this scene, the effect of artificiality abounds. Not surprisingly, Felix becomes part of the inanimate setting, a prop ("pink as a waxwork" [163]), while Hermann himself performs the main part: "Placing one foot on the footboard of the car and like an enraged tenor slashing my hand with the glove I had taken off, I glared steadily at Felix" (163). As in the scene of his sexual dissociation, life turns into opera: "all was rumble and thunder in the orchestra between my vocal outbursts . . . That fragment of opera came to an end, and the broadcast speaker resumed in his usual voice" (163–64). As Hermann prepares Felix for "the great moment" (165), the latter is increasingly dehumanized. In Hermann's memory, after the shot, time slows down ("that puff of smoke, hanging in midair, then displaying a transparent fold and vanishing slowly" [171]) until it stops completely, breaking into discrete elements, to mark the exact moment of Felix's death: "the way Felix fell; for he did not fall at once; first he terminated a movement still related to life, and that was a full turn almost; he intended, I think, swinging before me in jest, as before a mirror; so that, inertly bringing that poor piece of foolery to an end, he (already pierced) came to face me, slowly spread his hands as if asking: 'What's the meaning of this?'—and getting no reply, slowly collapsed backward" (171). In this sentence, with its convoluted and extended syntax, time is both retarded and spatialized, as if the sentence itself were a perfect manifestation of Hermann's treatment of reality. Once again, the heightened theatricality of the description reappears, and the act of murder is presented as staged by Hermann and performed by Felix. In this context, the latter's imagined

Chapter Three

question about meaning symbolically reveals the real motivation behind Hermann's murderous enterprise.

In killing Felix, Hermann imagines himself to be God, the giver and taker of life. As Felix turns, the movement is still part of Felix's life and, as if propping one mirror against the other, Hermann imagines Felix imagining Hermann to be his perfect reflection. The moment Felix is dead, however, Hermann begins to feel the spinning of the Earth: "and then the rotation of the earth made itself felt" (171). This *is* Hermann's crowning achievement, and the description marks the moment with solemn and quasi-religious details: the hat falls off Felix's "crown," "all present bared their heads," and the air is filled with "persistent singing" in the English text (171) and "ringing" (suggestive of tolling bells) in the Russian text.

Through murder, Hermann finally achieves what he believes to be the perfect solution in his quest for form. In the passage that follows, the relationship Hermann constructs between death and creativity, between life and text, but also between writing and his project, reaches its apogee:

> There are mysterious moments and that was one of them. Like an author reading his work over a thousand times, probing and testing every syllable, and finally unable to say of this brindle of words whether it is good or not, so it happened with me, so it happened—But there is the maker's secret certainty; which never can err. At that moment when all the required features were fixed and frozen, our likeness was such that really I could not say who had been killed, I or he. And while I looked, it grew dark in the vibrating wood, and with that face before me slowly dissolving, vibrating fainter and fainter, it seemed as if I were looking at my image in a stagnant pool. (171–72)

Earlier in the novel, as Hermann prepares to write Felix the first letter, he compares the mirror reflection that writing leaves on the blotting paper to the similarity that he perceives exists between him and Felix:

> The pen supplied by the State screeched and rattled, I kept thrusting it into the inkwell, into the black spit therein; the pale blotting paper upon which I leaned my elbow was all crisscrossed with the imprints of unreadable lines. Those irrational characters, preceded as it were by a minus, remind me always of mirrors: minus X minus = plus. It struck me that perhaps Felix too was a minus I, and that was a line of thought of quite astounding importance, which I did wrong, oh, very wrong, not to have thoroughly investigated. (117)

Here Hermann comes close to recognizing the true source behind his mystification: the resemblance between him and Felix is both imaginary and irrational and has an internal rather than an external source. Similarly, Hermann distinguishes between two kinds of memory that fuel his endeavors. There is rational memory and irrational memory, the former insisting on the difference between him and Felix, the latter on their identity: "the following night my rational memory did not cease examining such minute flaws, whereas with the irrational memory of my senses I kept seeing, despite everything, myself, my own self, in the sorry disguise of a tramp, his face motionless, with chin and cheeks bristle-shaded, as happens to a dead man overnight" (117). In comparing the passages describing Hermann after the murder and his writing, we can say that there is a similar mirror-like relationship between them: if the former compares writing to life, the latter does the opposite, comparing life to writing. The horizontal axis separating the original text from the blotting paper now separates Hermann (alive) and Felix (dead). The comparison is strengthened as we realize that in the background of Hermann's description of the murder, there is a visual image of Felix's dark body against the white of the snow. The two passages differ, of course, since after the murder the ambivalence is gone as Hermann no longer questions or hides his desire: having killed Felix, Hermann believes he has attained the authority and control that comes with authorship, "the maker's secret certainty; which never can err" (172).

THE ETHICS OF INTERSUBJECTIVITY

Of course, err Hermann does, and the seeds of his failure are already present in the description of his triumph. Hence, the pool of his Narcissus fantasy is *stagnant*, a description that suggests not only the final stability of similarity between him and Felix but also stasis, death. Most importantly, Hermann's expression of accomplishment with which he confirms the likeness is heavy with foreshadowing: "our likeness was such that really I could not say who had been killed, I or he" (172). Indeed, it is hard to say who has been killed, as we see Hermann become increasingly imprisoned in the identity of Felix as he ends up losing his own. As Hermann, he can lie and make up stories; but as Felix, he is stuck with a single one. Killing Felix robs Hermann's identity of potentiality, pinning the mask on him, as if it were the only face possible:

> I love violets and music. I was born at Zwickau. My father was a bald-headed bespectacled shoemaker, and my mother was a washerwoman with scarlet hands....
> And all over again from the beginning, with new absurd details.... Thus, a reflected image, asserting itself, laid its claims. Not I sought a refuge in a foreign land, not I grew a beard, but Felix, my slayer. (176)

Chapter Three

The sense of the loss of selfhood becomes explicit in Hermann's last nightmare, in which Lydia betrays him and he finds himself powerless, since he—as Hermann—officially does not exist anymore:

> I at last found Lydia, who was hiding from me and who now coolly declared that all was well, she had got the inheritance all right and was going to marry another man, "because, you see," she said, "you are dead." I woke up in a terrific rage, my heart pounding madly: fooled! helpless!—for how could a dead man sue the living—yes, helpless—and she knew it! (199)

The powerlessness Hermann experiences in the dream (which he, the most resilient of literary characters, characteristically attempts to laugh off) is about the loss of his public identity, indicated here—consciously or not—by his realization that he would be unable to protect himself in court. The importance of conducting one's life among others similarly becomes apparent as Hermann admits the lack of similarity between himself and Felix's passport photo. As an object that has no other purpose than to officially validate one's identity by *others*, the passport becomes another marker of reality's social nature in the novel. Both photos belong in the public realm; hence, how they are seen by others is a reality check that Hermann stubbornly refuses to accept. Indeed, as the end of the novel shows, the side effects of the murder are devastating for Hermann: instead of bringing him the control he seeks, the murder forces him to accept the intersubjective nature of any act of signification, as well as his dependence on others. Even before he is caught, Hermann is imprisoned by the interpretations of others. Or, to put it differently, the interpretative imprisonment precedes and prefigures the physical one. This is yet another point of thematic concurrence between Dostoevsky and Nabokov: as *Despair* reaches its denouement, the metaphysical issues of the novel reveal their social underside. Hermann, like Raskolnikov in *Crime and Punishment* and Stavrogin in *Demons*, must realize that the desire for control is indistinguishable from the desire for recognition.

Like everything in this novel about doubles, the meaning of "recognition" doubles after the murder. Hence, on the one hand, Hermann bemoans the refusal of investigators and journalists "to recognize [him] in the corpse of [his] flawless double" and, on the other hand, he undertakes the writing of his memoirs "in order to obtain recognition" (194). Indeed, after the murder, the connection between the project of killing Felix and writing and Hermann's dependence on the opinion of others becomes apparent. Instead of the liberation he so desperately seeks, Hermann finds his "vast vacant soul" filled with "a sterile and hideous confusion" anticipating "a certain extraordinary, madly happy, all-solving moment . . . of an artist's triumph; of pride, deliverance, bliss" (183). When it fails to come, he compares the police and the media to vindictive "literary critic[s]" (191). Finally, his inability to tolerate the interpretation of others spurs another round of his creative activity, this time in writing.

The irony here is similar to that of *Crime and Punishment*, where Raskolnikov understands his desire for recognition as proof that he lacks the autonomy required for the status of an extraordinary person. While it is true that the two novels bear a structural resemblance, the difference between them is that in the second part of *Crime*'s epilogue, Raskolnikov not only accepts the ethical demands of intersubjectivity but also willingly submits to the external authority of the ideal other, symbolized by his momentous kneeling before Sonia. *Despair* does not offer Hermann such an opportunity for a spiritual and ethical reprieve. Hermann's attempt to "author" reality continues until the novel's last breath. The English-language addition to the Russian ending brings this point home. Hermann cannot stop aestheticizing life, and at the end, as he is watched by others, he continues to perform by once again switching mediums:

> I have peeped again. Standing and staring. There are hundreds of them—men in blue, women in black, butcher boys, flower girls, a priest, two nuns, soldiers, carpenters, glaziers, postmen, clerks, shopkeepers . . . But absolute quiet; only the swish of their breathing. How about opening the window and making a little speech. . . .
> "Frenchmen! This is a rehearsal. Hold those policemen. A famous film actor will presently come running out of this house. He is an arch-criminal but he must escape. You are asked to prevent them from grabbing him. This is part of the plot. French crowd! I want you to make a free passage for him from door to car. Remove its driver! Start the motor! Hold those policemen, knock them down, sit on them—we pay them for it. This is a German company, so excuse my French. Les preneurs de vues, my technicians and armed advisers are already among you. Attention! I want a clean getaway. That's all. Thank you. I'm coming out now." (211–12)

Hence, while *Crime and Punishment* still allows for the existence of the transcendental signified on the character level, in *Despair* it exists only as a marker of authorial activity. The third-person narrative in Dostoevsky's novel makes it possible to frame Raskolnikov's redemption outside of his consciousness. In *Despair*, the position of outsideness has been relegated to the authorial presence in the text, that is, the traces Nabokov leaves of a consciousness that can belong only to the implied author. This, in turn, gives rise to a reading of the novel as a story of aesthetic imposture. Hermann's crimes are aesthetic ones par excellence: he is a bad author who tries to usurp the position of authorship from its rightful owner but fails. The metaphysical and the aesthetic hierarchies are analogous to each other, but there is no cause-and-effect relationship between them: a just punishment awaits Hermann at the end of the novel as Nabokov kicks the usurper out of the authorial heaven.[50]

Yet, what separates Nabokov from Dostoevsky is not that one operates in the domain of ethics and the other in that of aesthetics but in how each employs the authorial function in his prose, which influences the range of the reader's ethical responses to the act of reading. It is important to understand that Nabokov does not abandon ethical concerns by switching his focus from the material reality to the textual one; on the contrary, he consciously investigates the ethical consequences that acts of signification and representation have on authors and readers, tellers and listeners.

Therefore, I argue that for Nabokov the "theological model" is important inasmuch as it becomes the source for the power dynamic that is inherent in any creative act and, specifically, in narrative prose. In this sense, the creative activity of Nabokov's narrators such as Hermann, Humbert, or Kinbote has a metaphysical origin: it strives to regain a lost authenticity by endowing the world with meaning and order that it no longer possesses. While Dostoevsky makes the religious sources of this loss explicit, Nabokov constructs post-Christian fictive worlds, in which the metaphysical scale of the loss remains not only unacknowledged but also unrecognized by their protagonist-narrators. Still, this loss can be perceived through the overwhelming sense of metaphysical anxiety exhibited in these characters' narratives, which they attempt to quell by seizing control over signification, insisting that the identity between reality and their representation of it is nonarbitrary.

Furthermore, Nabokov's engagement of his readers' ethics depends on their recognition that the power dynamic between the protagonist-narrator and the other characters (including the narratee) is both analogous and contiguous to the one that informs the intersubjective relationships created by the text itself, encompassing the figures of implied author and reader. In short, the reader's complicity in the aesthetic and physical violence that takes place in Nabokov's prose comes with her awareness that by revealing the unethical nature of the creative activity of his narrators, Nabokov compromises the authorial function itself.

To better understand the role of metaphysics in Nabokov's narrative ethics, it might be productive to compare it to that of Dostoevsky, since Nabokov's protagonist-narrators are of the same kin as Dostoevsky's metaphysical rebels. Dostoevsky frames his characters' ideological dialogues within nonverbal, iconic, Christian imagery that seeks to (but rarely does) direct his characters toward a nonviolent resolution of their metaphysical and social conflicts and a subsequent reintegration into the rightful order through their submission to the authority of Christ. Nabokov's attitude toward the

The Metaphysics of Authorship

transcendental signified is much more ambivalent. On the one hand, for Nabokov, the theological hierarchy indeed informs the distribution of power within the relationships created by acts of representation. In his fiction, the figure of the implied author holds all the reins, both through the romantic notion of the artist as a divine creator and within the network of relationships structured by narrative prose, such as author-characters and author-reader. At the same time—and in *Despair* Nabokov achieves this by creating a metaphoric relationship between writing and crime/cruelty—authorship (as long as we are speaking about human authors) is a false transcendental signified, and any attempt to endow it with such a status is exposed as unethical and futile. Hence, for Nabokov, writing is predicated on both presence and absence, and to insist that in writing one can achieve an unmediated presence of being unavoidably results in violence. The reader's ethical engagement with Nabokov's fiction begins with the realization that Nabokov exposes his protagonists' pretensions for authorial control on the level of content while on the formal level leaving his readers in the presence of an authorial consciousness that claims to retain all control over signification for itself. Such a bifurcation within Nabokov's conceptualization of the authorial function—duplicated, in turn, in the authorial aspirations of his protagonists-narrators (artists/creators on the one hand, unethical impostors on the other)—accounts for the choice of first-person narratives in such novels as *The Eye*, *Despair*, *Lolita*, *Pnin*, and *Pale Fire*. It also explains why Nabokov's own extratextual remarks in prefaces and interviews often have a strong tinge of that very *"poshlust"* he so ardently attempted to eradicate in his readers.[51] It is hardly accidental that Nabokov's preface to the English text of *Despair* reads as if it could have easily been penned by Hermann himself. The authorial figure who demands unambiguous submission from the readers is Nabokov's best mystification.[52] No wonder it has commanded such critical respect.

Therefore, we can say that *Despair* creates a link—symptomatic, I would argue, of modernism—between the crisis of mimesis and the metaphysical crisis; it also provides a compelling critique of violence by making apparent the relationship between aesthetic and physical violence—a topic that dominates Nabokov's creative output. *Despair* sets the protagonist's demiurgic desire to usurp authorship against his utter inability to control the account of events, to secure their interpretation within his own subjectivity. As such, the wind that we encounter at both ends of Hermann's narrative is not only a marker of authorial consciousness but also symbolic of the proliferation of meaning, of the semantic openness and permeability of any text. Hence, while the "aesthetic" argument insists that in *Despair*—as elsewhere—Nabokov's goal is to reinstate the proper order by punishing the author-impostor and expelling him from the garden of Eden in which there

Chapter Three

can be no author other than Nabokov, I argue that in Hermann Nabokov creates a parody of authorship itself, bringing forward the ethical implications of the fulfillment of the subject's desire for meaning produced through acts of representation.

Hence, Hermann combines in himself the figure of a gnostic poet who—as Lachmann suggests—exposes reality's inherent falseness and lack of authenticity by reassembling it and that of an impostor who wants to usurp full control of his narrative, to be the ultimate creator of his universe and to secure for his narrative the function of the transcendental signified. In this doubling, Hermann reveals his propinquity to such Dostoevskian protagonists as Raskolnikov and Stavrogin.[53] Both play out the roles of reformers and usurpers of life, whose tragedy is the inability to tell the difference between the one and the other. In *Despair*, Hermann's kinship with Stavrogin is hinted at by the former's persistent thoughts of suicide by hanging—"I have exactly twenty-five kinds of handwritings, the best (i.e., those I use the most readily) being as follows: a round diminutive one . . . ; then *a suicide's hand, every letter a noose*, every comma a trigger"[54]—although here, of course, the *textual* rather than physical reality moves into the foreground. Dostoevsky associates Stavrogin's terrifying freedom with metaphysical *emptiness*; similarly, after the murder, Hermann states that his "vast vacant soul" is filled with "a sterile and hideous confusion" (183). This emptiness is also referenced in Hermann's other nightmare, in which he finds himself in a symbolically heavy empty room watching himself in preparations for suicide:

> For several years I was haunted by a very singular and very nasty dream: I dreamed I was standing in the middle of a long passage with a door at the bottom, and passionately wanting, but not daring to go and open it, and then deciding at last to go, which I accordingly did; but at once awoke with a groan, for what I saw there was unimaginably terrible; to wit, a perfectly empty, newly whitewashed room. That was all, but it was so terrible that I never could hold out; then one night a chair and its slender shadow appeared in the middle of the bare room—not as a first item of furniture but as though somebody had brought it to climb upon it and fix a bit of drapery, and since I knew whom I would find there next time stretching up with a hammer and a mouthful of nails, I spat them out and never opened that door again. (46)[55]

Just like Raskolnikov and Stavrogin, Hermann exhibits a yearning for metaphysical freedom while being completely subjugated by the mechanism of his metaphysical desire, whose function he does not understand. This split becomes apparent after Hermann's nightmare of the worm-like dog, when he suddenly decides to "take the advice of fate" and abandon his plan of killing Felix.[56] Even as Hermann imagines himself free to leave the hotel room

The Metaphysics of Authorship

and Felix behind forever, he almost immediately (even if not completely consciously) interprets his actions as if they were governed by a mechanism over which he has no control at all. He is bound to return:

> Really, what a fascinating thought; to take the advice of fate and, now, at once, leave that room, forever leave and forget, and spare my poor double . . . Thus an adolescent, after yielding once again to a solitary and shameful vice, says to himself with inordinate force and clearness: "That's finished for good; from this time forth, life shall be pure; the rapture of purity"; thus, after having voiced everything, having lived through everything in advance and had my fill of pain and pleasure, I was now superstitiously keen to turn away from temptation for ever. (97)

In *Despair*, this internal split between Hermann's perception of his demiurgic powers and his utter lack of control over his actions becomes apparent if we compare his fantasy of himself as an instrument of Fate, as he randomly chooses one of the girls playing marbles to post his letter to Felix, to his desperate feeling of dependence on the dictating man he sees outside his window. Here is Hermann imagining himself as Fate incarnate:

> I selected the younger of the two . . . and, patting her on the head, I said: "Look here, my dear, my eyes are so weak that I'm afraid of missing the slit; do, please, drop this letter for me into the box over there . . .
> . . . She will grow up, that child . . . and she will never know in what an eerie business she had served as go-between.
> Then, also, there is another likelihood: fate, not suffering such blind and naïve brokerage, envious fate with its vast experience, assortment of confidence tricks, and hatred of competition, may cruelly punish that little maiden for intruding, and make her wonder—"Whatever have I done to be so unfortunate?" and never, never, never will she understand. (124–25)

Here, he contemplates the stranger in the building across from him:

> I remember, I shook off that numbness, put the little book back into my pocket, took out my keys, was about to lock up and leave—was leaving, but then stopped in the passage with my heart going pit-a-pit. . . . No, it was impossible to leave. . . . I returned to the room and stood awhile by the window looking at the house opposite. Lamps had already lit up there, shining upon office ledgers, and a man in black, with one hand behind his back, was walking to and fro, presumably dictating to a secretary I could not see. Ever and anon he appeared, and once, even, he stopped at the window to do some thinking, and then again turned, dictating, dictating, dictating. (57)

Chapter Three

In both of these passages, but especially in the latter one, Nabokov once again closely connects the themes of metaphysical anxiety and aestheticized reality. What is significant here is not just the range of Hermann's responses—from turning one of the girls into a character in the first passage to becoming a character himself in the second—but also his growing awareness of how strongly writing figures into social power dynamics, as well as the ethical implications of this realization. In the first passage, the reasons behind Hermann's demonic attempt to orchestrate events are nothing less than to clear his conscience ("But my conscience is clear. Not I wrote to Felix, but he wrote to me; not I sent him the answer, but an unknown child" [125]). Paradoxically, Hermann seeks to escape the responsibility that comes with authorship, as he simultaneously envisions himself to be the agent of fate. Hermann's convenient (and quite possibly sincere) blindness to his form-shaping activity is yet another point of kinship between Nabokov and Dostoevsky, whose characters likewise show formidable blindness to their measure of responsibility. If the pawnbroker of "The Meek One" is unable to see the full extent of his participation in his wife's suicide, Hermann avoids taking responsibility for his actions by believing (or pretending) to be not the author, but a character:

> Why, what is this talk about trouble, when it is the harmony of mathematical symbols, the movement of planets, the hitchless working of natural laws which have a true bearing upon the subject? My wonderful edifice grew without my assistance; yes, from the very start everything had complied with my wishes; and when now I asked myself what to write to Felix, I was hardly astonished to find that letter in my brain, as ready-made there as those congratulatory telegrams with vignettes that can be sent for a certain additional payment to newly married couples. It only remained to inscribe the date in the space left for it on the printed form. (121)

The passage in which Hermann observes a dictating man through the window shows his distant awareness of how intrinsic intersubjective power dynamics are to the process of writing, as he imagines himself to be a product and an instrument of another's unforgiving will. As in the moments preceding his initial encounter with Felix, here the internal processes of Hermann's consciousness are indistinguishable from the external ones, although Nabokov carefully avoids validating a reading that interprets the external vision as a projection of the internal state. The logic of this scene is that of a *mise en abyme*, rather than an allegory, as the black book with Felix's address is reflected in the figure of "a man in black." Notably, if this is a manifestation of the authorial consciousness, it is a human, not a godly one. Its equality in ontological status to Hermann is underlined by the mirror-like composition

The Metaphysics of Authorship

of the opposing window frames. In the image of the dictating man, we have the most direct indication that the internal mechanism of desire governing Hermann's actions is intersubjective: his desire will forever be that other remaining outside of his control, that other whose authority Hermann is unable to shake off any more than he is able to secure meaning in the text he is creating. Visualizing the man's activity as "dictating" rather than "writing," Hermann comes closest to understanding the full futility of his endeavor to become the only author of his own life, a position that would also endow his life with the authenticity he seeks to secure. Hermann's vision of the man in black is a precursor of the grand catastrophe to follow; it is a premonition that his pretensions of control are illusory. The man in black becomes yet another instance of demonic possession, another authorial ring in Nabokov's *mise-en-abyme* universe, a figure of the nonidentical double tormenting the subject in a world without authenticity.

In *Despair*, Nabokov creates a protagonist-narrator who insists that his vision of reality be uncontested. For Hermann, the relationship between the signifier and the signified must be of a complete and nonarbitrary identity. It is precisely this kind of identity he imagines between himself and Felix. His belief in this perceived identity is such that he is unable to accept the difference between himself and Felix even after it is announced in the newspapers: "For I look like my name, gentlemen, and it fits me as exactly as it used to fit him. You must be fools not to understand" (193). Hermann's project fails because reality will always refuse to fit within a singular point of view, a single subjectivity. If we follow Nabokov's notion that "reality is a . . . subjective affair,"[57] we have to conclude that reality depends on everyone's subjectivity, that any subjectivity is irreplaceable and necessary in the project of understanding and representing life. The tragic joke of the novel is that as Hermann insists on the identity between himself and Felix, he, of course, loses his own unique identity.

It is common in the criticism of this novel to point to the aesthetization of reality as Hermann's main transgression. Hermann's crime, such criticism holds, is in refusing to differentiate between physical and textual reality. Yet, for Nabokov, reality always possesses a textual presence: it exists inasmuch as one can assign meaning to it, and aestheticizing it is one way among many of doing so. If this is true, then doubling can be said to be reality's governing principle, and finding patterns and similarities between events, things, and people, as well as classifying concepts and ordering life, must be inherent to the human activity of "attaining" reality. At the same time, Nabokov insists on the redeeming power of the misprint and misalignment. While Lachmann sees the imagined identity between Hermann and Felix as a personified trope, in *Despair* Nabokov asserts that the opposite is also true: creating a trope runs the risk of dehumanizing someone. The

Chapter Three

ethical tension of *Despair* (and even more so of *Lolita*) depends on the subject's ability to maintain the ambivalence of the trope, a recognition that it contains both difference *and* sameness, absence *as well as* presence, and that the distance between the two always has a social dimension. By depicting Hermann's endeavors in the novel as both futile and violent, Nabokov does not suggest that what might protect us from becoming a Hermann is a forced abstinence from treating reality as if it were a text. Instead, the novel compels the reader to accept responsibility for the potential violence in any aesthetic act by recognizing the role she plays in it.[58]

THE SAVING GRACE OF MISRECOGNITION

While Hermann accepts neither the loss of the transcendental signified nor the responsibility for his attempts to regain it, the novel includes a passage in which such features as misalignment, misprint, and mis-identity that we have identified as Nabokov's "saving grace" become—for a brief time—the governing principle of Hermann's actions and observations. This passage's singularity in the novel warrants an extended quote. Arriving in Tarnitz, Hermann rents a room in the hotel where he contemplates his project. He begins with a plea to God, hoping, for the first time, that the identity between him and Felix has been imagined. This moment of partial self-awareness gives rise to the following:

> I went to the window and looked out: there was a dreary courtyard down there, and a round-backed Tartar in an embroidered skullcap was showing a small blue carpet to a buxom barefooted woman. Now I knew that woman and I recognized that Tartar too, and the patch of weeds in one corner of the yard, and that vortex of dust, and the Caspian wind's soft pressure, and the pale sky sick of looking on fisheries.
> At that moment there was a knock, a maid entered with the additional pillow and the cleaner chamber pot I had demanded, and when I turned to the window again it was no longer a Tartar whom I saw there but some local peddler selling braces, and the woman was gone. But while I looked there started afresh that process of fusion, of building, that making up of a definite remembrance; there reappeared, growing and clustering, those weeds in a corner of the yard, and again red-haired Christina Forsmann, whom I had known carnally in 1915, fingered the Tartar's carpet, and sand flew, and I could not discover what the kernel was, around which all those things were formed, and where exactly the germ, the fount—suddenly I glanced at the decanter of dead water and it said "warm"—as in that game when you hide objects; and very possibly I should have finally found the trifle, which, unconsciously no-

ticed by me, had at once set going the engine of memory (or, again, I should not have found it, the simple, nonliterary explanation being that everything in that provincial German hotel chamber, even the view, vaguely and uglily resembled something seen in Russia ages ago) had I not thought of my appointment; and that made me draw on my gloves and hurry out.[59]

As Hermann walks down the street, he continues to observe the correspondences between past and present:

> I turned down the boulevard, past the post office. A brutal wind was blowing and chasing leaves—scurry, cripples!—athwart the street. In spite of my impatience I was as observant as usual, noting the faces and trousers of passersby, the tramcars which seemed like toys compared to the Berlin ones, the shops, a giant's top hat painted on a peeling wall, signboards, the name of a fishmonger: Carl Spiess, reminding me of one Carl Spiess whom I used to know in that Volga village of my past and who likewise sold spitchcocks.
>   At last, reaching the end of the street, I saw the bronze horse rearing and using its tail for a prop, like a woodpecker, and if the duke riding it had stretched out his arm with more energy, the whole monument in the murky evening light might have passed for that of Peter the Great in the town he founded. On one of the benches an old man was eating grapes out of a paper bag; on another bench sat two elderly dames; an invalid old woman of enormous size reclined in a Bath chair and listened to their talk, her round eyes agog. Twice and thrice did I go round the statue, observing as I went the snake writhing under that hind hoof, that legend in Latin, that jackboot with the black star of a spur. Sorry, there was really no snake; it was just my fancy borrowing from Tsar Peter—whose statue, anyway, wears buskins. (68)

As images from the past fold into the present, Hermann perceives a series of identities, none of which he produces consciously. These are offered to him by some higher authority, and it is telling that the wind, which in *Despair* is a sign of authorial presence, accompanies his walk through Tarnitz. The wind, as I suggested previously, is also a sign of the instability of meaning, a symbol of semiotic slippage, and as Hermann enters the tobacconist's store he encounters another fake double, in which both the difference from and the similarity to the original become apparent:

> Just above it was one of Ardalion's still-life pictures: a tobacco pipe, on green cloth, and two roses.
>   "How on earth did you—?" I asked with a laugh. She did not understand at first, and then answered:
>   "My niece painted it—my niece who died recently."

Chapter Three

> Well, I'm damned! (thought I). For had I not seen something very similar, if not identical, among Ardalion's pictures? Well, I'm damned! (69)

Nabokov frames the extended passage I quoted above with two instances of seemingly unconscious slips of Hermann's tongue that reveal the metaphysical undercurrent of his wanderings through the town. What begins with Hermann's impulsive plea to God to be delivered from having to go through with his plan ends with an emphatic (and unwitting) confirmation of Hermann's status as "damned." Most importantly, the passage above is remarkable for the sets of associations that are strikingly specific and at the same time completely arbitrary. Nabokov emphasizes the double nature of the process of *re*-membering (doubly doubled, in fact, since we are now following it by reading Hermann's memoirs): it is driven by the opposing forces of recognition and *mis*-perception. Here Hermann's "engine of memory" gives rise to what Andrew Field called "one moment of Proustian sublimity" in the novel.[60] Hermann's memory creates correspondences that are similar in their spontaneity to his discovery of the identity between himself and Felix. Yet, here these correspondences possess one feature that the similarity he discovers between himself and Felix does not: they are both exact *and* fleeting. The folds in time that appear in front of Hermann's gaze vanish almost as soon as he notices them, and unlike his encounter with Felix, here he does not attempt to hold on to them in order to insist on the permanent stability of the momentary perception. This passage is strikingly similar to Nabokov's famous credo in *Speak, Memory*, in which he describes his relationship to time:

> I confess I do not believe in time. I like to fold my magic carpet, after use, in such a way as to superimpose one part of the pattern upon another. Let visitors trip. And the highest enjoyment of timelessness—in a landscape selected at random—is when I stand among rare butterflies and their food plants. This is ecstasy, and behind the ecstasy is something else, which is hard to explain. It is like a momentary vacuum into which rushes all that I love. A sense of oneness with sun and stone. A thrill of gratitude to whom it may concern—to the contrapuntal genius of human fate or to tender ghosts humoring a lucky mortal.[61]

The difference between Nabokov and Hermann lies not in the separation of physical and textual realities but in the attitude each takes toward the transcendental signified. While Hermann attempts to control his perceptions, to be simultaneously in charge of fate and absolved of responsibility, the "sense of oneness," of complete identity with the world, fills Nabokov with gratitude toward the unnamed but omniscient authority. This sense of

The Metaphysics of Authorship

unity is, of course, the polar opposite of what Hermann experiences with his practice of dissociation. Submitting to it, Nabokov consciously frames the experience as a scene of address: it is pointedly intersubjective. Neither the authority over nor authorship of the text of nature belongs to Nabokov. It is this understanding, perhaps, that constitutes "the kernel" that Hermann fails to discover, yet here, in this passage quoted earlier, he comes closest to accepting what I would call the principle of "unstable identity," which recognizes identity as an impermanent gift without any further purpose. Noticeably, Hermann's narrative of his perceptions in Tarnitz also bears close resemblance to how Nabokov portrays the experiences of his son at the end of the autobiography: both are involved in a game called "Find What the Sailor Has Hidden" (310). Unlike his creator, however, Hermann refuses to recognize the duality inherent in any creative act; he cannot accept that the game is both artificial and divine.

Nevertheless, in playing this "catch and release" of identity as he continues on to the meeting with Felix, Hermann—unwittingly and unwillingly—allows his life to be the text in which he is simply a character, and he accepts that the identity he believes exists between him and Felix might be subjective and arbitrary after all. It is hardly accidental that Nabokov concludes Hermann's observations with a vision of another game, as the two girls playing marbles, rolling the "iridescent orb into a tiny pit,"[62] become a reimagining of the Fates. The image of the orb in the pit is highly symbolic here, since, as an image of an eye, it points to the second most important instrument of Hermann's activity in the novel (the writing hand being the first). Walking down Kelly Road, he is pure observation and stops short of negating the possibility that reality can have other authors besides him. It is against the playful concentration of the girls that Hermann recognizes the true burden of his plan:

> I stood under the porch and looked at two little girls playing marbles; rolling by turn the iridescent orb ... in order that the marble should trickle into a tiny pit in the ground under a double-trunked birch tree; as I stood looking at that concentrated, silent and minute game, I somehow found myself thinking that Felix could not come for the simple reason that he was a product of my imagination, which hankered after reflections, repetitions, masks, and that my presence in a remote little town was absurd and even monstrous. (69–70)

The novel's plot, however, requires that Hermann reject this opportunity to abandon his project. One of the many links connecting Hermann with Dostoevsky's characters is that his obsession with originality supplements his desire for authorial control. Rakitin, Ivan, and the Underground Man are the most obvious points of comparison here. Rakitin and Ivan accuse Alyosha of plagiarism, and the Underground Man cannot bear Liza's accusation

Chapter Three

that he has a "bookish" imagination. In *The Brothers Karamazov*, Alyosha's "plagiarism" is a sign of spiritual health: he is not afraid to model his behavior on those he holds in high esteem. The desire for originality and the fear of being like someone else are connected in *The Brothers Karamazov* to pride. Alyosha's most famous act of "plagiarism" is his kiss of Ivan, which he "steals" from Jesus's kiss of the Grand Inquisitor in Ivan's poem. Unlike Alyosha, Hermann cannot tolerate being a character in someone else's story. Unlike Nabokov, he concludes by rejecting the anonymous workings of fate as derivative:

> Nor am I quite certain of the exceptionality of the aforesaid phenomena. Every man with a keen eye is familiar with those anonymously retold passages from his past life: false-innocent combinations of details, which smack revoltingly of plagiarism. Let us leave them to the conscience of fate and return, with a sinking heart and dull reluctance, to the monument at the end of the street. (70)

While Hermann—his keen eye notwithstanding—fails to recognize the reappearance of these girls again as he considers sending Felix the letter with an invitation for their final meeting later in the novel, the reader must not. This doubling is especially significant, since, as I discussed above, during the second encounter Hermann imagines *himself* to be an agent of fate by asking one of the girls to drop the letter into the mailbox for him. The comparison of the girls to the Fates is intensified here, as the reader acknowledges the parallelism of action: instead of dropping the marble into a pit, the girl drops Hermann's letter into the mailbox. Such subtle authorial intrusions are a trademark of Nabokov's prose, and the reader's interpretation of Nabokov's texts depends in large measure on detecting them and understanding their intent. Yet, they also highlight the ethical tensions of the novel, since the reader must also recognize that the patterning activity of the author is quite similar to that of the protagonist-narrator. The implied author of *Despair* declares the nonarbitrary identity to be crucial for the "correct" reading of the novel at the same time as he announces the same assertion by the protagonist-narrator to be unethical. In identifying with the author to take an ethical stance against the novel's compromised narrator, the reader simultaneously identifies with Hermann. Hence, on the one hand, the novel proposes that what might protect us from becoming Hermann is the acceptance of the boundaries being blurry, of arbitrariness, of the loss of the transcendental signified, yet, on the other hand, it introduces an authorial consciousness, whose legitimacy depends on the reader's acceptance of its transcendental status. Through the course of reading, the reader must first face the unethical usurpation of authorship by the single subjectivity of the protagonist-narrator, only to land in the snares of the similarly controlling subjectivity of the authorial figure. To exempt this authorial presence from responsibility would be the same as to condone Hermann's authorial aspirations.

While embracing its own affirmation of unstable identity, the novel contains the opposite reading as well. Hermann's project is doomed not only because there will always be others to contest his account but also because the law of absolute identity is deadly to the true nature of life. As the novel shows through a series of interconnected metaphors, reality always exceeds any single subjective account of it. Felix refuses to fit into Hermann's clothes, just as the walking stick inscribed with the victim's name will always "stick out." While the inscription on the stick is crucial to the plot of the story, the symbolic meaning of Hermann's fateful oversight is just as clear: the stick becomes metonymic proof that the proliferation of meaning cannot be avoided and that the other can never be completely "consumed" by representation. Finally, the narrative itself refuses to fit into the neat structure Hermann prepares for it and at the end explodes into a diary. That Hermann's project is about control over the narrative of his life is emphasized as he desperately attempts to provide a "neat" ending to the story, imagining the loose ends tied up in a manner that is most advantageous for him. Whether or not this fake ending, which Hermann "concoct[s] . . . according to a classic recipe" (179), can be seen as Nabokov's own argument for a "loose, baggy monster" as the most appropriate form for the modern novel, the point that *Despair* makes about the role of subjectivity in the novel is clear: a single subject's point of view—be it the point of view of a protagonist-narrator or the third-person point of view of an omniscient narrator—is incapable of containing the world of the novel within its horizon. Such an assertion of noncoincidence, as well as the ethical implications of its rejection, can be seen as Nabokov's critique of the subject's universalist aspirations. It also forces the reader to recognize the ambivalence contained within acts of authorship driven by the subject's desire for metaphysical stability and the violence that it inevitably brings along.

Chapter Four

The Dangers of Aesthetic Bliss: The Double Bind of Language in *Bend Sinister*

ON THE REAL AND THE IMAGINED (NABOKOV AND DOSTOEVSKY I)

"Art is a divine game," explains Nabokov in his lecture on Dostoevsky, and the "delight" we experience in a work of art is the result of a system of checks and balances, in which the harmony between authenticity and constructedness is crucial.[1] True artistic creation has a divine origin and endows us with the power to feel the joy of the creative act. But since, technically speaking, art is "all make-believe" and "the people on stage . . . are not actually murdered," readers can allow themselves to enjoy "participating in an elaborate and enchanting game" (106). Because art and reality exist in immediate proximity to each other, their relationship is not only metaphorical but metonymic as well, and the contiguity between them creates a risk of encroachment. The measure of the artist's originality is in how successfully he can keep the constructed world of his creation separate from the real one without compromising the plausibility of the make-believe.

Continuing to discuss Nabokov's narrative ethics in this chapter, I begin by addressing the differences between Dostoevsky's and Nabokov's conceptualizations of verbal art. I argue that, unlike Dostoevsky, Nabokov envisions this practice as both mimetic and self-referential. Such duality inevitably complicates an ethical inquiry into Nabokov's texts, since it threatens to invalidate our mimetic identification with his characters. Yet, what makes the affinity between Nabokov's and Dostoevsky's narrative ethics so close is Nabokov's attention to the ethical significance of the intersubjective relationships binding together author, characters, and readers. To argue this point, I analyze the complex hierarchies established by the formal distribution of discourse between author and characters in chapter 7 of *Bend Sinister*. I end by suggesting that an ethical inquiry that puts Nabokov's authorial persona on a par with his characters gives the tension inherent in his artistic practice its proper due.

The Dangers of Aesthetic Bliss

The delight in art—or, as Nabokov calls it in his Dostoevsky lecture, "spiritual vibration"—belongs to writers and readers alike (106). The writer enjoys creating a world that strives to compete in complexity with the one we live in; and yet, since this new world is not real, readers are able to take pleasure in the writer's genius and not be "disgusted or horrified" by the characters' tragic demise (106). The reader's pleasure comes from being part of what Peter J. Rabinowitz calls the "narrative audience" and the "authorial audience" at the same time.[2] The former—the imagined audience of the narrator (but not the author)—believes in the reality of the narrated world and attends to the realistic layer of the text; the latter attempts to make sense of the work of fiction that contains it, aware that it is just that, a fiction, and focuses on the aesthetic properties of the text. In his lecture on Dostoevsky, Nabokov argues that while the simultaneous presence of both audiences is necessary for reading, in order to enjoy the text, readers ultimately must let the authorial audience have the final word.[3]

Among the main reasons that Nabokov lists for his dislike of Dostoevsky is precisely his aesthetic imbalance, the source of which he finds in Dostoevsky's excessive "excursions into the sick souls of his characters."[4] For Nabokov, as Rabinowitz might have put it, Dostoevsky sins on the side of the narrative audience. He collapses the delicate balance between art and our reality by overwhelming his readers with emotions of disgust and morbidity. Dostoevsky's preference for "criminal reportage" over "aesthetic achievement" brings his prose too close to home and belongs in a newspaper, rather than in a work of art (160). The discreteness of both worlds is not a given, and in order to work, the relationship between the artist and his world, and between him and God should be, to use a mathematical term, one of conformity: the writer relates to his work, as God to his. Still, there is always a danger of interpermeation, as elements of one world seep into another. For Nabokov, as for Tolstoy, whose artistry Nabokov praises in the following lecture, this leakage is caused by none other than the reader's empathy. Unlike Tolstoy, however, who insists in *What Is Art?* that true art is emotionally infectious (hence, its danger) and who bases the distinction between "good" and "bad" art on the moral quality of the emotion the artwork carries, Nabokov advocates for the aesthetic quality of art whose emotional charge is intentionally staged and is able to titillate the reader with aesthetic pleasure without overwhelming her. The blood spilled in works of art must coagulate, as Alexander Blok would have it, into cranberry juice only; otherwise, with the safety net of artificiality gone, the reader's pleasure too quickly acidifies into feelings of disgust and horror. The source of Dostoevsky's bad artistic judgment is his disrespect for the borders that separate the world of his characters from the world inhabited by real people, by us in fact. One might say that for Nabokov, such writing may be plagiarizing the outside world instead of creating one. Nabokov blames Dostoevsky for destroying the tension that exists between the two worlds at the cost of artistic originality.

Furthermore, Dostoevsky not only smuggles the nonfiction of the newspaper into the fictive world of his novels, he also exploits his reader's interest by exposing her to the most pathological manifestations of the human mind and spirit, as if the unremitting display of mental pathology is an adequate reflection of our souls' depths. Dostoevsky's characters are both too real and too exaggerated for Nabokov's taste. Dostoevsky has nothing to tell us about the human condition because his characters—"poor, deformed, warped souls," as Nabokov calls them—are "no longer human" (107).

To illustrate this point, Nabokov seeks a temporary alliance with the psychoanalysis he so notoriously hated, drawing on an article about Dostoevsky by S. Stephenson Smith and Andrei Isotoff published in the *Psychoanalytic Review* in 1939. Among the mental afflictions of Dostoevsky's characters, Nabokov lists epilepsy (Dostoevsky's epileptics are Myshkin, Smerdyakov, Kirillov, and Nelli in *The Insulted and the Injured*); senile dementia (General Ivolgin); hysteria (a quartet of females: two Lizas—Khokhlakova from *The Brothers Karamazov* and Tushina from *Demons*—Nastasya Filippovna from *The Idiot*, and Katerina Ivanovna from *Crime and Punishment*); and psychopathology (Stavrogin, Rogozhin, Raskolnikov, Ivan Karamazov, and numerous other unnamed characters, who are completely mad). Setting aside the exasperating idiosyncrasy of Nabokov's assessments of Dostoevsky's prose, we can say that they do touch upon one of the major issues in our discussion of narrative ethics, namely, the relationship between the fictional world of the novel and the "real" space in which the novels are being read.

In his lecture on Dostoevsky, Nabokov portrays the relationship between works of art and real life as both isomorphic and mimetic. From the point of view of the creator, it is isomorphic: art is not subservient to life, but as long as we accept the comparison of the author to God, it is analogous to it. This point is both traditional and modernist, since Nabokov puts an equal accent on the divine qualities of authorship and the construction of the product: art is divine, but, like art, nature is "created."[5] However, from the point of view of the reader—or, to be more precise, from the point of view of the reader's emotional involvement—the relationship between art and life is that of a copy to an original: life is real, while art is a construction and can be enjoyed precisely because it is make-believe.

The reader's emotional response—however vaguely Nabokov defines it—is where Nabokov's aesthetics merge with ethics. Earlier in the lecture, Nabokov makes a distinction between sentimentality and sensitivity as two human qualities in which an aesthetic element becomes the source for ethical (or unethical) judgments and actions. A sensitive man, says Nabokov, "is never a cruel person";[6] sentimentality, on the other hand, has been the trait of many a dictator. It is sentimentality, imprudently taken up by Dostoevsky from Western sentimental and gothic fiction, combined with religious exaltation that, in Nabokov's view, makes Dostoevsky's prose ethically inferior (102–3). Sentimentality lacks discernment, and Nabokov attributes Dostoevsky's ethical inadequacy to his aesthetic shortcomings, his resort to *poshlost* in order to wrench from his reader a viscerally compassionate response.

It is hard to say whether Nabokov advocates moderation in art because it affords us an emotional distance from which our study of life can become more subtle and discerning or because such moderation simply increases the effect of verisimilitude, allowing the reader to more easily accept Nabokov's deceptive realism. His famous statement on the moral value of *Lolita*—and fiction in general—in the novel's afterword contains a definition of art in which "curiosity, tenderness, kindness" is followed by "ecstasy," which is hardly a state of restraint.[7] We might ultimately better understand Nabokov's criticism of Dostoevsky if we compare their diverging visions of art and its purpose. Dostoevsky's prose is explicitly mimetic, even if he is interested in expressions of *internal* life, that is, processes hidden from plain view. In Dostoevsky's art, the extraordinary manifestations of the laws and dynamics governing an individual's internal life—the fantastic quality of Dostoevsky's realism—are symptoms through which—and this is part of the artist's aim—he can reveal the spiritual disease that has engulfed the Russian intelligentsia of the late nineteenth century and then work out a cure that would stop it from turning into a nationwide and worldwide epidemic. For Nabokov, however, art plays a double function: it represents reality and, at the same time, has no outside referent, existing as an autonomous mechanism. Its representational function is part of the conjurer's legerdemain.

Without keeping in mind this double nature of Nabokov's art, it would be hard to make sense of his statements that both repudiate and recognize the humanity of his characters. Hence, in the afterword to *Lolita*, defending himself against the imagined charge of spending his time "among such depressing people" as his characters, Nabokov rejoins that "the only discomfort . . . [he] really experienced was to live in . . . [his] workshop among discarded limbs and unfinished torsos" (316). At the same time, as Brian Boyd reports: "Nabokov once said, Lolita came second in his list of those he admired most as people. Top of the list came Pnin, another courageous victim."[8] It would be hard to argue that the reputed humanity of Lolita or Pnin is just an effect of fiction, masterfully managed for the sake of the narrative audience and not grounded in their creator's emotional and ethical view of life.

The most common way of dealing with the tension contained within the double-tiered structure of Nabokov's works is to separate aesthetics and ethics and to designate the former as a function of the authorial audience and the latter as one of the narrative audience. Hence, Nabokov's validation of his characters' humanity is there to please those who tilt the balance toward the narrative audience; Nabokov's insistence that his prose lacks referentiality and purpose is for those who favor the authorial audience. The seesaw of criticism then aligns its readings either with the narrative or the authorial audience, or argues for the importance of maintaining the tension between them and between aesthetics and ethics.[9]

In his nonfiction writing, Nabokov clearly comes out on the side of the authorial audience. As he explains in "Good Readers and Good Writers," while a major writer combines the functions of a storyteller, a teacher, and an enchanter, "it is the enchanter in him that predominates and makes him a major writer."[10] The function of enchantment, however, is not there to trick the reader into suspending disbelief and giving in to the pleasures of verisimilitude. On the contrary, enchantment is all rhetoric and zero veracity: in order to grasp the "individual magic of [the writer's] genius," continues Nabokov, we must "study the style, the imagery, the pattern of his novels or poems" (5–6).

Yet, if we are to accept Nabokov's instruction to shift our reading focus from the realistic layer of the text (narrative audience) to its aesthetic dimension (authorial audience), are we obliged to accept a concomitant dismissal of any ethical inquiry into his prose? In other words, what is our responsibility for the work of fiction once the suspension of disbelief wears thin? For Rabinowitz, who put the division of audiences into theoretical circulation, the relationship between the two poles is straightforward: "It would seem that the greater the distance between authorial and narrative audiences (the less realistic the novel in our new definition), the less impact a moral lesson learned by the narrative audience is likely to have on the authorial audience."[11] In his nonfiction writing, Nabokov often takes positions that contradict each other on this matter, but for the most part he resists any and all attempts to assign a moral lesson to his prose. In his fiction, however, matters are more ambiguous, and the neat division between authorial audience and narrative audience—as well as between aesthetics and ethics—is not as easy to uphold.

ON WRITING AND TRANSLATION

The passage to which I turn next is an excellent example of such ambiguity. It comes from *Bend Sinister*, arguably one of Nabokov's most political texts, and is lodged within chapter 7, which at first glance has little to do with the novel's preoccupation with politics. In fact, most of this chapter is a meditation on decidedly apolitical subjects: Krug comes to Ember, and the two proceed to discuss Ember's indignation at having to advise on the state's

The Dangers of Aesthetic Bliss

production of *Hamlet* and then his own translation of the play. It is true that, in part, their conversation addresses the effects of the state's control of artistic production: hence, Ember's complaint that the production of *Hamlet* has been corrupted by the nationalistic and racist "study" of the play by the appropriately named Professor Hamm, whose conception the state adopts as official.[12] The real hero of Hamm's *Hamlet* is Fortinbras; the book's embrace of the active and victorious warrior instead of the indecisive prince is the reason behind the state's interest in producing the play.[13] Still, Hamm's reading is "balanced" by another take on the play, this one by an American film director whom Krug meets on a train in the United States. Playing one vulgarity off against another, Nabokov's point—at least on the surface—is quite clear: stretching the play in search of "thrills" or forcibly compressing it into a political allegory is equally Procrustean.[14] Submission, which Krug a bit later identifies as the necessary precondition for any translation, is clearly not an operative principle in either of these translations for the stage or screen. To force the play into the vise of mass appeal, whether the masses are crass American moviegoers or the ideologically set-up victims of an authoritarian dictatorship, is to inevitably corrupt its meaning.[15] Among the possible evils that threaten art, bad politics does not necessarily stand out. Krug and Ember parody these (mis)interpretations of *Hamlet* and amuse themselves by proposing their own takes on the play, which are no less preposterous. Then, Ember reads aloud excerpts from his own translation of *Hamlet*; these are interrupted by Krug's meditations on the nature of translation:

> As he sits listening to Ember's translation, Krug cannot help marveling at the strangeness of the day. . . . He listened to the rich-toned voice (Ember's father had been a Persian merchant) and tried to simplify the terms of his reaction. Nature had once produced an Englishman whose domed head had been a hive of words; a man who had only to breathe on any particle of his stupendous vocabulary to have that particle live and expand and throw out tremulous tentacles until it became a complex image with a pulsing brain and correlated limbs. Three centuries later, another man, in another country, was trying to render these rhythms and metaphors in a different tongue. This process entailed a prodigious amount of labour, for the necessity of which no real reason could be given. It was as if someone, having seen a certain oak tree (further called Individual T) growing in a certain land and casting its own unique shadow on the green and brown ground, had proceeded to erect in his garden a prodigiously intricate piece of machinery which in itself was as unlike that or any other tree as the translator's inspiration and language were unlike those of the original author, but which, by means of ingenious combinations of parts, light effects, breeze-engendering engines, would, when completed, cast a shadow exactly similar to that of Individual T—the same out-

line, changing in the same manner, with the same double and single spots of suns rippling in the same position, at the same hour of the day. From a practical point of view, such a waste of time and material (those headaches, those midnight triumphs that turn out to be disasters in the sober light of the morning!) was almost criminally absurd, since the greatest masterpiece of imitation presupposed a voluntary limitation of thought, in submission to another man's genius. Could this suicidal limitation and submission be compensated by the miracle of adaptive tactics, by the thousand devices of shadography, by the keen pleasure that the weaver of words and their witness experienced at every wile in the warp, or was it, taken all in all, but an exaggerated and spiritualized replica of Paduk's writing machine?[16]

Krug's thoughts are not quite on writing and, since the novel emphasizes Krug's fictionality, they are not quite Nabokov's either; nor are they necessarily endorsed by the narrator of the novel, "an anthropomorphic deity." The space created here—between translation and writing, but also between character, narrator, and author—is part of the complex interplay of proximity and distancing that Nabokov is staging in this chapter. All this has a direct bearing on our discussion of Nabokov's narrative ethics.

To start with, Krug's thoughts on translation in the passage above have numerous similarities to Nabokov's statements on literature in his lecture on Dostoevsky. The affinity between this passage and the lecture lies in the sets of relationships each constructs: between the work of art and reality in Nabokov's lecture, and between the translation and original in Krug's reflections. Krug stresses the constructedness of translation (it is a complex mechanism built by the translator), its goal being elsewhere (in the shadow thrown by the mechanism rather than the mechanism itself), and the exact identity between the effect of the original work (the shadow of the oak tree) and the effect of the translation (the shadow thrown by the mechanism). Compare this to the points made by Nabokov in his Dostoevsky lecture: literature is a construction (its deaths are illusory), yet it deceives us into thinking otherwise (part of us believes in the deft illusion) and requires the participation of the reader. Similarly, Krug portrays translation as an act of *mimetic* creation (even as the task of representation is shifted onto the shadow of the tree), while the original work—*Hamlet*—simply exists as a living organism ("a certain oak tree").

In Krug's analogy, the boundary between writing and translation, between emanation and representation, is purposefully blurred, as the original itself is announced to be a product of "Nature." Krug begins by imagining Shakespeare, whose "domed head" houses "a hive of words" and whose breath enlivens "any particle of his stupendous vocabulary." Hence, Shakespeare appears as both a living organism *and* nature's artifact, and as such, the initial position of *Hamlet* as original to the translation's copy becomes ambiguous. The double nature of Nabokov's art that we discussed above is preserved here, since Shakespeare is said to be a product of Nature, yet he possesses a divine attribute, namely, the ability to breathe life into words. Finally, form performs content here as Krug's description undertakes the very action he ascribes to Shakespeare, as the particles of Krug's depiction also "expand and throw out tremulous tentacles until it [becomes] a complex image with a pulsing brain and correlated limbs." The domed head housing a hive of words metamorphoses into the dome of an oak tree, whose branches take the place of "tremulous tentacles." As the passage progresses, the original image grows and transforms: Shakespeare becomes both a metonym and a metaphor for his works, *Hamlet* in particular. But, just as the distinction between the functions of contiguity and comparison becomes unstable here, so too does the initial difference between the translation and the original. The repeated stress on complexity in Krug's portrayal of Shakespeare and in his description of the mechanism of translation, underscoring the constructedness of both, strengthens this effect.

Obscuring the difference between writing and translation works both ways: the translation acquires the features of the original work of art, while art may now be seen as a secondary or derived product. This process ultimately includes Nature, which is seen here as a creator comparable to both artist and translator: Nature creates with organic matter, and the artist/translator creates with inorganic matter. This *mise-en-abyme* effect generates a series of structures that are simultaneously independent of one another while existing in a relationship of mimetic tension—Nature is to Shakespeare what Shakespeare is to *Hamlet* and what *Hamlet* is to its translation. Each is concurrently similar to and different from the others. In this passage, where form is indistinguishable from content, Nabokov creates the image of an *organic mechanism* that gives birth to another mechanism whose function is identical to the original and which—through this act of creation—becomes part of the original mechanism, and so on. The power of this image is intensified by Krug's insistence that the creator's goal should not be the object itself but its shadow. The shadow, however, is more than a placeholder for the final goal of the translation: in accordance with the complex rhetorical economy of this passage, it enters into the interplay of its tropes. Inasmuch as its exact replication constitutes the goal of the translation, the shadow becomes the marker of identity between the original and the copy. At the same time, it also functions as a metaphor of difference, indicating the loss incurred between the original and its translation. Finally, the shadow can be seen as a metaphor of deception, once again indicating the inherent constructedness of what we assume to be an authentic creation.

Nabokov's own criteria for a successful translator similarly blur the difference between original and translation. Thus, in "The Art of Translation" Nabokov requires of the translator "as much talent, or at least the same kind of talent as the author that he chooses."[17] Most importantly, the translator's task appears to be not so different from the artist's; the translator must "possess the gift of mimicry and be able to act, as it were, the real author's part, by impersonating his tricks, demeanor and speech, his ways and his mind, with the utmost degree of verisimilitude" (319–20). The qualities of mimicry and deception unite all three: nature, artist, and translator. As Boyd reports, Nabokov told his mother in 1925 that writers were "translators of God's creation, his little plagiarists and imitators, [who] dress up what he wrote, as a charmed commentator sometimes gives an extra grace to a line of genius."[18]

Krug clearly inherits the notion of the deceptive quality of art—which signifies the simultaneous constructedness and originality of the artistic product—from his own creator, who in "Good Readers and Good Writers" insists that Nature is yet another version of an anthropomorphic deity. Its acts and processes are analogous to those employed by writers of fiction: "Every great writer is a great deceiver, but so is that arch-cheat Nature. Nature always deceives. From the simple deception of propagation to the prodigiously sophisticated illusion of protective colors in butterflies or birds, there is in Nature a marvelous system of spells and wiles."[19] The *mise en abyme* effect through which original and translation are seen as receding reflections of each other is similarly picked up in Nabokov's discussion of the ever-elusive nature of reality in this 1972 interview:

> What is that reality? Reality is a very subjective affair. I can only define it as a kind of gradual accumulation of information; and as specialization. If we take a lily, for instance, or any other kind of natural object, a lily is more real to a naturalist than it is to an ordinary person. But it is still more real to a botanist. And yet another stage of reality is reached with that botanist who is a specialist in lilies. You can get nearer and nearer, so to speak, to reality; but you never get near enough because reality is an infinite succession of steps, levels of perception, false bottoms, and hence unquenchable, unattainable. You can know more and more about one thing but you can never know everything about one thing: it's hopeless.[20]

In this passage, Nabokov underscores the ultimate subjectivity of perception.[21] As a tool for approximating reality, art invariably carries a double function: it is both an act of pure creation and a human product. It functions as an instrument through which the artist undertakes the search for reality, and yet it is the very thing that separates him from its attainment.

In other words, art retains the mark of sacrality that upholds its status as an autonomous, self-contained entity, while simultaneously announcing its secondariness and lack of authenticity. It is both an original *and* a translation. For Krug, whether or not this is an aporetic duality in which each of the elements is incompatible with the other remains an open question. After all, there is nothing that guarantees the presence of reality—even if it is unattainable—behind the innumerable veils of deception. In Krug's conceptualizations, the translator's unquestionable obedience to the task of "imitation" carries the risk that it will be nothing but that.

Krug's anxiety materializes at the end of the passage as he compares the translator to a "spiritualized replica of Paduk's writing machine."[22] The similarity between the description of the padograph and the translator's labor, in Krug's account of it, is no doubt intentional:

> You supplied the inventor with numerous specimens of your penmanship, he would study the strokes and the linkage, and then turn out your individual padograph. The resulting script copied exactly the average "tone" of your handwriting while the minor variations of each character were taken care of by the several keys serving each letter. Punctuation marks were carefully diversified within the limits of this or that individual manner, and such details as spacing and what experts call "clines" were so rendered as to mask mechanical regularity. (69)

In describing the padograph, the narrator does not cease to stress the averageness and the ultimate lack of depth in both the padograph ("Although, of course, a close examination of the script never failed to reveal the presence of a mechanical medium" [69]) and its users ("one purchaser after another enjoyed the luxury of seeing the essence of his incomplex personality distilled by the magic of an elaborate instrument" [69]). For Krug, however, the risk lies not so much in the creation of an inferior artistic product, but in a potential inability to discern the difference between the two practices, which are both dependent on the suppression of freedom. The total submission of the translator—what Krug calls a "suicidal" erasure of individuality in the service of the task—feels uncomfortably close to the obedience that the tyrant demands from his subjects.

The stress on the translator's unconditional surrender to the authority of the original points to Krug's awareness that the practice of translation and, by extension, of art inevitably involves a distribution of power and a construction of social hierarchies and, as such, becomes a likely site of tension and struggle. Nabokov proceeds to clinch the idea that the relationships between author and text, or translator and translation, or author and reader carry ethical and political significance. Krug's anxious meditations over the balance of power in artistic production and its possible consequences are

Chapter Four

immediately followed by Ember's apprehensive conferral of authority upon his friend: "'Do you like it, do you accept it?' asked Ember anxiously" (120).

Pointing out the link between the politics of the novel and its aesthetics, Eric Naiman argues that *Bend Sinister* "most conclusively establishes an affinity between totalitarianism and art."[23] He similarly sees Krug's definition of the translator's task as an allegory of the creative process but interprets Krug's apprehension about the translator's wasted efforts ("such a waste of time and material") as Nabokov's inscription of his own anxieties about the autonomy—and uselessness—of art. In Naiman's argument, *Bend Sinister* becomes Nabokov's experiment in taking two of the most important principles of his own creative practice to their logical conclusion. Naiman observes that in the novel, "authorial control and uselessness" find their representation as "totalitarianism and excrement" (70). I agree with his insight that, for Nabokov, poetics is not separate from hermeneutics and should neither be omitted from the discussion of Nabokov's ethics and politics, nor, conversely, become a prooftext of his unambivalent embrace of individual freedom. At the same time, while preoccupied with correcting the overzealous efforts of Nabokov critics who see the novel—and Nabokov's artistic efforts in general—as a paean to art's resistance to ideology, Naiman too easily swerves to the opposite extreme and simplifies the complex treatment of power relations that make up Nabokov's aesthetics in the novel. What Naiman misses is the deep contradictions inherent in Nabokov's aesthetics, which simultaneously affirm art's authenticity *and* lack of originality, reject mimesis *and* depend on it, and assert the complete autonomy of its medium *and* insist on submission to a higher power.

CORRUPTION AND INTERRUPTION: LANGUAGE IN *BEND SINISTER*

In chapter 7 of *Bend Sinister*, the Shakespeare chapter, all these contradictions manifest themselves both thematically (through the development of the theme of language as an ambiguous tool whose use can bring about both freedom and subjugation) and architectonically (by focusing the reader's attention on the power dynamic between the different subjectivities in the novel). Almost free of plot (except for Ember's brutal arrest at the end), the Shakespeare chapter asks the reader to attend to the formal designs of the text and the ethical costs incurred in structuring discursive relationships in the novel. Hence it becomes a stage on which the novel's ethics and politics are performed. Together, the chapter's thematics—from the narrator's discussions of Shakespeare, to the different takes on *Hamlet*, and then to the excerpts of various translations of the play—and its architectonics indicate

The Dangers of Aesthetic Bliss

Nabokov's acute awareness of the ethical nature of the experience of narrative prose and the responsibilities to which this experience calls those who participate in it.

While at first glance the *Hamlet* conversation between Krug and Ember may seem like a short-lived refuge that the two find from the intrusions of the state, a careful reading reveals deep correspondences between the social relations instituted in Padukgrad and those that exist among the authorial figure, the narrator, and the characters. This connection between the novel's content and its form becomes especially apparent if we consider that Ember's removal from his apartment at the end of the chapter by Hustav and his "henchwoman" Mrs. Bachofen prefigures Krug's extraction from the end of the novel by its authorial agent, the anthropomorphic deity. What shocks the most is the ease with which each act is performed. The complete collapse of Ember's life happens just as suddenly and quickly as the collapse of the diegetic world of the novel when the authorial figure contrives to save his protagonist. The special position of chapter 7 in the novel, its obvious dramatic quality, enhanced by the narrator's stage directions throughout, and the promptness with which Ember disappears from its "set" all attest to the terrifyingly obvious correlation between political tyranny and art: Paduk's regime deals with its subjects as if they were characters in a novel.

Reinforcing the parallelism between the discursive dynamics of the novel and the ones that sustain Paduk's totalitarian state is the structural linkage between the narrator's surplus of vision vis-à-vis the characters and the state's mechanisms of surveillance. Krug's remark about the undercover police agents, who appear disguised as organ-grinders ("They do not play but they do glance upwards"),[24] as well as his observation about the similar direction of the gaze of the Padukgrad clergy ("I know of only one other profession . . . that has that upward movement of the eyeballs" [121]), points to vision/surveillance as an important operative faculty in the construction of Padukgrad's subjects. But if the totalitarian hierarchy of Paduk's state is revealed through vision (directed upward), the same hierarchy is manifested in the authorial figure, the self-announced deity of the novel, who watches *his* subjects from on high: "and the secret spectator (some anthropomorphic deity for example) surely would be amused by the shape of human heads seen from above" (147).[25] In chapter 7, Krug and Ember might have found an escape—even if a temporary one—from the nightmarish reality of the state; this, however, only highlights their constant supervision by the authorial consciousness.

Such an analogy between the authorial and totalitarian modes of control is in line with Naiman's argument. Still, Nabokov's prose resists strict allegorizing, and *Bend Sinister* is no exception. Nabokov does indeed make a connection between artistic and political control, but a closer look at the relationship between the narrator and the characters in the Shakespeare chapter points to a crucial difference between an artist and a tyrant, no matter how provocatively tempting this comparison might seem. This difference aligns with the one that Krug believes to exist between the padograph and a translation. And it is this difference, as I hope to show, that constitutes the kernel of Nabokov's *narrative ethics*.

While the direct object of the chapter is Krug and Ember's discussion of *Hamlet* and its translations, Nabokov's handling of it is much more self-aware. From the chapter's very beginning, Nabokov continually drives home the point that the semantic scope of any verbal utterance can never be neutral; it is inevitably open to subjective distortion and perversion. The importance for Nabokov of this seemingly simple notion emerges if we consider once again the multivalence of the "shadow" metaphor with which he defines the effect of art. An intangible product of matter, shadows exist in between surfaces; likewise, the goal of art lies outside the text itself and is rooted in the reader's engagement with it. Moreover, shadows lack stability and permanence—submerged in the flow of time, they are inevitably susceptible to change. Likewise, language, Nabokov insists, can never be abstract and is always submerged in history—or rather, history itself can be understood as the strata of discursive statements, each of which exists in a state of dynamic tension with the previous one, trying to incorporate, add to, or annul it. By making the reader cognizant of how the numerous voices in the Shakespeare chapter interact with one another, Nabokov puts into practice his beliefs about the ever-elusive true nature of reality—so elusive, in fact, that we can only contend with our different takes on it. Any attempt to capture reality discursively will always fall short, since, as Krug suggests, language is already a translation, a shadow with an absent referent.

Hence, in the chapter, language is depicted as an ambiguous instrument that searches for presence but is only able to announce absence. To emphasize this point, Nabokov frames the chapter with two absences, one at each end: Olga's in the beginning and Ember's at the end (with Krug's announcement of the Maximovs' arrest in between). The pun with which the narrator introduces the chapter's two main themes ("The Shakespearean one rendered in the *present*" and "Olga's monstrous *absence*")[26] is the first indication of the way language is going to function here—as a presence that can neither compensate for Olga's death nor even adequately render the emotional extent of her absence. Words seem lacking in contrast to action; as the narrator explains, Ember's awkwardness in the face of Krug's tragedy only showcases "a miserable defeat in the case of philosophers and poets accustomed to believe that words are superior to deeds" (106). Nor can the chapter's tenuous *present* prepare the characters for the horror that is about to occur in their immediate *future*—Ember's arrest. Noticeably, the narrator's statement about the deficiency of words vis-à-vis action is echoed by Hustav, who parodies the idea by contrasting philosophy and poetry with pure physicality: "Poetry and philosophy must brood, while beauty and strength—your apartment is nicely heated, Mr. Ember" (127).

At the same time, even while language is shown to be inferior to action (inasmuch as Olga's death can be seen as an "act") and unable to prevent violence, it also becomes an instrument of ethical and political resistance. The conversation between Krug and Ember is one of the few instances in the novel where the characters are able to affirm—if only for a short time—their creative freedom against the regime and its official dogma. The affinities between political corruption in Shakespeare's Denmark and Padukgrad, as well as between Hamlet and Krug, are not accidental.[27] Ultimately, the dialogue carried on by the two friends about Shakespeare and his play can be seen as political resistance against Paduk's regime in the same way that Hamlet's *inaction* can be seen as a mode of resistance against the corruption of power in Denmark: the dialogue retards the plot progression, each knot of which is marked by the increasing violence of the state apparatus against Krug and his loved ones. Words might indeed be inadequate at uncovering the essence of reality or preventing natural (Olga) or human-inflicted (Ember, David) violence—the link between natural and political violence is underscored once again in the passage on translation: "Krug had recently lost his wife. A new political order had stunned the city"[28]—but words are all Ember and Krug have at the moment, and—seeing that Ember is about to perish in one of Padukgrad's prisons—words are all that these two will ever have again. The distance between the narrator's acceptance of the inadequacy of language and Hustav's perverse affirmation of physical strength's superiority over words confirms the ambiguous status of language in this chapter: it corrupts—but it also creates communion.

The Shakespearean theme proper begins by announcing Shakespeare to be one of the most talented practitioners of language *and* a symbol of that elusive truth which language fails to grasp—the goal of the human quest is not the discovery of truth but the search for it. The distorted quote from the book of Proverbs, which the narrator attributes to Shakespeare, testifies to the same sentiment: "The person who said (not for the first time) that the glory of God is to hide a thing, and the glory of man is to find it" (106).[29]

The theme of the receding original is heralded by the narrator's speculations about Shakespeare's real identity, and the chapter starts with the narrator having fun with the Francis Bacon-as-Shakespeare theory. Just as with the layers of interpretations and translations of *Hamlet* later on, the narrator's focus here is the verbal sedimentation deposited throughout history, the recorded traces that both point to the original and deviate from it. The playwright's name itself is a product of history, hence "Shakespeare" appears only in its variable forms here ("Shaxpere" and "Shagspere"), stressing the notion that any record is going to be mediated by human presence, a double and a translation, in place of the authentic original: "He begets doubles at every corner. His penmanship is unconsciously faked by lawyers who happen to write a similar hand" (106; notice again the veiled reference to writing corrupted by the padograph).[30] It is quite telling that the only time the name "Shakespeare" appears in the chapter is when it is voiced by the representatives of the regime, Dr. Hamm and Hustav, the literary hack and the policeman. In the case of Hamm, at least, such adherence to the "standard" form of the spelling becomes a symptom not only of the exploitation of the name (and, by extension, the art) of Shakespeare in the service of politics, but also of the pretense that one can arrive at a definitive interpretation of the play, an idea that is antithetical to the understanding of art as a shadow, a translation.

Language inevitably breeds doubles; it veils truth as it attempts to grasp it, if only because it is uttered by subjects whose vision is by definition limited. The obvious consequence of this idea is verbal pollution and excess. Not surprisingly, Hamm's vision of an uncorrupted Denmark includes his (and the state's) desire to cleanse language of any ambiguity: *"verbum sine ornatu"*—the reduction of language's complexity to the point where it becomes "intelligible to man and beast alike, and accompanied by fit action."[31] The critique of Hamm's position implies that the word inflicts the most violence when it insists on the incorruptibility and authenticity of its message.[32] In contrast, the chapter advances the notion of the word as ornate and "protean" (yet another fittingly chosen epithet for Shakespeare and his art), whose meaning changes according to its historical context and its speaker. The chapter develops the motif of Shakespeare's protean art as Krug and Ember elaborate on the river theme and portray Ophelia as a "rivermaid," "a mermaid of Lethe, a rare water serpent, *Russalka letheana* of science."[33] The theme indirectly lends itself to the idea that art thrives on the multivalence and fluidity of meanings; to insist that an objective and singular interpretation of the work of art is possible is useless at best and potentially dangerous. The recognition that any verbal expression can only approximate the truth becomes the foundation of Nabokov's narrative ethics in the novel; it is also what separates the anthropomorphic deity of the novel from the tyrant of Padukgrad.

Hence, instead of the "correct" reading of *Hamlet*, the chapter presents different misreadings of the play by Hamm and the American movie director, which are then, in turn, taken up by Ember and Krug, who adopt Hamm's interpretative methods and push them toward absurdity.[34] Two wrongs make a very particular right here, since the difference between the two approaches is not simply a matter of intent but of one's attitude toward language—which in the case of Ember and Krug includes an awareness of

The Dangers of Aesthetic Bliss

language's inherent ambiguities. While the novel clearly identifies Hamm's interpretation as perverse, the status of the American film director's ideas on how to turn *Hamlet* into a film is more ambiguous.[35] Reporting them to Ember, Krug is able to divert his friend's attention from the increasing misery of their lives under the new regime. While making fun of the crude literalness of the filmmaker's approach, Krug's account also initiates a round of scintillating and intentionally absurd insights into *Hamlet* between the two friends. The only purpose of the linguistic games the two conduct with such virtuosic irreverence is the pleasure of the game itself, and for a short while Ember is able to forget about the unhappiness outside. Yet, in the end, the whole exercise proves to be palliative at best, and the fantasy of art's autonomy is broken here by the novel's insistence on its untenability. Krug and Ember's private realm is decidedly not airtight and cannot shield the two from the inevitable intrusions of the state, just as Krug's dreams and private fantasies cannot adequately protect him from the reality of Olga's death. By the time Paduk's agents invade Ember's apartment at the end of the chapter, similar invasions of reality have already occurred on the level of Ember's consciousness, as thoughts about the state's production of the play interrupt the fun the two are having and, eventually, put a stop to it. This, again, underscores the correspondence between the political conflict on the level of content and the tension that exists among the different discursive layers in the chapter.

With each consecutive take on *Hamlet*, Nabokov intensifies the effect of this layering but also exposes language as a site of struggle. Krug and Ember's games are obviously parodic and seek to restore justice to the play by intensifying (hence, ridiculing) the "verbal plague" that Nabokov in his introduction to the novel identifies as paronomasia. Yet, whether such a reductio ad absurdum is enough to serve as protection from "the contagious sickness" of paronomasia or whether Krug and Ember's sincere enjoyment of it betrays their own weakness for its pleasures remains open to interpretation.[36] After all, when accepting that paronomasia is the most direct manifestation of a triumph of form over content, we should similarly recognize it as an appropriate emblem of verbal aesthetics. Even setting aside Nabokov's own predilection for linguistic acrobatics, we need to acknowledge that the distinction between the language *in* the novel and the language *of* the novel is unstable at best.[37] Once again, language in the chapter reveals itself to be ethically ambiguous. Paradoxically, while the formal functions of language are proclaimed to be signs of ideological perversity, it is the formal mastery of the authorial figure that purports to protect the novel's protagonists from the ideological menace of Ekwilism. This point is crucial to the novel's final twist, since, while for Krug and especially for Ember, the superiority of aesthetics over politics fails to provide sufficient protection from the crude force of the

Chapter Four

regime, it is by declaring the novel to be nothing but an aesthetic artifact that the author secures his control over the fate of the novel's protagonist.

The same indeterminacy is found in the excerpts of different translations of *Hamlet*, each of which stresses not only the distance between the translation and the original but also the inherent ambiguity of language: the gains and losses that, in accordance with the rest of the chapter, accompany any utterance.[38] With each consecutive translation the original becomes less and less discernible:

> But enough of this, let us hear Ember's rendering of some famous lines:
>> *Ubit' il' ne ubit'? Vot est' oprosen.*
>> *Vto bude edler: v rasume tzerpieren*
>> *Ogneprashchi i strely zlovo roka—*
>
> (or as a Frenchman might have it:)
>> *L'égorgerai-je ou non? Voici le vrai problème.*
>> *Est-il plus noble en soi de supporter quand même*
>> *Et les dards et le feu d'un accablant destin—*
>
> Yes, I am still jesting. We now come to the real thing.
>> *Tam nad ruch'om rostiot naklonno iva,*
>> *V vode iavliaia list'ev sedinu;*
>> *Guirliandy fantasticheskie sviv*
>> *Iz etikh list'ev—s primes'u romashek,*
>> *Krapivy, lutikov—*
>
>> (Over yon brook there grows aslant a willow
>> Showing in the water the hoariness of its leaves;
>> Having tressed fantastic garlands
>> of these leaves, with a sprinkling of daisies,
>> Nettles, crowflowers—)
>
> You see, I have to choose my commentators.
>
> Or this difficult passage:
>
> *Ne dumaete-li Vy, sudar', shto vot eto* (the song about the wounded deer), *da les per'ev na shliape, da dve kamchatye rozy na proreznykh bashmakakh, mogli by, kol' fortuna zadala by mne turku, zasluzhit' mne uchast'e v teatralnoi arteli; a, sudar'?*
>
> Or the beginning of my favourite scene: . . .[39]

The effect of "layering" that I mentioned earlier abounds here. It is achieved not only by the unclear boundaries between the translation and the original but also by the increasingly complicated relationship between the different voices present here. Does the first excerpt (*"Ubit' il' ne ubit'?"*) belong to Ember, and is the second (*"L'égorgerai-je ou non?"*) the corrupted French version of the original English? In the novel's introduction, Nabokov is quite clear on this point:

> Ember . . . gives his friend a sample of the three first lines of Hamlet's soliloquy (Act III, Scene I) translated into the vernacular (with a pseudo-scholarly interpretation of the first phrase taken to refer to the contemplated killing of Claudius, i.e., "is the murder to be or not to be?"). He follows this up with a Russian version of part of the Queen's speech in Act IV, Scene VII (also not without a built-in scholium) and a splendid Russian rendering of the prose passage in Act III, Scene II, beginning, 'Would not this, Sir, and a forest of feathers . . .'" (xvi)

In the text of the novel proper, however, determining who says what becomes increasingly less clear. The narrator's use of "still" in "I am still jesting" implies that the speaker is the same as in the narrator's direct address to the reader right before the excerpt and that the joke at the expense of "pseudo-scholars" is indeed his, not Ember's, although there is still the possibility that this is really Ember's voice and the jesting refers to his and Krug's previous ridiculing, especially if we take into account the loose punctuation that precedes this statement. The recognizable Russian (*"Ubit' il' ne ubit'"*) in this version of Hamlet's monologue is a paronomastic pun on (and an almost complete semantic inversion of) the original. The introduction states that this is a continuation of Ember's (or is it the narrator's?) mockery of overzealous readers like Hamm: "a pseudo-scholarly interpretation" in the guise of a translation (xvi).[40] Yet, since the punning (*to be—ubit'* or *byt'—ubit'*) exists only in Russian (or, supposedly, in that "mongrel blend of Slavic and Germanic" spoken in Padukgrad), it must follow that the French is, in fact, a translation of a translation and, moreover, one that translates Hamlet's monologue into an existent language from a nonexistent one.

Furthermore, the translation from Act IV, Scene VII that the narrator promises to finally be "the real thing" is written in Russian with Latin characters. The novel's introduction attests to as much ("He follows this up with a Russian version of part of the Queen's speech in Act IV, Scene VII" [xvi]).[41] Still, the purpose of all this remains unclear, as well as whether this is indeed Nabokov's Russian or Ember's rendering of "the colloquial Russian" spoken in Padukgrad.[42] To make matters even more complex, we have Nabokov's translation of this same passage from 1930 that differs substan-

Chapter Four

tially (but not necessarily in quality) from the one offered here.[43] We cannot say with certainty whose version we have here: Ember's or the narrator's. If it is the latter, can we surmise that we have an example here of Nabokov's conscious distancing of himself from "the anthropomorphic deity" of the novel? Whether or not Nabokov is simply following editorial convention by printing the Russian in the Latin alphabet, this introduces yet another kind of distortion that involves an interplay between the visual form (the Latin script) and the "audible" content (the Russian). On the one hand, the translation, whose meaning might be incomprehensible to the English-language reader, invites her to experience the foreign without *translating* it. This creates a vertigo effect—the English-language reader is prompted to read the translation as if it were an original. On the other hand, retaining the Latin alphabet for the translation offers the *shadow* of the original. The translation of the translation into English that immediately follows intensifies still more the effect of ambiguity created by this simultaneous toing and froing by introducing yet another layer: do we understand this as a literal translation of the Russian that precedes it? In that case, its appearance further confirms the Russian as the likely original. Or, since the English prose rendering is, after all, a *double translation*, are we to see this as an indicator of the irreducible distance that *any* translation travels from the original, the corruption that *any* translation imposes on a poetic text? The absence of the original (*Shakespeare's* "original"!) is emblematic here; all we are left to contend with is an interplay of distortions and shadows.

Through the various layers and types of misinterpretations and mistranslations, the chapter creates the effect of a nonexistent (or at least inaccessible) original. That the original passage itself is so well known increases the sense of deliberateness with which Nabokov is operating here. In his introduction to the novel, Nabokov connects form to politics by explaining away the series of translation distortions as one of the symptoms of the political regime of Padukgrad: "Problems of translation, fluid transitions from one tongue to another, semantic transparencies yielding layers of receding or welling sense are as characteristic of Sinisterbad as are the monetary problems of more habitual tyrannies."[44] The reader's knowledge of the original, in this case, and her ability to measure the level of deviation from it turn each attempt at translation into a (pseudo)commentary on the text, what Nabokov calls "a built-in scholium" (xvi), which in turn requires its own commentary in order to be properly understood (provided by the introduction), and so on. Yet, even if we agree that a translation—which successfully hides and corrupts the original instead of revealing it—is a by-product of tyranny, we still have to ask whether or not Nabokov's intention here is to make the reader aware that the bend sinister is emblematic not only of Padukgrad but of art in general, and that tyranny—as the unlawful usurpation of power by the hands of a ruler—is a constituent feature of any artistic production.

Here too, however, we can see that the function of the *Hamlet* translations is laden with the same ambiguity in Nabokov's conception of language that I discussed earlier. The inaccessibility of the original elevates its status to a sacred object, a linguistic taboo, protected by layers of masks. Hence, another goal of the translations is not so much to allow the reader to get close to the original but to signal the insurmountable distance that exists between them.

Almost twenty years after *Bend Sinister*, in his translation of *Eugene Onegin*, Nabokov explained his choice of the literal mode of translation over the paraphrastic and lexical ones in terms that are strikingly similar to Krug's thoughts on translation. The goal of any translation should be the re-creation of the effect of the original; hence, the literal translation is meant to render "as closely as the associative and syntactical capacities of another language allow, the exact contextual meaning of the original."[45] "Only this," states Nabokov unequivocally, "is the true translation" (1: viii). What determines this choice is Nabokov's mistrust of the paraphrastic method, which betrays the original on both sides of the translator-reader divide, since it offers "a free version of the original with omissions and additions prompted by the exigencies of form, the conventions attributed to the consumer, and the translator's ignorance" (1: vii). A literal translation, however, aims to protect the original from abuse by either the subjective arbitrariness of the paraphrastic translator or the bowdlerizing taste of the consuming public. Hence, Krug validates the translator's task by advocating his or her submission to the authority of the original, just as Nabokov speaks of the sacrifices he had to make in order to remain faithful to Pushkin: "In fact, to my ideal of literalism I sacrificed everything (elegance, euphony, clarity, good taste, modern usage, and even grammar) that the dainty mimic prizes higher than truth" (1: x). Moreover, as Judson Rosengrant argues, to reproduce the effect of the original and convey its "contextual and connotative meaning," the literal translator has "to provide some sort of compensatory apparatus—a massive scholarly and linguistic commentary . . . in order to ensure the carrying over into the second language of as much as possible of the original text and context."[46] As Rosengrant convincingly demonstrates, however, even with the addition of the commentary, Nabokov, in his translation of Pushkin, "was not . . . able to reach his own austere but noble standard" (25).[47]

We can conjecture that, even as Nabokov chooses a different method, his aim in *Bend Sinister* is the same as in his translation of *Eugene Onegin*. Hiding the original Shakespeare under layers of paraphrastic attempts, Nabokov points to the inevitable distortion inherent in any act of translation. Just as in Nabokov's conceptualization of "reality," the original remains forever inaccessible. With each layer, the translation increases the distance from the original, while simultaneously conveying its complexity and untranslatability. "Fluid transitions from one tongue to another, semantic transparencies yielding layers of receding or welling sense" might very well be "characteristic of Sinisterbad," and yet they simultaneously act as a cover, safeguarding the integrity of the original and raising its status.[48]

The next instance of translation from *Hamlet*, from a "difficult passage" in Act III, Scene II, presents the reader with similar problems. The novel's introduction calls this bit "a splendid Russian rendering of the prose passage,"[49] and the translator's efforts here are similarly in line with the literalist Nabokov. Nevertheless, in the absence of any appropriate commentary, the outdated *"fortuna zadala mne turku,"* while purporting to re-create a comparable distance between the contemporary reader and the original ("if the rest of my fortunes turn Turk with me"), threatens to render the passage incomprehensible.

Importantly, Nabokov links the relationship between translation and original that he develops here to the relationship between narrator and characters and, finally, to the power dynamics present on the level of the novel's plot. The chapter's building blocks are interruptions and corruptions; hence, the narrator establishes his possession of the discourse by interrupting Krug and Ember's playful mockery: "But enough of this, let us hear Ember's rendering of some famous lines" (118). As I already mentioned, beginning with this first bit (*"Ubit' il' ne ubit'"*), it becomes increasingly difficult to hear Ember's voice from behind the voice of the narrator. Ultimately, the reader cannot with certainty tell whether the authorship of any part of either the commentary or the translation that follows belongs to Ember. It is clear that this is not free indirect discourse—an example of which occurs in Krug's contemplation on translation immediately following the translation sampling—but rather an instance of one voice absorbing or covering over the voice of another. The effect produced is the exact opposite of free indirect discourse: in the latter we expect to find a character's voice taking over the voice of narration, but here the voice of the narrator overpowers and replaces the voice of the character.

The force of this device becomes even stronger once we accept that Ember's translation might simply be muffled by the narrator's pouring out of samples. Yet, the narrator's control of discourse is not absolute or permanent. Just as the narrator finally decides to give the floor to Ember ("Or the beginning of my favourite scene: . . ."), Krug takes over: "As he sits listening to Ember's translation, Krug cannot help marveling at the strangeness of the day." Once again, Nabokov draws the reader's attention to the power dynamic between the voices present in the chapter by pointing out that Ember's voice might *not be strong enough* to be heard: "[Krug] listened to the rich-toned voice (Ember's father had been a Persian merchant) and tried to simplify the terms of his reaction."[50] Still, while Krug's meditation hides Ember's translation beneath it, his subsequent commentary on it shows that his attention is equally attuned to the passage in question: "'I think it is wonderful,' said Krug, frowning. He got up and paced the room. 'Some lines need oiling,' he continued, 'and I do not like the colour of dawn's coat—I see 'russet' in a less leathery, less proletarian way, but you may be right" (120). Krug's thoughts cover over Ember's voice, and yet they simultaneously reveal the presence of the original *in its absence*, just as the samples of translation by the narrator do earlier, in a strategy that turns out to be the main constructive principle of this chapter—a strategy that goes back to the two friends' attempts to hide Olga's unredeemable absence underneath their discussion of Shakespeare.

The weakness that makes Ember's *translating* voice inaudible is of special importance here, since it resonates with Krug's insistence that the translator's "submission to another man's genius" is a prerequisite for a successful result. As might be expected, Krug's thoughts are immediately followed by Ember's appeal—"'Do you like it, do you accept it?' asked Ember anxiously" (120), indicating that he submits to Krug's critical authority as well, and that perhaps his "submission" is to be understood more generally. The parallels between Ember's submission (consciously to Krug here and unawares to the narrator earlier) and his arrest are too strong to ignore. By having the muting of Ember's voice precede his final exit from the novel at the end of the chapter, Nabokov once again highlights the correspondence between the political hierarchy of Padukgrad and the hierarchy of relationships between the narrator and the characters.

Nabokov creates an association between the power relations established by Paduk's tyranny and those that exist among the various *voices* in the chapter by marking virtually all instances of the state's trespassing into the intimate space of Ember's apartment as *aural*. Hence, the regime makes its initial appearance in the guise of two organ-grinders who spy through Ember's windows. Krug's comment on the "absurd duality" of this "very emblem of oneness" can be read as an echo of his earlier thoughts on the tension between original and translation—and the danger of the latter becoming a mere copy of the former (121). Krug seems to be aware of this echo as well: "There is something familiar about the whole thing, something I cannot quite disentangle—a certain line of thought . . ." The unnecessary doubling of the organ-grinders is emblematic of their affiliation with the regime. This "politicized" superfluity can be traced back to the author's statements in the introduction on the political dimension of paronomasia, identified as verbal excess. Ember's suggestion that their silence is caused by their fear of competition and their seeming discomfort by "one of them butt[ing] into

Chapter Four

the other's beat" is similarly evocative of the earlier rivalry over translation samples during which the narrator "butts" into Ember's beat so successfully as to mute it completely (121). The entrance of Hustav and his secretary is likewise announced as a *phonic* invasion: "The remote sound of the doorbell interrupted him" (122). Ember's hypothesis about the reason behind his arrest is remarkable in this respect: "It is because I did not open my windows when those very loud speakers were on yesterday" (125). Needless to say, while mistaken in detail, Ember hits the nail on the head symbolically: the loudspeakers that threaten to forever block out any other speech are a perfect image for the violence of the state, whose official ideology seeks to overpower any individual's voice.

It is tempting to draw direct parallels between the voice of Ekwilism and the voice of the narrator: both are equally overpowering. Indeed, the results of the translation sampling and Hustav's visit are not that different: the former overtakes Ember's voice narratively, while the latter overtakes him physically, by removing his speaking body from the apartment and the novel. Yet, upon closer examination, it becomes evident that the real authority lies elsewhere and that the narrator's possession of it is not as fixed as it seems at first. While for the most part there is little to suggest that the entity which Nabokov refers to in the introduction as an "anthropomorphic deity impersonated by me" is not in full control of the novel, there are places where the narrator's authority is clearly not unconditional. Consider, for example, the following passage from the beginning of chapter 7:

> Describe the bedroom. Allude to Ember's bright brown eyes. Hot punch and a touch of fever. His strong shining blue-veined nose and the bracelet on his hairy wrist. Say something. Ask about David. Relate the horror of those rehearsals. (106)

This list of commands suggests that there is a certain organizing principle to the prose, a formal imperative that supersedes the seemingly absolute control of the narrator. The stance of the narrator here is also one of submission, and perhaps it is the recognition of his own limits that unites the narrator's voice in the last three sentences in the quote above with Ember's, which is clearly the "weakest link" in the chain of voices in the chapter. In another instance of the narrator's submission to the formal imperative, we encounter a complete reversal of the hierarchy when Ember's presence unmistakably overpowers the narrator's intentions: "So [Ember] prefers to talk shop. Last chance of describing the bedroom. Too late. Ember gushes. He exaggerates his own gushing manner" (107). Indeed, it is hardly accidental that the most powerful voice in the novel, that of the author-narrator, frequently exhibits its kinship with one of the weakest voices, the translator Ember's.

One of the most interesting "mergings" of the two consciousnesses occurs as Hustav affirms the state's domination over its subjects:

> "But this is ridiculous!" cried Ember, "I cannot just jump into my clothes. I must have a bath first, I must shave."
> "There is a barber at the nice quiet place you are going to," remarked the kindly Hustav. "Come, get up, you really must not be so disobedient."
> (How if I answer "no"?)
> "I refuse to dress while you are all staring at me," said Ember. (125–26)

On the one hand, here the narrator once again announces his presence *as a participating subject*, exposing the fictionality of the scene. On the other hand, since Hustav's order is addressed to Ember, the case can be made that the parenthetic attempt at resistance may belong to Ember as well. A third option would suggest that we have here an instance of the collective consciousness of Ember and the narrator. Unsettling the fixed hierarchy between the voices of narrator and characters, such shifts similarly disrupt the correspondence between the political dimension of the novel and the architectonics of the text. One of the reasons for the shifting locus of authority in the chapter could be that Nabokov preserves the ultimate seat of power for art itself, the transcendental signified that is both morally incorruptible (since it exceeds subjectivity) and apolitical, inasmuch as it renders any comparison between the tyranny of the state and the tyranny of the author invalid. Yet, whether or not the remark in parentheses—even if it does belong to the narrator—is solely rhetorical or indeed entertains a real alternative remains unclear. And can we question the validity of the formal imperative that allows the anthropomorphic deity to save the protagonist at the novel's end, but not his family or his best friend in the novel's middle portions? One is reminded here of Peter Brooks's argument that the movement of the plot is directed by its desire for the right death, avoiding the wrong deaths of the middle (see "Freud's Masterplot: A Model for Narrative" in Brooks's *Reading for the Plot: Design and Intention in Narrative*). In *Bend Sinister*, we have the choice of the right salvation over the wrong one, but the underlying plot structure still confirms Brooks's hypothesis. The recognition of the subconscious energies of the plot (which are similarly anthropomorphized in Brooks's argument) further challenges the authority of the novel's anthropomorphic deity. Moreover, the selection of framing imagery in the chapter strongly suggests that the formal imperative might not be able to completely transcend the novel's politics after all. Hence, the potential penetration of state propaganda (through the apartment's windows) and Hustav's entry into the apartment (through its doors) are clearly in a metaphoric relationship to the intrusion of plot into the otherwise plotless portion of the text, imply-

Chapter Four

ing once again that the forces governing the distribution of discourse in the novel and the novel's politics are interdependent.[51]

What drives this ambiguity in the power dynamic between the different voices of the chapter is a complex series of metonymic and metaphoric correspondences but also slippages between the voice of the narrator, who stands above the action of the novel, and the different voices within the narrative (including those of Krug and Ember, to be sure, but also of Paduk and his henchmen, the ideology of the regime, the Catholic Church, and so on). As a result, narrative discourse in *Bend Sinister* emerges as a site of tension and struggle, in which artistic control is governed by the same will to power that underlies Paduk's political tyranny. Yet, what separates the artist from the tyrant—and this, as I argued above, can be related to what distinguishes the translator from the padograph—is Nabokov's heightened awareness of how the wiles of artistic practice entangle its subjects and make them complicit with authority. In *Bend Sinister*, Nabokov endows language itself with an *ethical* function by defining it as an instrument by which a narrative subject seeks power. Awareness of the role that language plays in forging the novel's ethics does not allow the reader to escape its ethical bind and urges her to accept responsibility for the discursive violence of her own (interpretative) engagement with the text.

At the same time, however, there are several instances in the chapter in which the authorial figure's relationship to power is markedly different. These are the moments in which the narrator, instead of seeking narrative dominion over other characters, submits either to the voices of others or to the formal imperative of the prose. In general, in this chapter, submission—of either the translator to the original or of the artist to the aesthetic imperative of art—is shown to be an integral part of artistic practice and helps to establish a community held together by the same aesthetic (and political) sensibilities. Such is the communion between the philosopher and the translator, Krug and Ember. Submission, however, can also be seen as an act that reveals one's moral compass; it stands as a principle, adherence to which designates an awareness of the ethical demands of the prose and the acceptance of one's inevitable participation in the struggle for who controls discourse in the novel. Thus, the narrator's submission to the force of Ember's voice, allowing it—even if temporarily—to be heard over and against other discourses (political or personal) that seek to mute the subject, becomes an expression of the narrator's affinity with the victim. This submission introduces a relationship to power that is noticeably different from the one that enables the narrator to extract Krug from the novel at its closure.[52] The chain—established by the narrator's submission to Ember, who submits his translation efforts to Krug, while the latter confirms that the act of submission is the sine qua non of translation, with all three submitting to the

168

creative genius of Shakespeare, who in turn submits to the forces of nature, being like nature himself—institutes a community based on interdependence and mutual responsibility. Here the aesthetics and ethics of the novel come as close to each other as they ever will.

And yet the tension that informs the relationship among aesthetics, ethics, and politics in the novel ultimately remains in place. The question of whether submission to the formal imperative of the prose—even if it is understood as an act informed by the novel's narrative ethics—implies the abnegation of political resistance remains as unresolved as the question of the correspondence between narrative control and political oppression. As I have argued throughout this chapter, such indeterminacy can be traced back to Nabokov's complex conception of verbal art. This conception, on the one hand, stipulates that the energies forming relationships in life and art have an inevitable attraction toward each other and, on the other hand, asserts art's complete autonomy from life. Nabokov's narrative ethics, however, *can be* determined as the tension between the two poles of such a conceptualization: between control and submission, political resistance and ethical responsibility, authenticity and constructedness.

THE DELICATE BALANCE OF METALEPSIS

That Nabokov considered the use of metalepsis at the end of *Bend Sinister* to be of extraordinary significance is evident from a letter to Donald B. Alder in which he announced it to be "a device never yet attempted in literature."[53] Judging by his commentary to "The Vane Sisters" in 1959, some twelve years after the publication of *Bend Sinister*, metalepsis did not lose its power for Nabokov. As he writes to the readers of *Encounter*, "nothing of this kind has ever been attempted by any author" (286).[54] Nabokov once again confirms the singular power of the metaleptic gesture in his footnote to "The Vane Sisters" included in the collection *Tyrants Destroyed and Other Stories*: "this particular trick can be tried only once in a thousand years of fiction. Whether it has come off is another question."[55] In the short story, the metaleptic movement points in a direction opposite to the one in the novel: in *Bend Sinister*, the author descends into the world of his characters; while in "The Vane Sisters," the character invades the consciousness of the narrator. In the novel, the metalepsis is intentionally obvious, while in the story, its effect depends on its postponed discovery. Structurally, however, both instances perform a similar function: they direct the reader's attention to the presence of the text's metafictive plane as they break down its diegetic borders.

These two metaleptic moments can help us to appreciate the delicate balance in Nabokov's fiction between modernist and realist poetics. At one

Chapter Four

end, we sense Nabokov's apprehension over such an *explicit* use of the device in *Bend Sinister*: the intrusion of the "divine power"[56] may invalidate the integrity of the novel's character-driven diegetic world, with metalepsis turning it into all but a construction, a product of the author's rhetorical bag of tricks. At the other end, as in "The Vane Sisters," the danger lies in the metalepsis remaining undiscovered, even by Nabokov's most attentive readers. And yet, Nabokov's texts—at least his English-language ones—firmly insist on the existence of *both* planes—the diegetic and the extradiegetic—by peppering the prose with metaleptic traces, injecting the presence of the authorial figure into the text covertly enough not to shatter the reader's suspension of disbelief yet making this presence perceptible to Nabokov's ideal reader.

The pervasiveness of metaleptic tendencies in Nabokov's fiction raises the question of the risks inherent in the tension between the two tiers of Nabokov's art: how does the presence of the extradiegetic plane inform Nabokov's narrative ethics? After all, do the metaleptic gestures not threaten the characters, depriving them of life by pointing to the ultimate constructedness of the diegetic world?[57] This kind of objectification can be compared to what Bakhtin termed monologism, that is, the apotheosis of the author's valuational center at the expense of the characters, the tyrannical dominance of the authorial consciousness over all others.

One of the more typical critical approaches to the presence of both extradiegetic and diegetic planes in Nabokov's fiction has been to treat it as an aesthetic exercise in Gnosticism.[58] Armed with Vera Nabokov's assertion that the leitmotif of Nabokov's art is "otherworldliness,"[59] such criticism considers the double-tiered structure of the prose and its consequences as a reflection of and a meditation on our own metaphysical situation. In exposing the fictive nature of his literary worlds, Nabokov hints at the constructedness of our own lives, asking readers to contemplate their own origins. But instead of leading to an investigation of the power dynamic that governs the construction of the subject, such an approach reaffirms a belief in Nabokov's metaphysical essentialism.[60] The divine status of the author vis-à-vis his characters becomes an invitation to stop and look for the presence of the otherworldly dimension in our own lives.

As I have argued in this chapter, however, Nabokov's complex conceptualization of language and writing renders problematic such an unambiguous ascription of divine status to art. The metaleptic gestures make the boundary between the language *of* the novel (the extradiegetic level of the text) and the language *in* the novel (the diegetic level) too unstable and the intrusion of the authorial figure in the text too frequent to align the author-characters pair with God-humans. To categorize the co-presence of the diegetic and extradiegetic levels in Nabokov's prose as an inquiry into the limits (and potentiality) of our knowledge about our ends and origins risks bringing to a stasis the dynamic tension between the modernist and the realist poetics of his texts. Even if we disregard Nabokov's strong aversion to translating formal matters into matters of content, we can agree that such critical pursuits neutralize any ethical inquiry into his texts by making it a derivative of whatever textual metaphysics we accept on faith. In contrast, in my discussion of Nabokov's narrative ethics, I aimed to bring out the constructionist Nabokov by treating the metaphysical underpinnings of the subject-construction that his double-tiered texts advance as an ethical problem rather than an epistemological given.[61] The ontological hierarchy that metaleptic gestures and traces make explicit is equally suggestive of the metaphysical aspirations present in the narrative formation of the subject, and can be understood as a critique of the power struggle and violence that inevitably accompany it.[62] While this view can be understood in terms of the knowledge that comes with the experience of reading Nabokov, the fact that it subjects the author's participation to a hard scrutiny makes for knowledge of a quite different kind. As Debra Malina aptly observes: "if, as the constructionist view has it, the subject external to these novels is the internal subject of cultural, familial, and self narratives, if it is produced in and by its stories just as the novels' characters are in and by theirs, the dynamics of the metaleptic cycle might apply to the construction of real subjects as well as fictional ones."[63] Last, but by no account least, an ethical inquiry that takes as its starting point an analysis of the power dynamic that extends across different narrative planes presupposes a diachronic rather than a synchronic reading, questioning rather than accepting the teleological drive of the plot as well as the teleological implications of the hierarchically structured narrative.[64]

CONCLUSION: ON AESTHETICS AND ETHICS (NABOKOV AND DOSTOEVSKY II)

Such an understanding of Nabokov's narrative ethics allows us once again to address the similarities and differences between Nabokov and Dostoevsky. Both authors treat the language *of* the novel and *in* the novel as a socially and historically determined phenomenon that shapes the relationships between participating subjects. Not unlike that of Dostoevsky, Nabokov's narrative ethics challenges the reader to accept responsibility for the discursive violence by becoming aware of the "dialogic" (to use Bakhtin's term) and often conflictual nature of discourse in narrative fiction. Both Dostoevsky and Nabokov share the notion that the characters' will to power manifests itself through discursive exchange among them, and this notion becomes the foundation for these authors' narrative ethics. For Dostoevsky, however, while language is laden with potential violence, there is still the possibility of a release from dialogic rivalry, even if it is paradoxically located outside of language, as silence becomes one of the main attributes of the transcendental signified. Dostoevsky's prose contains iconic and nonverbal images of Christian ethics that serve as signposts, directing the characters' (and eventually the reader's) journey from the novel's *is* to its *ought-to-be*. Nabokov's prose retains Dostoevsky's conception of language as the site of the struggle through which characters determine their social and ethical standing vis-à-vis themselves and one another. But in Dostoevsky's prose, Christ is unambiguously the transcendental signified; in Nabokov, by contrast, the function of the transcendental signified is folded back onto the work of art itself, with the figure of the author as its quasi-divine creator. Dostoevsky's narrative ethics can be defined as the distance between the divine silence of Christ and the all-too-human word; in Nabokov, the word becomes the vessel of both divine and human signification. At first glance, the ontological instability this creates seems like it could be resolved by fastening one's point of view to the epistemological boundary that separates the word *of* the prose from the word *in* the prose. The author's word is divine; the characters' word is human. The difference here would correspond to Rabinowitz's distinction between authorial and narrative audiences. Yet, keeping the two apart is hardly possible, since the boundary separating the worlds of the text and the author in Nabokov's prose is distinctly and consciously porous. The interpermeability of the two realms inevitably leads to the aporetic ambiguity of language we have analyzed throughout this chapter. Straddling, as it were, both sides of the diegetic divide, the author invades the world of the prose, directly affecting its narrative dynamics by participating in it in the guise of the authorial figure.

In reading Nabokov, we are in the presence of two simultaneous rhetorical strategies: on the one hand, characters strive to seize control of representation (with *Despair*, *Lolita*, and *Pale Fire* as the most representative examples); on the other hand, the authorial figure makes all such attempts obsolete by revealing the prose to be nothing but an aesthetic artifact (as in *Invitation to a Beheading*, *The Gift*, and *Transparent Things*, to name a few texts in which this function is paramount). Treating the author as a special kind of character leads us to align authorial control with other modes through which power manifests itself on the level of content, such as political tyranny, while moments of authorial submission can be evaluated as acts of accepting ethical responsibility. An awareness of epistemological instability, on the one hand, and of the author's "role" in narrative violence, on the other, calls upon the reader to mull over her responsibility for her own discursive participation with the text. Such an analysis pushes back against Nabokov's assertions of the autonomy of art, in which he maintains that authorial control over works of art transcends both ethics and politics and should not be evaluated by either. Whether there was any tongue in Nabokov's cheek in proclaiming such an impossible authorial freedom and how conscious he was that this claim is in itself an ethical position, and hence subject to ethical inquiry, we will probably never know. For the reader, compliance with Nabokov's insistence on keeping aesthetics and ethics in separate cages in order to partake of aesthetic delight is conditional on a kind of submission (even if it is dressed up in Nabokov's nonfiction as companionship).[65] In the case of *Bend Sinister*, however, as a formative characteristic of the relationship between author and reader, submission immediately plunges the reader back into the *ethical* and *political* world of the novel. In my discussion of Nabokov, I have argued that to understand ethical inquiry as one of the main tracks on this epistemological Mobius strip is to endow Nabokov's prose with the relevance it deserves. Reading Nabokov, one has to contend not so much with the incompatibility of aesthetics and ethics and the necessity of choosing one over the other, as with the productive tension of their antagonistic co-presence.

Conclusion

AFTER ATTEMPTING TO fit yet another puzzle piece into the story of the protagonist's life, the narrator of *Sebastian Knight* begins to understand that his quest to grasp the essence of his half-brother in a biography might, after all, fail. The realization comes to V. through an inner voice:

> That Voice in the Mist rang out in the dimmest passage of my mind. It was but the echo of some possible truth, a timely reminder: don't be too certain of learning the past from the lips of the present. Beware of the most honest broker. Remember that what you are told is really threefold: shaped by the teller, reshaped by the listener, concealed from both by the dead man of the tale.[1]

This passage neatly captures the lines of distortion present in any storytelling; it also asks us to think of the relationships among listeners, tellers, and characters, relationships that are structured by the narrative, while always surpassing it as well. The unfortunate state of the protagonist in the above passage becomes that insurmountable obstacle which prevents V. from obtaining his innermost secrets; it also points to the dangers intrinsic to narrative acts: the desire to bring a character to life through the telling of that character's story might prove deadly for its subject.

This ambivalence toward narrating resurfaces once again toward the end of the book as V. describes Sebastian's last novel or, what might be the same thing, the one he himself is currently composing. In a somewhat ominous image, the dead man *becomes* the tale, or, to put it differently, the possibility of the tale is conditional on the status quo of the man. To exist, the tale must have him dead:

> A man is dying, and he is the hero of the tale; but whereas the lives of other people in the book seem perfectly realistic (or at least realistic in a Knightian sense), the reader is kept ignorant as to who the dying man is, and where his

deathbed stands or floats, or whether it is a bed at all. The man is the book; the book itself is heaving and dying, and drawing up a ghostly knee. (173)

A confirmation of Peter Brooks's adage that "all narrative may be in essence obituary"[2] as well as Bakhtin's statement that "my birth, . . . and . . . my death are events that occur neither in me nor for me,"[3] here the connection between narrative and human life is announced to be not only mimetic (as with the secondary characters of Sebastian's book) but also that of a *mise en abyme*: the former repeats the subconscious energies of the latter. As might be expected, the novel both confirms such perfect congruence and announces it to be illusory. The "absolute truth," "the answer to all questions of life and death"[4] that such a narrative promises, slips away from its readers in a final moment of authorial hesitation:

> At this last bend of his book the author seems to pause for a minute, as if he were pondering whether it were wise to let the truth out. He seems to lift his head and to leave the dying man, whose thoughts he was following, and to turn away and to think: Shall we follow him to the end? . . . We shall. . . . And we turn and bend again over a hazy bed, over a grey, floating form—lower and lower. . . . But that minute of doubt was fatal: the man is dead. (178)

If narrative, as Nabokov suggests here, operates within the economy of attainment and loss, then our ethical engagement with the text must begin with an acceptance of responsibility for the inevitable costs incurred in the pursuit of the elusive presence that narrating promises. A central hypothesis of my book has been that Nabokov's preoccupations with the risks of storytelling, especially those associated with acts of representation and interpretation—"shaped by the teller, reshaped by the listener"—allow us to see him as a constitutive part of a literary-philosophical constellation that also includes Dostoevsky and Bakhtin. All three, I have argued, are especially attuned to the power hierarchies and dynamics formed by the distribution of narrative discourse and the moral temptations it presents to those who participate in it.

Among the three, the notion that aesthetic activity directed toward the subject might lead to that subject's unmaking was put forth most explicitly and radically by Bakhtin in his wartime notebooks, especially in a short text that the editors of Bakhtin's collective works titled "Rhetoric to the Extent That It Lies . . ." ("Rhetoric"). Written in the mid-1940s, this text contains what are probably Bakhtin's most sobering reflections on the way language—or what Bakhtin calls "the word"—affects the formation of the subject. In "Rhetoric," aesthetic representation is inevitably wrought with violence, and, inasmuch as it is a constituent of any interaction, so is the subject's relationship with the other. Unlike Bakhtin's earlier work (such as "Toward a Philosophy of the Act" or *Problems of Dostoevsky's Art*), here the other's word about the human subject is neither a gift of love nor an invitation to a dialogue of ideas, but an attempt to "devour" and "consume" him. The word seeks to materialize the subject, turn him or her into an object, a thing, as if by framing the unbound and unfinalizable I-for-myself, representation deprives the subject of its spiritual element, imprisoning him within the walls of matter.

In Bakhtin's notes, we can witness a later stage in the evolution of his aesthetic philosophy, which, as I have argued, was directly influenced by Dostoevsky's innovative solutions on how to endow aesthetic activity with ethical value. Bakhtin's awareness of the word's power to deprive the subject of freedom and of the dangers hidden in acts of representation first appears explicitly in his original Dostoevsky book, where he splits verbal art into monologic and polyphonic—the former inevitably subjugating, the latter releasing and complicating the subject. The dispiriting nature of "Rhetoric" comes, in part, from the absence of such a division. The violence of the word is no longer rooted in the other's attitude—monologic or dialogic—but in the other's very position vis-à-vis the subject. Originating in outsideness (*vnenakhodimost'*), the word seeks to destroy the subject; its opposite is not a dialogic word, but silence. The word in these notes is a totalizing and a totalitarian force: it, on the one hand, decentralizes the subject and, on the other hand, tempts the other with an empty seat of power at the center. The notes also make it clear why literature has been Bakhtin's most consistent preoccupation. For Bakhtin, the relationship between author and character becomes the model for all intersubjectivity. Aesthetic activity gives form and meaning not only to human interaction but also to what constitutes the ethical limits of interpersonal experience. As Bakhtin elliptically states in "Rhetoric": "The image of a human being as the central image of all fictional literature. Tendencies in the creation of this image, the ethics of literature."[5] For Bakhtin, literature is much better equipped to deal with the crisis of authority and the conflation of authority with authorship that becomes a salient factor determining the formation of the modern subject. The "ethics of literature" guides Bakhtin's search for the human in a world full of characters.

In this book, I have argued that this search for "the image of the human being"—or, to use Dostoevsky's famous phrase, "the man in man"—is also the main concern of Dostoevsky's and Nabokov's fiction. Like Bakhtin, both authors attend to the word's representational power while acknowledging its potential to become an instrument of subjugation and domination. Moreover, in their prose, Dostoevsky and Nabokov investigate the sources behind narrative violence and insist that the responsibility for it must be shared not just among the characters but also by authors and readers.

Conclusion

Hence, my study of Dostoevsky's narrative ethics began with a suggestion that his evaluation of the risks involved in discursive aesthetic activity might be more closely aligned with the Bakhtin of "Rhetoric" than with the Bakhtin of *Problems of Dostoevsky's Poetics*. In the latter work, Bakhtin transfers Viacheslav Ivanov's "dialogic principle" from the relationships among the novels' characters to the relationship between author and hero, shifting his focus to the novels' *form*, that is, to Dostoevsky's aesthetics.[6] In Bakhtin's reading, Dostoevsky allows his characters freedom of self-expression and gives birth to the polyphonic novel by radically altering the relationship between author and hero, thus freeing his characters from authorial narrative representation. In my own examination of Dostoevsky's prose, I projected Bakhtin's analysis of authorial narrative representation back into the world of Dostoevsky's characters, while arguing that, for the most part, it retains the negative value assigned to it by Bakhtin in *Problems of Dostoevsky's Poetics*.[7]

Dostoevsky's authorial "silence" and the resulting narrative freedom of his characters can be traced to his Christian worldview, which understands freedom of moral choice as Christ's most important gift to humanity. Dostoevsky's protagonists, however, live in a world in which the belief in the unshakeable presence of a moral order in the world has been put to the test. In the absence of an unquestionable moral authority, the responsibility *of* and *for* the moral law falls on the characters' shoulders. The dialogic activity of the characters unfolds in the struggle between their desire to reconstitute the law and their desire for power, and must be resolved either as a freely chosen act of self-sacrifice and compassion or as an act of violence. Hence, Dostoevsky's Christian ethics realizes itself in the formal structures of his prose, defining the tense dynamic between the characters' unlimited dialogic freedom and their action. In this sense, Lydia Ginzburg's observation that "all of [Dostoevsky's heroes] have unlimited time at their disposal for their ideological adventures" requires a correction: their discursive freedom must in the decisive moment enter history and actualize itself in the world as an act.[8] Or, as Harpham would put it, the overdetermined ethics has to become the underdetermined morality.[9]

The ethical tension between discourse and action in Dostoevsky's prose endows the word—the dialogic exchanges between characters—with a morally ambiguous status. The discursive struggle for power between the characters often prefigures physical violence but can also be dissolved with an act of self-sacrifice and compassion. The "physical" and the "nonverbal" in Dostoevsky are invested with the potential to take his characters out of interpersonal struggles and, in this way, become moral limits that frame the verbal exchanges. Revealing the violence inherent in the narrative formation of the subject, such framing calls for responsibility from all parties sharing

Conclusion

the narrative experience: engaged in the dialogic exchange of ideas or the hermeneutic interpretation of the prose, the reader must become aware of her own *discursive* participation with the text in which discourse is marked as a moral category.

In "The Meek One," to take one example, the dialogic activity of the pawnbroker brings the narrator to truth, but at the same time it is exposed as the very instrument of his wife's destruction. By joining in the dialogue, however, even if only to pronounce her judgment upon the pawnbroker, the reader *nolens volens* becomes accountable for the destruction that the husband's word inflicted on his wife. The extreme case of such moral accenting in Dostoevsky's oeuvre, I have argued, is *The Idiot*, where the validity of any kind of interpretation, even the truest and the most accurate one, is exposed as ethically inadequate in comparison to nonverbal, participatory acts of repentance, such as Myshkin's vigil next to Rogozhin and the body of Nastasya Filippovna.

Like Dostoevsky's characters, the narrator-protagonists in Nabokov's fiction often experience the loss of authenticity. Unlike Dostoevsky, however, who explicitly points to the metaphysical source of such a loss, Nabokov's prose—as is often the case in modernist and postmodernist literature— stages a disruption of the mimetic relationship between the text and its referent. As a result, the loss in Nabokov's fiction originates with the characters' inherently uncertain ontological status: their humanness is simultaneously affirmed and denied depending on whether we attend to the intra- or extradiegetic levels of the prose. The authorial figure becomes the main agent driving this bifurcation and, by declaring himself as the only arbiter of textual value, the only force capable of reconstituting the law.

To reimagine the aesthetic sphere as the only place where the validity of the law can be reconstituted divests morality and politics of power. On the one hand, Nabokov's authorial figure, striving to control the production of meaning not only on the intradiegetic level but also vis-à-vis the reader, corresponds to the romantic notion of the author as a divine creator. On the other hand, the activity of this "anthropomorphic deity" closely parallels the romantic quests of Nabokov's protagonists, whose aesthetic pursuits over the course of the text are shown to be driven by demiurgic aspirations for power. The direct by-product of these pursuits is narrative and physical cruelty to others, such as Hermann's murder of Felix in *Despair* or Humbert's continuous rape and abuse of Dolores Haze in *Lolita*. Nabokov's implicit critique of romantic aesthetics is not unlike Dostoevsky's exposure of the selfish motivations hidden beneath romantic idealism. As Nabokov himself suggested, the goal of parodying authorial activity in his protagonists was purgation: by turning his characters into "monsters" on "a cathedral façade,"[10] Nabokov ensured that the qualities his art retains for itself continue to be "curiosity, tenderness, kindness, [and] ecstasy."[11]

Conclusion

Whether such strategies of exorcism can absolve the authorial figure of responsibility remains an open question. In my reading of the Shakespeare chapter in *Bend Sinister*, I have argued that the authorial figure must bear responsibility for his participation in the discursive violence of the text. Such treatment would not only maintain the ethical tension of the text but also require a similar acknowledgment of responsibility from the reader. Beyond the ability to perceive the extradiegetic bread crumbs left by the author, the diplopia one must possess when reading Nabokov requires an understanding that his definition of art contains its own double: the notion of art as a quasi-divine pursuit coexists with the vision of artistic activity as exclusively human, and the awareness of such coexistence must not be excluded from an ethical inquiry. As I suggested in my reading of *Despair*, the hubris of such protagonists as Nabokov's Hermann lies in their inability to tolerate such ambiguity, which feeds their desire for metaphysical certainty and aesthetic control.

It is here, in how each author connects the struggle for power among his characters to the aesthetic sphere, marking the acts of authoring and reading as ethical, that the similarities between Dostoevsky and Nabokov come into relief. As I argued in this book, what allows us to reveal this connection is Bakhtin's aesthetic philosophy that asks us to attend to the power relationships among the participants of narrative fiction: author, characters, and reader. Importantly, both Dostoevsky and Nabokov (albeit, each in his own way) point to the Russian literary tradition—and Pushkin in particular—as a direct source for their conceptualization of narrative ethics. Notably, in writing about Pushkin, Dostoevsky and Nabokov put forth a perspective that can only be called Bakhtinian *avant la lettre*.

Hence, in his famous Pushkin Speech delivered on June 20, 1880, at the Moscow University Society of Literature Lovers, Dostoevsky identified in Pushkin the quality that Bakhtin would later coin as "polyphony" with regard to Dostoevsky himself. For Dostoevsky, the most important characteristic of Pushkin's mature period is the poet's "absolutely unique" talent "to transform his spirit into the spirit of other nations."[12] Paradoxically—but in full accordance with Dostoevsky's philosophy—Pushkin's ability to allow the other to reveal himself fully without authorial intrusion becomes a guarantee of the poet's originality. Dostoevsky explicitly connects Pushkin's *artistic* skill at discovering "the man in man" of other epochs and cultures with the *moral* and *spiritual* qualities of the Russian people: "without enmity . . . , but with complete love we assimilated into our soul the geniuses of other nations, all of them, without making tribal preferences, instinctually knowing how, from the very first step, to discern and remove contradictions, to forgive and reconcile differences. . . . It could be that to become a real Russian means only . . . to become a brother to all people, to become an all-man, if you wish" (147). In the speech, Pushkin's authorial position vis-à-vis his subjects is united with the Christian mission of the Russian people, as Dostoevsky envisioned it. It is easy to see that what Dostoevsky recognizes as Pushkin's "unique trait" is very similar to what Bakhtin announces to be the energizing principle behind Dostoevsky's particular brand of "realism." As Bakhtin writes in *Problems of Dostoevsky's Poetics*, "[Dostoevsky] solves his *new* task—'portraying all the depths of the human soul'—with 'utter realism'; that is, he sees these depths outside himself, in the souls of *others*.[13] As I argued in this book, such an authorial position is also a cornerstone of Dostoevsky's Christian narrative ethics. It allows Dostoevsky to designate narrative discourse as an ethical category, thus inviting the reader's understanding that her own *discursive* participation in the act of reading is an ethical act that calls for responsibility.

Pushkin's "polyphonic" poetics becomes an implicit inspiration behind Dostoevsky's artistic method. Similarly, it would be hard to overemphasize the influence of Pushkin on Nabokov, especially that of *Eugene Onegin*.[14] Nabokov's authorial presence in the worlds of his prose—both on the intra- and extradiegetic levels—could be traced to the adoption of numerous authorial masks in Pushkin's novel-in-verse, as well as the persistent metaleptic puncturing that becomes one of the most important strategies in *Eugene Onegin*'s composition.[15] It is in his early lecture on Pushkin, "Pushkin, or the Real and the Plausible," that Nabokov shows his Bakhtinian colors most explicitly, directly addressing the ethical implications of authorship.[16] Nabokov's two immediate concerns in the lecture are the difficulty of writing Pushkin's biography and of translating his poetry. Hence, Nabokov warns against "fictionized biographies," arguing that in taking the real life as its subject, they inevitably corrupt it: "the fictionizing biographer organizes his finds as best he can, and, since his best is generally a little bit worse than the worst of the author he is working on, the latter's life is inevitably distorted even if the basic facts are there."[17] The result, Nabokov says, "turns out to be plausible, but not true" (40). Nabokov compares the loss that occurs as one attempts to capture a "real" life in a text to the inevitable failure of translation: "at the approach of the translator's pen, the soul of that poetry immediately flies off, and we are left holding but a little gilded cage" (41). Contemplating Pushkin's biography and poetry, however, allows Nabokov to address the act of authorship in general: "Is it possible to imagine the full reality of another's life, to relive it in one's mind and set it down intact on paper? I doubt it: one even finds oneself seduced by the idea that thought itself, as it shines its beam on the story of a man's life, cannot avoid deforming it" (40).

The strength of Nabokov's suspicions about the possibility of capturing the real through writing is comparable only to his desire for doing so. As he puts it in the lecture, "one would therefore like to think that what we call art is, essentially, but the picturesque side of reality: one must simply be capable of seizing it" (42). Here, navigating between the inevitable risks of authorship and the pursuit of truth, Nabokov comes closest to what Bakhtin identifies as Dostoevsky's main artistic task: "to portray all the depths of the human soul."[18] Bakhtin explains that what lies behind Dostoevsky's insistence on being a realist and not a psychologist is the desire to escape "a degrading reification of a person's soul, a discounting of its freedom and its unfinalizability, and of that peculiar indeterminacy and indefiniteness which in Dostoevsky constitute the main object of representation" (61). It is perhaps in their aspiration to peer beyond discourses which obscure the truth and in their awareness that the act of peering inevitably engenders ethical responsibility that Dostoevsky and Nabokov come into the closest proximity of each other.

Both authors also require the reader to recognize her own responsibility in the process of interpretation. In this book, my argument has been that the distance between writing and reading, between telling and listening, between representation and interpretation, is the space of narrative ethics. Hence, the ethical lesson of reading fiction extends not only to transferring this awareness into the reader's interpersonal relationships with living, not fictional others but also, perhaps more importantly, to accepting that the boundaries between the acts of authoring, reading, and living are all but fluid.

Looking beyond the literary criticism that focuses solely on the aesthetics of the text, Martha Nussbaum proposed that "one of the things that makes literature something deeper and more central for us than a complex game, deeper even than those games, for example chess and tennis, that move us to wonder by their complex beauty, is that it speaks . . . *about us*, about our lives and choices and emotions, about our social existence and the totality of our connections."[19] If my own argument for narrative ethics had the misfortune of having to be condensed into a single statement, it would be this: at the core of our ethical engagement with literature is its ability to orchestrate and examine the relationships among authors, narrators, listeners, and readers. In this, discourse emerges not simply as the dye in an angiogram but as the very blood vessels of intersubjectivity, the building blocks from which the relationships in a work of fiction are being formed. Its distribution across intra- and extradiegetic levels of text creates the power dynamics that are ethical in nature inasmuch as they call the subjects involved in writing, narrating, and reading to responsibility.

To turn to literature as a guide for making ethical choices is to follow the philosopher Bernard Williams in doubting whether "the reality of complex moral situations can be represented by means other than those of imaginative literature."[20] Not only did the two subjects of my book spend their careers investigating moral quandaries without reducing them to prescriptive lessons and abstractions, but they also chose to leave the record of their inquiry in the highly specific and complex form that is narrative fiction.

Conclusion

In their prose, Dostoevsky and Nabokov consciously and rigorously explore narrative's unique ability to re-create the immediacy and force of interpersonal experience and reveal the violence that accompanies our narrative formation as a subject.

The violence we encounter in narrative fiction might be different from the more harrowing, horrible, and visceral violence of real life. Yet, as I have argued in this book, understanding one can teach us how to recognize our unwitting complicity in the designs of the other.

Notes

INTRODUCTION

Parts of the introduction were published as "Between Mourning and Melancholy: Narrative Ethics in Fyodor Dostoevsky and Witold Gombrowicz" in *Comparative Literature* 66, no. 2 (2014): 186–207.

1. Vladimir Nabokov, *The Real Life of Sebastian Knight* (New York: Vintage International, 1992), 88.
2. Adam Zachary Newton, *Narrative Ethics* (Cambridge, Mass.: Harvard University Press, 1995).
3. Geoffrey Harpham connects the revival of the ethical discourse to the exposure of collaborationist wartime writings by Paul de Man, which occurred on December 1, 1987: Harpham, *Shadows of Ethics: Criticism and the Just Society* (Durham, N.C.: Duke University Press, 1999). In the theoretical earthquake at the end of 1987, Harpham sees a shift in the establishment's focus from an a-personal, discursive language and text-based analysis to the relationships of personal responsibility between the authors and readers of texts.
4. Todd F. Davis and Kenneth Womack, "Preface: Reading Literature and the Ethics of Criticism," in *Mapping the Ethical Turn: A Reader in Ethics, Culture, and Literary Theory*, ed. Todd F. Davis and Kenneth Womack (Charlottesville: University Press of Virginia, 2001), ix–x.
5. Martha Nussbaum, *Love's Knowledge: Essays on Philosophy and Literature* (Oxford: Oxford University Press, 1990), 23–24.
6. Tobin Siebers, *The Ethics of Criticism* (Ithaca, N.Y.: Cornell University Press, 1988), 1.
7. Nussbaum, *Love's Knowledge*, 171. Elaborating new pathways for ethical literary criticism, Nussbaum suggests that by taking into account literary form, ethical analysis can escape the violence inherent in both humanist and formalist approaches to literature: "It has been easy enough to feel that ethical writing must do violence to the literary work. Of course, it should have been obvious that to concentrate on form to the neglect of the work's sense of life and choice is not a solution, only violence of a different sort. It should have been recognized that neither sort of violence is required" (172).

8. Siebers, *Ethics of Criticism*, 4. The introduction to the collection *Critical Ethics* argues that "the ethical is a category that was neglected for a considerable period, through the 1960s, 1970s, and 1980s, in part because it was felt to have been surpassed and discredited. The Left regarded ethics as a liberal humanist apology for the bourgeois subject, while poststructuralists tended to treat most ethical discourse as contaminated with metaphysics": Dominic Rainsford and Tim Woods, "Introduction: Ethics and Intellectuals," in *Critical Ethics: Text, Theory and Responsibility*, ed. Dominic Rainsford and Tim Woods (New York: St. Martin's Press, 1999), 3. For the evolution of our understanding of the moral sphere from the Enlightenment to our day and how it affects the contemporary critical situation, see Alasdair MacIntyre, *After Virtue* (Notre Dame, Ind.: University of Notre Dame Press, 2007). For the reasons behind contemporary theory's critique of ethical criticism, see Harpham, *Shadows of Ethics*.

9. Siebers, *Ethics of Criticism*, 10. A recognition of critical theory's motivations as ethical brings out what David Parker coined as "the ethical unconscious" of theory and makes possible a discussion of theory's participation in today's debate on the importance of ethics. See his *Ethics, Theory, and the Novel* (Cambridge: Cambridge University Press, 1994).

10. Nussbaum, *Love's Knowledge*, 105.

11. Nussbaum, *Love's Knowledge*, 171.

12. Wayne Booth, *The Company We Keep: An Ethics of Fiction* (Berkeley: University of California Press, 1988).

13. Booth, *Company We Keep*, 488.

14. As Charles Altieri observes, Nussbaum wants literature to be both distinct from and supplemental to moral philosophy, yet her efforts end up curtailing the reach of both, since "the very role of supplement undercuts the concreteness by making it dependent on abstractions and undercuts the abstractions by making them dependent for their realization on something that philosophy apparently cannot provide on its own": Altieri, "Lyrical Ethics and Literary Experience," in *Mapping the Ethical Turn: A Reader in Ethics, Culture, and Literary Theory*, ed. Todd F. Davis and Kenneth Womack (Charlottesville: University Press of Virginia, 2001), 45. For an excellent critique of Nussbaum's attempt to secure the authority of reason over affect, see chapter 5 of Altieri's *Particulars of Rapture: An Aesthetics of the Affects* (Ithaca, N.Y.: Cornell University Press, 2003).

15. Altieri, "Lyrical Ethics," 45.

16. Altieri, "Lyrical Ethics," 46.

17. This, of course, is especially relevant for Dostoevsky's prose, in which emotional extremes are the law of the land.

18. Altieri, "Lyrical Ethics," 50–53.

19. Altieri, "Lyrical Ethics," 50–53.

20. Altieri, "Lyrical Ethics," 52.

21. Altieri, *Particulars of Rapture*, 25.

22. Altieri, *Particulars of Rapture*, 25.

23. As Caryl Emerson pointed out in a personal conversation, "what is curious about Bakhtin is his indifference to the power dynamics in 'evaluations.'" By turning his attention to the author-character power dynamics in his Dostoevsky scholarship, inasmuch as it strives to avoid a discussion of ideological positions or worldviews, Bakhtin chooses a fundamentally formalist approach. Still, in his book on Dostoevsky, the "valuational" position of the creator is present.

24. Mikhail Bakhtin, "The Problem of Form, Content, and Material in Verbal Art," in *Art and Answerability: Early Philosophical Essays by M. M. Bakhtin*, ed. Michael Holquist and Vadim Liapunov, trans. Vadim Liapunov and Kenneth Brostrom (Austin: University of Texas Press, 1990), 264, emphasis in the original. See the analysis of this essay, as well as the evolution of Bakhtin's attitude toward formalism, in Caryl Emerson's "Perezhiv temnotu stalinskoi nochi, Bakhtin vnov' razmyshliaet o formalizme," *Matica Srpska Journal for Slavic Studies* 92 (2017). On the difference between Bakhtinian and formalist aesthetics, see Emerson's essay "Shklovsky's ostranenie, Bakhtin's vnenakhodimost' (How Distance Serves an Aesthetics of Arousal Differently from an Aesthetics Based on Pain)," *Poetics Today* 26, no. 4 (winter 2005).

25. Caroline Levine, *Forms: Whole, Rhythm, Hierarchy, Network* (Princeton, N.J.: Princeton University Press, 2017), 14.

26. Levine, *Forms*, 14.

27. Levine, *Forms*, 16. While absent from Levine's argument, any "new formalism" must come with the reassessment of the legacy of the Russian formalists. Revealing the political dimension of formalist aesthetics, Svetlana Boym aligns Shklovsky's use of estrangement with Hannah Arendt's notion of freedom as something that is "'fundamentally strange' that pushes us beyond 'routinization and automatization of the modern life'": Boym, "Poetics and Politics of Estrangement: Victor Shklovsky and Hannah Arendt," *Poetics Today* 26, no. 4 (winter 2005): 582. Reading Shklovsky with Arendt allows Boym to interpret estrangement not as an artistic device but as an "art of survival and a practice of freedom and dissent" (582). Similarly, in *The Aesthetics of Anarchy: Art and Ideology in the Early Russian Avant-Garde* (Berkeley: University of California Press, 2012), Nina Gourianova revisits Shklovsky's notion that the goal of art—through estrangement—is to liberate us from our tendency to take the world for granted. Gourianova sets Shklovsky's estrangement, which provokes the cultural consumer into the role of an active cocreator, against Sergei Eisenstein's montage of attractions, an approach that seeks to ideologically manipulate the consumer.

28. Graham Pechey, "Philosophy and Theology in 'Aesthetic Activity,'" in *Bakhtin and Religion: A Feeling for Faith*, ed. Susan M. Felch and Paul J. Contino (Evanston, Ill.: Northwestern University Press, 2001), 51. Not to be confused by the taxonomy of terms, this to me still seems an argument for Bakhtin's

reimagining of Kantian ethics into an ethics of intersubjectivity: Mikhail Bakhtin, "Author and Hero in Aesthetic Activity," trans. Vadim Liapunov, in *Art and Answerability: Early Philosophical Essays by M. M. Bakhtin*, ed. Michael Holquist and Vadim Liapunov (Austin: University of Texas Press), 1990. For Pechey, aesthetics "tempt[s] ethics away from 'morality' and toward an ontology of the uniquely situated body" (Pechey, "Philosophy and Theology," 52).

29. Newton, *Narrative Ethics*, 17–18.

30. Newton, *Narrative Ethics*, 18.

31. For an example of ethical criticism grounded in structuralist poetics, see James Phelan's *Living to Tell About It: A Rhetoric and Ethics of Character Narration* (Ithaca, N.Y.: Cornell University Press, 2005). Phelan develops a notion of rhetorical ethics based on the narratological communication model of Seymour Chatman, Peter J. Rabinowitz, and Wayne Booth, among others.

32. Heather Love, "Close but Not Deep: Literary Ethics and the Descriptive Turn," *New Literary History* 41, no. 2 (spring 2010): 375.

33. For a discussion of parody in Nabokov's use of Dostoevsky, see George Nivat's "Nabokov and Dostoevsky," in *The Garland Companion to Vladimir Nabokov*, ed. Vladimir E. Alexandrov (London: Routledge, 1995). Katherine Tiernan O'Connor suggests that Nabokov's "total engagement" with Dostoevsky can be seen as an example of the anxiety of influence, and that in *Lolita* Nabokov thoroughly reworks themes from *Crime and Punishment*: O'Connor, "Rereading Lolita: Reconsidering Nabokov's Relationship with Dostoevskij," *Slavic and East European Journal* 33, no. 1 (1989): 66. In comparative studies of Nabokov and Dostoevsky, a value judgment favoring the former over the latter is not uncommon. Thus, comparing *Lolita* with "The Meek One," Julian Connolly states that "Nabokov appropriated some of the most striking elements of Dostoevsky's story, only to fashion from them a work that far outstrips his predecessor's achievement in complexity and scope": Connolly, "Nabokov's Dialogue with Dostoevsky: *Lolita* and 'The Gentle Creature,'" *Nabokov Studies* 4 (1997): 16. In "Dostoevski and Vladimir Nabokov: The Case of *Despair*" (in *Dostoevski and the Human Condition after a Century*, ed. Alexey Ugrinsky, Frank S. Lambasa, and Valija K. Ozolins [New York: Greenwood, 1986]), Connolly suggests that Nabokov's engagement with Dostoevsky in *Despair* extends beyond mere parody and argues that there are strong characterological parallels between Hermann and the Underground Man and Raskolnikov. Alexander Dolinin argues that Nabokov's relationship to Dostoevsky underwent a change from his Russian to American periods. A cautious acknowledgment of Dostoevsky's merits combined with his aversion to Dostoevsky's Russian epigones in the 1930s gave way to his forceful dislike of the Dostoevsky fad among the American intelligentsia in the 1960s; see Dolinin's "Nabokov, Dostoevsky, and 'Dostoevskyness,'" *Russian Studies in Literature* 35, no. 4 (1999). Stephen Blackwell's important article "Dostoevskian Problems in Nabokov's Poetics" (in *From Petersburg to Bloomington:*

Essays in Honor of Nina Perlina, ed. John Bartle, Michael C. Finke, and Vadim Liapunov [Bloomington, Ind.: Slavica, 2012]) demonstrates the applicability of Bakhtinian insights to Nabokov's first-person narratives (137–54). Francisco Picon's dissertation, "Bakhtin and Nabokov: The Dialogue That Never Was" (Columbia University, New York, 2016), similarly posits Dostoevsky as a common source for Nabokov's and Bakhtin's critique of monologism. In "Nabokov and Dostoevsky: Good Writer, Bad Reader?" (in *Nabokov and the Question of Morality: Aesthetics, Metaphysics, and the Ethics of Fiction*, ed. Michael Rogers and Susan Elizabeth Sweeney [New York: Palgrave Macmillan, 2016]), Connolly takes Nabokov's criticism of Dostoevsky to task by showing that Nabokov fails "to provide a serious analysis of Dostoevsky's poetics, either by investigating the grounds on which his novels are structured or by asking why his narrative voices display such distinctive traits and rhythms" (45).

34. Sergei Davydov argues that Dostoevsky's ethical preoccupations in *Crime and Punishment* become aesthetic ones in *Despair*; see his "Dostoevsky and Nabokov: The Morality of Structure in *Crime and Punishment* and *Despair*," *Dostoevsky Studies* 3 (1982). Galina Patterson asserts that in writing Hermann as Goliadkin, Nabokov punishes his antihero for "aesthetic blindness": Patterson, "Nabokov's Use of Dostoevskii: Developing Goliadkin 'Symptoms' in Hermann as a Sign of the Artist's End," *Canadian Slavonic Papers* 40, nos. 1–2 (1998): 109. For a more general discussion of how Nabokov enacts the shift from realism to modernism, see Jean-Philippe Jaccard's "Bukvy na snegu ili vstrecha dvukh oznachaemykh v glukhom lesu," in *Literatura kak takovaia* (Moscow: Novoe literaturnoe obozrenie, 2011). For a different way of bringing Nabokov and Dostoevsky together into the sphere of ethical inquiry, see David Rampton's "Critical Choices: Reading Nabokov's *Despair*" (*Forum for Modern Language Studies* 38, no. 1 [January 2002]), which argues that the content of Nabokov's prose, that is, the unethical acts of his characters, is as important as its form. Rampton develops a similar argument in *Vladimir Nabokov: A Critical Study of the Novels* (Cambridge: Cambridge University Press, 1984).

35. In *Nabokov, Perversely* (Ithaca, N.Y.: Cornell University Press, 2010), Eric Naiman argues that Nabokov corners his readers into accepting moral responsibility by forcing on them the responsibility for enjoying—on the extradiegetic level—the same kind of perverse linguistic sexual deviancy that his characters participate in on the intradiegetic level. Leland de la Durantaye's *Style Is Matter: The Moral Art of Vladimir Nabokov* (Ithaca, N.Y.: Cornell University Press, 2007) begins by addressing the anxiety of being the proper Nabokov reader—hermeneutically, but also ethically—by highlighting the moral dangers that lie in wait for anyone about to experience *Lolita*: "What sort of attention should we pay and what sort of intelligence should we apply to a work of art that recounts so much love, so much loss, so much thoughtlessness—and across which flashes something we might be tempted to call evil?" (6). The introduction

to Rodgers and Sweeney's recent collection of articles on the subject, *Nabokov and the Question of Morality*, gives a succinct yet thorough account of scholarship that since the beginning of 1980s has paid attention to the moral quandaries in Nabokov's prose.

36. Mikhail Bakhtin, *Problems of Dostoevsky's Poetics*, trans. and ed. Caryl Emerson (Minneapolis: University of Minnesota Press, 1984), 55.

37. Vladimir Nabokov, *Strong Opinions* (New York: Vintage International, 1990), 95.

38. Fyodor Dostoevsky, *The Brothers Karamazov: A Novel in Four Parts with Epilogue*, trans. Richard Pevear and Larissa Volokhonsky (New York: Vintage Classics, 1990), 289.

39. Sarah Young, *Dostoevsky's "The Idiot" and the Ethical Foundations of Narrative: Reading, Narrating, Scripting* (London: Anthem, 2004), 17.

40. Mikhail Bakhtin, *Toward a Philosophy of the Act*, trans. Vadim Liapunov (Austin: University of Texas Press, 1993), 40.

41. Alexander Dolinin, "Nabokov, Dostoevsky, and 'Dostoevskyness,'" *Russian Studies in Literature* 35, no. 4 (1999): 45.

42. Marijeta Bozovic shows how Nabokov's translation and commentary to *Eugene Onegin* and *Ada* become necessary elements in a two-step process of literary self-fashioning, the goal of which was the reshaping and mastering of the European modernist tradition: Bozovic, *Nabokov's Canon: From "Onegin" to "Ada"* (Evanston, Ill.: Northwestern University Press, 2016). For Nabokov, Pushkin becomes "a model for how to make new out of old, advanced out of belated, and central out of marginal" (12). Nabokov applies the blueprint of strategic cultural appropriation he finds in *Eugene Onegin* to *Ada*, using the novel to forge a new canon of modernist literature that consists of "great English, French, and Russian triads," with Nabokov at its helm (13).

43. Nikolai Gogol, *Selected Passages from Correspondence with Friends*, trans. Jesse Zeldin (Nashville, Tenn.: Vanderbilt University Press, 1969), 248–49. In the chapter "On the Essence of Russian Poetry and on Its Originality," poetry is contrasted with prose but also stands as a metonym for literature.

44. For discussion of the interrelationship between church, state, and literature in Gogol's *Selected Passages*, see Vladimir Markovich's "O nekotorykh paradoksakh knigi Gogolia *Vybrannye mesta iz perepiski s druz'iami*," in *Fenomen Gogolia: Materialy Yubileinoi mezhdunarodnoi nauchnoi konferentsii, posviashchennoi 200-letiu so dnia rozhdeniia N.V.Gogolia*, ed. M. N. Virolainen and A. A. Karpova (St. Petersburg: Petropolis, 2001). Markovich explains the duality in Gogol's attitude toward literature partially by the influence of German romantic aesthetics, which conceptualizes "literary creativity as theurgy, a joint action by a human being and God," and partially by the resistance—characteristic of the Russian culture of the 1840s—to the romantic "elevation of art above any other social ideas and relationships, above morality and religion" (382).

Notes to Pages 14–15

45. Nikolai Gogol, "An Author's Confession," in *Sobranie sochinenii v shesti tomakh*, vol. 6 (Moscow: Gosudarstvennoe izdatel'stvo khudozhestvennoi literatury, 1953), 208–9.

46. Gogol, "An Author's Confession," 209. Anne Lounsbery attributes Gogol's anxiety about his readers to the ambiguous effects of the advent of print culture in 1840s Russia: "Gogol was keenly aware that in the brave new world of print culture, the Russian author who published his works sent them out alone into a world of largely incompetent readers whose responses he could neither predict nor guide. And yet Gogol also knew that the act of sending a printed book out into the world conferred unprecedented power upon the work of art": Lounsbery, *Thin Culture, High Art: Gogol, Hawthorne, and Authorship in Nineteenth-Century Russia and America* (Cambridge, Mass.: Harvard University Press, 2007), 127.

47. Gogol, "An Author's Confession," 210.

48. Gogol, "An Author's Confession," 210.

49. Gogol, "An Author's Confession," 211.

50. Markovich, "O nekotorykh paradoksakh," 383.

51. See Alexei Vdovin for a detailed discussion of the development of Russian literary criticism as a main force in the process of canon-formation in the first half of the nineteenth century. According to Vdovin, by the mid-1830s, Russian literary critics with Belinsky at the helm began to play a decisive role in shaping the hierarchy and history of Russian literature. Influenced by the aesthetic philosophy of Friedrich Schlegel, Belinsky proposed the concept of "the head of literature"—a figure who, appointed by the critic, would crown the historic development of Russian literature, most fully embodying the "spirit of the nation." Having announced Gogol to be "the head of literature" in 1835, Belinsky "dethroned" Gogol after the quarrel over *Selected Passages* in 1847: Vdovin, *Kontsept 'Glava literatury' v russkoi kritike 1830kh–1860kh godov* (Tartu, Estonia: Tartu University Press, 2011), 76. The first chapter of Irina Paperno's *Chernyshevsky and the Age of Realism: A Study in the Semiotics of Behavior* (Stanford, Calif.: Stanford University Press, 1988) succinctly outlines the history of the tense relationship between Russian literary critics and writers in the 1840s and 1860s. For a summary of the power struggle between Russian literary critics and writers at this time, see also Igor Kondakov, "Pokushenie na literaturu: O bor'be literaturnoi kritiki s literaturoi v russkoi kul'ture," *Voprosy literatury* 2 (1992).

52. Scholars treat *Selected Passages* and Belinsky's response to it as the symbolic inception of the growing encroachment of ideology upon literature in Russia, as well as for the expansion of the prescriptive tendencies in Russian letters. Kondakov treats Belinsky's lunge against Gogol as an initial attempt by Russian literary criticism to subjugate fictional literature, which culminated in the ideological demands made by the Soviet critical apparatus (Kondakov, "Pokushenie na literaturu"). Markovich, on the contrary, draws a direct line from *Selected*

Passages to the regulatory aesthetics of socialist realism (Markovich, "O nekotorykh paradoksakh").

53. Vissarion Belinskii, "Pis'mo k N.V. Gogoliu ot 15 iulia n. st. 1847 goda," in *V. G. Belinskii: Pro et Contra: Lichnost' i tvorchestvo Belinskogo v russkoi mysli (1848–2011)*, ed. D. K. Burlak (St. Petersburg: Izdatel'stvo russkoi khristianskoi gumanitarnoi akademii, 2011), 56.

54. Yuri Tynianov writes that "the reading of the letter and copying it . . . became one of the main charges against Dostoevsky during the Petrashevsky trial": Tynianov, *Dostoevskii i Gogol': K teorii parodii* (Petrograd: Opoiaz, 1921), 28.

55. For a summary of Belinsky's philosophical evolution in relation to Dostoevsky, see chapter 14, "Belinsky and Dostoevsky: II," of Joseph Frank's *Dostoevsky: The Seeds of Revolt, 1821–1849* (Princeton, N.J.: Princeton University Press, 1986). While somewhat dated, Valerii Kirpotin's *Dostoevskii i Belinskii* (Moscow: Khudozhestvennaia literatura, 1976) similarly conveys Dostoevsky's deep ambivalence toward Belinsky.

56. Joseph Frank defines the philosophy of the radical critics as an "all-embracing materialism, an ethics of Utilitarian egoism, and a naive belief in science and rationality as entirely sufficient to unravel the complexities of the human condition": Frank, *Dostoevsky: The Stir of Liberation, 1860–1865* (Princeton, N.J.: Princeton University Press, 1986), 6. Nabokov describes this evolution in terms that are even less generous: "Whatever his naive shortcomings as an appraiser of artistic values, Belinsky had as a citizen and as a thinker that wonderful instinct for truth and freedom which only party politics can destroy—and party politics were still in their infancy. At the time his cup still contained a pure liquid; with the help of Dobrolyubov and Pisarev and Mikhaylovski it was doomed to turn into a breeding fluid for most sinister germs": Vladimir Nabokov, *Gogol* (Norfolk, Va.: New Directions, 1944), 128.

57. Fyodor Dostoevsky, *The Idiot*, trans. Richard Pevear and Larissa Volokhonsky (New York: Vintage Classics, 2003), 394.

58. Fyodor Dostoevsky, "G-n -Bov i vopros ob iskusstve" in vol. 18 of *Polnoe sobranie sochinenii v tridtsati tomakh* (Leningrad: Nauka, 1972–90), 94. All translations from the Russian of this edition are my own. *Polnoe sobranie* is hereafter cited as *PSS* in the notes.

59. Dostoevsky, "G-n -Bov i vopros ob iskusstve," 94.

60. Dostoevsky, "G-n -Bov i vopros ob iskusstve," 94. On Dostoevsky's understanding of the ideal of beauty, especially in the context of "Mr. –bov," see Robert Louis Jackson, *Dostoevsky's Quest for Form* (New Haven, Conn.: Yale University Press, 1966).

61. Dostoevsky, "G-n -Bov i vopros ob iskusstve," 78.

62. Dostoevsky, "[Zapisnaia knizhka 1863–1864 gg.]" in vol. 20 of *Polnoe sobranie sochinenii v tridtsati tomakh* (Leningrad: Nauka, 1972–90), 172–75, italics in the original.

63. Gogol wrote his draft response to Belinsky's letter between the end of July and the beginning of August 1847. Torn into pieces, but saved by Gogol, the unsent letter was discovered among Gogol's papers by Pantaleimon Kulish, Gogol's first biographer and the editor of the first posthumous edition of his collected works. Kulish put together the torn pieces and published the draft in an incomplete form, with censored omissions and numerous textual inaccuracies, in the second volume of his biography *Zapiski o zhizni Nikolaia Vasil'evicha Gogolia* [*Notes on the Life of Nikolai Gogol*] (St. Petersburg: Yulius Shtauf, 1856), 108–13. While Kulish omits Belinsky's name for reasons of censorship, the publication of Gogol's response to Belinsky from August 10, 1847, next to the draft makes its addressee obvious for anyone familiar with the correspondence between Belinsky and Gogol. Dostoevsky knew of and used Kulish's edition of Gogol's works, hence, there is no reason to doubt that he read Kulish's biography. The reconstructed full text of the draft was published for the first time in the Soviet edition of Gogol's collected works in 1952 (see Nikolai Gogol, *Polnoe sobranie sochinenii* [Moscow: Izdatel'stvo Akademii nauk SSSR, 1937–52]).

64. Dostoevsky, "G-n -Bov i vopros ob iskusstve," 81.

65. In *Dostoevsky's Secrets: Reading Against the Grain* (Evanston, Ill.: Northwestern University Press, 2009), Carol Apollonio exposes the pathology of the dreamer figure in the seemingly innocent narrator of Dostoevsky's early novella "White Nights."

66. Kulish, *Zapiski*, 112.

67. In *Dostoevskii i Gogol'*, Tynianov mentions that the inclusion of Gogol's previously unpublished letters in Kulish's edition of the collected works played a considerable role in the critical reevaluation of Gogol's legacy, particularly as a result of Chernyshevsky's review of the edition. He argues, however, that Dostoevsky's negative opinion of *Selected Passages* remained the same (28–29). I am not aware whether Tynianov was familiar with Kulish's *Zapiski* (which included Gogol's draft, while the collected works edition did not).

68. Kristin Vitalich suggests that in *The Village of Stepanchikovo*, Dostoevsky enacts a struggle with Gogol over literary mastery: Vitalich, "*The Village of Stepanchikovo*: Toward a (Lacanian) Theory of Parody," *Slavic and East European Journal* 53, no. 2 (2009).

69. Dostoevsky, "I.S. Aksakovu," in vol. 30.1 of *Polnoe sobranie sochinenii v tridtsati tomakh* (Leningrad: Nauka, 1972–90), 225–26.

70. Dostoevsky, "*Svistok* i *Russkii Vestnik*," in vol. 19 of *Polnoe sobranie sochinenii v tridtsati tomakh* (Leningrad: Nauka, 1972–90), 109.

71. Robert Louis Jackson similarly proposes to reconcile the dialogic unfinalizability in Dostoevsky's prose with his Christian ethics through the idea of *permanent striving* toward finalization. Distinguishing the ethical value of the verbal mode of expression from the visual one, Jackson argues that what directs and attracts the characters is visual, not verbal, inspiration. While the voice in-

creasingly becomes the characteristic of the *horizontal*, human world, the image is strongly associated with the *vertical* dimension of Dostoevsky's Christian hierarchy of values. For Jackson, the two distinct dimensions of Dostoevsky's writing correspond to Dostoevsky's double relation to his novelistic world. While on the horizontal plane he comes out as "a man with a point of view" (and is not structurally different from any of his characters), the vertical plane is a reflection of Dostoevsky's artistic self, which allows him to orchestrate the ideological quests of his characters in the same way that Bakhtin's Christ "organizes and subdues" different voices of the novel. "In both roles," writes Jackson, "Dostoevsky acknowledges the unfinalized nature of human experience and striving, the permanent reality of freedom and uncertainty, dialogue and dilemma, in this world": Jackson, *Dialogues with Dostoevsky: The Overwhelming Questions* (Stanford, Calif.: Stanford University Press, 1993), 284–85.

72. Harpham, *Shadows of Ethics*, 29, emphasis in the original.

73. Geoffrey Galt Harpham, *Getting It Right: Language, Literature, and Ethics* (Chicago: University of Chicago Press, 1992), 165.

74. Fyodor Dostoevsky, *Notes from Underground* (New York: Vintage, 1993), 10.

75. In arguing that Bakhtin's reading of Dostoevsky is informed by the latter's Christian ethics, Jackson suggests that the polyphonic Dostoevsky "acts out" Christ by altruistically allowing his characters to talk without authorial intervention (see his "Bakhtin's Poetics of Dostoevsky" in *Dialogues with Dostoevsky*).

76. Nabokov brings up the scene between Sonya and Raskolnikov as evidence of Dostoevsky's blatant and cliché-ridden emotional manipulation of the reader in his lecture on Dostoevsky; see Vladimir Nabokov, *Lectures on Russian Literature* (New York: Harcourt Brace Jovanovich, 1980).

77. In her monograph *The Gift of Active Empathy: Scheler, Bakhtin, and Dostoevsky* (Evanston, Ill.: Northwestern University Press, 2016), Alina Wyman has convincingly argued that among Dostoevsky's heroes, Alyosha Karamazov is alone able to participate and engage others in relationships that are both rewarding and ethically sound.

78. Vladislav Khodasevich, "O Sirine," in *V. V. Nabokov: Pro i contra*, vol. 1, ed. B. V. Averin et al. (St. Petersburg: Izdatel'stvo russkogo khristianskogo gumanitarnogo instituta, 1997), 243.

79. David Packman treats *Lolita* as a modernist text that allegorizes practices of reading. As such, it "engages in a kind of self-representation, for it is its own referent": Packman, *Vladimir Nabokov: The Structure of Literary Desire* (Columbia: University of Missouri Press, 1982), 35. This turns the novel into a text meant to heighten the reader's awareness of engaging with a textual construction. Consider, for example, this passage, in which Packman discusses Humbert's masturbation scene: "However, quite another, more formal view of the matter is certainly possible. The Russian Formalist notion of motivation per-

mits this other view, from which moral implications are absent. One might say that Lolita has indeed been 'safely solipsized' in that she has become a functional element in the construction of a sequence, a bit of narrative" (53).

80. Michael Wood, *The Magician's Doubts: Nabokov and the Risks of Fiction* (Princeton, N.J.: Princeton University Press, 1994), 57.

81. Vladimir Nabokov, *The Annotated Lolita*, ed. Alfred Appel, Jr. (New York: Vintage, 1991), 312.

82. The most obvious of these are *Despair* and *Lolita*, but Nabokov's narrator's cruelty extends into *Pnin*, as well as such late novels as *Ada*. For the discussion of the narrator's "monologizing" tendencies in *Pnin*, see Stephen Blackwell's "Dostoevskian Problems." In "Kant's Eye: *Ada*, Art, Ethics," which is the third chapter of *Vladimir Nabokov and the Poetics of Liberalism* (Evanston, Ill.: Northwestern University Press, 2011), Dana Dragunoiu evaluates Van's cruelty toward Lucette against Nabokov's engagement with Kant's moral philosophy. Dragunoiu accepts that deception constitutes a core of Nabokov's artistic practice, but distinguishes between two kinds of deception—an immoral one which is associated with lying and paraphrastic translation, while the other, which is linked to "the natural idiom of art and nature, take[s] dignity and autonomy as [its] point of departure" (165). Dragunoiu proceeds to argue that the same difference persists in Nabokov's separation of life and art, and art and politics: "Unlike the enchanting deceptions of art, which seek to expand human consciousness by making it aware of its uniqueness and freedom, political deception drives the human spirit into the ground" (167). Yet, the problem of applying Kant, whose aesthetics are integrally connected to his ethics, to someone like Nabokov, who takes great pains to separate the two, is that one has to immediately start accounting for exceptions. Hence, Dragunoiu argues—quite accurately, I believe—that Mademoiselle's deception of the narrator in *Speak, Memory* is "strikingly *artistic*" (166, italics in the original) just because it is kind, but Dragunoiu refuses to accept that this example contradicts the strict epistemological divisions she proposes earlier. As it is, Nabokov's texts demand a kind of ethics that posits the irreplaceability of experience as its cornerstone; and the Bakhtinian approach, with its stress on the uniqueness of interpersonal experience, seems to be much better suited for it than the Kantian one (see note 28 of this chapter for my adjustments to Pechey's explanations for the differences between Bakhtin and Kant).

83. For this view, see Ellen Pifer, *Nabokov and the Novel* (Cambridge, Mass.: Harvard University Press, 1980).

84. See Leland de la Durantaye's *Style Is Matter*.

85. Vladimir Nabokov, *Despair* (New York: Vintage International, 1989), xiii.

86. De la Durantaye, *Style Is Matter*, 14.

87. As Naiman argues, "while depicting aestheticizing and . . . condemning [illicit] connections in the form of characters' sexual practices, Nabokov encour-

ages and even trains his readers to make illicit . . . and often libidinally charged interpretive associations as an essential step in understanding his texts" (Naiman, *Nabokov, Perversely*, 8). Similarly, in combining the Girardian model of mimetic desire and Peter Brook's suggestion that "thematic representations of desire in the novel reflect and refract a desire that motivates its telling and reception," Christopher S. Weinberger argues that the ethical reading of Nabokov depends on our recognition and acceptance of the analogy between the two tiers of the text: Weinberger, "Critical Desire and the Novel: Ethics of Self-Consciousness in Cervantes and Nabokov," *Narrative* 20, no. 3 (October 2012): 282.

88. Maurice Couturier, "Censorship and the Authorial Figure in *Ulysses* and *Lolita*," *Cycnos* 12, no. 2, "Nabokov: At the Crossroads of Modernism and Postmodernism" (1995): 30.

89. Vladimir Nabokov, *Strong Opinions* (New York: Vintage International, 1990), 19; cited in Couturier, "Censorship and the Authorial Figure," 40.

90. Maurice Couturier, "The Near-Tyranny of the Author: *Pale Fire*," in *Nabokov and His Fiction: New Perspectives*, ed. Julian W. Connolly (Cambridge: Cambridge University Press, 1999), 64.

91. Couturier, "Censorship and the Authorial Figure," 41.

92. As in, for example, Ellen Pifer's case, who, taking to heart Nabokov's condemnation of his protagonist in the preface to *Despair*, completely discounts Hermann's verbal artistry. In order to resuscitate the appreciation of Hermann's sparkling verbosity, David Rampton makes a case for disregarding Nabokov's extratextual writing on his prose (see his "Critical Choices").

93. Nabokov, *Strong Opinions*, 16.

94. Zadie Smith, *Changing My Mind: Occasional Essays* (New York: Penguin, 2009), 51.

95. Couturier, "Near-Tyranny of the Author," 66.

96. Michel de Montaigne, *Works of Michael de Montaigne*, vol. 2, trans. W. Hazlitt (New York: Hurd and Houghton, 1859), 17.

97. Wood, *Magician's Doubts*, 76.

98. Vladimir Nabokov, *Bend Sinister* (New York: Vintage International, 1990), 116.

99. Vladimir Nabokov, *The Stories of Vladimir Nabokov* (New York: Alfred A. Knopf, 1995), 659.

100. Nabokov, *Bend Sinister*, 117.

101. This, of course, is one of the more common ways of reading Nabokov. For its concise formulation (with the reader's task implied), see Alexander Dolinin: "Nabokov's peculiar strategy that he used sparingly but persistently throughout his mature work is to create a discrepancy or a tension between *syuzhet* and *fabula* of a text through enigmatizing certain important elements of the latter . . . Relevant information related to the omitted event (or events) is encrypted in the *syuzhet* as a kind of intratextual riddle (often supported by intertextual ref-

erences), and specifically marked clues to the pertinent code are implanted into the text": Dolinin, "The Signs and Symbols in Nabokov's 'Signs and Symbols,'" *Zembla*, https://www.libraries.psu.edu/Nabokov/dolinin.htm.

102. Andrew Gibson, *Postmodernity, Ethics, and the Novel: From Leavis to Levinas* (London: Routledge, 1999), 32.

103. In the afterword to *Lolita*, Nabokov writes that the first "shiver of inspiration" for the novel was "prompted by a newspaper story about an ape in the Jardin des Plantes, who, after months of coaxing by a scientist, produced the first drawing ever charcoaled by an animal: this sketch showed the bars of the poor creature's cage" (Nabokov, *Annotated Lolita*, 311).

104. Nabokov, *Annotated Lolita*, 259. Humbert's original proposes that "sex is but the ancilla of art" (259).

105. The Bakhtinian reading of Nabokov's prose that I am proposing here is not terra incognita. There have been a number of critical inquiries that explored the connection between the philosopher and the writer. Pekka Tammi describes Nabokov as an ultimate antipolyphonist: "We may talk of a pronouncedly *anti-polypohonic* feature in [Nabokov's] writing: *an overriding tendency to make explicit the presence of a creative consciousness behind every fictive construction*": Tammi, *Problems of Nabokov's Poetics: A Narratological Analysis* (Helsinki: Suomalainen Tiedeakatemia, 1985), 100, emphasis in the original. While Tammi does not pursue the implications of Nabokov's authorial control of the text, the Bakhtinian framework he proposes allows us to productively bring the authorial figure into the fold of literary analysis in order to understand the ethical implications of the complex relationship between the monologic strategies of the author and the monologism of his narrating protagonists. This is the direction I take up in my study here. In *Nabokov's Early Fiction*, Connolly employs Bakhtinian analysis to point out the monologizing strategies of Nabokov's characters. Similarly, in "Dostoevskian Problems," Blackwell points out that when applied to Nabokov's first-person narratives, the Bakhtinian approach reveals "an uncanny affinity with the devices and themes that Nabokov appears to have valued in Dostoevsky and sought to elaborate in his own fiction" (138). In exploring the characters' Bakhtinian quest for narrative freedom in Nabokov's first-person narratives such as *The Eye, Despair, The Gift, The Real Life of Sebastian Knight, Lolita*, and *Pnin*, Blackwell finds in these novels "characters whose self-definitions are formed against a vivid backdrop of the possibility of being described or defined by someone else's words" (141). In his dissertation "Bakhtin and Nabokov," Picon takes this inquiry further to argue that Nabokov's first-person protagonists not only struggle to retain their freedom, but also attempt to usurp the authorial position. Picon argues for the intrinsic connection between the aesthetic and physical crimes of such narrators as Hermann in *Despair* and Humbert Humbert in *Lolita*. As Picon puts it, "Nabokov posits a conception of monologism as a moral transgression against the other, a conception with

equally valid and compelling permutations across conceptual and philosophical boundaries: at the level of narrative as representation of the world, it is a hermeneutic crime that falsifies and distorts the epistemological underpinnings of a world made up of multiple consciousnesses; at the level of interpersonal ethics, monologism is the metaphor for acts that can lead to the literal silence of others" (214). Blackwell makes a persuasive case for Zina as the first—and most perceptive—of *The Gift*'s readers and proposes a Bakhtinian correlation between aesthetic and interpersonal experiences: "Thus, it turns out that to read lovingly is, at the very least, analogous to actual love between two people": Stephen Blackwell, *Zina's Paradox: The Figured Reader in Nabokov's "Gift"* (New York: Peter Lang, 2000), 102. Using the Bakhtin of "Author and Hero" as his philosophical springboard, Blackwell argues that Nabokov insists that "love . . . is a principle of necessity in both artistic and 'human' relationships" (103). Basing my reading of Nabokov on the Bakhtinian blurring of the boundary between ethical and aesthetic experiences, I suggest instead that the "principle of necessity" in reading and authoring the other is not love but *responsibility*. After all, it would be hard to argue that the Chernyshevsky of Fyodor's book is a product of love. The shift from love to responsibility, in my opinion, corresponds to the shift in Bakhtinian thought from "Author and Hero" to *Problems of Dostoevsky's Poetics*. None of the above-mentioned scholars—and this is where my study differs from theirs—address the relationship between the monologism of the author and the monologism of the characters.

106. After all, it is hardly accidental that most of Sybil's otherworldly visitors are writers.

CHAPTER ONE

1. As Gary Saul Morson writes, the relation between hero and author in a polyphonic novel "allows the hero to be truly free, capable of surprising not only characters but also the author . . . In some crucial respects the polyphonic author—not just the narrator—resembles just another character. Strange as it may seem, the Dostoevskian hero is not wholly the author's product; once created, he has a life of his own": Morson, *Narrative and Freedom: The Shadows of Time* (New Haven, Conn.: Yale University Press, 1994), 91.

2. As Caryl Emerson observes, in Bakhtin's vision of the polyphonic novel, "once a dialogue of ideas . . . becomes the common denominator between author, hero, and reader, more space opens up for the reader. Readers can participate actively—which is to say, non-vicariously, on an equal plane—in the narrative": Emerson, *The First Hundred Years of Mikhail Bakhtin* (Princeton, N.J.: Princeton University Press, 1997), 128.

3. In *Christianity in Bakhtin: God and the Exiled Author* (Cambridge: Cambridge University Press, 1998), Ruth Coates recuperates Bakhtin as a Protestant

Notes to Pages 37–38

Christian. With less enthusiasm and more skepticism, in *Mikhail Bakhtin: An Aesthetic for Democracy* (Oxford: Oxford University Press, 1999), Ken Hirschkop similarly explains the meaning-bestowing activity of the author by Bakhtin's Christian ethics: "The author can love the other and only the other because distance between the two is a presupposition of Christian ethics, according to which the believer demands the 'cross for himself and happiness for others.' What appears to be the result of a phenomenological investigation—the gap between I and other—turns out to be an axiom of Christian ethics" (66). Yet, while arguing that Bakhtin in his later writing turns from sacrifice to reciprocity, Hirschkop also quickly discounts it: "To the extent that he persuades us that the other can be redeemed by some judicious combination of phenomenological inspection and aesthetic deftness, we are apt to see his call for divine aid as redundant, and the possibility of salvation as not the gift of God but a *promesse de bonheur* [promise of happiness] built into historical life" (67). In *Gift of Active Empathy*, Wyman argues that the Incarnation is essential to the ethics of Bakhtin's architectonics (see especially 14–41).

4. Bakhtin, *Toward a Philosophy*, 107; qtd. in Coates, *Christianity in Bakhtin*, 45.

5. Bakhtin, "Author and Hero," 56.

6. For Pechey, the incarnation of Christ as an embodied consciousness allows us to view "the 'religious event'" as "paradigmatic for aesthetic activity: structurally similar in the strict non-coincidence of constituent consciousnesses, prayer and ritual differ from the aesthetic event only in that the author is not any other (human) other but the (divine) Other of all of us" (Pechey, "Philosophy and Theology," 51).

7. Dostoevsky, "Zapisi literaturno-kriticheskogo i publitsisticheskogo kharaktera iz zapisnoii tetradi 1880–1881 gg.," in vol. 27 of *Polnoe sobranie sochinenii v tridtsati tomakh* (Leningrad: Nauka, 1972–90), 56–85.

8. See the "Introduction" for the text of the entry in Dostoevsky's 1864 notebook where he records this thought after the death of his first wife.

9. Bakhtin, "Author and Hero," 56, italics in the original.

10. Daphne Erdinast-Vulcan, *Between Philosophy and Literature: Bakhtin and the Question of the Subject* (Stanford, Calif.: Stanford University Press, 2013), 14.

11. The most recent criticism of Bakhtin's suppositions about the inherent hierarchy between author and character comes from Irina Sandomirskaia, who reads the aesthetic activity of the Bakhtinian author as violence par excellence, not because there exists a different, less harmful way of representing the other, but because Bakhtin refuses to acknowledge it as such. Or, at least, the Bakhtin of "Author and Hero" does so. In Sandomirskaia's reading, Bakhtin's evaluation of the ethics of authorship begins to change by the 1940s, as expressed in his wartime notebooks. (See Irina Sandomirskaia, *Blokada v slove: Ocherki*

kriticheskoi teorii i biopolitiki iazyka [Moscow: Novoe literaturnoe obozrenie, 2013], 111–72.) For a translation and a scholarly reading of Bakhtin's notebooks in the context of his philosophy and the evolution of the author-hero relationship, see the recent forum "The Dark and Radiant Bakhtin: Wartime Notes," in the *Slavic and East European Journal* 61, no. 2 (2017).

12. Coates, *Christianity in Bakhtin*, 86.

13. Malcolm Jones, *Dostoevsky and the Dynamics of Religious Experience* (London: Anthem, 2005), 146.

14. A quick summary of Bakhtin's definition of polyphony might be helpful here. According to Bakhtin, in the monologic novel the horizon of the hero's consciousness is limited by the very fact that it belongs to someone who is a literary creation, not a real person. The hero is a product of the author's imagination; thus he cannot achieve full autonomy vis-à-vis a creator. In the polyphonic novel, on the other hand, the strict hierarchy between author and hero has been dismantled. Polyphony, in Bakhtin's terms, does not stand for a multiplicity of different voices in the novel, but defines the effect produced once these voices are no longer united within the mental scope of a singular (monologic) authorial consciousness. Hence, the ethical and religious beliefs espoused in Dostoevsky's nonfictional writing have no place in his novels. Or, to put it differently, they can have a voice, but that voice takes its place in the chorus of his characters' voices (sometimes embodied in one or another character) and does not (and structurally cannot) have ideological superiority over them. The division of literature into Dostoevsky and everyone else is much stronger in Bakhtin's original Dostoevsky book, while the second one includes an extensive chapter treating the Dostoevsky novel, in Michael Holquist's words, "as the purest expression of what always had been implicit in [the history of the genre]": Holquist, "Introduction," in Mikhail Bakhtin, *The Dialogic Imagination: Four Essays by M. M. Bakhtin*, trans. Caryl Emerson and Michael Holquist, ed. Michael Holquist (Austin: University of Texas Press, 1981), xxxi. In such "middle period" works as "Discourse in the Novel" Bakhtin argues that heteroglossia—the multitude of voices—is the distinguishing characteristic of the modern novel.

15. In his preparatory notes for *Problems of Dostoevsky's Poetics*, Bakhtin insists that the position of the polyphonic author is still that of outsideness; what is different in the polyphonic novel is the relationship of the author toward his hero: "The new position of the author in the polyphonic novel, revealing in a person the different 'I-for myself,' which is infinite and unfinalizable, does not destroy the image, since *the authorial position of outsideness* remains in full force. What changes is the topos of this outsideness and the content of the surplus" ("Dostoevsky, 1961," in Mikhail Bakhtin, *Sobranie sochinenii v semi tomakh* [Moscow: Izdatel'stvo russkie slovari iazyki slavianskoi kultury, 1997–2012], vol. 5: 367. The translation from the Russian is mine).

16. This is what Coates (*Christianity in Bakhtin*) calls "the exiled author"

(20). See also Robert Louis Jackson's comparison of the author's changed position with respect to Christ in "Bakhtin's Poetics of Dostoevsky and Dostoevsky's 'Declaration of Religious Faith'" (in *Dialogues with Dostoevsky*).

17. Natalia Reed, in a Girardian reading of Bakhtin's *Problems of Dostoevsky's Poetics*, proposes that far from protecting the hero from authorial violence, Bakhtin achieves the opposite effect by "scapegoating" monologic discourse, that is, by letting the polyphonic author off the hook and projecting all narrative violence onto the novels' monologic heroes: Reed, "The Philosophical Roots of Polyphony: A Dostoevskian Reading," in *Critical Essays on Mikhail Bakhtin*, ed. Caryl Emerson (Boston: G. K. Hall, 1999), 117–52. See also Mark Lipovetsky: "Either Bakhtin consciously demonizes the monologic word to free it from any violence that is also inherently present in the 'communicative'—dialogic—model of truth, or the monologic word becomes the only reality that exists for Bakhtin, and the dialogic discourse is nothing but wishful thinking . . . an intellectual utopia, masterfully performed on not quite dialogic Dostoevsky": Mark Lipovetsky and Irina Sandomirskaia, "Kak ne 'zavershit" Bakhtina," *Novoe literaturnoe obozrenie* 79 (2006).

18. Bakhtin, *Problems of Dostoevsky's Poetics*, 68, emphasis in the original.

19. As Caryl Emerson puts it: "For he [Bakhtin] suspects that it was not form that the formalists really cared about: in their role as 'specifiers,' what they cared about was matter, shaped material" (Emerson, "Perezhiv temnotu stalinskoi nochi," 43, translation from Russian is mine).

20. Emerson similarly observes that "*Problems of Dostoevsky's Poetics*, admittedly 'formalist' in its reluctance to pass judgment on the ideology and moral virtue of Dostoevsky's plots, is also remarkably free of ethical or metaphysical problems even in the formal realm of language. The tortured verbal moves of the underground man . . . ultimately represent for Bakhtin a celebration of unrealized potential and the right to postpone forever the final word": Emerson, "Word and Image in Dostoevsky's Worlds: Robert Louis Jackson on Readings That Bakhtin Could Not Do," in *Freedom and Responsibility in Russian Literature: Essays in Honor of Robert Louis Jackson*, ed. Elizabeth Cheresh Allen and Gary Saul Morson (Evanston, Ill.: Northwestern University Press, 1995), 253.

21. Bakhtin, *Problems of Dostoevsky's Poetics*, 40.

22. Caryl Emerson, "Editor's Preface," in Mikhail Bakhtin, *Problems of Dostoevsky's Poetics*, ed. and trans. Caryl Emerson (Minneapolis: University of Minnesota Press, 1984), xxxii.

23. Mikhail Bakhtin, "Toward a Reworking of the Dostoevsky Book," in *Critical Essays on Dostoevsky*, ed. Robin Feuer Miller (Boston: G. K. Hall, 1986), 287.

24. Michael Holquist, *Dialogism: Bakhtin and His World* (London: Routledge, 1990), 17.

25. Bakhtin delineates the differences between hidden and overt polemics by making a distinction between the object of each: "Overt polemic is . . . directed at another's discourse . . . In the hidden polemic, however, discourse is directed toward an ordinary referential object, naming it, portraying, expressing, and only indirectly striking a blow at the other's discourse, clashing with it, as it were, within the object itself" (Holquist, *Dialogism*, 196).

26. Dostoevsky, *The Idiot*, 309–10.

27. Bakhtin, *Problems of Dostoevsky's Poetics*, 242.

28. Caryl Emerson, "Zosima's 'Mysterious Visitor': Again Bakhtin on Dostoevsky, and Dostoevsky on Heaven and Hell," in *A New Word on The Brothers Karamazov*, ed. Robert Louis Jackson (Evanston, Ill.: Northwestern University Press, 2004), 159.

29. Dostoevsky, "Zapisi literaturno-kriticheskogo i publitsisticheskogo kharaktera iz zapisnoii tetradi 1880–1881 gg.," in vol. 27 of *Polnoe sobranie sochinenii v tridtsati tomakh* (Leningrad: Nauka, 1972–90), 56–85; quoted in Bakhtin, *Problems of Dostoevsky's Poetics*, 97–98.

30. Bakhtin, *Problems of Dostoevsky's Poetics*, 87.

31. Fyodor Dostoevsky, *Crime and Punishment* (New York: Vintage, 1993), 70.

32. In a Nietzschean reading of Bakhtin, Michael Andre Bernstein identifies ressentiment as one of the underlying causes of dialogism in Dostoevsky. In Bernstein's account, Dostoevsky's characters experience dialogue as entrapment, which triggers "rage and *ressentiment* in [those] who must endure that endless chatter of already uttered utterances": Bernstein, "The Poetics of Ressentiment," in *Rethinking Bakhtin: Extensions and Challenges*, ed. Gary S. Morson and Caryl Emerson (Evanston, Ill.: Northwestern University Press, 1989), 208. Bernstein's reassessment of dialogic activity designates Dostoevsky's characters' discursive activity as a portrayal of "the most disturbing modern metaphysics of evil" (208). For a Schelerian reading of ressentiment in *Notes from the Underground*, see Wyman, *Gift of Active Empathy*.

33. Dostoevsky, "[Zapisnaia knizhka 1863–1864 gg.]" 172.

34. I am indebted to Caryl Emerson for this point.

35. Emerson, "Word and Image in Dostoevsky's Worlds," 257.

36. Fyodor Dostoevsky, *A Writer's Diary* (Evanston, Ill.: Northwestern University Press, 1993), 1:677.

37. Bakhtin, *Problems of Dostoevsky's Poetics*, 55.

38. Dostoevsky, *A Writer's Diary*, 1:677.

39. Quoted in Bakhtin, *Problems of Dostoevsky's Poetics*, 97.

40. Robin Feuer Miller, *Dostoevsky and The Idiot: Author, Narrator, and Reader* (Cambridge, Mass.: Harvard University Press, 1981), 45.

41. Dostoevsky, *The Brothers Karamazov*, 109.

42. Discussed in Emerson, *First Hundred Years*, 130.

43. Dostoevsky, *A Writer's Diary*, 1:652, emphasis in the original.

44. On Dostoevsky's views on suicide, see Irina Paperno's *Suicide as a Cultural Institution in Dostoevsky's Russia* (Ithaca, N.Y.: Cornell University Press, 1997).

45. Harriet Murav notices other biblical references that the pawnbroker fails to recognize: "The Christological imagery of the scene resonates with an earlier passage, in which the narrator pokes his finger into the spoonful of blood next to her body, like doubting Thomas who pokes his finger into Jesus": Murav, "Reading Women in Dostoevsky," in *A Plot of Her Own*, ed. Sona Stephan Hoisington (Evanston, Ill.: Northwestern University Press, 1995), 50. The narrator's description of the "dessert-spoon of blood" spilled out of his wife's body becomes another marker of his interpretative limits (Dostoevsky, *A Writer's Diary*, 1:716, translation amended). Throughout the narrative, but also during his marriage, the pawnbroker interprets life through the framework of economic value.

46. See Irina Paperno's discussion of this point in *Suicide as a Cultural Institution*, 178–82.

47. Commenting on Dostoevsky's analysis of Liza Herzen's death, Murav states that "Dostoevsky constructs Liza Herzen as a heroine with an idea, and as a heroine who produces discourse" ("Reading Women in Dostoevsky," 53).

48. In Murav's words, Dostoevsky "gives the correspondent a lesson in how to read what Bakhtin calls 'the word with a sidelong glance'" ("Reading Women in Dostoevsky," 54). For Murav, this is an example of Dostoevsky's generosity toward the young woman: "In this reading of the suicide note, we can see Dostoevsky's dialogic address to the woman inside the woman, to paraphrase the much-quoted line from his 1880 notebooks: 'with utter realism to find the man in man'" (54). I agree with Murav that Dostoevsky's generous analysis uncovers the hidden logic in Liza Herzen's note, yet also argue that this is generosity with a purpose, allowing Dostoevsky to launch a critique of discourse based on materialist philosophy.

49. Writing on Dostoevsky's views on suicide, Paperno suggests that for Dostoevsky the suicide was a symptom of a generational malaise. See *Suicide as a Cultural Institution*.

50. Paperno, *Suicide as a Cultural Institution*, 179–80. In her reading, Paperno focuses on the pernicious side effects of materialist philosophy on the generation of the 1860s, but does not address the formal elements of Liza Herzen's discourse.

51. Dostoevsky, *A Writer's Diary*, 1:653.

52. Dostoevsky, "Varianty," in vol. 23 of *Polnoe sobranie sochinenii v tridtsati tomakh* (Leningrad: Nauka, 1972–90), 325.

53. Dostoevsky, *A Writer's Diary*, 1:653.

54. Dostoevsky responds here to Saltykov-Shchedrin.

55. In *Dostoevsky and the Riddle of the Self* (Evanston, Ill.: Northwestern University Press, 2017), Yuri Corrigan makes a convincing argument that with-

out the self's ability "to discover the collectively shared indwelling sources of the psyche" (148), Dostoevsky's characters are consigned to an aggressive "mutual consumption as the direct consequence of the disappearance of an essential indwelling principle" (29).

56. Dostoevsky, *A Writer's Diary*, 1:654.

57. The letter is discussed in the "Introduction."

58. This aspect of the story was analyzed in detail by L. M. O'Toole, who states that "in ['The Meek One"] the essential theme is not, as in classic short stories by Pushkin, Turgenev or Chekhov, confined to the facts and relationships narrated (*l'histoire*), but spills over into the process of narration (*le discours*)": O'Toole, "Structure and Style in the Short Story: Dostoevsky's *A Gentle Spirit*," in *F.M. Dostoevsky (1821–1881): A Centenary Collection*, ed. Leon Burnett (Oxford: Holdan, 1981), 5.

59. Compare O'Toole: "We are challenged not only on the level of *l'histoire*, as in most prose fiction, but on the level of *le discours*" ("Structure and Style," 11).

60. Dostoevsky, *A Writer's Diary*, 1:678.

61. Peter Brooks, *Body Work: Objects of Desire in Modern Narrative* (Cambridge, Mass.: Harvard University Press, 1993), 7.

62. As Harriet Murav observes, "The husband is far more concerned with an explanation of his own actions than those of his dead wife. He is absorbed in himself and what will happen to him, while the 'meek one' enters and leaves the story as a corpse" ("Reading Women in Dostoevsky," 47).

63. Dostoevsky, *A Writer's Diary*, 1:689.

64. See Bakhtin, "Author and Hero": "We take into account the background behind our back, that is to say, all that which in our surroundings, we do not see and do not know directly and which has no direct axiological validity for us, although it is seen and known by others and has validity for others—all that, in other words, which constitutes the background against which, as it were, others perceive us axiologically, against which we stand forth for them. Finally, we also anticipate and take into account what will happen after our death—the outcome of our life as a whole (no longer for us, of course, but for others)" (15–16).

65. Bakhtin, *Problems of Dostoevsky's Poetics*, 290.

66. This is Marina Mizzau's reading. As she puts it, silence in the story becomes "a paradoxical mode of communication": Mizzau, "A Double-Voiced Silence," in *The Lonely Mirror*, ed. Sandra Kemp and Paola Bono (London: Routledge, 1993), 65.

67. Aaron Fogel, "Coerced Speech," in *Rethinking Bakhtin: Extensions and Challenges*, ed. Gary S. Morson and Caryl Emerson (Evanston, Ill.: Northwestern University Press, 1989), 175.

68. Murav, "Reading Women in Dostoevsky," 48.

69. As Murav writes: "The death of the 'meek one' not only precipitates but is a necessary condition for the construction of the hero's 'confessional self-

utterance' . . . The husband's existence as discourse depends on the body lying on the table" ("Reading Women in Dostoevsky," 48).

70. Dostoevsky, *A Writer's Diary*, 2:700, emphasis in the original.
71. Dostoevsky, "[Zapisnaia knizhka 1863–1864 gg.]," 172.
72. Dostoevsky, *A Writer's Diary*, 1:693.
73. I am indebted to Natalia Reed for this comment.
74. Dostoevsky, *A Writer's Diary*, 1:689.
75. Robert Louis Jackson, *The Art of Dostoevsky: Deliriums and Nocturnes* (Princeton, N.J.: Princeton University Press, 1981), 256.
76. Dostoevsky, *A Writer's Diary*, 1:713.
77. Fogel, "Coerced Speech," 177.
78. Dostoevsky, *A Writer's Diary*, 1:710–11.

CHAPTER TWO

Chapter 2 was previously published in a somewhat different form as "From Violence to Silence: Vicissitudes of Reading (in) The Idiot" in *Slavic Review* 72, no. 3 (Fall 2013): 552–72.

1. Dostoevsky, *The Idiot*, 579–80.
2. Bakhtin, *Problems of Dostoevsky's Poetics*, 7.
3. Avital Ronell, *Stupidity* (Urbana: University of Illinois Press, 2002), 174.
4. Dostoevsky, *The Idiot*, 581–83, emphasis in the original.
5. Ronell, *Stupidity*, 176.
6. Bakhtin, "Toward a Reworking of the Dostoevsky Book," 249.
7. Emerson, "Word and Image in Dostoevsky's Worlds," 253.
8. Caryl Emerson, "Prefatory Comments on 'Toward a Reworking of the Dostoevsky Book,'" in *Critical Essays on Dostoevsky*, ed. Robin Feuer Miller (Boston: G. K. Hall, 1986), 245, emphasis in the original.
9. Jackson, *Dialogues with Dostoevsky*, 283.
10. But also see Emerson: "Bakhtin's passion for the horizontally projected dialogic word comes at the cost of Dostoevsky's more vertical gestures, those leaps into iconic or transfigured time-space in the form of personal conversion or collective apocalypse" (Emerson, "Word and Image in Dostoevsky's Worlds," 253).
11. For a thorough discussion of the differences between Jackson's and Bakhtin's approaches to Dostoevsky, see Emerson, "Word and Image in Dostoevsky's Worlds."
12. Mikhail Epstein, *Slovo i molchanie: Metafizika russkoi literatury* (Moscow: Vysshaya shkola, 2006), 268.
13. For an informative discussion on the duality of silence in *The Brothers Karamazov*, see Jones, *Dynamics of Religious Experience*, 103–47.
14. Dostoevsky, *The Idiot*, 385.

Notes to Pages 88–95

15. See the "Introduction" for an elaboration of Geoffrey Harpham's conceptualization of the importance of plot for literary ethics.

16. Jones, *Dynamics of Religious Experience*, 92.

17. Dostoevsky, *Brothers Karamazov*, 108.

18. Malcolm Jones, *Dostoevsky after Bakhtin: Readings in Dostoevsky's Fantastic Realism* (Cambridge: Cambridge University Press, 1990), 181.

19. Robin Feuer Miller makes the important point, however, that Zosima's life comes to the reader as "a product of indirection, of multiple layers of mediation": Robin Feuer Miller, *The Brothers Karamazov: Worlds of the Novel* (New Haven, Conn.: Yale University Press, 1992), 74. For a discussion of Alyosha's "word about the other" that does not finalize the other, see Wyman, *Gift of Active Empathy*.

20. See Feuer Miller's *Dostoevsky and The Idiot* and Jones's *Dostoevsky after Bakhtin*.

21. Newton, *Narrative Ethics*, 19.

22. Jones, *Dostoevsky after Bakhtin*, 142.

23. Young, *Dostoevsky's "The Idiot,"* 17.

24. See chapter 1 for a fuller articulation of this notion.

25. Dostoevsky, *The Idiot*, 309.

26. J. M. Coetzee, "Confession and Double Thoughts: Tolstoy, Rousseau, Dostoevsky," *Comparative Literature* 37, no. 3 (1985): 222.

27. Paul de Man, *Blindness and Insight: Essays in the Rhetoric of Contemporary Criticism* (Minneapolis: University of Minnesota Press, 1983), 11.

28. Dostoevsky, *The Idiot*, 308.

29. Coetzee, "Confession and Double Thoughts," 226.

30. Ronell, *Stupidity*, 175.

31. Young, *Dostoevsky's "The Idiot,"* 93.

32. Dostoevsky, "[Zapisnaia knizhka 1863–1864 gg.]," 172–75. Emphasis in the original. See the "Introduction" for a fuller text of this entry.

33. Jones, *Dostoevsky after Bakhtin*, 183.

34. Dostoevsky, *The Idiot*, 36.

35. Val Vinokur, *The Trace of Judaism: Dostoevsky, Babel, Mandelstam, Levinas* (Evanston, Ill.: Northwestern University Press, 2008), 18.

36. See Vinokur, *Trace of Judaism*, 15–34.

37. Emmanuel Levinas, *Totality and Infinity* (Pittsburgh, Pa.: Duquesne University Press, 1969), 23; cited in Vinokur, *Trace of Judaism*, 17.

38. Vinokur, *Trace of Judaism*, 22.

39. In her feminist reading of the novel, Nina Pelican Straus makes a similar point by addressing the tension between Dostoevsky's desire to "save women 'through Christ'" and a "dramatized apprehension of the ways Christianity makes that wish impossible to fulfill": Straus, "Flights from *The Idiot*'s Womanhood," in *Dostoevsky's "The Idiot": A Critical Companion*, ed. Liza Knapp (Evanston, Ill.: Northwestern University Press, 1998), 107.

Notes to Pages 95–102

40. Fyodor Dostoevsky, *Selected Letters of Fyodor Dostoevsky*, trans. Andrew R. MacAndrew, ed. Joseph Frank and David I. Goldstein (New Brunswick, N.J.: Rutgers University Press, 1987), 68.

41. Vinokur, *Trace of Judaism*, 20.

42. See Dostoevsky, "[Zapisnaia knizhka 1863–1864 gg.]," 175.

43. Vinokur uses Tolstoy (and *Anna Karenina*) as a foil for Dostoevsky. It is perhaps useful to compare Tolstoy's ambivalence toward language as a tool of communication in this novel (but also in *War and Peace*—especially in the hunt scene) to Dostoevsky's more radical stance in *The Idiot* (as argued here).

44. Walter Benjamin, "Dostoevsky's *The Idiot*," in *Selected Writings*, vol. 1, ed. Marcus Bullock and Michael W. Jennings (Cambridge, Mass.: Belknap Press of Harvard University Press, 1996), 80.

45. Dostoevsky, *The Idiot*, 308.

46. Benjamin, "Dostoevsky's *The Idiot*," 81.

47. Dostoevsky, *The Idiot*, 426.

48. Jill Robbins, *Altered Reading: Levinas and Literature* (Chicago: University of Chicago Press, 1999), 12.

49. Dostoevsky, *The Idiot*, 227.

50. See David Bethea, "*The Idiot*: Historicism Arrives at the Station," in *Dostoevsky's "The Idiot": A Critical Companion*, ed. Liza Knapp (Evanston Ill.: Northwestern University Press, 1998); and Caryl Emerson, "Problems with Baxtin's Poetics," *Slavic and East European Journal* 32, no. 4 (winter 1988).

51. Dostoevsky, *The Idiot*, 610.

52. See, for example, Andrew Wachtel, "Dostoevsky's *The Idiot*: The Novel as Photograph," *History of Photography* 26, no. 3 (2002); and Nariman Skakov, "Dostoevsky's Christ and Silence at the Margins of *The Idiot*," *Dostoevsky Studies* 13 (2009).

53. For a discussion of the anachronistic, Enlightenment nature of this interpretation, see Jeff Gatrall's "Between Iconoclasm and Silence: Representing the Divine in Holbein and Dostoevsky," *Comparative Literature* 53, no. 3 (summer 2001).

54. Dostoevsky, *The Idiot*, 218.

55. See Coetzee, "Confession and Double Thoughts," for a more thorough discussion of the nature of confessions in Dostoevsky in general and in *The Idiot* in particular. For a somewhat different reading of this scene, see Skakov, "Dostoevsky's Christ and Silence."

56. Skakov, "Dostoevsky's Christ and Silence," 132.

CHAPTER THREE

1. See Richard Rorty, "The Barber of Kasbeam: Nabokov on Cruelty," in *Contingency, Irony, and Solidarity* (Cambridge: Cambridge University Press, 1989).

Notes to Pages 102–104

2. Tackling the problem of Nabokov's double-tiered prose, Naiman proposes that the relationship between the diegetic and extradiegetic levels of Nabokov's texts is more isomorphic than hierarchical. The intensity of characters' engagement on the level of content translates into the intensity of the reader's engagement on the level of form. Hence, on the realist, diegetic plane of the text we witness "the tortured urgency of the conversations and internal debates that are so compelling in the heroes of Dostoevsky, Tolstoy, and, in some cases, Chekhov" (these revolve around questions of morality); on the extradiegetic, modernist plane a similar intensity directs the reader's "concerns whether he is a good reader and, implicitly, whether Nabokov is worth reading" (Naiman, *Nabokov, Perversely*, 9). Still, Naiman circumscribes "the moral questions about life" within the character-driven *content*, while letting the reader deal with "procedural [questions] about reading" that Nabokov poses on the level of *form* (9). Naiman does leave a loophole for an ethical inquiry that incorporates the formal features of the prose: "these questions about reading, which take the place of the old moral ones about living, do not obliterate their predecessors; indeed, the Russian literary heritage both inspires and shadows his work, so that scholars of Nabokov continue to worry not only about whether they are good enough readers but also about whether being a good reader is enough" (9). However, from the perspective of narrative ethics, such independence of content from form is not possible even in a seemingly realist Dostoevsky.

3. As I discussed in chapter 1, the evolution of Bakhtin's thought on this matter begins with celebrating the sacrifice of the hero by the priestly author in his early works (as in "Author and Hero") and progresses to the gradual self-exclusion of the authorial voice from the polyphonic text and the restriction of the authorial function to the orchestration of characters' voices that Bakhtin finds in Dostoevsky.

4. Nabokov, *Strong Opinions*, 95.

5. Nabokov, *Annotated Lolita*, 52.

6. David Packman connects reading of/in *Lolita* with Humbert's desire for Lolita in *Structure of Literary Desire*.

7. See Alfred Appel, Jr., "Notes," in Vladimir Nabokov, *The Annotated Lolita*, ed. Alfred Appel Jr. (New York: Vintage, 1991), 362.

8. Nabokov, *Annotated Lolita*, 316.

9. Julian Murphet reimagines the gradual progression from realist to modernist literature as a tension between the unity of the character and "the inherent multiplicity of a complex structure of signification": Murphet, "The Mole and the Multiple: A Chiasmus of Character," *New Literary History* 42, no. 2 (2011): 256. In Murphet's argument, the discovery of the infinitely rich internal world of the protagonist by the realist novel is also what ultimately makes the unity of that world unsustainable. Murphet claims that modernism inaugurates its existence by producing texts that become aware of the multiplicity held together

Note to Page 104

by their characters' proper names. For Murphet, the explosion of what he calls "the multiple" coincides with, but is also an effect of, a paradigmatic shift caused by the arrival of cinema as a new narrative medium. The dialectic relationship between literature and film requires a synthesis, an understanding of modernist literature that does not end with an insight that human interactions can be sufficiently understood through the theory of two-dimensional object-relations. Hence, in modernist and postmodernist literature, the reader's attention had to shift from the consciousness of the characters to the consciousness of the author that makes itself present not so much in the ironic distance between form and content, but between intra- and extradiegetic levels of narration.

10. Consider, for example, the recent analysis of *Pale Fire* in John Frow's study of characterization. After successfully showing that attempts to secure the meaning of the text on the intradiegetic level are reductive, Frow concludes that these attempts suffer from an "inability to move beyond diegetic accounts of character in order to treat characters as textually based effects": Frow, *Character and Person* (Oxford: Oxford University Press, 2014), 31. Instead, he suggests that we shift our attention to "the compositional level where characters work as allotropes, no longer fully distinct but forming patterns of interaction and of thematic connection" (31). This move obviously takes us out of the critical dead end, but it also eliminates any tension present on the novel's diegetic level. By dissolving any notion of subjectivity into the novel's "structure," such readings risk reaching their own interpretative dead end: "At this level of structure, [Kinbote's] reality is an effect of the modality of the textual world to which he belongs, and of the intermodal play between the novel's worlds" (32). Not unreasonably, Frow dismisses Brian Boyd's proposal that Kinbote is haunted by the ghost of Hazel; see Brian Boyd, *Nabokov's "Pale Fire": The Magic of Artistic Discovery* (Princeton, N.J.: Princeton University Press, 1999), 173 (cited in Frow, *Character and Person*, 31). What Frow does not notice, however, is that this hypothesis desperately hopes to fasten the production of meaning in the novel to a *consciousness*, even if it doesn't belong to a living being inhabiting the world of the novel. Symptomatically, Frow does direct our attention to the consciousness of the character, who manipulates the text on the extradiegetic level—Nabokov himself. Frow makes no attempt, however, to either recognize this character's ambiguous ontological status or to account how his presence is connected to the novel's diegesis. In Boyd's resolve to resort to Hazel's ghostly consciousness one can sense, on the one hand, the desire to bypass the text's refusal to find ontologic security on its diegetic level, and, on the other hand, the fear of crossing over the diegetic level in order to include the figure of the author into one's discussion of the novel's dynamics. Similarly to Frow, Couturier suggests that abandoning the diegetic level of the text opens the path to interpretation: "So long as I remain within the text, I am merely describing the novel but remain unable to interpret it. Shade and

Kinbote are not the prime enunciators of the text but the author's paradoxical masks" (Couturier, "Near-Tyranny of the Author," 64).

11. See, for one such example, the second chapter of Sergei Davydov's *Teksty-matrioshki Vladimira Nabokova* (Munich: Otto Sagner, 1982).

12. Nabokov, *Despair*, 101–3.

13. For the thematic motifs between *Despair* and *Notes from Underground*, see Connolly's "The Function of Literary Allusion in Nabokov's *Despair*," *Slavic and East European Journal* 26, no. 3 (autumn 1982). Connolly argues that the intertextuality of the novel is meant "to underscore the fallacy of Hermann's conception of himself as an author by highlighting his status as a literary character," as well as to "remind the reader of the high degree of artifice that is involved in the making of a Nabokov novel, and thus expose a basic cornerstone of the writer's conception of art itself" (310).

14. Davydov suggests that the wind signifies authorial presence (*Teksty-matrioshki*, 81–82).

15. Nabokov, *Despair*, 5. The original Russian-language text is *Otchayanie*, vol. 3 of *Sobranie sochinenii v chetyrekh tomakh* (Moscow: Izdatel'stvo "Pravda," 1990).

16. Ellen Pifer in *Nabokov and the Novel*, for example, argues that Hermann is guilty of treating reality as if it were a text.

17. Andrew Field similarly connects aesthetics and metaphysics as he comments on Hermann's metaphysical ruminations on the existence of God: "This argument is over authorship, and Hermann is striving to establish himself as the primary author of everyone and everything around him while at the same time freeing himself from any possible similar control": Field, *VN: The Life and Art of Vladimir Nabokov*, 3rd ed. (New York: Crown, 1986), 236.

18. Nabokov, *Despair*, 7–8. In Russian the religious connotations are even stronger as Hermann announces that he witnesses a miracle (*chudo*).

19. Nabokov, *Speak, Memory* (New York: Vintage International, 1989), 125.

20. For other similarities between *Despair* and *Speak, Memory*, see chapter 5 of John Burt Foster Jr.'s *Nabokov's Art of Memory and European Modernism* (Princeton, N.J.: Princeton University Press, 1993), 97, where he proposes that Hermann's search for the double can be compared to the process of poetic production that Nabokov outlines in his memoirs.

21. Imbuing his morally corrupt characters with his own worldview is a trait that Nabokov shares with Dostoevsky. As Thomas R. Frosch suggests, "Nabokov in his fictional and nonfictional utterances has created a composite literary persona . . . His heroes . . . tend to be more or less perverse or absurd inflections of his own voice": Frosch, "Parody and Authenticity in *Lolita*," in *Nabokov's Fifth Arc: Nabokov and Others on His Life's Work*, ed. J. E. Rivers and Charles Nicol (Austin: University of Texas Press, 1982), 174. Frosch argues that in *Lolita* Nabokov puts the romantics' quest for "uniqueness and authenticity" on trial, not only exposing Humbert's desire for authenticity as metaphysical, but also showing its

ultimate futility: "All he can achieve is parody. When he calls himself a poet, the point is not that he's shamming us but that he fails. Authenticity eludes him, and he loses out to history" (179). Frosch goes on to suggest that Nabokov's strategy of creating a parody of a romantic hero in Humbert is one of control: Nabokov exorcises himself onto Humbert in order to himself have a shot at creating a new form of a romantic novel: "We might say that Nabokov must kill off a bad romantic and a bad artist in Humbert in order for his own brand of enchantment to exist" (184).

22. As Renate Lachmann points out, Hermann is a character who has lived through "a catastrophe of signification" which he describes in "gnostic terminology": Lachmann, "Semiotika mistifikatsii: *Otchaianie* Nabokova," in *Hypertext Отчаяние, Сверхтекст Despair: Studien zu Vladimir Nabokovs Roman-Rätsel*, ed. Igor' Smirnov (Munich: Die Welt der Slaven, vol. 9, 2000), 47. (All translations from Russian in this article are my own.)

23. Alexander Dolinin identifies the sources of Hermann's lack of originality in Nabokov's attack against the "epigonic eclecticism" he discerned in contemporary modernist literature where, in Yuri Tynianov's words, "boundary lines between writers have been erased; writers are getting fluid" (Dolinin, "The Caning of Modernist Profaners," *Zembla*, https://www.libraries.psu.edu/Nabokov/dolil.htm). The object of Nabokov's parody is not Dostoevsky per se, but his numerous imitators. This argument, however, stresses Nabokov's aesthetic concerns while downplaying the thematic and philosophical correspondences between Dostoevsky's and Nabokov's protagonists.

24. Nabokov, *Despair*, 22.

25. Davydov, *Teksty-matrioshki*, 61.

26. Nabokov, *Despair*, 25.

27. It is instructive to compare Hermann's overtly *aestheticized* sexual activity with Bakhtin's description of the dynamic of a sexual act in "Author and Hero": "In the sexual approach to the other's body, my own body and the other's merge into one flesh, but this unitary flesh can be only an inner flesh. To be sure, this merging into one inner flesh is an ultimate limit toward which my sexual attitude tends in its purest form; in reality, it is always complicated by aesthetic moments that derive from my loving admiration of the other's body, and, consequently, by form-giving, constructive energies as well. In this case, however, the formation of aesthetic value through these energies is only a means and does not attain autonomy and fullness" (51–52). For Bakhtin, sexual activity is governed by "carnal desire, pleasure, gratification" (51), which makes "my own body and the other's merge into one flesh, but this unitary flesh can be only an inner flesh" (51). It still, however, retains "aesthetic moments that derive from my loving admiration of the other's body, and, consequently, by form-giving, constructive energies as well" (51–52). In Hermann's case, the balance has radically shifted: he experiences his sexual activity primarily as an aesthetic act.

Notes to Pages 111–122

28. Nabokov, *Despair*, 19.
29. Nabokov, *Annotated Lolita*, 308.
30. Nabokov, *Despair*, 16.
31. Dostoevsky, *Brothers Karamazov*, 26.
32. Dolinin suggests that by having Hermann distort Pushkin in this and other texts throughout the novel, Nabokov exposes his protagonist's distance from genuine artistry (see Dolinin, "The Caning of Modernist Profaners").
33. Nabokov, *Despair*, 141.
34. The first quote might be another reference to *Notes from Underground*, in which the Underground Man accuses his ideological opponents of passing off "a chicken coop" for the Crystal Palace. The Underground Man directs his critique of rational egoists at their attempts to fit the complexities of life into an inferior abstract utopia. The second quote could be a subtle reference to the pawnbroker from Dostoevsky's "The Meek One," who similarly desires to "spend the rest of [his] life somewhere in the Crimea, on the south coast, among the mountains and vineyards" (Dostoevsky, *A Writer's Diary*, 1:686).
35. Nabokov, *Despair*, 31.
36. Connolly argues that "to liberate their authorial potential, Nabokov's characters seek to shed that aspect of their identity that functions as a character": Julian W. Connolly, *Nabokov's Early Fiction: Patterns of Self and Other* (Cambridge: Cambridge University Press, 1992), 147. In Connolly's argument, in order to become an author, Hermann projects his identity of a character onto Felix and then murders him, "thereby unleashing his own authorial center" (147). While similar to mine, Connolly's reading concentrates on the aesthetic side of Hermann's project, which he does not connect to the metaphysical one ("Hermann does not describe his role in metaphysical terms" [147]).
37. Nabokov, *Despair*, 36.
38. Nabokov, *Otchayanie*, 354, emphasis added.
39. Nabokov, *Despair*, 43.
40. I am indebted to Caryl Emerson for this point.
41. Emily Dickinson, *Final Harvest: Emily Dickinson's Poems* (Boston: Little, Brown, 1961), 298.
42. Nabokov, *Despair*, 103.
43. Davydov similarly observes that the six days of writing a novel references the Old Testament, supporting the idea of Hermann as a demiurgic impostor: "Six days—are the six days of creation during which Hermann's novel is born" (*Teksty-matrioshki*, 82). Another reference to the Old Testament is hidden in character names that together *almost* refer to a tetramorph: Hermann (man), Orlovius (eagle), Ardalion (lion). The irony, of course, is that regardless of what Hermann thinks of her ("well knowing how stupid, forgetful and clumsy"), Lydia is no cow, and the joke is on Hermann.
44. Lachmann connects the ontological and semantic instabilities of the text

by arguing that Hermann's mystification (and self-mystification, since he, more than anyone, believes in his and Felix's complete coincidence) is an example of a personified trope, since it ambivalently points to both similarity and difference and in which the similarity—as with baroque metaphors—has an oxymoronic quality. (See Lachmann, "Semiotika mistifikatsii," 43–52.) Lachmann defines a trope as a mechanism which "seemingly protects from rupture, upheavals, and vacillations that threaten the connection between the sign and the object . . . by creating artificial iconicity and invented similarity" (46). As Lachmann argues, by killing Felix, Hermann destroys the ambivalent nature of the trope, which simultaneously insists on similarity and difference: "the murder of the other—the double, who does not resemble his murderer—becomes the death of the trope, leading to the loss of the semantic balance and the artificial order" (46).

45. Nabokov, *Despair*, 67.

46. Claire Rosenfield, "*Despair* and the Lust for Immortality," *Wisconsin Studies in Contemporary Literature* 8, no. 2 (spring 1967): 181.

47. Nabokov, *Despair*, 122.

48. Davydov, *Teksty-matrioshki*, 62. Davydov points out that in Nabokov's world, the leaves of trees often become a metaphor for pages of the manuscript (82).

49. Nabokov, *Despair*, 66.

50. Comparing *Despair* with *Crime and Punishment*, Davydov interprets Hermann's actions as a rebellion against the rightful order, but projects it into the aesthetic dimension: "*Despair* is . . . a novel . . . in which the main character behaves with loathsome caddishness as he tries to usurp for himself the authority of the author, and to behave in such a way in the temple of Nabokov's art is an unforgivable sin" (Davydov, "Dostoevsky and Nabokov"). Davydov contrasts Hermann's aesthetic rebellion with Raskolnikov's ethical one, and, accordingly, reimagines Dostoevsky's ethical universe as Nabokov's aesthetic one. Such a separation of aesthetics and ethics and the exclusion of the latter from analysis seem to me deficient. First of all, declaring Hermann a bad author disregards a rather obvious point about his (the arrogant boasting notwithstanding) undeniable stylistic mastery. Hermann's manuscript, while certainly perverse, is also aesthetically pleasurable. While the pleasure of the text becomes an unavoidable part of discussing *Lolita*, the stylistic mastery of *Despair* is, as a rule, overlooked in criticism. (For a refreshing exception, see Rampton's "Critical Choices.") More importantly, such an analysis fails to account for the ethical tension of the novel, in which writing and crime seem to be in a metaphoric relationship with each other, and both have roots in metaphysical despair. As I have shown above, in the novel, writing is a correlative to the desire for control over signification. Hence, if we agree that Hermann's despair comes from his realization of the inability to attain such control and that the reader's despair comes from our realization that such attempts are inevitably wrought with violence, the issue of Nabokov's authorial control over the text of *Despair* becomes much more problematic.

By shifting from "authority" to "authorship" without recognizing the implications of such a structural adaptation and replacing ethics with aesthetics, Davydov's argument stays within the rigid framework of structuralism, which insists on the incompatibility of the two realms. Much closer to my understanding of Nabokov's use of metaphysics in the novel is Lachmann's suggestion that Hermann can be interpreted as a radical gnostic poet who exposes the artificiality, the incompleteness, and the inadequacy of the world. Similarly important is her suggestion that Nabokov-the-author is a figure of the same order as both Hermann and demon-mystificator: "Nabokov with his poetic gnosticism turns out to be a mystificator even as he parodies mystification" (Lachmann, "Semiotika mistifikatsii," 47).

51. "Poshlust" is Nabokov's ingenious translation of the Russian *poshlost*, a word that, as Svetlana Boym writes "encompasses triviality, vulgarity, sexual promiscuity, and a lack of spirituality": Boym, *Common Places: Mythologies of Everyday Life in Russia* (Cambridge: Harvard University Press, 1994), 41.

For a brutal and brilliant critique of Nabokov's haughtiness in his "Commentary" to his translation of *Eugene Onegin*, see Alexander Gershenkron, "A Manufactured Monument?" *Modern Philology* 63, no. 4 (May 1966): 336–47.

52. Brian Boyd explains the "irascible and arrogant Nabokov persona" of the prefaces as the author's protective spell against "the curiosity-seekers who might think they could intrude on his time simply because he had become famous": Boyd, *Vladimir Nabokov: The American Years* (Princeton, N.J.: Princeton University Press, 1991), 477.

53. Rampton, "Critical Choices," 75–87.

54. Nabokov, *Despair*, 80. Another possible interpretation of the "hanging" motif could be the foreshadowing of punishment that awaits Hermann once he is caught. Whether subconsciously or through the consciousness of the implied author, Hermann imagines the gallows as he looks at his portrait by Ardalion: "All this—against an ambitious background hinting at things that might have been either geometrical figures or gallow trees . . ." (56).

55. Davydov interprets this scene as a reference to *Crime and Punishment* (see "Dostoevsky and Nabokov").

56. Nabokov, *Despair*, 97.

57. Nabokov, *Strong Opinions*, 11.

58. Susan Elizabeth Sweeney argues that in engaging with Nabokov's fiction, the reader's moral sensibility is affected by the lack of resolution in the novels for the crimes committed by its protagonists. Such open-endedness, writes Sweeney, invites the reader to *"rhetorically"* carry out her own justice prepared by the similar rhetorical adjudication of their crimes by the protagonists: Sweeney, "Whether Judgments, Sentences, and Executions Satisfy the Moral Sense in Nabokov," in *Nabokov and the Question of Morality: Aesthetics, Metaphysics, and the Ethics of Fiction*, ed. Michael Rogers and Susan Elizabeth Sweeney

(New York: Palgrave Macmillan, 2016), 169, emphasis in the original. My argument can be seen as diametrically opposite: the reader must accept responsibility for her rhetorical participation with the text in which physical violence is prepared by the protagonists' rhetorical desires.

59. Nabokov, *Despair*, 67–68.
60. Field, *VN*, 228.
61. Nabokov, *Speak, Memory*, 139.
62. Nabokov, *Despair*, 69.

CHAPTER FOUR

1. Nabokov, *Lectures on Russian Literature*, 106.
2. See Peter J. Rabinowitz's "Truth in Fiction" (*Critical Inquiry* 4, no. 1 [autumn 1977]); and his "Lolita: Solipsized or Sodomized? or, Against Abstraction—in General" in *A Companion to Rhetoric and Rhetorical Criticism*, ed. Walter Jost and Wendy Olmsted (Malden, Mass.: Blackwell, 2004). "The reader's experience of fiction . . . is thus always at least double: we can treat the work neither as what it is nor as what it appears to be, but must hold these competing (and mutually incompatible) perspectives simultaneously in our consciousness" (Rabinowitz, "Lolita: Solipsized or Sodomized?" 329).
3. In "Lolita: Solipsized or Sodomized?" Rabinowitz equates symbolizing with solipsizing and argues that by tipping the scale toward the authorial audience, the reader commits a rhetorical rape of Lolita. Aligning with the narrative audience allows Rabinowitz "moral indignation," yet it deprives the novel and its reader of its powerful meta-fictional apparatus. As I argue in this chapter, the connection between Humbert's solipsistic strategies and the critics' symbolizing ones first and foremost points to the reader's inevitable complicity in reading fiction, not in her ability to call rape a rape.
4. Nabokov, *Lectures on Russian Literature*, 106.
5. The comparison with Mandelstam is apt here. Mandelstam begins his treatise on poetry, "Conversation about Dante," with a similar insistence on isomorphism between nature and poetry: "Poetry is not a part of nature, not even its best or choicest part, let alone a reflection of it . . . ; rather, poetry establishes itself with astonishing independence in a new extra-spatial field of action, not so much narrating as acting out nature by means of its arsenal of devices, commonly known as tropes": Mandelstam, "Conversation about Dante," in *The Complete Critical Prose and Letters*, trans. Jane Gary Harris and Constance Link, ed. Jane Gary Harris (Ann Arbor, Mich.: Ardis, 1979), 397. Unlike Nabokov, for whom such isomorphism becomes evidence of art's divine attributes, Mandelstam uses it to argue for poetic evolution and suggests that scholarship on poetics would benefit from the natural sciences.
6. Nabokov, *Lectures on Russian Literature*, 103.

Notes to Pages 147–152

7. Nabokov, *Annotated Lolita*, 325.

8. Boyd, *Nabokov: The American Years*, 237.

9. For an example of the "ethical" reading, see Rabinowitz's own article "Lolita: Solipsized or Sodomized?" For the "aesthetic" reading that insists on treating Nabokov's novels as allegories on art, see Jean-Philippe Jaccard's "Bukvy na snegu."

10. Vladimir Nabokov, *Lectures on Literature* (New York: Harvest, 1980), 5.

11. Rabinowitz, "Truth in Fiction," 132.

12. In the Russian cultural context, the biblical Ham at first becomes a common slur for the lower class and then, more generally, synonymous with vulgarity and lack of polish and culture. The novel includes a number of characters whose names all contain the mark of what Nabokov ingeniously translated as *"poshlust"* in one way or another; symptomatically, all of them are intellectuals in the service of the totalitarian state: Dr. *Ham*mecke, the director of the Institute for Abnormal Children, where Krug's son is tortured and killed, and one of the elders of the regime, Sc*ham*m (italics added).

13. Nabokov's observations on Padukgrad's interest in *Hamlet* astutely reflect the conditions of the play's reception in Stalin's Russia. Arkady Ostrovsky states that Stalin disliked *Hamlet* especially for the protagonist's hesitancy. Yet, as Ostrovsky puts it, what precluded Soviet directors from staging either of the Northern tragedies was bigger than Stalin's personal tastes: "neither *Hamlet* nor *Macbeth* answered the optimistic spirit of the time. . . . Tragic conflict was ruled out by the style of socialist realism": Ostrovsky, "Shakespeare as a Founding Father of Soviet Realism: The Soviet Affair with Shakespeare," in *Shakespeare in the Worlds of Communism and Socialism*, ed. Irena R. Makaryk and Joseph G. Price (Toronto: University of Toronto Press, 2006), 61–62. Commenting on the history of *Hamlet* in the Soviet Union, Arthur P. Mendel states much more unequivocally that "Stalin liquidated Hamlet: there was no place in the closed society for one who questioned and vacillated": Mendel, "Hamlet and Soviet Humanism," *Slavic Review* 30, no. 4 (December 1971): 734. Interest in the play resurged during the Thaw era.

14. Nabokov, *Bend Sinister*, 112.

15. Compare Boyd's statement in his analysis of the novel: "*Bend Sinister* defends the freedom of the individual mind not only against dictatorships abroad but against the coercion of mass culture or mass mobilization at home or anywhere else": Boyd, *Nabokov: The American Years*, 96.

16. Nabokov, *Bend Sinister*, 119–20.

17. Nabokov, *Lectures on Russian Literature*, 319.

18. Brian Boyd, *Vladimir Nabokov: The Russian Years* (Princeton, N.J.: Princeton University Press, 1990), 245, as cited by Elizabeth Klosty Beaujour in "Translation and Self-Translation," in *The Garland Companion to Vladimir Nabokov*, ed. Vladimir E. Alexandrov (New York: Routledge, 1995), 716. Beau-

jour argues that "while Nabokov admires and is touched by mimicry and imitation in nature . . . , he despises mimicry in human beings and in art" (716). I insist, however, that mimicry, deception, and lack of authenticity are as integral to Nabokov's conception of art as originality, difference, and authenticity. Nabokov does not so much "despise mimicry" as he despises human attempts to pass off mimicry as originality. As I show below, what Nabokov rejects is the inability to hold on to the ambivalence inherent in art: for him, art lacks authenticity and simultaneously insists on it.

19. Nabokov, *Lectures on Literature*, 5.
20. Nabokov, *Strong Opinions*, 10–11.
21. In her analysis of this passage, Jacqueline Hamrit argues that Nabokov's understanding of deception as a tool of nature does not presuppose a vision of reality as a "mere simulacrum," and that for Nabokov "reality is there, exists, consists, insists but is 'unattainable'": Hamrit, *Authorship in Nabokov's Prefaces* (Newcastle upon Tyne, Eng.: Cambridge Scholars, 2014), 35–36.
22. Nabokov, *Bend Sinister*, 120.
23. Naiman, *Nabokov, Perversely*, 47.
24. Nabokov, *Bend Sinister*, 121.
25. Taking stock of the author's use of cinematic metaphors in *Bend Sinister*, Beverly Gray Bienstock suggests a correlation between the author as "artistic tyrant—as *auteur*" and the Padukgrad regime's ideological and manipulative use of film, but she stops short of exploring the implications of this comparison: Bienstock, "Focus Pocus: Film Imagery in *Bend Sinister*," in *Nabokov's Fifth Arc: Nabokov and Others on His Life's Work*, ed. J. E. Rivers and Charles Nicol (Austin: University of Texas Press, 1982), 128.
26. Nabokov, *Bend Sinister*, 106, emphasis added.
27. Such is, as numerous commentators have pointed out, the similarity of the physical descriptions between "fat" Krug and "fat" Hamlet. On the other similarities between Krug and Hamlet, see Herbert Grabes's "Nabokov and Shakespeare: The English Works," in *The Garland Companion to Vladimir Nabokov*, ed. Vladimir E. Alexandrov (London: Routledge, 1995). For the thematic analogies and allusions between the novel and the play, see also Samuel Schuman, "Something Rotten in the State: *Hamlet* and *Bend Sinister*," *Russian Literature Triquarterly* 24 (1990); and Frances H. Assa, "Krug and Hamlet," *Nabokovian* 59 (2007).
28. Nabokov, *Bend Sinister*, 119.
29. Nabokov transforms Proverbs 25:2: "It is the glory of God to conceal a thing: but the honour of kings is to search out a matter."
30. None of the six surviving signatures contains the spelling of the name accepted today. For a discussion of Shakespeare's extant signatures, see Edward Maude Thompson, *Shakespeare's Handwriting: A Study* (Oxford: Clarendon, 1916).
31. Nabokov, *Bend Sinister*, 109.

32. Marijeta Bozovic suggests that Nabokov's attitude toward Pushkin was based on a similar awareness of language's inherent impurity. In wresting Pushkin away from what he considered to be gross misreadings, Nabokov invents his own. "The difference," writes Bozovic, "lies in the stark admission that this is at best a plausible Pushkin" (Bozovic, *Nabokov's Canon*, 52).

33. Nabokov, *Bend Sinister*, 113, 114.

34. L. L. Lee traced Hamm's interpretation to *A New Variorum Edition of Shakespeare* (see Lee, *Vladimir Nabokov* [Boston: Twayne, 1976], 107). Edited by Horace Howard Furness, this edition contains a dedication that in the context of *Bend Sinister* seems very suggestive and sinister enough: "To the 'German Shakespeare Society' of Weimar, a representative of a people whose recent history has proved once for all that 'Germany is *not* Hamlet'": H. H. Furness, ed., *A New Variorum Edition of Shakespeare* (Philadelphia: J. B. Lippincott, 1877), iii, emphasis in the original.

35. The complexity of this segment has been reflected in the criticism. Hence, Schuman writes that "[Nabokov] is affirming that grotesque literary criticism and revision is more than poor playing of an intellectual game: it is a reflection of a deformed and deforming, inhuman, vision of the world" ("Something Rotten in the State," 209). Susan Elizabeth Sweeney, on the contrary, has argued that the linguistic games that Krug and Ember play are not different from those between Nabokov and Wilson, and that "their correspondence features similar wordplay, learned wit, and multilingual puns": Sweeney, "Sinistral Details: Nabokov, Wilson, and Hamlet in *Bend Sinister*," *Nabokov Studies* 1 (1994): 182. Michael H. Begnal identifies Joycean references in this passage and proposes that "the hawkfaced shabby man" that Krug meets in America might be a stand-in for Joyce or Stephen Dedalus: Begnal, "*Bend Sinister*: Joyce, Shakespeare, Nabokov," *Modern Language Studies* 15, no. 4 (autumn 1985).

36. Nabokov, *Bend Sinister*, xv.

37. On linguistic codes in *Bend Sinister* in particular, see, for example, D. Barton Johnson's "Nabokov as Gnostic Seeker: The Mystery of Infinite Consciousness in *Bend Sinister*" (in Johnson, *Worlds in Regression: Some Novels of Vladimir Nabokov* [Ann Arbor, Mich.: Ardis, 1985]), where Johnson deciphers linguistic clues in order to reveal hidden patterns and motifs that support the metaphysical reading of the novel. Johnson does not discuss the implications of Krug and Ember's proclivity for linguistic games in light of the connection the introduction makes between paronomasia and tyranny.

38. Using Uspensky's notion of "point of view on the phraseological plane," Richard Patteson suggests that the parenthetical inclusion of translations from the Ekwilist language into real ones indicates the presence of the authorial perspective: Patteson, "Nabokov's *Bend Sinister*: The Narrator as God," *Studies in American Fiction* 5, no. 2 (autumn 1977): 244. While this hypothesis might be true, it stops short of indicating the authorial *intent* in choosing this or that par-

ticular language. My analysis seeks to elucidate the potential rhetorical strategies behind multilayered translation practices, at least in this passage.

39. Nabokov, *Bend Sinister*, 118–19.

40. In her reading of this passage, Christine Raguet-Bouvart suggests that the parodic perversion of the first line of Hamlet's monologue points to the author's death at the translator's hands, once the production and the translation of the play are forced to align with the needs of the regime ("Ember, Translator of Hamlet," *Zembla*, https://www.libraries.psu.edu/Nabokov/raguetb1.htm). The author's introduction argues for a less politicized reading: "a pseudo-scholarly interpretation of the first phrase [is] taken to refer to the contemplated killing of Claudius, i.e., 'is the murder to be or not to be?'" (Nabokov, *Bend Sinister*, xvi).

41. In "The Art of Translation," Nabokov ridicules what is most probably Andrei Kroneberg's translation of this passage, which "gives Ophelia richer flowers than the poor weeds she found" (316) and becomes an example of the worst transgression Nabokov identifies in the practice: "the third, and worst, degree of turpitude is reached when a masterpiece is planished and patted into such a shape, vilely beautified in such a fashion as to conform to the notions and prejudices of a given public" (*Lectures on Russian Literature*, 315).

42. Drawing parallels between the novel and the Nabokov-Wilson correspondence, Sweeney states that Nabokov argued that "Russian and English iambs are quite similar," while Wilson disagreed ("Sinistral Details," 185). The inclusion of the Queen's speech here could be Nabokov's attempt to demonstrate the point.

43. "Есть ива у ручья, к той бледной иве,
    склонившейся над ясною водой,
    она пришла с гирляндами ромашек,
    крапивы, лютиков, лиловой змейки,
    зовущейся у вольных пастухов
    иначе и грубее, а у наших
    холодных дев—перстами мертвых." (Nabokov published this excerpt in Russian in the periodical *Rul'* on October 19, 1930.)

44. Nabokov, *Bend Sinister*, xvi.

45. Vladimir Nabokov, trans., *Eugene Onegin: A Novel in Verse*, by Aleksandr Pushkin, trans. and commentary by Vladimir Nabokov, 4 vols. (New York: Bollingen Foundation, 1964), 1: viii.

46. Judson Rosengrant, "Nabokov, Onegin, and the Theory of Translation," *Slavic and East European Journal* 38, no. 1 (spring 1994): 15–16.

47. Drawing on the articles by Douglas J. Clayton ("The Theory and Practice of Poetic Translation in Pushkin and Nabokov") and Clarence Brown ("Nabokov's Pushkin and Nabokov's Nabokov"), Beaujour suggests that "Nabokov did not wish the monolingual English-language reader to have the illusion that he could experience the *living* Pushkin" ("Translation and Self-Translation,"

717), making the translation "deliberately 'adversionary,' turning the target language toward the source, deforming English grammar with malign satisfaction" (717–18).

48. Nabokov, *Bend Sinister*, xvi. Compare, for example, the translated excerpt of Act IV, Scene VII, in which the Russian translation is retranslated, word for word, back into English prose, to Nabokov's treatment of the multilingual layering in *Eugene Onegin*. As Beaujour observes, to cite one example, Nabokov translates Pushkin's parody of Dmitriev—which is itself a "paraphrase of a French translation of a line by Pope"—quite literally "rather than returning to Pope, thus depriving the English language reader of the ability to recognize some echo . . ." ("Translation and Self-Translation," 718).

49. Nabokov, *Bend Sinister*, xvi.

50. Nabokov, *Bend Sinister*, 119.

51. Brian D. Walter, albeit from a different perspective, draws similar parallels between Hustav's intrusion and the novel itself. In Walter's provocative argument, Nabokov's "political novel"—not unlike Hustav—"comes dressed in civilian clothing": Walter, "Two Organ-Grinders: Duality and Discontent in *Bend Sinister*," in *Discourse and Ideology in Nabokov's Prose*, ed. David H. J. Larmour (London: Routledge, 2002), 37.

52. In "'Perplex'd in the Extreme': Moral Facets of Vladimir Nabokov's Work," *Nabokov Studies* 2 (1995), Gerard de Vries makes a similar argument that, for Nabokov, "it is the survivor who is [morally] inferior" (140).

53. Vladimir Nabokov, *Selected Letters, 1940–1977* (New York: Harcourt Brace Jovanovich, 1989), 50. I follow Gérard Genette's definition of metalepsis as "any intrusion by the extradiegetic narrator or narratee into the diegetic universe (or by diegetic characters into a metadiegetic universe, etc.), or the inverse": Genette, *Narrative Discourse: An Essay in Method* (Ithaca, N.Y.: Cornell University Press, 1983), 234–35. In my discussion of metalepsis in Nabokov's fiction, I use the word to include all the traces of authorial presence in the text.

54. "The Vane Sisters" was first published in 1959 in an issue of the *Hudson Review*, where Nabokov's short note warning the readers to look for the coded message precedes the text of the story.

55. Nabokov, *Stories of Vladimir Nabokov*, 655.

56. Nabokov, *Selected Letters*, 50.

57. Debra Malina similarly suggests that the consequences of the ontologic breach of borders that occurs during metalepsis has a direct bearing on the ethics of the relationship that binds author and characters: "Because it traverses an ontological hierarchy, metalepsis has the power to endow subjects with great or lesser degrees of 'reality'—in effect, to promote them into subjectivity and demote them from it": Malina, *Breaking the Frame: Metalepsis and the Construction of the Subject* (Columbus: Ohio University Press, 2002), 4.

58. Notice, for example, the chapter titles of D. Barton Johnson's study

Notes to Pages 170–171

Worlds in Regression: Some Novels of Vladimir Nabokov, which are indicative of this approach: "Nabokov as Maze Maker," "Nabokov as Literary Cosmologist," "Nabokov as Gnostic Seeker."

59. Vera Nabokov, "Predislovie k sborniku V. Nabokov 'Stikhi' (1979)," in *V. V. Nabokov: Pro i contra*, vol. 1, ed. B. V. Averin et al. (St. Petersburg: Izdatel'stvo russkogo khristianskogo gumanitarnogo instituta, 1997), 342.

60. Consider a recent example of such commentaries on the authorial presence in Nabokov's prose: "This recurrent motif (Nabokov is to his created world as God is to his) makes no sense unless Nabokov is at the very least willing to imagine a universe in which that God exists": Samuel Schuman, "Nabokov's God; God's Nabokov," in *Nabokov and the Question of Morality: Aesthetics, Metaphysics, and the Ethics of Fiction*, ed. Michael Rodgers and Susan Elizabeth Sweeney (New York: Palgrave Macmillan, 2016), 77.

61. For an alternative argument, which chooses to trust the statements of Nabokov's authorial persona, see Zoran Kuzmanovich's dissertation, "The Fine Fabric of Deceit: Nabokov and His Readers" (University of Wisconsin, Madison, 1988). Writing of Nabokov's notion of transcendence, Kuzmanovich suggests that it affords us with a vision of Nabokov's ethics: "The counterintuition, voiced by the various schools of poststructuralism, is that all such transcendence is at best an illusion, at worst a disguise and a distortion of the writer's and reader's will to power. And though neither intuition can be proven rationally at the expense of the other, the first at least holds out the possibility of tenderness, kindness, and ecstasy. The second does not even hold out the promise of surprise" (87). This to me does not either sufficiently interrogate Nabokov's essentialist claims or make use of a poststructuralist discussion of ethics. I, on the contrary, claim that subjecting Nabokov's authorial persona to a poststructuralist critique opens a pathway to a more productive discussion of Nabokov's narrative ethics.

62. For a reading that similarly examines the power dynamic that exists between different narrative planes, but reaches different conclusions from mine, see Yael Levin, "Metalepsis and the Author Figure in Modernist and Postmodernist Fiction," *Twentieth Century Literature* 62 (2016). Levin locates the difference between modern and postmodern literatures in the paradigmatic shift in their respective use of metalepsis. In modernist literature, Levin argues, the metaleptic gesture—such as Nabokov's inclusion of the "anthropomorphic deity" in the narrative of *Bend Sinister*—only *seems* to endow the characters with freedom, while in fact it "serves to underline the power relations at work—consolidating the creative agency of he who stands outside the diegesis" (294–95). Levin identifies the postmodernist moment as one that renders the metalepsis obsolete and "collaps[es] diegetic levels into each other" (295). This leaves the readers "with only a single, flat world, [in which] the identity of the creative agent must be determined by the participating actors" (295). As a result of this shift, "authority is no longer the mark of a conventionally predetermined stratifi-

cation but the product of a careful thematic negotiation of power that takes place within the diegesis" (295). Like my own, Levin's framework can be traced back to Bakhtin's elaborations on the architectonics of fiction. At stake is the question of characters' ontologic freedom; but, in my opinion, to make it dependent on the postmodern obsolescence of metalepsis is to oversimplify the issue. Metalepsis is scarcely the only device through which authors can explore the power dynamic between author and character. Moreover, I take issue with Levin's assertion that metalepsis in modernist fiction cements the ontological authority of author over character. In *Bend Sinister*, for example, Nabokov's metaleptic gestures simultaneously consolidate and problematize authorial control by associating them with political tyranny. By including the metalepsis in *Bend Sinister* into the wider parameters of our ethical inquiry, we can see that Nabokov uses it to make the reader aware of the ethical costs incurred in breaking the diegetic distance that separates the reader (as well as the authorial figure) from the characters, eventually asking the reader to share the responsibility for this state of affairs.

63. Malina, *Breaking the Frame*, 19–20. Malina's object of inquiry is the prose of Beckett, Christine Brook-Rose, and Angela Carter, but I would argue that her understanding of the awareness that metalepsis brings to our understanding of subject-formation can be productively applied to Nabokov as well.

64. As Malina indicates, a "further shift away from an essentialist concept of the self and its desire toward a more purely constructionist vision leads [us] to locate narrative's violent tendency not in its end but in its *middle*, its *process*—in the constant reconstruction of subjects and realities necessary for their continued existence" (*Breaking the Frame*, 19, emphasis in the original).

65. On the fears and anxieties of "being a bad reader" (*Nabokov, Perversely*, 109), see Naiman's convincing argument in "Hermophobia (On Sexual Orientation and Reading Nabokov)," where interpretative anxiety is tied to insecurities connected with sexual acts. On authorial control in *Bend Sinister* proper, see Brian D. Walter's "Two Organ-Grinders," in which he argues that writing a political satire prevents Nabokov from an "*empathetic* relationship between the writer and the reader" and that "in the case of this novel, the authorial need for control takes on revealing urgency" (29).

CONCLUSION

Parts of the conclusion were published as "In Search of the Human: Bakhtin's Wartime Notebooks" in *Slavic and East European Journal* 61, no. 2 (Summer 2017): 233–54.

1. Nabokov, *Sebastian Knight*, 50.

2. Peter Brooks, *Reading for the Plot: Design and Intention in Narrative* (Cambridge, Mass.: Harvard University Press, 1992), 95.

3. Bakhtin, "Author and Hero," 105. For Bakhtin, in becoming an event for the other, death can be a celebration of life. As Caryl Emerson points out, in the Bakhtin of "Author and Hero," "death is what makes the other available; it is a gift. But the 'gift' is not, of course, free: personal loss is the price we pay for this gift of wholeness from the other": Emerson, "The Tolstoy Connection in Bakhtin," in *Rethinking Bakhtin: Extensions and Challenges*, ed. Gary S. Morson and Caryl Emerson (Evanston, Ill.: Northwestern University Press, 1989), 163. As I have argued in this book, and others elsewhere, for Bakhtin in his Dostoevsky book, consummation acquires darker overtones and requires accountability.

4. Nabokov, *Sebastian Knight*, 176.

5. Bakhtin Forum, "The Dark and Radiant Bakhtin," 213.

6. In his 1911 essay "Dostoevsky and the Tragic Novel," Viacheslav Ivanov asserted that the foundation of Dostoevsky's realism is not knowledge but "penetration," a process through which the other is perceived not as an object to be described and understood, but as a subject: Ivanov, "Dostoevsky i roman-tragediia" (accessed online). The guiding principle of Dostoevsky's art and the ethical task of his characters, Ivanov claimed, is an affirmation "with one's whole will and understanding of the other's being: 'thou art.'" Georgii Fridlender suggests that Ivanov's work gave Bakhtin a "decisive impetus": Fridlender, "Dostoevskii i Viacheslav Ivanov," in *Dostoevsky: Materialy i issledovaniia*, vol. 11 (St. Petersburg: Nauka, 1994), 132.

7. With the possible exception of *The Brothers Karamazov*. See Wyman's discussion of Alyosha Karamazov as the most successful carrier of the nonviolent word in *Gift of Active Empathy*.

8. Lydia Ginzburg, *On Psychological Prose* (Princeton, N.J.: Princeton University Press, 1991), 260.

9. See the "Introduction" for a full discussion of this point.

10. Nabokov, *Strong Opinions*, 19.

11. Nabokov, *Annotated Lolita*, 315.

12. Dostoevsky, "Pushkin. (Ocherk)" in vol. 26 of *Polnoe sobranie sochinenii v tridtsati tomakh* (Leningrad: Nauka, 1972–90), 146.

13. Bakhtin, *Problems of Dostoevsky's Poetics*, 61, emphasis in the original.

14. For the most recent study of Pushkin's prominent place in Nabokov's pantheon of writers, see Bozovic, *Nabokov's Canon*.

15. Marcus Levitt comments that the presence of the narrator-creator in *Eugene Onegin* "challenges us . . . with . . . the contradictions [that] underscore the inevitability of mediation: 'reality' is always filtered through culture, convention, language, and it is the understanding of this necessary limitation that enables the poet's creative manipulations": Marcus Levitt, "Evgenii Onegin," in *The Cambridge Companion to Pushkin*, ed. Andrew Kahn (Cambridge: Cambridge University Press, 2006), 45. This understanding of Pushkin is very close to Nabokov's perception of reality which I discussed in chapter 4.

16. Nabokov presented the lecture publicly in 1937 and published it in *Nouvelle Revue Française* on March 1 of the same year.

17. Vladimir Nabokov, "Pushkin, or the Real and the Plausible," *New York Review of Books*, March 31, 1988, 39.

18. Bakhtin, *Problems of Dostoevsky's Poetics*, 60.

19. Nussbaum, *Love's Knowledge*, 345.

20. Bernard Williams, *Morality: An Introduction to Ethics* (New York: Harper, 1972), xi.

Bibliography

Altieri, Charles. "Lyrical Ethics and Literary Experience." In *Mapping the Ethical Turn: A Reader in Ethics, Culture, and Literary Theory*, edited by Todd F. Davis and Kenneth Womack, 30–58. Charlottesville: University Press of Virginia, 2001.
———. *Particulars of Rapture: An Aesthetics of the Affects*. Ithaca, N.Y.: Cornell University Press, 2003.
Apollonio, Carol. *Dostoevsky's Secrets: Reading Against the Grain*. Evanston, Ill.: Northwestern University Press, 2009.
Appel, Alfred, Jr. "Notes." In Vladimir Nabokov, *The Annotated Lolita*, edited by Alfred Appel Jr., 319–457. New York: Vintage, 1991.
Assa, Frances H. "Krug and Hamlet." *Nabokovian* 59 (2007): 14–19.
Auden, W. H. "*The Shield of Perseus*: Dingley Dell and the Fleet." In *The Dyer's Hand and Other Essays*, 407–28. New York: Random House, 1968.
Bakhtin Forum. The Dark and Radiant Bakhtin: Wartime Notes. *Slavic and East European Journal* 61, no. 2 (Summer 2017).
Bakhtin, Mikhail. "Author and Hero in Aesthetic Activity." Translated by Vadim Liapunov. In *Art and Answerability: Early Philosophical Essays by M. M. Bakhtin*, edited by Michael Holquist and Vadim Liapunov, 4–256. Austin: University of Texas Press, 1990.
———. *Problems of Dostoevsky's Poetics*. Edited and translated by Caryl Emerson. Minneapolis: University of Minnesota Press, 1984.
———. *Sobranie sochinenii v semi tomakh*. Moscow: Izdatel'stvo russkie slovari iazyki slavianskoi kultury, 1997–2012.
———. *Toward a Philosophy of the Act*. Translated by Vadim Liapunov. Austin: University of Texas Press, 1993.
———. "Toward a Reworking of the Dostoevsky Book." In *Critical Essays on Dostoevsky*, edited by Robin Feuer Miller, 247–64. Boston: G. K. Hall, 1986.
Barthes, Roland. S/Z. Translated by Richard Miller. Oxford: Blackwell, 1990.
Bataille, Georges. *Literature and Evil*. Translated by Alastair Hamilton. London: Calder and Boyars, 1973.

Beaujour, Elizabeth Klosty. "Translation and Self-Translation." In *The Garland Companion to Vladimir Nabokov*, edited by Vladimir E. Alexandrov, 714–24. New York: Routledge, 1995.

Begnal, Michael H. "*Bend Sinister*: Joyce, Shakespeare, Nabokov." *Modern Language Studies* 15, no. 4 (Autumn 1985): 22–27.

Belinskii, Vissarion. "Pis'mo k N.V. Gogoliu ot 15 iulia n. st. 1847 goda." In *V. G. Belinskii: Pro et Contra: Lichnost' i tvorchestvo Belinskogo v russkoi mysli (1848–2011)*, edited by D. K. Burlak, 55–63. St. Petersburg: Izdatel'stvo russkoi khristianskoi gumanitarnoi akademii, 2011.

Benjamin, Walter. "Dostoevsky's *The Idiot*." In *Selected Writings*, vol. 1, edited by Marcus Bullock and Michael W. Jennings, 78–81. Cambridge, Mass.: Belknap Press of Harvard University Press, 1996.

Bernstein, Michael A. "The Poetics of Ressentiment." In *Rethinking Bakhtin: Extensions and Challenges*, edited by Gary S. Morson and Caryl Emerson, 197–223. Evanston, Ill.: Northwestern University Press, 1989.

Bethea, David. "*The Idiot*: Historicism Arrives at the Station." In *Dostoevsky's "The Idiot": A Critical Companion*, edited by Liza Knapp, 130–90. Evanston, Ill.: Northwestern University Press, 1998.

Bienstock, Beverly Gray. "Focus Pocus: Film Imagery in *Bend Sinister*." In *Nabokov's Fifth Arc: Nabokov and Others on His Life's Work*, edited by J. E. Rivers and Charles Nicol, 171–87. Austin: University of Texas Press, 1982.

Blackwell, Stephen. "Dostoevskian Problems in Nabokov's Poetics." In *From Petersburg to Bloomington: Essays in Honor of Nina Perlina*, edited by John Bartle, Michael C. Finke, and Vadim Liapunov, 137–54. Bloomington, Ind.: Slavica, 2012.

———. *Zina's Paradox: The Figured Reader in Nabokov's "Gift."* New York: Peter Lang, 2000.

Booth, Wayne. *The Company We Keep: An Ethics of Fiction*. Berkeley: University of California Press, 1988.

Boyd, Brian. *Nabokov's "Pale Fire": The Magic of Artistic Discovery*. Princeton, N.J.: Princeton University Press, 1999.

———. *Vladimir Nabokov: The American Years*. Princeton, N.J.: Princeton University Press, 1991.

———. *Vladimir Nabokov: The Russian Years*. Princeton, N.J.: Princeton University Press, 1990.

Boym, Svetlana. *Common Places: Mythologies of Everyday Life in Russia*. Cambridge, Mass.: Harvard University Press, 1994.

———. "Poetics and Politics of Estrangement: Victor Shklovsky and Hannah Arendt." *Poetics Today* 26, no. 4 (Winter 2005): 581–611.

Bozovic, Marijeta. *Nabokov's Canon: From "Onegin" to "Ada."* Evanston, Ill.: Northwestern University Press, 2016.

Bibliography

Brooks, Peter. *Body Work: Objects of Desire in Modern Narrative.* Cambridge, Mass.: Harvard University Press, 1993.

———. *Reading for the Plot: Design and Intention in Narrative.* Cambridge, Mass.: Harvard University Press, 1992.

Coates, Ruth. *Christianity in Bakhtin: God and the Exiled Author.* Cambridge: Cambridge University Press, 1998.

Coetzee, J. M. "Confession and Double Thoughts: Tolstoy, Rousseau, Dostoevsky." *Comparative Literature* 37, no. 3 (1985): 193–232.

Connolly, Julian W. "Dostoevski and Vladimir Nabokov: The Case of *Despair*." In *Dostoevski and the Human Condition after a Century*, edited by Alexey Ugrinsky, Frank S. Lambasa, and Valija K. Ozolins, 155–62. New York: Greenwood, 1986.

———. "The Function of Literary Allusion in Nabokov's *Despair*." *Slavic and East European Journal* 26, no. 3 (Autumn 1982): 302–13.

———. "Nabokov and Dostoevsky: Good Writer, Bad Reader?" In *Nabokov and the Question of Morality: Aesthetics, Metaphysics, and the Ethics of Fiction*, edited by Michael Rogers and Susan Elizabeth Sweeney, 33–49. New York: Palgrave Macmillan, 2016.

———. "Nabokov's Dialogue with Dostoevsky: *Lolita* and 'The Gentle Creature.'" *Nabokov Studies* 4 (1997): 15–36.

———. *Nabokov's Early Fiction: Patterns of Self and Other.* Cambridge: Cambridge University Press, 1992.

Corrigan, Yuri. *Dostoevsky and the Riddle of the Self.* Evanston, Ill.: Northwestern University Press, 2017.

Couturier, Maurice. "Censorship and the Authorial Figure in *Ulysses* and *Lolita*." *Cycnos* 12, no. 2, "Nabokov: At the Crossroads of Modernism and Postmodernism" (1995): 29–43.

———. "The Near-Tyranny of the Author: *Pale Fire*." In *Nabokov and His Fiction: New Perspectives*, edited by Julian W. Connolly, 54–72. Cambridge: Cambridge University Press, 1999.

Davis, Todd F., and Kenneth Womack. "Preface: Reading Literature and the Ethics of Criticism." In *Mapping the Ethical Turn: A Reader in Ethics, Culture, and Literary Theory*, edited by Todd F. Davis and Kenneth Womack, ix. Charlottesville: University Press of Virginia, 2001.

Davydov, Sergei. "Dostoevsky and Nabokov: The Morality of Structure in *Crime and Punishment* and *Despair*." *Dostoevsky Studies* 3 (1982). http://sites.utoronto.ca/tsq/DS/03/157.shtml.

———. *Teksty-matrioshki Vladimira Nabokova.* Munich: Otto Sagner, 1982.

de la Durantaye, Leland. *Style Is Matter: The Moral Art of Vladimir Nabokov.* Ithaca, N.Y.: Cornell University Press, 2007.

Deleuze, Gilles. *Cinema 2: The Time-Image.* Translated by Hugh Tomlinson and Robert Galeta. London: Athlone, 1989.

Bibliography

de Man, Paul. *Blindness and Insight: Essays in the Rhetoric of Contemporary Criticism*. Minneapolis: University of Minnesota Press, 1983.

Denischenko, Irina, and Alexander Spektor. "Forum Introduction." *Slavic and East European Journal* 61, no. 2 (Summer 2017): 189–201.

de Vries, Gerard. "'Perplex'd in the Extreme': Moral Facets of Vladimir Nabokov's Work." *Nabokov Studies* 2 (1995): 135–52.

Dickinson, Emily. *Final Harvest: Emily Dickinson's Poems*. Boston: Little, Brown, 1961.

Dolinin, Alexander. "The Caning of Modernist Profaners." *Zembla*. https://www.libraries.psu.edu/Nabokov/doli1.htm.

———. "Nabokov, Dostoevsky, and 'Dostoevskyness.'" *Russian Studies in Literature* 35, no. 4 (1999): 42–60.

———. "The Signs and Symbols in Nabokov's 'Signs and Symbols.'" *Zembla*. https://www.libraries.psu.edu/Nabokov/dolinin.htm.

Dostoevsky, Fyodor. *The Brothers Karamazov: A Novel in Four Parts with Epilogue*. Translated by Richard Pevear and Larissa Volokhonsky. New York: Vintage Classics, 1990.

———. *Crime and Punishment*. New York: Vintage, 1993.

———. *Demons*. Translated by Richard Pevear and Larissa Volokhonsky. New York: Vintage Classics, 1995.

———. *Great Short Works of Fyodor Dostoevsky*. New York: Harper Perennial Modern Classics, 2004.

———. *The Idiot*. Translated by Richard Pevear and Larissa Volokhonsky. New York: Vintage Classics, 2003.

———. *Notes from Underground*. New York: Vintage, 1993.

———. *Polnoe sobranie sochinenii v tridtsati tomakh*, vols. 1–30. Leningrad: Nauka, 1972–90.

———. *Selected Letters of Fyodor Dostoevsky*. Translated by Andrew R. MacAndrew, edited by Joseph Frank and David I. Goldstein. New Brunswick, N.J.: Rutgers University Press, 1987.

———. *A Writer's Diary*. Evanston, Ill.: Northwestern University Press, 1993.

Dragunoiu, Dana. *Vladimir Nabokov and the Poetics of Liberalism*. Evanston, Ill.: Northwestern University Press, 2011.

Emerson, Caryl. "Editor's Preface." In Mikhail Bakhtin, *Problems of Dostoevsky's Poetics*, edited and translated by Caryl Emerson, xxix–xliii. Minneapolis: University of Minnesota Press, 1984.

———. *The First Hundred Years of Mikhail Bakhtin*. Princeton, N.J.: Princeton University Press, 1997.

———. "Perezhiv temnotu stalinskoi nochi, Bakhtin vnov' razmyshliaet o formalizme." *Matica Srpska Journal for Slavic Studies* 92 (2017): 39–57.

———. "Prefatory Comments on 'Toward a Reworking of the Dostoevsky Book.'" In *Critical Essays on Dostoevsky*, edited by Robin Feuer Miller, 243–46. Boston: G. K. Hall, 1986.

Bibliography

———. "Problems with Baxtin's Poetics." *Slavic and East European Journal* 32, no. 4 (Winter 1988): 503–25.

———. "Shklovsky's ostranenie, Bakhtin's vnenakhodimost' (How Distance Serves an Aesthetics of Arousal Differently from an Aesthetics Based on Pain)." *Poetics Today* 26, no. 4 (Winter 2005): 637–64.

———. "The Tolstoy Connection in Bakhtin." In *Rethinking Bakhtin: Extensions and Challenges*, edited by Gary S. Morson and Caryl Emerson, 149–70. Evanston, Ill.: Northwestern University Press, 1989.

———."Word and Image in Dostoevsky's Worlds: Robert Louis Jackson on Readings That Bakhtin Could Not Do." In *Freedom and Responsibility in Russian Literature: Essays in Honor of Robert Louis Jackson*, edited by Elizabeth Cheresh Allen and Gary Saul Morson, 245–65. Evanston, Ill.: Northwestern University Press, 1995.

———. "Zosima's 'Mysterious Visitor': Again Bakhtin on Dostoevsky, and Dostoevsky on Heaven and Hell." In *A New Word on The Brothers Karamazov*, edited by Robert Louis Jackson, 155–79. Evanston, Ill.: Northwestern University Press, 2004.

Epstein, Mikhail. *Slovo i molchanie: Metafizika russkoi literatury*. Moscow: Vysshaya shkola, 2006.

Erdinast-Vulcan, Daphne. *Between Philosophy and Literature: Bakhtin and the Question of the Subject*. Stanford, Calif.: Stanford University Press, 2013.

Field, Andrew. *VN: The Life and Art of Vladimir Nabokov*. 3rd edition. New York: Crown, 1986.

Fogel, Aaron. "Coerced Speech." In *Rethinking Bakhtin: Extensions and Challenges*, edited by Gary S. Morson and Caryl Emerson, 173–96. Evanston, Ill.: Northwestern University Press, 1989.

Foster, John Burt, Jr. *Nabokov's Art of Memory and European Modernism*. Princeton, N.J.: Princeton University Press, 1993.

Frank, Joseph. *Dostoevsky: The Seeds of Revolt, 1821–1849*. Princeton, N.J.: Princeton University Press, 1986.

———. *Dostoevsky: The Stir of Liberation, 1860–1865*. Princeton, N.J.: Princeton University Press, 1986.

Fridlender, Georgii. "Dostoevskii i Viacheslav Ivanov." In *Dostoevsky: Materialy i issledovaniia*, vol. 11: 132–44. St. Petersburg: Nauka, 1994.

Frosch, Thomas R. "Parody and Authenticity in *Lolita*." In *Nabokov's Fifth Arc: Nabokov and Others on His Life's Work*, edited by J. E. Rivers and Charles Nicol, 171–87. Austin: University of Texas Press, 1982.

Frow, John. *Character and Person*. Oxford: Oxford University Press, 2014.

Furness, Horace Howard, ed. *A New Variorum Edition of Shakespeare*. Philadelphia: J. B. Lippincott, 1877.

Gatrall, Jeff. "Between Iconoclasm and Silence: Representing the Divine in Holbein and Dostoevsky." *Comparative Literature* 53, no. 3 (Summer 2001): 214–32.

Genette, Gérard. *Narrative Discourse: An Essay in Method*. Ithaca, N.Y.: Cornell University Press, 1983.

Gershenkron, Alexander. "A Manufactured Monument?" *Modern Philology* 63, no. 4 (May 1966): 336–47.

Gibson, Andrew. *Postmodernity, Ethics, and the Novel: From Leavis to Levinas*. London: Routledge, 1999.

Ginzburg, Lydia. *On Psychological Prose*. Translated and edited by Judson Rosengrant. Princeton, N.J.: Princeton University Press, 1991.

Gogol, Nikolai. *Polnoe sobranie sochinenii*. Moscow: Izdatel'stvo Akademii nauk SSSR, 1937–52.

——. *Selected Passages from Correspondence with Friends*. Translated by Jesse Zeldin. Nashville, Tenn.: Vanderbilt University Press, 1969.

Gourianova, Nina. *The Aesthetics of Anarchy: Art and Ideology in the Early Russian Avant-Garde*. Berkeley: University of California Press, 2012.

Grabes, Herbert. "Nabokov and Shakespeare: The English Works." In *The Garland Companion to Vladimir Nabokov*, edited by Vladimir E. Alexandrov, 496–510. London: Routledge, 1995.

Hamrit, Jacqueline. *Authorship in Nabokov's Prefaces*. Newcastle upon Tyne, Eng.: Cambridge Scholars, 2014.

Harpham, Geoffrey Galt. *Getting It Right: Language, Literature, and Ethics*. Chicago: University of Chicago Press, 1992.

——. *Shadows of Ethics: Criticism and the Just Society*. Durham, N.C.: Duke University Press, 1999.

Hirschkop, Ken. *Mikhail Bakhtin: An Aesthetic for Democracy*. Oxford: Oxford University Press, 1999.

Holquist, Michael. *Dialogism: Bakhtin and His World*. London: Routledge, 1990.

——. *Dostoevsky and the Novel*. Evanston, Ill.: Northwestern University Press, 1977.

——. "Introduction." In Mikhail Bakhtin, *The Dialogic Imagination: Four Essays by M. M. Bakhtin*, translated by Caryl Emerson and Michael Holquist, edited by Michael Holquist, xv–xxxiii. Austin: University of Texas Press, 1981.

Ivanov, Viacheslav. "Dostoevsky i roman-tragediia." http://az.lib.ru/i/iwanow_w_i/text_0010.shtml.

Jaccard, Jean-Philippe. "Bukvy na snegu ili Vstrecha dvukh oznachaemykh v glukhom lesu." In *Literatura kak takovaia*, 58–88. Moscow: Novoe literaturnoe obozrenie, 2011.

Jackson, Robert Louis. *The Art of Dostoevsky: Deliriums and Nocturnes*. Princeton, N.J.: Princeton University Press, 1981.

——. *Dialogues with Dostoevsky: The Overwhelming Questions*. Stanford, Calif.: Stanford University Press, 1993.

——. *Dostoevsky's Quest for Form*. New Haven, Conn.: Yale University Press, 1966.

Johnson, D. Barton. *Worlds in Regression: Some Novels of Vladimir Nabokov.* Ann Arbor, Mich.: Ardis, 1985.
Jones, Malcolm. *Dostoevsky and the Dynamics of Religious Experience.* London: Anthem, 2005.
———. *Dostoevsky after Bakhtin: Readings in Dostoevsky's Fantastic Realism.* Cambridge: Cambridge University Press, 1990.
Khodasevich, Vladislav. "O Sirine." In *V. V. Nabokov: Pro i contra*, vol. 1, edited by B. V. Averin et al., 238–44. St Petersburg: Izdatel'stvo russkogo khristianskogo gumanitarnogo instituta, 1997.
Kirpotin, Valerii. *Dostoevskii i Belinskii.* Moscow: Khudozhestvennaia literatura, 1976.
Kondakov, Igor. "Pokushenie na literaturu: O bor'be literaturnoi kritiki s literaturoi v russkoi kul'ture." *Voprosy literatury* 2 (1992): 75–127.
Kulish, Panteleimon. *Zapiski o zhizni Nikolaia Vasil'evicha Gogolia*, vol. 2. St. Petersburg: Yulius Shtauf, 1856.
Kuzmanovich, Zoran. "The Fine Fabric of Deceit: Nabokov and His Readers." Ph.D. dissertation, University of Wisconsin, Madison, 1988.
Lachmann, Renate. "Semiotika mistifikatsii: *Otchaianie* Nabokova." In *Hypertext Отчаяние. Сверхтекст Despair. Studien zu Vladimir Nabokovs Roman-Rätsel*, edited by Igor' Smirnov, 43–52. Munich: Die Welt der Slaven, vol. 9, 2000.
Lee, L. L. *Vladimir Nabokov.* Boston: Twayne, 1976.
Levin, Yael. "Metalepsis and the Author Figure in Modernist and Postmodernist Fiction." *Twentieth Century Literature* 62 (2016): 289–308.
Levinas, Emmanuel. *Totality and Infinity.* Pittsburgh, Pa.: Duquesne University Press, 1969.
Levine, Caroline. *Forms: Whole, Rhythm, Hierarchy, Network.* Princeton, N.J.: Princeton University Press, 2017.
Levitt, Marcus. "Evgenii Onegin." In *The Cambridge Companion to Pushkin*, edited by Andrew Kahn, 41–56. Cambridge: Cambridge University Press, 2006.
Lipovetsky, Mark, and Irina Sandomirskaia. "Kak ne 'zavershit' Bakhtina." *Novoe literaturnoe obozrenie* 79 (2006): 7–38. http://magazines.russ.ru/nlo/2006/79/li1.html.
Lounsbery, Anne. *Thin Culture, High Art: Gogol, Hawthorne, and Authorship in Nineteenth-Century Russia and America.* Cambridge, Mass.: Harvard University Press, 2007.
Love, Heather. "Close but Not Deep: Literary Ethics and the Descriptive Turn." *New Literary History* 41, no. 2 (Spring 2010): 371–91.
MacIntyre, Alasdair. *After Virtue.* 3rd edition. Notre Dame, Ind.: University of Notre Dame Press, 2007.
Malina, Debra. *Breaking the Frame: Metalepsis and the Construction of the Subject.* Columbus: Ohio University Press, 2002.

Mandelstam, Osip. "Conversation about Dante." In Osip Mandelstam, *The Complete Critical Prose and Letters*, translated by Jane Gary Harris and Constance Link, edited by Jane Gary Harris, 397–442. Ann Arbor, Mich.: Ardis, 1979.

Markovich, Vladimir. "O nekotorykh paradoksakh knigi Gogolia *Vybrannye mesta iz perepiski s druz'iami*." In *Fenomen Gogolia: Materialy Yubileinoi mezhdunarodnoi nauchnoi konferentsii, posviashchennoi 200-letiu so dnia rozhdeniia N.V.Gogolia*, edited by M. N. Virolainen and A. A. Karpova, 373–87. St. Petersburg: Petropolis, 2001.

McHale, Brian. *Postmodernist Fiction*. New York: Methuen, 1987.

Mendel, Arthur P. "Hamlet and Soviet Humanism." *Slavic Review* 30, no. 4 (December 1971): 733–47.

Miller, Robin Feuer. *The Brothers Karamazov: Worlds of the Novel*. New Haven, Conn.: Yale University Press, 1992.

———. *Dostoevsky and The Idiot: Author, Narrator, and Reader*. Cambridge, Mass.: Harvard University Press, 1981.

Mizzau, Marina. "A Double-Voiced Silence." In *The Lonely Mirror*, edited by Sandra Kemp and Paola Bono, 64–82. London: Routledge, 1993.

Montaigne, Michel de. *Works of Michael de Montaigne*, vol. 2. Translated by W. Hazlitt. New York: Hurd and Houghton, 1859.

Morson, Gary Saul. *The Boundaries of Genre: Dostoevsky's "Diary of a Writer" and the Traditions of Literary Utopia*. Evanston, Ill.: Northwestern University Press, 1981.

———. *Narrative and Freedom: The Shadows of Time*. New Haven, Conn.: Yale University Press, 1994.

Murav, Harriet. "Dora and the Underground Man." In *Russian Literature and Psychoanalysis*, edited by Daniel Rancour-Laferriere, 417–30. Amsterdam: J. Benjamins, 1989.

———. "Reading Women in Dostoevsky." In *A Plot of Her Own*, edited by Sona Stephan Hoisington, 44–57. Evanston, Ill.: Northwestern University Press, 1995.

Murphet, Julian. "The Mole and the Multiple: A Chiasmus of Character." *New Literary History* 42, no. 2 (2011): 255–76.

Nabokov, Vera. "Predislovie k sborniku V. Nabokov 'Stikhi' (1979)." In *V. V. Nabokov: Pro i contra*, vol. 1, edited by B. V. Averin et al., 342–43. St. Petersburg: Izdatel'stvo russkogo khristianskogo gumanitarnogo instituta, 1997.

Nabokov, Vladimir. *The Annotated Lolita*. Edited by Alfred Appel, Jr. New York: Vintage, 1991.

———. "The Art of Translation" in *Lectures on Russian Literature*. New York: Harcourt Brace Jovanovich, 1980, 315–22.

———. *Bend Sinister*. New York: Vintage International, 1990.

———. *Despair*. New York: Vintage International, 1989.

———, trans. *Eugene Onegin: A Novel in Verse*, by Aleksandr Pushkin, trans-

lated and commentary by Vladimir Nabokov. 4 vols. New York: Bollingen Foundation, 1964.
———. *Gogol*. Norfolk, Va.: New Directions, 1944.
———. *Lectures on Literature*. New York: Harvest, 1980.
———. *Lectures on Russian Literature*. New York: Harcourt Brace Jovanovich, 1980.
———. *Otchayanie*, vol. 3 of *Sobranie sochinenii v chetyrekh tomakh*. Moscow: Izdatel'stvo "Pravda," 1990.
———. "Pushkin, or the Real and the Plausible." *New York Review of Books*, March 31, 1988, 38–42.
———. *The Real Life of Sebastian Knight*. New York: Vintage International, 1992.
———. *Selected Letters, 1940–1977*. New York: Harcourt Brace Jovanovich, 1989.
———. *Speak, Memory*. New York: Vintage International, 1989.
———. *The Stories of Vladimir Nabokov*. New York: Alfred A. Knopf, 1995.
———. *Strong Opinions*. New York: Vintage International, 1990.
———. "Translator's Introduction." In Alexander Pushkin, *Eugene Onegin: A Novel in Verse*, edited and translated by Vladimir Nabokov. 4 vols. Princeton, N.J.: Princeton University Press, 1975.
Naiman, Eric. "Kalganov." *Slavic and East European Journal* 58, no. 3 (Fall 2014): 394–418.
———. *Nabokov, Perversely*. Ithaca, N.Y.: Cornell University Press, 2010.
Newton, Adam Zachary. *Narrative Ethics*. Cambridge, Mass.: Harvard University Press, 1995.
Nietzsche, Friedrich. *Thus Spoke Zarathustra*. Translated by Walter Kaufmann. New York: Vintage, 1966.
Nivat, George. "Nabokov and Dostoevsky." In *The Garland Companion to Vladimir Nabokov*, edited by Vladimir E. Alexandrov, 714–24. London: Routledge, 1995.
Nussbaum, Martha. *Love's Knowledge: Essays on Philosophy and Literature*. Oxford: Oxford University Press, 1990.
O'Connor, Katherine Tiernan. "Rereading Lolita: Reconsidering Nabokov's Relationship with Dostoevskij." *Slavic and East European Journal* 33, no. 1 (1989): 64–77.
Ostrovsky, Arkady. "Shakespeare as a Founding Father of Soviet Realism: The Soviet Affair with Shakespeare." In *Shakespeare in the Worlds of Communism and Socialism*, edited by Irena R. Makaryk and Joseph G. Price, 56–83. Toronto: University of Toronto Press, 2006.
O'Toole, L. M. "Structure and Style in the Short Story: Dostoevsky's *A Gentle Spirit*." In *F. M. Dostoevsky (1821–1881): A Centenary Collection*, edited by Leon Burnett, 1–36. Colchester, Eng.: University of Essex, 1981.

Packman, David. *Vladimir Nabokov: The Structure of Literary Desire*. Columbia: University of Missouri Press, 1982.

Paperno, Irina. *Chernyshevsky and the Age of Realism: A Study in the Semiotics of Behavior*. Stanford, Calif.: Stanford University Press, 1988.

———. *Suicide as a Cultural Institution in Dostoevsky's Russia*. Ithaca, N.Y.: Cornell University Press, 1997.

Parker, David. *Ethics, Theory, and the Novel*. Cambridge: Cambridge University Press, 1994.

Patterson, Galina. "Nabokov's Use of Dostoevskii: Developing Goliadkin 'Symptoms' in Hermann as a Sign of the Artist's End." *Canadian Slavonic Papers* 40, nos. 1–2 (1998): 107–24.

Patteson, Richard. "Nabokov's *Bend Sinister*: The Narrator as God." *Studies in American Fiction* 5, no. 2 (Autumn 1977): 241–53.

Peace, Richard. "Dostoevsky and 'The Golden Age.'" *Dostoevsky Studies* 3 (1982): 61–78.

Pechey, Graham. *Mikhail Bakhtin: The Word in the World*. London: Routledge, 2007.

———. "Philosophy and Theology in 'Aesthetic Activity.'" In *Bakhtin and Religion: A Feeling for Faith*, edited by Susan M. Felch and Paul J. Contino, 47–62. Evanston, Ill.: Northwestern University Press, 2001.

Phelan, James. *Living to Tell about It: A Rhetoric and Ethics of Character Narration*. Ithaca, N.Y.: Cornell University Press, 2005.

Picon, Francisco. "Bakhtin and Nabokov: The Dialogue That Never Was." Ph.D. dissertation, Columbia University, New York, 2016.

Pifer, Ellen. *Nabokov and the Novel*. Cambridge, Mass.: Harvard University Press, 1980.

Rabinowitz, Peter J. "Lolita: Solipsized or Sodomized? or, Against Abstraction—in General." In *A Companion to Rhetoric and Rhetorical Criticism*, edited by Walter Jost and Wendy Olmsted, 325–39. Malden, Mass.: Blackwell, 2004.

———. "Truth in Fiction." *Critical Inquiry* 4, no. 1 (Autumn 1977): 121–41.

Raguet-Bouvart, Christine. "Ember, Translator of Hamlet." *Zembla*. https://www.libraries.psu.edu/Nabokov/raguetb1.htm.

Rainsford, Dominic, and Tim Woods. "Introduction: Ethics and Intellectuals." In *Critical Ethics: Text, Theory, and Responsibility*, edited by Dominic Rainsford and Tim Woods, 1–19. New York: St. Martin's Press, 1999.

Rampton, David. "Critical Choices: Reading Nabokov's *Despair*." *Forum for Modern Language Studies* 38, no. 1 (January 2002): 75–87.

———. *Vladimir Nabokov: A Critical Study of the Novels*. Cambridge: Cambridge University Press, 1984.

Reed, Natalia. "The Philosophical Roots of Polyphony: A Dostoevskian Reading." In *Critical Essays on Mikhail Bakhtin*, edited by Caryl Emerson, 117–52. Boston: G. K. Hall, 1999.

Bibliography

Robbins, Jill. *Altered Reading: Levinas and Literature*. Chicago: University of Chicago Press, 1999.

Rodgers, Michael. "The Will to Disempower? Nabokov and His Readers." In *Nabokov and the Question of Morality: Aesthetics, Metaphysics, and the Ethics of Fiction*, edited by Michael Rodgers and Susan Elizabeth Sweeney, 51–69. New York: Palgrave Macmillan, 2016.

Rodgers, Michael, and Susan Elizabeth Sweeney. "Introduction: Nabokov's Morality Play." In *Nabokov and the Question of Morality: Aesthetics, Metaphysics, and the Ethics of Fiction*, edited by Michael Rodgers and Susan Elizabeth Sweeney, 1–18. New York: Palgrave Macmillan, 2016.

Ronell, Avital. *Stupidity*. Urbana: University of Illinois Press, 2002.

Rorty, Richard. *Contingency, Irony, and Solidarity*. Cambridge: Cambridge University Press, 1989.

Rosenfield, Claire. "*Despair* and the Lust for Immortality." *Wisconsin Studies in Contemporary Literature* 8, no. 2 (Spring 1967): 174–92.

Rosengrant, Judson. "Nabokov, Onegin, and the Theory of Translation." *Slavic and East European Journal* 38, no. 1 (Spring 1994): 13–27.

Sandomirskaia, Irina. *Blokada v slove: Ocherki kriticheskoi teorii i biopolitiki iazyka*. Moscow: Novoe literaturnoe obozrenie, 2013.

Schuman, Samuel. "Nabokov's God; God's Nabokov." In *Nabokov and the Question of Morality: Aesthetics, Metaphysics, and the Ethics of Fiction*, edited by Michael Rodgers and Susan Elizabeth Sweeney, 73–86. New York: Palgrave Macmillan, 2016.

———. "Something Rotten in the State: *Hamlet* and *Bend Sinister*." *Russian Literature Triquarterly* 24 (1990): 197–212.

Shneidman, N. N. *Dostoevsky and Suicide*. New York: Mosaic, 1984.

Siebers, Tobin. *The Ethics of Criticism*. Ithaca, N.Y.: Cornell University Press, 1988.

Skakov, Nariman. "Dostoevsky's Christ and Silence at the Margins of *The Idiot*." *Dostoevsky Studies* 13 (2009): 121–40.

Smith, Zadie. *Changing My Mind: Occasional Essays*. New York: Penguin, 2009.

Straus, Nina Pelican. "Flights from *The Idiot*'s Womanhood." In *Dostoevsky's "The Idiot": A Critical Companion*, edited by Liza Knapp, 105–29. Evanston, Ill.: Northwestern University Press, 1998.

Sweeney, Susan Elizabeth. "Sinistral Details: Nabokov, Wilson, and Hamlet in *Bend Sinister*." *Nabokov Studies* 1 (1994): 179–94.

———. "Whether Judgments, Sentences, and Executions Satisfy the Moral Sense in Nabokov." In *Nabokov and the Question of Morality: Aesthetics, Metaphysics, and the Ethics of Fiction*, edited by Michael Rogers and Susan Elizabeth Sweeney, 161–82. New York: Palgrave Macmillan, 2016.

Tammi, Pekka. *Problems of Nabokov's Poetics: A Narratological Analysis*. Helsinki: Suomalainen Tiedeakatemia, 1985.

Thompson, Edward Maude. *Shakespeare's Handwriting: A Study*. Oxford: Clarendon, 1916.

Tynianov, Yuri. *Dostoevskii i Gogol': K teorii parodii*. Petrograd: Opoiaz, 1921.

———. "O parodii." In *Poetika, Istoriia literatury, Kino*, 284–310. Moscow: Nauka, 1977.

Vdovin, Alexei. *Kontsept 'Glava literatury' v russkoi kritike 1830kh–1860kh godov*. Tartu, Estonia: Tartu University Press, 2011.

Vinokur, Val. *The Trace of Judaism: Dostoevsky, Babel, Mandelstam, Levinas*. Evanston, Ill.: Northwestern University Press, 2008.

Vitalich, Kristin. "*The Village of Stepanchikovo*: Toward a (Lacanian) Theory of Parody." *Slavic and East European Journal* 53, no. 2 (2009): 203–18.

Wachtel, Andrew. "Dostoevsky's *The Idiot*: The Novel as Photograph." *History of Photography* 26, no. 3 (2002): 205–15.

Walter, Brian D. "Two Organ-Grinders: Duality and Discontent in *Bend Sinister*." In *Discourse and Ideology in Nabokov's Prose*, edited by David H. J. Larmour, 24–40. London: Routledge, 2002.

Wasiolek, Edward. *Dostoevsky: The Major Fiction*. Cambridge, Mass.: MIT Press, 1964.

Weinberger, Christopher S. "Critical Desire and the Novel: Ethics of Self-Consciousness in Cervantes and Nabokov." *Narrative* 20, no. 3 (October 2012): 277–300.

Williams, Bernard. *Morality: An Introduction to Ethics*. New York: Harper, 1972.

Woloch, Alex. *The One vs. the Many: Minor Characters and the Space of the Protagonist in the Novel*. Princeton, N.J.: Princeton University Press, 2003.

Wood, Michael. *The Magician's Doubts: Nabokov and the Risks of Fiction*. Princeton, N.J.: Princeton University Press, 1994.

Wyman, Alina. *The Gift of Active Empathy: Scheler, Bakhtin, and Dostoevsky*. Evanston, Ill.: Northwestern University Press, 2016.

Young, Sarah J. *Dostoevsky's "The Idiot" and the Ethical Foundations of Narrative: Reading, Narrating, Scripting*. London: Anthem, 2004.

Index

aesthetics: Bakhtin on, 2–3, 6–8, 35, 185n24; Dostoevsky's, 35, 41, 57–58, 171–72; and ethics, 6–7, 31–33, 102–3, 108, 147–48, 171–72, 211n50; formalist, 40, 185n24, 185n27; Kantian, 3, 193n82; and metaphysics, 102, 108–9, 208n17; Nabokov's, 102–3, 108, 132, 146, 147–48, 154, 171–73, 177; of the novel, 169; romantic, 178, 188n44; and subject, 102–3, 175–76; verbal, 159
Aksakov, Ivan, 19, 69
Alder, Donald B., 169
alterity, 2, 8–9, 65, 95, 97, 100
Altieri, Charles, 5–6, 29, 184n14
Appel, Alfred, 104
art: autonomy from life, 169; delight in, 145–46; Nabokov on, 104–5, 154, 156, 172–73, 179; as original and translation, 152–54
"Art of Translation, The" (Nabokov), 152, 217n41
audience: authorial vs. narrative, 145, 147–48, 172, 213n3; for character's thoughts, 68, 70, 75, 76–77; dialogue with, 75
author: accidental, 110; and characters, 2, 10–11, 20, 24, 27, 29–33, 105–8, 133, 155, 165–67, 172–73; control over creation, 1, 10, 27, 31–32, 103–4, 154, 172–73, 195n105; and discourse distribution, 9, 144–73; and God, 112, 146; and hero, 7, 32, 37, 196n1, 206n3; implied, 12, 30, 57–59, 132–33, 142–43; as presence in prose, 25; as quasi-divine, 172; and reader, 10–12, 24, 29–33, 172–73; and relationships, 153–54; responsibility of, 10–12, 24–25, 27, 29–33, 136, 172–73, 176–77

"authored" condition, 10, 44, 47, 76, 122
authority: and authorship, 23, 31–32, 37, 105, 108, 129, 176, 211n50, 220n62; and Bahktin, 176; of characters, 10, 49, 163, 165; of Christ, 47, 132; contested, 68; in Dostevsky, 75, 86, 91, 132, 177; distribution of, 23, 27; higher, 140; moral, 22, 177; in Nabokov, 105, 131–33, 137, 139–41, 153–54, 163, 165–68; of narrator, 166; and original, 153–54; transcendental, 58, 121–22
"Author's Confession" (Gogol), 13–15, 189n46

Bacon, Francis, 157
Bakhtin, Mikhail: on aesthetics, 2–3, 6–8, 35, 185n24; characterization theory of, 103; Christian viewpoint of, 36–37, 196n3; in constellation with Dostoevsky and Nabokov, 1–3, 10–12, 24, 175–82; on death, 72–73; on the dialogic, 20–22, 42–45, 72–73, 171, 177, 200n32; and Dostoevsky, 7–8, 10, 20–21, 24, 29, 34–49, 52, 175–82; and Dostoevsky-Nabokov comparison, 24–28, 31–33, 175–82; Emerson on, 42, 185n23, 196n2, 199n19, 203n10, 221n3; on language, 175–77; and "The Meek One," 36–42, 52; on monologism, 170; neglect of the physical, 40–41; on plot/dialogue relationship, 50; on polyphony, 11, 34–35, 39, 179, 198n14; on speaker-listener relationship, 2; on subject, 45–46; on unfinalizability, 84. See also *Problem of Dostoevsky's Poetics, The*; *Problems of Dostoevsky's Art*; "Rhetoric to the Extent That It Lies . . ."; "Toward a Philosophy of the

235

Index

Act"; "Toward a Reworking of Dostoevsky's Book"
Barthes, Roland, 28
Belinsky, Vissarion, 15–16, 189nn51–52, 190n56, 191n63
Bend Sinister (Nabokov): critics of, 154; Ember character in, 148–50, 154–68; Krug character in, 148–65, 168, 214n12, 215n27, 216n35; language in, 154–69; metalepsis in, 169–71; plot in, 154, 167–68; as political text, 12, 148–49, 155–56, 165–66; reader of, 173; Shakespeare in, 149–51, 154–65, 214n13; structure of, 151; totalitarianism in, 154–56
Benjamin, Walter, 96
Blok, Alexander, 145
Body of the Dead Christ in the Tomb, The (Holbein), 22–23, 88, 99–101
Booth, Wayne, 5–6, 57, 186n31
Borisova, Mar'ia, suicide of, 59–61, 63, 65, 74
Boyd, Brian, 147, 152, 207n10
Brooks, Peter, 167, 175
Brothers Karamazov, The (Dostoevsky): characters in, 78, 88, 115, 192n77; Christ in, 38–39, 87; and *Despair*, 142; faith in, 22–23, 67, 88; God in, 115–16; Grand Inquisitor character in, 87, 88, 142; Karamazov characters in, 22, 38, 67, 78, 88, 115, 142, 146; mental affliction in, 146; Zosima character in, 10, 22, 33, 38, 50, 88, 204n19

characters: and author, 2, 10–11, 20, 24, 27, 29–33, 105–8, 133, 155, 165–67, 172–73, 197n11; bodily components of, 39–40; control and, 94, 103–4, 172–73; dialogic relationships among, 81; and discourse distribution, 9, 144–73; discursive components of, 20–22, 39–42; Dostoevsky's, 34–51, 81–82, 86–87, 91–92, 145–46, 177; internal struggles of, 91–92; Nabokov's, 24–25, 167–69, 172–73, 178–79; narrator and, 105–6, 167; power struggles among, 179–82; vs. real people, 145; and responsibility, 10–11, 24, 137; scapegoating of, 27, 58; will to power of, 171–72
Chernyshevsky, Nikolai, 15, 191n67, 196n105

Christ: Bahktin and, 37, 192n71, 197n6; Dostoevsky on, 10, 17, 21, 37–39, 46–47, 49, 59, 65, 67, 75, 81, 85, 87, 94–96, 172, 177; ethical position of, 37–38; Gogol on, 14; Holbein painting of, 22–23, 88, 99–101; image of, 87, 94, 100; Nabokov and, 132
Coates, Ruth, 37, 38
coercion, dialogic, 23, 73, 81
Coetzee, J. M., 91–92
Conan Doyle, Arthur, 123–24
Conrad, Joseph, 81
Contemporary, The (journal), 15
Couturier, Maurice, 27, 28, 207n10
crime: and aesthetic ambition, 10; and art, 32; and discourse, 97; rhetorical, 25; and writing, 10, 11–12, 25–26, 124–25, 128, 133
Crime and Punishment (Dostoevsky): alienation in, 18; characters in, 18, 23, 48; Christianity in, 22; consciousness in, 84; and *Despair*, 130–31, 211n50; dialogue and action in, 48–49; and *The Idiot*, 84, 92; mental affliction in, 146; Raskolnikov character in, 22, 45, 48–49, 80–81, 84, 85, 92–93, 130–31, 146, 186n33, 192n76, 211n50; Sonya character in, 22, 23, 45, 48, 49–50, 89, 92–93, 192n76; as third-person narrative, 80–81; word in, 92–93
criticism: and audience, 148; ethical, 3 7–8, 32, 181, 183n3, 183n7, 184nn8–9, 186n31; literary, 3–6, 104, 137, 181

Darwin, Charles, 109
Davis, Todd, 3
Dead Souls (Gogol), 14
death: of author, 31; Christ's, 22–23; in *Despair*, 122–29; and language, 156–57, 159; and narrative, 174–75; right vs. wrong, 167; as spectacle, 41; by suicide, 58–70, 79–80
de Man, Paul, 92
Demons (Dostoevsky), 130, 146
Despair (Nabokov): characters in, 26, 172, 179; and *Crime and Punishment*, 130–31, 211n50; criticism of, 137–38; death in, 122–29; detective novel in, 109–10; doubling in, 125–26, 130–31; *ekphrasis* in, 113, 119; ethics of intersubjectiv-

236

Index

ity in, 129–38; Hermann character in, 11–12, 26, 105–43, 178–79, 186n33, 194n92, 210n43, 212n54; hierarchical relationship of author and character in, 105; implied author in, 132–33, 142–43; Lydia character in, 108–13, 125–26, 130, 210n43; misrecognition in, 138–43; murder in, 120, 127–31, 178; Nabokov's presence in, 105–8; narrative ethics in, 102–43; physical dimension in, 108–13; plot in, 108–9, 137; preface to, 133; Russian original texts of, 107, 115, 116, 118; structure of, 111, 124, 136–37; themes of, 125, 127; time in, 117–19; violence in, 133–39; wordplay in, 119–20; writing in, 11–12, 110–12, 114–15, 119–20, 124–25, 128, 133

dialogism: Bahktin on, 20–22, 42–45, 171, 177, 200n32; among characters, 81; and coercion, 23, 73, 81; and hierarchy of exchanges, 81; and discursive violence, 171–72; in Dostoevsky, 20–24, 42–50, 70–82, 86–87, 171–72, 178, 200n32; and spirituality, 87–88; and truth, 41

dialogue: Bakhtinian model for, 72–73; internal vs. external, 44–45; in the novel, 88–89; vs. plot, 47–51; and silence, 100–101; and subject, 176

Dickinson, Emily, 121–22

diegesis and extradiegesis: as divide, 172–73; levels of, 104–5, 178, 181; in reading, 180; in text, 104–5, 106, 169–71, 206n2, 207n10

discourse: critical, 3–6; distribution between author, character, and reader, 9, 144–73, 175–76; persistence after death, 72–73; postmodern, 3–4; of the self, 56; and silence, 101; and struggle, 168; and truth, 92

discursive participation: ethical cost of, 11, 12, 23–24; and human life, 95–96; and responsibility, 32–33, 36, 177–80; and violence, 91, 98

Dobroliubov, Nikolai, 15–19

Dolores Haze character, 25, 26, 103, 178

Dostoevsky, Fyodor: "aesthetic revolution" of, 89; and author-character dynamic, 21–22, 24–25, 31–32; and Bakhtin, 7–8, 10, 20–21, 24, 29 34–49, 52, 175–82; "carnivalistic" overtones in, 41; Christian ethics of, 3, 7–8, 17–20, 22–24, 46–47, 49–51, 57–59, 69–70, 84–89, 94–96, 99–101, 172, 177–78, 180, 191n71, 192n75; in constellation with Bakhtin and Nabokov, 1–3, 10–12, 24, 175–82; critical writings of, 15–20, 68; and dialogism, 20–24, 42–50, 70–82, 86–87, 171–72, 178; and discourse distribution, 9, 175–76; Emerson on, 50, 86, 199n20; and Gogol, 13–15, 18–19, 191nn67–68; importance of, 12–13; journalism of, 19, 59, 69; and language, 172; and literary critics, 15–18; mental afflictions in, 146; metaphysics in, 132–33; and monologism, 39, 69; moral philosophy of, 94; and Nabokov (see Dostoevsky and Nabokov, comparison of); narrative ethics of, 11–12, 32–33, 55–56, 74, 103, 171–73, 177, 180; narrative imperative of, 57–59; narrators in, 36, 53–58, 60, 70–81, 83, 84, 90; notebooks of, 95; plot in, 36, 40–42, 91, 199n20; prose of, 20–22, 31–32, 35, 146–47, 172, 177–78, 182; protagonists in, 134; Pushkin Speech by, 179–80; scholarship on, 40; on socialism, 115; and spirituality, 87–88. See also *Brothers Karamazov, The*; *Crime and Punishment*; *Demons*; *Idiot, The*; *Insulted and the Injured, The*; "Legend of the Grand Inquisitor, The"; "Meek One, The"; "Mr.–bov and the Question of Art"; *Notes from Underground*; "Sentence, The"; "Two Suicides"; *Village of Stepanchikovo, The*; *Writer's Diary, A*

Dostoevsky and Nabokov, comparison of: authorial function in, 13, 141; characters in, 136, 141–42, 179–82, 208n21; conceptualizations of verbal art in, 143–48; in constellation with Bakhtin, 175–82; ethics of intersubjectivity in, 130–35, 176; God in, 115–16, 121–22; narrative ethics in, 2–3, 9–13, 32–33, 132–33, 171–73, 176–82, 187n34; prose in, 31; protagonists in, 105–6, 134; and randomness of existence, 117, 118; responsibility in, 176–79; subject in, 176–82

ekphrasis, 113, 119

Ember character, 148–50, 154–68

Index

Emerson, Caryl: on Bakhtin, 42, 185n23, 196n2, 199n19, 203n10, 221n3; on Dostoevsky, 50, 86, 199n20; on the novel, 46
Encounter magazine, 169
Epstein, Mikhail, 87
Erdinast-Vulcan, Daphne, 38
ethical, the: dilemmas in, 5–6; and engagement with literature, 181–82; fiction and, 5–6, 181; language and, 168; in narrative act, 2; and power, 171–73
ethics: and aesthetics, 6–7, 31–33, 102–3, 108, 147–48, 171–72, 196n3, 211n50; Aristotelian, 4; Christian, 3, 5, 7–8, 17–20, 22–24, 46–47, 49–51, 57–59, 69–70, 84–89, 94–96, 99–101, 172, 177–78, 191n71, 192n75; of form, 13–20; hermeneutic, 8; of intersubjectivity, 129–38; Kantian, 7, 193n82; Levinasian, 94–98; in literary studies, 3–6; narrational, 8; narrative (*see* narrative ethics); representational, 8; and truth, 52–57
Eugene Onegin (Pushkin), 163–64, 180, 218n48
Eye, The (Nabokov), 133, 195n105

fiction: authorial presence in, 104–5; and ethical dilemmas, 5–6; and ethical inquiry, 8; and ethical theory, 4; hierarchies of representation in, 2–3; plot in, 20–21; and reality, 54; and responsibility, 10–11, 24–25, 181–82; sentimental, 147; violence of, 182
Field, Andrew, 140
Fish, Stanley, 103
Fogel, Aaron, 73, 81
Fonvisina, N. D., 95
form: and content, 54, 155, 171; in *Despair*, 124–25, 128; emotional-volitional relationship and, 7; ethics of, 13–20; in "The Meek One," 51–52, 54–56
formal features: and aesthetics, 35; of Dostoevsky's prose, 57; in "The Idiot," 86; in "The Meek One," 74–75; of Nabokov's prose, 206n2; and polyphony, 21–22
freedom: artistic, 17; aesthetic, 19–20; authorial, 43, 173; of characters, 35, 38–40, 48, 89, 103–4, 177, 195n105; dialogic, 36, 73; discursive, 20–23; narrative, 177; of readers, 28, 89; and responsibility, 31, 34, 86; of subject, 176

Gibson, Andrew, 31
Gift, The (Nabokov), 172, 195n105
Ginzburg, Lydia, 177
Gnosticism, 170
God: as giver and taker of life, 128; longing for, 115–16; as ultimate author, 112; and writer, 145, 146
Gogol, Nikolai: and Belinsky, 15–16, 18–19, 189n51, 191n63; on Christ, 14; and Dostoevsky, 13–15, 18–19, 191nn67–68. *See also* "Author's Confession"; *Dead Souls*; *Selected Passages from Correspondence with Friends*
"Good Readers and Good Writers" (Nabokov), 148, 152
Grand Inquisitor character, 87, 88, 142

Hamlet (Shakespeare): in *Bend Sinister*, 149–51, 154–65, 214n13, 217n40
Harpham, Geoffrey, 20–21, 48, 177, 183n3
Heart of Darkness (Conrad), 81
Hermann character, 11–12, 26, 105–43, 178–79, 186n33, 194n92, 210n43, 212n54
Herzen, Alexander, 36, 58, 62–63, 69
Herzen, Lisa, suicide of, 36, 58–67, 69
hierarchy: of author, character, and reader, 23–24, 68, 106, 133, 155, 165, 166–67, 197n11, 198n14; Christ in, 47; of dialogic exchange, 81; evolutionary, 68; language and, 92; ontological, 171, 218n57; political, 165
Holbein, Hans, 22–23, 88, 99–101
Holquist, Michael, 42
Hugo, Victor, 54
Humbert character, 25, 26, 28, 31, 103–4, 111–13, 132, 178, 192n79, 195n105, 208n21, 213n3

identity, unstable vs. absolute, 138–43
Idiot, The (Dostoevsky): Christian ethics in, 84–89, 94–95; conflict in, 16; and *Crime and Punishment*, 84, 92; critical views of, 83–84; dialogic activity in, 43–44, 87–89; discursive participation in, 11, 91, 95, 98; formal features in, 86; image of Christ in, 22–23, 87–88, 99–101; interpretation of, 89–90, 101, 178; language in, 91–96; mental affliction in, 146; Nabokov and, 121; narrative incoherence of, 97–98; re-

Index

pentance in, 178; salvation in, 67; "scripting" in, 11, 91, 93; silence in, 99–101
imagination: dialogic, 35, 73; moral, 2, 13; and reality, 111
Insulted and the Injured, The (Dostoevsky), 146
interpretation: and Dostoevsky, 57, 61, 63, 64; ethical demands of, 2, 8–9, 33; of *The Idiot*, 86, 89–90, 101; and Nabokov, 25, 28; by reader, 56, 101
Invitation to a Beheading (Nabokov), 172
Isotoff, Andrei, 146
Ivanov, Viacheslav, 34–35, 177, 221n6

Jackson, Robert Louis, 80, 86–87
Jones, Malcolm, 38, 88, 90, 93, 94
jouissance, 28, 31
Judaism, 94

Kariakin, Yuri, 59
Kavelin, Konstantin, 47
Khodasevich, Vladislav, 25
Krug character, 148–65, 168, 214n12, 215n27, 216n35

Lachmann, Renate, 119, 134, 137–38, 210n44
language: as ambiguous, 156–57; in *Bend Sinister*, 154–69; and distribution of power, 12; fallen, 91–94; and hierarchy, 92; and self, 95–96; and violence, 158, 171–72
Last Day of a Condemned Man, The (Hugo), 54
"Legend of the Grand Inquisitor, The" (Dostoevsky), 21, 38, 216n35, 216n37, 217n40
Levinas, Emmanuel, 8, 94–98
literature: as choice-making, 4–5; ethical engagement with, 181–82; ethical inquiry in, 7–9; formal characteristics of, 4; Nabokov on, 150; postmodern, 178, 207n9, 219n62; Russian, 12–15; second-rate, 106–7; and spiritual regeneration, 13
Lolita (Nabokov), afterword to, 25,104, 195n103; characters in, 172, 178, 195n105, 208n21; and *Despair*, 111, 113, 137–38, 211n50; Dolores Haze character in, 25, 26, 103, 178; as first-person narrative, 133; Humbert character in, 25, 26, 28, 31, 103–4, 111–13, 132, 178, 192n79, 195n105, 208n21, 213n3; inspiration for, 31; Lolita character in, 103–4, 111–12; moral value of, 147; narrator of, 25–26, 28; reading in, 103, 192n79
Lolita character, 103–4, 111–12
Love, Heather, 8–9
Lydia character, 108–13, 125–26, 130, 210n43

Malina, Debra, 171, 220n63
Mandelstam, Osip, 3, 213n5
Mapping the Ethical Turn (Davis and Womack), 3
Marxism, 115
meaning: articulation of, 53–54; and authorial figure, 176, 178–79; in *Despair*, 103–43; in *The Idiot*, 85, 90–94; and language, 91–94; and order, 118, 119; production of, 28, 30–31, 6–68, 103; and reading, 8, 90; totality of, 1; and translation, 162–63; and violence, 98; and writing, 113
"Meek One, The" (Dostoevsky): Bakhtin and, 36–42, 52; and *Despair*, 117, 118, 136; dialogic in, 178; as first-person narrative, 80–81; formal features in, 74–75; narrator's voice in, 70–82; nonfictional sources of, 59; preface to, 51–52, 53–54; reader of, 28; suicide in, 11, 36, 58, 59–69
metalepsis, 169–71, 218n53, 218n 57, 219n62, 220n63
metaphysics: and aesthetics, 102, 108–9, 112, 208n17; and authenticity, 178; of authorship, 102–43; and crisis of mimesis, 133–34; and death, 122–29; in Dostoevsky, 132–33; in Nabokov, 132–33, 202n50; in narrative ethics, 132–33; and narrative formation of subject, 171; religious, 23; textual, 171
Miller, Robin Feuer, 57, 90, 98
mise-en-abyme structure, 111, 124, 136–37, 151, 152, 175
misrecognition, 138–43
modernism, 10, 12, 25, 27, 104, 117, 133, 146, 169, 206n9
monologism: Bakhtin on, 170, 199n17; and Dostoevsky, 39, 69; and Nabokov, 170; and subject, 176; and truth, 78

239

Index

Montaigne, Michel de, 28
morality: Christian, 89; Dostoevsky's, 56, 177; Enlightenment notions of, 4; Nabokov and, 26; as "non-ethical," 20–21
Moscow University Society of Literature Lovers, 179
"Mr.–bov and the Question of Art" (Dostoevsky), 16–18
Murav, Harriet, 73–74, 201n45
Myshkin character, 11, 22, 23, 43–44, 49, 83–101, 146, 178

Naiman, Eric, 27, 154, 155, 187n35, 193n87, 206n2
Nabokov, Vera, 170
Nabokov, Vladimir: on art, 104–5, 154, 156, 172–73, 179; on artist's role, 12; and author-character dynamic, 24–25, 195n105; authorial figure in, 32–33, 103–5, 145–46, 172, 178–79, 219n61; conceptualization of verbal art, 143–48, 169; in constellation with Bakhtin and Dostoevsky, 1–3, 10–12, 24, 175–82; criticism of, 104, 137–38, 154, 170; on Darwin, 109; diegesis and extradiegesis in, 104–5, 106, 169–71, 207n10; and discourse distribution, 9, 175–76; and Dostoevsky (see Dostoevsky and Nabokov, comparison of); Dostoevsky, comment on, 2–3, 9–10, 122–23, 144–47, 150, 186n33; ethics of intersubjectivity in, 130–35; on language, 12; on literature, 150; metalepsis in, 169–71, 218n53, 218n57, 219n62, 220n63; meta-narrative in, 104–5; metaphysics in, 132–33, 202n50; *mise-en-abyme* structure in, 111, 124, 136–37, 151, 152, 175; and monologism, 170, 195n105; and morality, 26; narrative ethics of, 11–12, 32–33, 102–43, 156–57, 169–73; narrators in, 1, 10, 12, 25–26, 28–31, 33, 102, 105–8, 132, 133, 166–69, 193n82; nonfiction writing of, 148; and otherworldly dimension, 170; power dynamics in, 154, 168; prose of, 10, 12–13, 25, 31, 103, 148, 170–73, 178, 182, 206n2; on psychoanalysis, 146; and Pushkin, 163–64, 180–81, 216n32; reader of, 24–33, 173, 194n101; on reality, 1, 25, 104–12, 123–25, 152–53, 156, 163–64; Russian language, use of, 107, 115, 118, 125, 128, 131, 160–64, 217n43; as satirist, 26; on time, 140; on translation, 152, 160–65. See also *Bend Sinister*; *Eye, The*; *Gift, The*; "Good Readers and Good Writers"; *Invitation to a Beheading*; *Lolita*; *Pale Fire*; *Pnin*; "Pushkin, or the Real and the Plausible"; *Real Life of Sebastian Knight, The*; "Signs and Symbols"; *Speak, Memory*; *Transparent Things*; *Tyrants Destroyed and Other Stories*; "Vane Sisters, The"

narrative: and the body, 74–75; danger of, 174–75; form in, 54–55; in formation of subject, 171, 177–78, 181–82; genealogy of, 2–3; instability of, 118–19; and liminal states, 6; limits of for author, 1–2; meta-, 104–5; as re-creating experience, 182; structure of, 29–33

narrative ethics: artist/tyrant difference in, 156–57, 162–63, 168; Dostoevsky's, 11–12, 32–33, 55–56, 74, 103, 171–73, 177, 180; and ethical engagement with literature, 181–82; and fictional vs "real," 146; in Nabokov-Dostoevsky comparison, 32–33, 103–4, 146, 171–73, 176–82; Nabokov's, 102–43, 156–57, 169–71; Newton on, 2, 8–9; and polyphony, 179–82; proximity vs. distancing in, 150; triadic structure in, 8

Narrative Ethics (Newton), 2

narrator: authority of, 166; as character, 105–6; in Dostoevsky, 36, 53–58, 60, 70–81, 83, 84, 90; hierarchy and, 167–69; in Nabokov, 1, 10, 12, 25–26, 28–31, 33, 102, 105–8, 132, 133, 166–69, 193n82; relationship with author and reader, 57–59, 76, 81

Nastasya Filippovna character, 83, 84, 87, 90–100, 146, 178

New Criticism, 3

Newton, Adam Zachary: on narrative ethics, 2, 8–9; on responsibility, 90; on surplus attention, 2

Notes from Underground (Dostoevsky), 18, 21; Christian ideal in, 50

novel, the: aesthetics of, 169; dialogic in, 50, 88–89; diegesis and extradiegesis in,

Index

170–71; form of, 177; polyphony in, 21–22, 34–35, 39, 72–73, 196n1, 198n14
Nussbaum, Martha, 3–6, 181, 183n7, 184n14

other: and self, 94–98

Packman, David, 25, 27, 31, 192n79, 206n6
Pale Fire (Nabokov), 133, 172, 207n10
paronomasia, 159, 165–66, 216n37
Pechey, Graham, 7, 185n28, 193n82, 197n6
Peter the Great, 13, 139
pleasure: at expense of others, 33; production of, 5; of reading, 27–29, 145, 148, 211n50
plot: Brooks on, 167; and diachronic reading, 171; and dialogic activity, 36, 47–51, 157; in Dostoevsky, 36, 40–42, 91, 199n20; and discourse, 22; and ethics, 20–21, 23; in Nabokov, 108, 117, 118, 124, 137, 141, 143, 154, 164
Pnin (Nabokov), 133, 193n82, 195n105
polyphony: of author, 40, 53, 78, 86; Bakhtin on, 11, 34–35, 39, 179, 198n14; in Dostoevsky, 11, 21–22, 34–35, 39, 44, 72–73, 89–90, 179; and narrative ethics, 179–82; in novel, 21–22, 34–35, 39, 72–73, 196n1, 198n14; and Pushkin, 179
power dynamics: among characters, 179–82; and ethical inquiry, 171–73; in Nabokov, 154, 168; and subject, 168–69; in text, 105, 132–33, 136
Problem of Dostoevsky's Poetics, The (Bakhtin), 34–49, 177, 180, 198n15
Problems of Dostoevsky's Art (Bakhtin), 38, 39, 176
prose: dialogic activity and plot in, 36, 47–50, 157; Dostoevsky's, 20–22, 31, 36, 50–51, 146–47, 172, 177–78; experience of, 31–32; hierarchy within, 22; Nabokov's, 10, 12–13, 25, 31, 103–4, 148, 170–73, 178, 182, 195n105, 206n2; philosophy in, 7–8
Proverbs, book of, 157
Psychoanalytic Review, 146
Pushkin, Aleksandr: Dostoevsky and, 179–80; Nabokov and, 116, 163–64, 180–81, 188n42, 210n32, 216n32, 218n48; and polyphony, 179. See also *Eugene Onegin*; "Shot, The"
"Pushkin, or the Real and the Plausible" (Nabokov), 180–81
Pushkin Speech by Dostoevsky, 179–80

Rabinowitz, Peter J., 145, 148, 172, 213n3
rape, 28, 178, 210n32
Raskolnikov character, 22, 45, 48–49, 80–81, 84, 85, 92–93, 130–31, 146, 186n33, 192n76, 211n50
reader: and discourse distribution, 9; Dostoevsky's, 23–24; exploited, 146; in hierarchy with author and character, 23–24, 68, 106, 133, 173; implied, 31, 132–33; interpretation by, 101, 181–82; as judicious spectator, 6; Nabokov's, 24–33, 173, 194n101; and production of meaning, 103–4; recognizing equivalences by, 4–5; responsibility of, 10–11, 24, 31, 53–53, 81, 176–77, 181–82; and text, 27, 74–75, 89–91
reading: by characters, 109–10; diachronic, 171; ethical costs of, 8–9; of Nabokov, 173; pleasure of, 27–29; and realistic vs. aesthetic in text, 148; structuralist analysis of, 8; as unifying, 3
Reading for the Plot (Brooks), 167
reality: aestheticization of, 137–38; Dostoevsky on, 55; Nabokov on, 1, 25, 104–12, 123–25, 152–53, 156, 163–64; as text, 108, 117–19, 125; and writing, 180–81
Real Life of Sebastian Knight, The (Nabokov), 1–2, 174–75, 195n105
religious faith, 36, 62–72, 81–82, 86–89
responsibility: author's, 10–12, 24–25, 27, 29–33, 136, 172–73, 176–77; characters', 10–11, 24, 137; for fiction, 148; Nabokov and, 155; of participants in the narrative act, 58; of reader, 10–11, 24, 31, 52–53, 81, 176–77, 181–82; and sin, 81–82; for truth, 96–97; for violence, 138
"Rhetoric to the Extent That It Lies . . ." (Bakhtin), 175–77
Robbins, Jill, 97
Ronell, Avital, 85, 92
Rorty, Richard, 26, 102
Rosenfield, Claire, 124
Rosengrant, Judson, 163–64

Index

Russia: Gogol on, 18; intelligentsia in, 147; moral crisis in, 11; religious philosophy in, 87
Russian formalists, 6–7, 185n27, 199n19
Russian language: Dostoevsky on, 56; Nabokov's use of, 107, 115, 118, 125, 128, 131, 160–64, 217n43
Russian literature, 12–20, 179–80, 189nn51–52

Saltykov-Shchedrin, Mikhail, 68
"scripting," 11, 91, 93
Selected Passages from Correspondence with Friends (Gogol), 13–15, 18–19, 188n44, 189nn51–52
"Sentence, The" (Dostoevsky), 61, 66–70
Shakespeare: in *Bend Sinister*, 154–65; as historical, 157–58, 162; and language, 157–58
"Shot, The" (Pushkin), 116
Siebers, Tobin, 3–4
"Signs and Symbols" (Nabokov), 30
silence: authorial, 177; Christ's, 87, 172; and the dialogic, 72–74, 81, 87–88, 96, 172, 176; as impossible, 65; narrative usurpation of, 10; and polyphony, 39; and reader, 11; and transcendental signified, 172; and truth, 92; types of, 100–101; and word, 99–101, 176
Skakov, Nariman, 101
Smith, S. Stephenson, 146
Smith, Zadie, 28
Sonya character, 22, 23, 45, 48, 49–50, 89, 92–93, 192n76
Speak, Memory (Nabokov), 24, 140, 193n82, 208n20
Stavrogin character, 81–82, 130, 134, 146
subject: aesthetics in construction of, 102–3; Bakhtinian, 45–46; desire for authenticity, 49; vs. language in critical discourse, 3–4; and the metaphysical, 113, 171; narrative formation of, 171, 177–78, 181–82; narrator as, 167; and power, 168–69; in relationship, 37; unmaking of, 175–76; and violence, 143, 176
suicide: in Dostoevsky, 11, 36, 48, 51–53, 55, 58–70, 73, 79–80, 100, 201nn48–50; and Nabokov, 121, 136

syuzhet and *fabula*, 30, 117–18, 123, 194n101

text: diegesis in, 104–5, 106, 169–71, 181–82; ethical engagement with, 175, 181; and meaning, 103–4; and reader, 27, 74–75, 89–91; realistic vs. aesthetic in, 148; reality as, 108, 117–19, 125
"Those—dying then" (Dickinson), 121–22
Tolstoy, Leo, 145, 205n43
totalitarianism, 154–56
"Toward a Philosophy of the Act" (Bakhtin), 176
"Toward a Reworking of Dostoevsky's Book" (Bakhtin), 42
translation: double, 162; Nabokov on, 152, 160–65; and writing, 148–54
Transparent Things (Nabokov), 172
tropes, ambiguity of, 137–38
truth: characters and, 20, 23; Christ and, 47; and consciousness, 51–57; dialogic search for, 41; and discourse, 92, 181; ethical value of, 52–57; and language, 158; monologic creator and, 78, 199n17; moral value of, 11; and narrative, 175, 178; responsibility for, 96–97; search for, 157
"Two Suicides" (Dostoevsky), 59–61
Tyrants Destroyed and Other Stories (Nabokov), 169

Underground Man character, 21, 49, 51, 55, 74, 106, 141–42, 210n34

"Vane Sisters, The" (Nabokov), 29–31, 169–70, 218n54
verbal utterance, semantic scope of, 156
Village of Stepanchikovo, The (Dostoevsky), 19, 191n68
Vinokur, Val, 94–95, 97, 98, 205n43
violence: aesthetic, 32–33, 46, 132, 133, 138, 197n11; and Christian morality, 85, 87–88; dialogic, 73, 81; discursive, 91, 94, 97, 101, 168, 171; and justice, 94; and language, 158; and meaning, 98; narrative, 12, 38, 58, 69, 81, 91, 172, 176–77, 179, 182, 199n17; physical, 38, 42, 91, 132, 133, 177, 213n58; political, 157, 166; of representation, 39; and the sub-

242

Index

ject, 143, 171, 176; and suicide, 65, 68–69; textual, 27

voice: author's, 39–40, 206n3; of characters, 113, 119, 127, 135, 156, 161–68, 198n14; double, 42–47, 59, 65; embodied, 95; ethical, 89, 94, 191n71; narrator's, 28, 51, 70–82, 90, 92, 96, 98, 166, 167–68

What Is Art (Tolstoy), 145
White, Katherine, 30
Williams, Bernard, 181
Womack, Kenneth, 3
Wood, Michael, 25, 29–30
word: dialogic, 88; divine and human in, 172; double-voiced, 42–47; and image, 86–87; and silence, 99–101; and subject, 175–76; and subjugation, 176–77

Writer's Diary, A (Dostoevsky): Christian beliefs in, 19; and "The Meek One," 11, 36, 51, 58, 59–61, 63–70, 75

writing: and crime, 10, 11–12, 25–26, 124–25, 128, 133; by machine, 153; and power dynamic, 136–37; and reality, 180–81; and sexuality, 110–12, 114–15, 119–20; and translation, 148–54

Young, Sarah, 11, 91, 93, 94

Zosima character, 10, 22, 33, 38, 50, 88, 204n19